First Among Men

First Among Men

GEORGE WASHINGTON
AND THE MYTH OF
AMERICAN MASCULINITY

Maurizio Valsania

Johns Hopkins University Press
Baltimore

Johns Hopkins University Press
2715 North Charles Street
Baltimore, Maryland 21218-4363
www.press.jhu.edu

Library of Congress Cataloging-in-Publication Data
Names: Valsania, Maurizio, 1965– author.
Title: First among men : George Washington and the myth of
    American masculinity / Maurizio Valsania.
Description: Baltimore : Johns Hopkins University Press, 2022. |
    Includes bibliographical references and index. |
Identifiers: LCCN 2021054973 | ISBN 9781421444475 (hard-
    cover) | ISBN 9781421444482 (ebook)
Subjects: LCSH: Washington, George, 1732-1799—Influence. |
    Masculinity—United States—History—18th century. |
    Presidents—United States—Biography. | United States—
    Social life and customs—1775-1783.
Classification: LCC E312.17.V35 2022 | DDC 973.4/1092 [B]—
    dc23/eng/20220413
LC record available at https://lccn.loc.gov/2021054973

A catalog record for this book is available from the British Library.

Special discounts are available for bulk purchases of this book. For more
information, please contact Special Sales at specialsales@jh.edu.

To Serenella

Visit the eighteenth century, and you will return with your head spinning, for it is endlessly surprising, inexhaustibly interesting, irresistibly strange.

ROBERT DARNTON, *George Washington's False Teeth*

❧

I do not think vanity is a trait of my character.

GEORGE WASHINGTON TO DR. JAMES CRAIK, March 25, 1784

Contents

❧

First Among Men

I

❧

The American Giant

The Great Nineteenth-Century Aggrandizing

On Christmas afternoon, 1776, Washington informed his rag-tag army that they would embark that night on a secret mission. The soldiers were stationed near McConkey's Ferry, Pennsylvania, where they had retreated after a series of defeats, the British having countered early losses in Boston with resounding victories in New York. Many of the men were wounded and sick, their numbers decimated by defections and a wave of de-enlistments in advance of Christmas. Supplies were scarce and morale low, and confidence in ultimate victory was ebbing fast. Perhaps it was for these reasons more than any tactical objective that Washington decided to launch a bold and unexpected counterattack against the enemy.

The weather was harsh that winter, and the British had withdrawn to New York to wait out the season until the next campaign. They'd left a troop of fifteen hundred Hessian soldiers across the Delaware to protect New Jersey. The Hessians had fought for the British in many colonial conflicts around the globe, and they were detested by the Americans for being paid mercenaries enforcing British rule. In preparation for the attack, Washington gathered reinforcements from other commanders, sufficient food supplies for a three-day foray, and a number of ferries and rowboats sturdy enough to transport his troops and heavy cannons. His plan was to cross the river in three waves and take the Hessian garrison by surprise.

After hours of delay, the men finally loaded up the boats and pushed off from shore around midnight. Washington himself led the first wave, riding in a wooden, flat-bottomed, double-ended watercraft known as a Durham boat because it was used by the nearby Durham Ironworks as a freighter. The wind and snow blew hard, and the river began to ice up, making the crossing even more treacherous. Though the sneak attack is heralded now as an illustration of dauntless courage and determination by brave revolutionaries, the sortie might have smacked of foolish desperation at the time. Many of the soldiers must have felt both daring and desperate as they made the crossing and prayed their boats would not capsize.

In one of the most famous paintings celebrating the Revolutionary War, *Washington Crossing the Delaware*, the general stands at the prow of one of those overladen rowboats, regal and stalwart, jaw lifted and eyes forward, eager to face all foes and meet the destiny before him. Though the wind tears at the American flag and chunks of ice batter the hull as the men strain at their oars, Washington himself is unaffected. He is an icon of the great nation struggling to be born. He is a hero without parallel. Washington's mind is crisp, but his body is even better. He stands for the eternal masculine. He is first among men.

This portrayal of Washington has been etched into our consciousness and the national mythos of the United States. Of the "Founding Fathers" and other significant figures in American history, Washington has been at once mythologized and simplified to an extent that places him beyond reproach but also beyond context, enshrined and sanctified.[1]

But rather than an emblem of the eternal masculine, Washington was a male of the eighteenth century. And he was a real human person: he felt pain and fear, suffered from physical hardships and ill-

nesses, experienced love and cruel loss, was
courageous but conscious of his own limits,
was both violent and caring, hard and soft, and
carefully crafted his own character and identity to project a highly refined public persona.[2]

*Washington Crossing the
Delaware*, by Emanuel Leutze,
1851. Courtesy of Metropolitan
Museum of Art, New York, NY.

The painting of Washington crossing the
Delaware was made in 1851, almost seventy-five years after the
events it depicted. The artist, Emanuel Leutze, was born in Germany in 1816. Of course, he had never met Washington. Accordingly, everything about the scene should be called into question. It's
highly implausible, for example, that Washington stood in the bow
of the boat as he was portrayed. It would have been foolish to do so,
and the military operation would have been marred by any jolt to
the boat that would plunge the general into the icy water. What's
more, the Durham boat Washington ferried in was longer than
depicted. It seems pedantic but also necessary to point out that the

sky at the time was not light but dark, and any posing Washington might have done would have gone completely unnoticed.

Like most art, the portrayal says more about the times and world in which the painter, not the subject, lived. In that sense, it's a masterpiece of realism. Leutze captures Washington perfectly through the lens of nineteenth-century preferences, sensibilities, stereotypes, and practices of masculinity. Leutze's Washington is barrel-chested, strong, and muscular. He is straightforward and unapologetic in his determination. He is defiant, self-preening, almost boorish. In this, he is no longer an eighteenth-century southern aristocrat. Leutze's Washington typifies the mood of American nationalism at the time, in the long aftermath of the War of 1812.[3]

That muscular patriotism infused the Jacksonian era, carried over into the expansionist agenda of the Polk administration, and fueled the territorial ambitions of the Mexican War. Leutze made Washington the incarnation of Manifest Destiny while wrapping him in 250 pounds of pure masculine vigor. More than delivering troops to battle the Hessians, Washington, in Leutze's painting, was metaphorically delivering superior republican institutions to inferior and effeminate neighbors, wherever the goddess of liberty decided to extend her reach.

As the symbolic father of a nation prizing strength and territorial expansion, Washington must by necessity remain the tallest, strongest, most athletic, and most virile of men. His conspicuous masculinity and unparalleled resolve seem not only natural but a moral imperative—even today. Indeed, many of Washington's modern biographers fall into the trap. They conjure an individual akin to the muscular giant found in *Washington Crossing the Delaware*—someone whose massive body "spread over a taut six-foot-four-and-a-half-inch frame," as Willard Sterne Randall writes.[4]

Other biographers dwell on this same conceit of physical prominence. Paul Johnson, for example, claims that Washington "inherited his physique" from his father, who was "a blond giant." John

Ferling says that Washington had "the striking look of what we would expect today in a gifted athlete." Richard Brookhiser quotes a female bodybuilder who, commenting on Washington's "well developed thighs," declares that he had "nice quads." Joseph Ellis likewise presents him as "physically majestic." While Washington's "internal muscularity" was impossible to see, his impressive "marvellous physique" was a show that everyone enjoyed.[5]

Ron Chernow's version of George Washington is still more spectacular. "A superb physical specimen, with a magnificent physique," Washington outdid every opponent. His body was "powerfully rough-hewn and endowed with matchless strength." To better render the idea, Chernow also provides cinematic close-ups: when Washington clenched his jaw, Chernow writes, "his cheek and jaw muscles seemed to ripple right through his skin." Washington, in conclusion, was "an exceptionally muscular and vigorous young man," with an "imposing face and virile form," "powerfully rough-hewn and endowed with matchless strength." His "wide, flaring hips with muscular thighs" made every woman, and more than one man, swoon.[6]

George Washington was in fact tall, but he was not 250 pounds of muscular energy. Nor did he match the fiercely virile and physically dominant nineteenth-century image by which he is remembered. Rather, he was distinctly eighteenth century in his masculinity, physicality, and outlook. Though eighteenth-century society was steeped in violence and brutality, it did not prize brute force or domination, boorishness, or recklessness. Moreover, athleticized male bodies did not appeal to the tastes of the time.[7]

The impression of Washington as equally at home while crossing semifrozen rivers or in the untamed wilderness and on muddy, blood-soaked battlefields is accurate. He was, after all, an outdoorsman and a soldier hardened by violence and extreme conditions. As a slaveowner, he benefited from the most brutal and violent institution ever contrived. At home in the finest surroundings, he was at the same time a gregarious, compassionate, unusually considerate man, sophisticated and refined in his tastes, sensitive in his relationships, and a leading connoisseur of fashion.

This well-roundedness is perhaps the most surprising aspect of the man to modern observers. But to his contemporaries, Washington was masculine *because* he combined doses of physicality and violence with a coiffed and perfumed style and a sensitive demeanor that would seem "feminine" to us now. The apparent contradiction between these elements did not detract from his virility. Americans have had difficulty grasping this since the nineteenth century. The real Washington embodied a much broader concept of masculinity.[8]

Leutze's Washington, just like any other image of Washington as a giant or a muscular athlete, is terribly overblown. Washington was his own man and strikingly distinct from such impressions. We can learn a great deal about masculinity, leadership, and America by studying him more intimately and accurately.

❧ Reverence for George Washington actually began around the end of the French and Indian War, in 1763. His feats during the Revolution and his sudden death, on December 14, 1799, elevated him to a transcendent status. Eulogies saluted the more-than-human man "as the deliverer and political saviour of our nation." He was "as Moses was to the Children of Israel" and, like Moses parting the Red Sea, he "conducted the Americans thro' seas of blood." Between December 1799 and February 1800, no fewer than 440 eulogies were delivered to an audience that could not get enough of Washington. He elicited more curiosity and popular acclaim in death than he had even in life.[9]

By the beginning of the nineteenth century, exaggerated accounts of Washington's superior athletic qualities were particularly appreciated, especially when they were delivered by those who might plausibly have seen him in the flesh. In 1775, ten-year-old Israel Trask had entered Colonel Mansfield's regiment as an army cook and a messenger. Years later, Trask recounted a brawl that broke out among the troops. Enter General Washington: "With the spring of a deer, he leaped from his saddle, threw the reins of his bridle into the hands of his servant, and rushed into the thickest of the melee, [and] with an iron grip seized two tall, brawny, athletic, savage-looking riflemen by the throat, keeping them at arm's length, alternately shaking and talking to them." The brawlers quickly realized they were no match for this giant of a general and ran off "at the top of their speed in all directions from the scene of the conflict." Did the episode occur? Trask, as an old man, can be forgiven for conjuring up a tall tale out of a dramatic moment that impressed him in childhood and delighted his listeners years later.[10]

With a similar bent toward exaggeration, in 1859, George Washington Parke Custis, grandson of Martha Washington and step-grandson of George Washington, claimed that the famous painter Charles Willson Peale told him about another display of explosive masculinity. The scene, allegedly, was Mount Vernon, December 1773. Several young gentlemen challenged themselves to see who could throw a heavy iron bar the greatest distance. "Suddenly the colonel appeared among us." Washington "requested to be shown the pegs that marked the bounds of our efforts; then, smiling, and without putting off his coat, held out his hand for the missile." The result was no contest at all. "No sooner . . . did the heavy iron bar feel the grasp of his mighty hand than it lost the power of gravitation, and whizzed through the air, striking the ground far, very far, beyond our utmost limits." It's all hearsay, of course, but imagine listeners encountering that story in the nineteenth century or even today; they would no doubt be impressed by the vivid details of such masculine prowess. While the other men were covered in sweat and dirt, "all stripped to the buff, with shirt sleeves rolled up," Washington remained clothed, dignified, and unruffled. Custis reported that Washington was nonchalant about his victory but couldn't resist poking his opponents with a last jab, an act of perfect braggadocio: "When you beat my pitch, young gentlemen, I'll try again."[11]

According to nineteenth-century testimonies, in even the most casual of affairs, Washington could never be less than titanic. When a log rolled out of the fire, another witness swears, Washington replaced it with ease using tongs in one hand. "The size of the heavy gum log & the facility with which he handled it, excited the notice of those present." After the general left the room, several of his "strong athletic" gentlemen guests tried to lift the log but to no avail. They had to join forces to manage it with shovel and tongs together.[12]

Recollections such as these are all too similar. On another occasion, we are told, a crowd gathered to watch a wrestling match. After overthrowing all challengers, the reigning champion put out a taunting call for nobler competitors. Washington, reading under a shade tree, heard the challenge and closed his book. "Without divesting himself of his coat," Washington started "grappling" with the champion. "The struggle was fierce but momentary." The champion of the arena turned defenseless in Washington's "lionlike" grasp: "I became powerless," this champion allegedly said, "and was hurled to the ground with a force that seemed to jar the very marrow in my bones." Washington then returned to his shady resting spot and resumed reading his book.[13]

Washington wrestled, hoisted, and tossed things, almost compulsively—men, iron bars, logs, and many other items. Parson Weems, a nineteenth-century biographer, was famous for inventing the legend of Washington and the cherry tree that features the apocryphal phrase "I cannot tell a lie." With similar flourish and just as little adherence to fact, Weems also recounted that Washington's brother-in-law Fielding Lewis "has been heard to say" that the strong man could throw a stone across the Rappahannock River, precisely "at the lower ferry of Fredericksburg." However, the river was much wider back then than it is now and likely spanned 440 feet. Even Weems thought that might be pushing it and suggested that it would be difficult to find any man alive who could still manage such a feat.[14]

George Washington Parke Custis echoed the story with a tale that Washington once hurled "a piece of slate, fashioned to about the size and shape of a dollar" over the Rappahannock, where it traveled "at least thirty yards on the other side." Custis also related that he threw another stone from the stream bed over the Natural Bridge in Virginia, about 215 feet in height. Such claims were repeated so many times that they became lodged in the popular imagination. Today, kids in school know that George was the one who could toss a silver dollar across the Potomac River from Mount Vernon, a distance of almost a mile. Not only is such a feat implausible but the silver dollar was not even minted until 1794.[15]

There was no limit to Washington's feats, no iron bar he couldn't toss, no champion wrestler he couldn't best, no sprawling river he couldn't span or cross. In the nineteenth century, Washington was called on to serve his country once more, this time as an exalted icon of impossible strength, the personification of a young nation swelling with its own sense of greatness. He had become straightforward, way too simple and predictable, a middle-class hero.[16]

Washington's Body

We show Washington more respect, not less, by acknowledging his complexities. As a human being, he was exceptionally malleable and adaptive. He didn't spring into life as a demigod or act like Superman. He worked hard to become the person he ended up being, leveraging the resources available to him in that quest. Some of his attributes were natural or God given, as they say. Some he adopted or developed in the context of his society, endeavoring to better himself according to the best guidance of the day. Other attributes he adopted out of necessity as he navigated the many crises he encountered in a notably eventful life. So, where do we start in understanding the true man?

In the early 2000s, the late James C. Rees, then executive director of Mount Vernon Estate and Garden, set out to free George Washington from the idealized and often simplistic or ridiculous characterizations of popular imagination. To that end, Rees launched a project to uncover the "real George Washington," the aim of which was to develop a more objective and accurate depiction of Washington's body so as to make the first president more approachable. Rees tapped the contributions of many experts. The curators at the National Portrait Gallery helped select what they believed were the most lifelike portraits. The forensic sketch artists at the Fairfax County Police Department's Center for Missing and Exploited Children applied their skill at aging and re-aging to determine Washington's appearance over the decades of his life. Anshuman Razdan and the Partnership for Research in Spatial Modeling at Arizona State University scanned materials to create a computer image of Washington out of data. Historical tailors like Henry Cooke, of Historical Costume Services, created garment reproductions.

Rees also recruited physical and forensic anthropologist Jeffrey H. Schwartz of the University of Pittsburgh and asked him to create life-size figures portraying Washington at three important ages: nineteen, forty-five, and fifty-seven. Since Washington's skeleton was not available as forensic evidence, Schwartz and his team had to work with laser scans of the bust and life mask made by French sculptor Jean-Antoine Houdon and with reproductions of Gilbert Stuart's, Charles Willson Peale's, Rembrandt Peale's,

and John Trumbull's portraits. They also incorporated a few sets of dentures and a selection of clothing. The three figures that Schwartz and his team produced have been on display at the Mount Vernon's Donald W. Reynolds Museum and Education Center since the fall of 2006.[17]

It is difficult to say whether the three mannequins produced by these techniques are ultimately accurate or rather sophisticated works of imagination and interpretation. These mannequins are certainly not Washington. Nevertheless, Schwartz's attempt is revolutionary in its use of science and facts. The mannequins represent a significant leap past other celebrated images and icons with which the public today is far too familiar.

Among the experts appointed by Rees for his project was Linda Baumgarten, the authority on American eighteenth-century clothing, at the time curator of textiles and costumes at Colonial Williamsburg. Her goal, in her words, was "to determine size parameters for George Washington's body through his clothing"—because individuals cannot be bigger than their clothes. Baumgarten studied and measured eleven garments held at the museum in Mount Vernon: three coats, five waistcoats, two pairs of breeches, and one pair of stockings. Waistcoats are uniquely revealing as they are intended to sit close to the body and even function as a stay. The cut of waistcoats in this period was close fitting; it did not allow a slumped posture but instead encouraged one to keep one's carriage upright and one's arms set back. Breeches are also interesting. Since belts were not in use in the eighteenth century, breeches reveal the actual girth of a person. Washington's remaining garments, as measured by Baumgarten, probably date from a limited period of Washington's life, between 1780 and 1799. It's possible that young Washington's waist was slightly narrower, although the measurements Washington himself sent to his tailors throughout his life show that he generally retained a consistent body shape.[18]

Very accurate dimensions and the true shape of Washington's real body are accessible to us—the measure of his masculinity, so to speak, is there for us to see. Yet astoundingly, Schwartz's and Baumgarten's methodologies and findings are largely ignored by modern Washington scholars—those very biographers who assure their public that he must have been a physical giant and an athletic superman. Schwartz's and Baumgarten's conclusions have not changed the public perception in any significant way. Nonetheless, the facts make it clear that Washington was not a "he-man" in the Hollywood sense. Noted movie star and former governor of California Arnold Schwarzenegger had a chest measurement of fifty-seven inches during his physical prime as a bodybuilder competitor. By contrast, Washington's "garment chest varied from a low of 35 inches," Baumgarten writes, "to 44 inches." His waist, she tells us, "was probably around 35 to 36 inches in the last quarter of the 18th century." In other words, Washington was not an overly muscular or heavy man, nor was he a V-shaped athlete. Today, he would probably "wear a modern forty to forty-two long," Baumgarten states. She adds, however, that "a modern suit is shaped differently."[19]

A modern suit is different because men's bodies, now, are different. Eighteenth-century bodies didn't go through workouts at the gym—no push-ups, no lifting with dumbbells or barbells. Washington's shoulders were narrower and more sloping than modern men's shoulders. His arms appear to have been much slimmer as well. In addition, while most men today allow their backs to settle in a natural, curved posture, eighteenth-century upper-class men idealized flat backs—the sort of posture notable in ballet dancers. Like his social contemporaries, Washington could have worn stays or a corset to pull his shoulders back, flatten the shoulder blades, and puff out the chest—unfortunately, no corset has been found, nor even a description of one. Unlike female corsets, male corsets did not pull the waist in but rather pulled the shoulders back and down, elongating the slope from the neck. Corsets also accentuated the natural inward curvature of the lower back and pushed the belly out.[20]

This is not how we think of athletic masculinity today. And the truth is more striking still. Washington's body was peculiar not only by the standards of the last two centuries but according to the observations of his contemporaries as well. It was shaped, sized, and even deformed in ways that are astonishing.

Washington's head was small, and his eyes sunk deep into their sockets, as the famous portrait by Charles Willson Peale suggests. A number of contemporaries noted the smallness of his head in proportion to the rest of his body. Captain George Mercer of the First Virginia Regiment declared that Washington's head was "well shaped, though not large." "His head is small, in which respect he resembles the make of a great number of his countrymen," Isaac Weld also wrote. "His head was not large in contrast to every other part of his body," David Ackerson confirmed. Surprisingly, Washington didn't see the problem. When he placed orders for hats, he requested that the milliner make sure they would "fit a pretty large head."[21]

George Washington, by Charles Willson Peale, ca. 1779–81. Courtesy of Metropolitan Museum of Art, New York, NY.

Edward Thornton, secretary of a British minister, also described Washington's head as very small. He found his sunken eyes, which, he said, had "nothing of fire or animation or openness in their expression," rather discomforting. The sockets were larger than usual, as the painter Gilbert Stuart reported to his contemporary Isaac Weld. Stuart also noted that the upper part of Washington's nose was broader than normal.[22]

In contrast, Washington's hands and feet were an oddity because they were outsized. George Mercer, in one of the first famous characterizations of the man, remarked on Washington's large extremities and observed that he was both big boned and

knobby in his joints. David Ackerson, who met Washington in 1779 during the war, claimed that "Washington's boots were enormous. They were number 13. His ordinary walking shoes were number 11. His hands were large in proportion, and he could not buy a glove to fit him and had to have his gloves made to order. . . . His finger-joints and wrists were so large as to be genuine curiosities." George Washington Parke Custis agreed: a plaster cast of Washington's right hand "would have been preserved in museum for ages as the anatomical wonder of the eighteenth century."[23]

The peculiarity did not stop there. Washington in the nude was a spectacle that not many got to behold or report on. But George Washington Parke Custis was one of those few—and, this time, we don't have reasons to suspect he was trying to aggrandize his hero. On a hot and humid morning, Custis entered Washington's study and found him "very much undressed." He did not see a modern athletic shape, with broad shoulders and narrow hips; the hips were as wide as the shoulders. Custis was especially disturbed to see that the center of Washington's chest was indented in a pronounced way: "This is an exception to the general rule laid down by anatomists, that, where the human frame possesses great muscular power, the chest should rather be rounded out and protuberant than indented."[24]

The description is telling. Like his upper-class contemporaries, Washington may have adopted a posture that flattened the back, pulled back the shoulders, and puffed out the chest. But he also suffered from a deformity of the thoracic wall, called pectum excavatum, which prevents the sternum and rib cage from growing normally. In severe cases, this deformity can hamper proper respiration and even cardiac function.

Custis was also surprised to note that Washington sported a belly. While not massive, it was noticeable and no six pack. But this would not have been a source of embarrassment or a point of criticism. A man of Washington's time would have not minded a pronounced belly or considered it unsightly. Since classical antiquity and until relatively recently, protruding bellies have communicated health and social status—virility, in a word. Aristocrats in Britain, France, and Italy gained weight intentionally through the excessive consumption of rich food. Moreover, several upper-class men avoided physical activity and spent their "energy," so to speak, in a relentless pursuit of leisure. Eating and drinking, playing cards, and attending society events absorbed them entirely. Accumulating weight and girth was tantamount to accumulating wealth and social power.

Washington, his belly notwithstanding, was not like that. He was active and remained slender, although we have to ask ourselves what "slender" actually meant. Captain George Mercer described a young man "weighing 175 lbs when he took his seat in the House of Burgesses in 1759," certainly a healthy weight. In 1779, the Marquis de Barbé-Marbois, secretary of the French legation, portrayed Washington as "well built, rather thin." Washington himself, as a much older man, declared that he estimated his weight to be "210 lbs," adding "without the Saddle," because the purpose of that estimate was to aid in his purchase of a horse, which is an indication that 210 pounds must have included the complete gear of the rider, crop, boots, and spurs. At any rate, if we compare these figures to the average white non-Hispanic American male over the age of twenty, Washington's weight does not seem remarkable. According to the National Health and Nutrition Examination Survey, such a man today weighs 198.8 pounds and stands around five feet, eight inches tall.[25]

What about Washington's height? Did the man fill the boots? Admirers think of Washington as a giant, taller than everyone around him. As his friend the Marquis de Lafayette wrote: "Although [Washington] was surrounded by officers and citizens the majesty of his figure and his height were unmistakable." But while Washington was by no means short, he was not a colossus, either.

Thomas Jefferson, for one, was taller—one inch more, probably two. Washington is often shown to be towering above everyone else, but those depictions are usually based on vague comparisons.[26]

Virginia regiment rolls show that the median height of mature male Virginia natives was five feet, eight inches tall. Hence, whether Washington could be considered "towering" remains an open question. In fact, according to the testimonial of Lieutenant Andreas Wiederhold, a Hessian officer, Washington was a very regular-sized man. The general, he wrote, "is not especially tall, but also not short, but rather of middle height with a good body." It should be noted that Hessians, particularly the officers, were typically tall by the standards of the day and were often the most impressive physical specimens in a room.[27]

But, again, this is the realm of comparisons and subjective evaluations. Let's move to figures. On December 15, 1799, the day after Washington died, Dr. Elisha Dick measured the corpse. He reported the very generous measure of six feet, three-and-one-half inches. But postmortem height is greater. A laid-out dead person is taller because of the lack of gravity pressing on the spine. Furthermore, in Washington's case, his body had spent hours in a very cold room. It could have been frozen and thus expanded by a few extra inches. Young and alive, as captain George Mercer testified, Washington was "6 feet 2 inches in his stockings." Custis, on the other hand, claimed that Washington himself declared that "in my best days . . . I stood six feet and two inches *in ordinary shoes*"— and in the eighteenth century shoes had heels.[28]

Six-foot-two may be a tad generous. David Humphreys, Washington's aide-de-camp from June 23, 1780, to December 23, 1783, and later his biographer, and private secretary at Mount Vernon and during the presidency in New York, recorded that Washington was "clear six feet high without his shoes." Likewise, Custis swore that Washington was precisely six feet tall when "laid out in death." Isaac Weld nudged that down a bit, claiming that "The height of his person is about five feet eleven." Claude Blanchard was convinced that Washington was, at best, "five feet, eight inches."[29]

Many of us are prone to exaggerate or minimize our personal measurements when we answer to others. But it's a different matter when we confide in our tailor. In 1761, young Washington instructed his representative, Richard Washington (no relation), to make a clothing purchase for him. Washington gave him leeway in making fashion choices, as he had confidence in the man's taste. He was, however, very concerned about fit and, accordingly, was scrupulously honest in his own measurements. To that end, he wrote, "for a further Insight I dont think it amiss to add that my stature is Six feet—otherwise rather slender than Corpulent."[30]

In a different letter of 1768, Washington made it clear to his English tailor, Charles Lawrence, that he did not want form-fitting vestments: "I have no doubts but you will choose a fashionable colourd Cloth as well as a good one & make it in the best taste to sit easy & loose." Washington preferred that his clothing should not be too snug, because tight clothes "always look aukward & are uneasy to the Wearer." Apparently, the clothes he had received from this tailor before were not exactly as he wished, and so he offered feedback: "I think you have generally sent my Cloaths too short & sometimes too tight." To ensure the tailor got it right this time, he thought it "necessary again to mention that I am full Six feet high which may be a good direction to you as to the length and as I am not at all inclind to be corpulent you might easily come at my size even if your measure of me shoud be lost."[31]

In conclusion, then, nothing in the records indicates that Washington was taller than six feet or six feet, one inch—give or take. Later in life, worn down by age, by the ordeals of two wars and two presidential administrations, he may have shrunk and settled in at a pinch less than six feet. The grandiose impressions of Washington's stature or strength must be due in large part to the power of his persona, his charisma. The extent of his personal impact on others over the decades seems to have enabled him to turn his relatively ordinary height and a slightly odd physique into something more meaningful and impressive. In fact, in Washington's day, too great height would have been seen as a hindrance for an upper-class man, an embarrassment on the dance floor and in gentle society.

Upper-class men who weren't blessed with imposing statures, bulging biceps, or shapely torsos didn't feel insecure. They wouldn't have known what to do with such a type of body or how to keep it in shape. Washington, like the other founders, didn't work out in the sense that we understand it today. Exercising isolated parts of the body was not contemporary practice. Taut figures, sculpted abdomens, and muscular chests might be sexy, appealing, healthy, or commendable today, but they weren't in Washington's time. This should not be disconcerting to anyone looking for virility in their hero. There is nothing natural about preferring specific body types or attributes over others, and nothing advantageous or "evolutionary" about it either. Despite present predilections, science shows that overweight people have more energy stored in their bodies, that short individuals fare much better in colder climates, and that taller people—no matter how striking or sexy—seem to be shorter lived. It is not nature but society that defines what is beautiful, attractive, and masculine or feminine.[32]

❧ Frederick Douglass's 1852 novella, *The Heroic Slave*, depicts the hero, Madison Washington, in the following way: "Madison was of manly form, tall, symmetrical, round, and strong. In his movements he seemed to combine, with the strength of the lion, a lion's elasticity. *His torn sleeves disclosed arms like polished iron.*" George Washington, on the other hand, didn't need arms like polished iron. He didn't need to bare his chest to be respected and feared.[33]

Washington is often presented as a strongman. But eighteenth-century upper-class manliness was more than a matter of how strong and sculpted the body was. Men like Washington belonged to a violent system. More importantly, they *governed* that system, while many other men were targeted by it. Lesser white men or men in bondage, at the opposite end of the spectrum, had not much else at their disposal than their laboring robust bodies. They could work or try to beat their opponents through fight and force—like boxing or wrestling. Men who were enslaved could also escape. These were the only resources through which these men could express their manliness.

To be feared and respected, Washington did not feel compelled to adopt what today would be called a "macho" stance. Washington played sports, but the sports he chose were, by and large, those traditionally connected with upper-class social rituals. While some in the English upper classes during the eighteenth century started to take an interest in boxing, barbells, and dumbbells, Washington remained indifferent. (It was not until the 1830s that boxing and bodybuilding would become popular in America.)[34]

The sports he partook in ranged from walking and horse riding to fencing, archery, cricket, hand tennis, billiards, fishing, hunting and fox hunting. However, none of these activities ever became an obsession. He did not train, practice, build his biceps, or hone and shape his body to better his physique or out of sheer competitiveness. His sports were not a means to an end; they were ends in themselves. In other words, Washington amused himself with sports but didn't use them to make his body stronger, more toned, or sexier.

His attitude to sports was typical of the time. His version of masculinity did not overly rely on "manly" features, except to an extent with respect to the legs. While Washington did not have the shoulders, deltoids, biceps, pectorals, and stomach of an athletically shaped strongman, he did have athletic legs—but athletic legs more like those of ballet dancer Rudolph Nureyev than of bodybuilder Arnold Schwarzenegger. In her book *You Never Forget Your First*, Alexis Coe makes fun of male biographers touting Washington's thighs—the "thigh men of dad history," she labels this group. But thighs, legs, and calves were important, especially among the eighteenth-century upper classes. While powerful arms were evidence of manual labor, well-proportioned legs signaled good horsemanship, and horses were both a useful means of transportation and symbol of social distinction and virility. Virginians, in particular, attached exceptional importance to horseback riding.[35]

Because horseback riding required good legs, breeches were tight in this period, designed to show off fine thighs, toned legs, and well-proportioned calves. While the calf itself did not need to be massive, some men nevertheless wore false calves of wool woven into their stockings to create a protrusion, as was fashionable during the 1780s—"downy calves," they were called. Young upperclass men were taught to bow in a genteel way, "to make a handsome leg," as a common expression went, which required an arch outward turn. Although it was commonly believed that a large calf was a sign of reproductive power, the point of this practice was not so much to showcase a man's fertility but to signal that the owner of said calf had received proper training in riding and dancing.[36]

Washington's limbs "were long," according to Custis, "large, and sinewy." But he didn't have massive calves: "In his lower limbs," Custis concluded, "he was what is usually called straight-limbed." Washington did not wear calf padding to primp this up, so his lower legs remained flat and straight. This did not mean, however, that he was in any way delicate or weak. His walk was "majestic," another observer noted.[37]

The goal was to show the leg in a way that adhered to the prescriptions of the famous William Hogarth in his *Analysis of Beauty* (1753). According to Hogarth, while the beauty of a woman was best expressed in the serpentine line around her waist, the beauty of a man was concentrated in the leg and the curve of the thigh. As Hogarth put it, the line of the male leg should go in a "flow from muscle to muscle along the elastic skin, as pleasantly as the lightest skiff dances over the gentlest wave." Muscular proportion and graceful elegance were prized in equal measures.[38]

Washington worked hard at developing and refining his movements. His relatively muscular legs allowed him to make jumps—repeated, high, quick but graceful jumps that would distinguish him either on the dance floor or on the battlefield. Eighteenth-century witnesses could "read" those legs immediately and find in them the promise of many achievements. His legs made him a model of both polite male comportment and military virility.[39]

≈ There is no universal quality that defines manliness or masculinity. Every era and culture has its own version, and sometimes it imposes those priorities and values on the past. This was the case in the nineteenth century when it came to Washington. The Continental Army general, founder of the republic, and first president was possibly the most important political leader of the eighteenth century, but wittingly or not, he was recast to serve the nineteenth century's need for a more straightforward muscular national hero. In this process of aggrandizement, the nuances and complexity of Washington's personality and character were greatly diminished. It is time to restore Washington to his own person, as a man in full.

PART I

Physical

2

❧

Testing Himself

A Boy

A 1939 painting by Grant Wood, titled *Parson Weems' Fable*, captures and makes fun of the cherry-tree legend, the story of a
six-year-old boy who could not tell his father a lie, that biographer
Parson Weems began circulating in 1806 in the fifth edition of his
book *The Life of Washington the Great*. In Wood's painting, the face
of the toddler is uncannily perfect. It's not a boy's face. It's not
open to many possible developments. There's no dynamism, no
uncertainties. George already resembles the sixty-four-year-old
man we see in Gilbert Stuart's 1796 *Athenaeum Portrait* (from
which the image on the one-dollar bill is also taken). In the background, everyone can see the two enslaved persons picking cher-
ries from a tree—a memento of the unpalatable truth that other
human beings were trapped in Washington's greatness.

Washington, Wood's painting suggests, has always been Washington. Indeed, for many Americans, Washington was never
young. He was never a suckling baby, a snot-nosed child, a saucy
toddler, or an adolescent who could have developed into a totally
different type of adult. But, obviously, George Washington *was* at
one time a boy, just like every other man. And as a boy, George had
neither the adult face nor the anachronistic mien and stiff posture

we see in Wood's rendering. He was not destined to be the icon he became.

Boyhood is an age of possibilities, uncertainties, and existential risks. The boy had been sent to the grammar school run by Reverend James Marye, the rector of St. George's Episcopal Church, in Fredericksburg, Virginia. He probably lived in the home of his half brother, Augustine "Austin" Washington Jr., in Westmoreland County, near Fredericksburg. The premature death in 1743 of Washington's father Augustine, perhaps of pancreatic cancer, had made it impossible for George to go to England and enroll in the Appleby Grammar School, in Appleby-in-Westmorland, Cumbria—as both his father and his older half brother Lawrence had done. George could have studied Latin, Greek, and other non-practical subjects. (Whether he would have liked this experience is quite another issue.) Eventually, he could have turned out a different type of adult.[1]

We do not have too much information about the true character and educational principles of George Washington's parents. Mary Ball, the mother, was herself an orphan. Her father, Joseph Ball, died when she was an infant. Her mother, Mary Johnson, remarried when Mary was twelve years old. Married in 1731 to Augustine Washington, Mary became a widow too soon, when she was thirty-four or thirty-six—not untypical, but harrowing nonetheless. Life was tough, even for relatively rich and privileged people.

Augustine, the father, was also an orphan. George Washington's grandfather, Captain Lawrence Washington, died when Gus, as he was known, was only four years old. We can suss out from this circumstance that Augustine, just like his famous son, must have learned from very early on to rely on himself. He must have been daring as a young boy. A slaveowner, Augustine considered brutality normal and unavoidable. But, at the same time, he bought and read books. Augustine's estate inventory shows that he amassed a library of about one hundred items—not very significant compared to other planters' libraries, but still noteworthy. He eventually became active in local politics and in the Anglican church. And he served as a county sheriff. Augustine was a businessman as well. In 1725, he started an iron works, the Accokeek Furnace, in Stafford County. He fathered ten children—the first four with his first wife, Jane Butler, and the other six with Mary Ball.[2]

Young George wasn't a bookish boy, a squeamish wonk, a bashful loner. He had no qualms about wreaking havoc. He may not have chopped the cherry tree of legend, but he knew how to operate the hatchet. He was also fond of knives, slingshots, and other tools and weapons often prized by boys. He didn't get a formal degree, but claiming that George was all instinct, little knowledge, and no books, as famous testimonies have done, is both unfair and incorrect. Thomas Jefferson, for one, wrongly contended that Washington was markedly subcultured, his education having been "merely reading, writing and common arithmetic." John Adams went even further and depicted Washington as embarrassingly ignorant. If we listen to Adams, Washington was "too illiterate, unlearned, unread, for his Station and reputation."[3]

But Washington's early education was intense, much above any elementary stage, however we choose to define "elementary." It covered geometry, geography, surveying, decimals, simple and compound interest, and trigonometry. What George accomplished with his tutors is nothing short of exceptional. He never became a trained philosopher or an academic, for sure, but he derived knowledge from books. Over the last two decades, scholars have dramatically reassessed young Washington's course of reading and have discovered that he possessed a lasting intellectual curiosity, that he gave a lot of thought to reading, learning, and ideas generally. He dealt with books all his life and drew pleasure from them. When George was nine, for example, he bought his first, Reverend Dr. Ofspring Blackall's *Sufficiency of a Standing Revelation in General, and of the Scripture Revelation in Particular* (1708), although he was too immature at the time, obviously, to understand Blackall's theological intricacies.[4]

As an adult, Washington ended up assembling a personal library of more than twelve hundred titles—nine hundred books and dozens of pamphlets and other publications. No matter what John Adams said, Washington was an active reader and a buyer of books. True as it is that he wasn't born into a family of intellectuals, his father and mother were both educated and owned and read books.[5]

Mary Ball Washington's personal library contained several devotional books, which were eventually passed on to her son. Mary was familiar with popular manuals such as John Scott's *Christian Life* (1647), Thomas Comber's *Short Discourses upon the Whole Common-Prayer* (1684), and James Hervey's *Meditations and Contemplations* (1746). She used to read aloud to her children, principally from Matthew Hale's *Contemplations Moral and Divine*

(1676). But do not picture this as dull. A grandson tells us what happened: Mary would sit in the parlor, especially on Sunday evenings, pick up the devotional book, and begin a recitation. The children would gaze with admiration and wonder at the "rude representations of saints and angels, and the joys of the redeemed, and shuddered at the sight of the skeleton death and devils with horns and hoofs, holding in their claws pitchforks of fire." Reading can be a very physical and emotional experience, just like wielding a hatchet, and George himself must have drawn from that experience a sense of adventure.[6]

Books sparked George's sense of adventure—or perhaps it was just the other way around, and the books young Washington happened to read only reinforced an audacity that was already there. He read stories of sailors and travelers. The library of his half brother Lawrence featured famous books such as Jonathan Swift's *Gulliver's Travels* (1726) and James Atkinson's *Epitome of the Art of Navigation, or, a Short, Easy, and Methodical Way to Become a Compleat Navigator* (1686). In the 1740s, George bought many others himself, including the sixth edition of George Anson's *A Voyage Round the World* (1749), the seventh edition of Andrew Michael Ramsay's *The Travels of Cyrus* (1745), and the fourth edition of Daniel Defoe's *A Tour Thro' the Whole Island of Great Britain* (1748). But he was already familiar with other classics as well, like Daniel Defoe's *Robinson Crusoe* (1719), a standard work read everywhere in the English-speaking world.[7]

George didn't go to England. Augustine left no significant inheritance, and Mary had to cut unnecessary expenses. She did her best to provide her progeny with a good life. But she was now a widow with five children between the ages of five and eleven, Charles, John Augustine, Samuel, Betty, and George—Mildred, the sixth and last child, had died in infancy. Furthermore, she decided not to remarry and this had economic implications for the entire family. As a *feme sole*, she had to take care of the estate, its fields, and crops, and order the necessary supplies; she also had to manage relations with merchants, neighbors, and enslaved persons. Upper-class widows didn't lack social power; they and other single women were a considerable economic and political force. In Virginia, they could buy and sell land—and they owned nearly 20 percent of the colony's total—negotiate contracts, and manage the household as they saw fit.[8]

Archaeological evidence shows that Mary was resourceful enough and was able to give her daughter and four sons a more or less comfortable life, even though George and his younger siblings had to grow up very quickly. This was not at all unusual in this time period, when parents frequently died prematurely. Because they had no adolescence to cocoon them, their transition from boyhood to maturity was abrupt.[9]

By their mid-teens, when boyhood biologically concludes, upper-class Southern youths had to show publicly they were fit to manage slaves, attend plantation business, and participate in such gentlemanly leisure activities as hunting and horse racing. On average, Southern boys had no time to linger about and get a degree. Formal school degrees did not help them to enter a profession. Indeed, these teenagers didn't need a profession to begin with. They lived out of their estates and had already all the necessary contacts. College degrees, consequently, were only ornamental—good if you had one, but you suffered no disadvantage if you didn't.[10]

  Psychologists and cognitivists seem to agree: the brain is not the sole cognitive resource human beings have in order to solve problems and make sense of the world. This means that the so-called mind is less localized "in the head" and more distributed throughout the body. ("Embodied cognition" is the technical phrase here.) The mind is corporeal. On top of that, the ingenuity, brightness, and spiritual life of certain people take on even more practical and corporeal forms than is typical. Such people are more active and more perceptive: in a corporeal sense, they are more intelligent; they are better at deciphering signs; they can better read the environment around them; they move better; they do more things; they are more courageous; and they do not get lost easily—literally.[11]

Young George was precisely this kind of person. At Ferry Farm—the 280-acre estate that featured an eight-room master house with several outbuildings on the opposite bank of the Rappahannock River from Fredericksburg—the boy spent his time outdoors. The Washingtons and their five young children had moved there in November 1738. A very physical boy, Washington primarily relied on his own body to discover the world. Especially during his formative years, knowing for him meant experiencing and acting rather than mulling over philosophical issues. Living for him meant going places and doing things. George went out; he cut down trees, although not the cherry tree.

The relatively big yet not fancy residence offered six-year-old George a world of possibilities, challenges, adventures. He familiarized himself with animals; he fished and hunted (killing entered the boy's world right away); and he saw enslaved persons doing every kind of chore. George went to visit the outlying quarters of Ferry Farm, consisting of around six outbuildings, because he had taken an interest in the "peculiarities" of these darker-skinned workers. He also ran little errands and performed tasks. Adults who had known Washington as this type of boy—starting with the prominent Thomas Fairfax, sixth lord and baron of Cameron, George's mentor and ultimate idol—grasped his inclination for spending "much life out of doors." "He is strong and hardy," Fairfax said, "and as good a master of a horse as any could desire."[12]

Ferry Farm made George realize that he was not the center of everything. At the bustling farm, the boy could easily measure himself against a bigger world—the river, to begin with. The Rappahannock was a real, powerful gateway into the unknown. Historian and archeologist Philip Levy has brilliantly described the scenes that the boy beheld: "The sound of ships' loading and unloading—even the chatting of the sailors and workers loading and unloading—would all drift into earshot. So, too, would the sounds of other peoples' lives."[13]

George was not pampered with luxuries or tricked into believing that life was easy and that he was destined to inherit the world. No one cosseted him by creating safe zones. No one kept him cloistered in a study room. And George, for his part, enthusiastically began to assess his potential and gauge his corporeal limits. He experienced his young self as both very real, material and fleshly, and as a merely one element of a much larger social and natural order. He realized death was a part of life. He grasped that pain and violence were inevitable and that some were born into endless night. If such intense experience begot his ambition and accentuated his curiosity and social drives, it also made him realize that the universe was large and confounding—overwhelming, in one word.

Lawrence and George discussed explorations and voyages. (The world, without GPS, was much larger and daunting back then.) Lawrence supported George's intrepidity and was a crucial character in his personal development. The two teamed up, and concocted many adventurous plans. One only has survived: that George would enter a life at sea.

Lawrence, the oldest living child of Augustine Washington and his first wife, Jane Butler, was not the daring and athletic type. He wasn't the prototypical adventurer. He seemed to disprove the idea that the mind is corporeal. He was very posh. More important, he visually looked like the perfect elite person. But although his narrow face, which featured a distinguished long straight nose and high nostrils and was accompanied by an aristocratic mien, seemed to be too soft, he was a military man—eighteenth-century style. He was a marine captain and later a major at the service of King George II during the war against Spain (the so-called War of Jenkins' Ear), between 1740 and 1743, under the dual command of Vice Admiral Edward Vernon and Brigadier General Thomas

Wentworth, on board the HMS Princess Caroline. In February 1741, he headed a Virginia military company in an attack against the Spanish on Cartagena (present-day Colombia). On that occasion, he became so fond of Vice Admiral Vernon that he decided to christen his home Mount Vernon. Despite

Lawrence Washington, by unknown artist, ca. 1743. Courtesy of Mount Vernon Ladies' Association, Mount Vernon, VA.

his softness and apparent "femininity," Lawrence's ego was big: unlike his younger brother George, he believed that he belonged among the best of the British and that he could conquer the whole world.[14]

Every biography recounts Lawrence's legendary plan to turn George into a sailor. The idea to place him in the entry-level position for aspiring Royal Navy officers was strongly supported by Lawrence's father-in-law, William Fairfax of Belvoir, cousin to Lord Fairfax, who was the customs collector for the South Potomac naval district. William Fairfax's second son, Thomas, had been placed in the Royal Navy in 1740 on a career path identical to that concocted for George; tragically, however, at the time when George's naval career was being planned, Thomas was already dead, having been killed in action against the French. But no one had gotten the news yet. In any case, George's mother struck the plan down. This time, she set a limit to George's daring and physical self-reliance. She had also written to her half brother in London, Joseph Ball, for advice. He was likewise skeptical and warned his half sister that older mariners and superiors would "Cut him & Slash him and use him like a Negro, or rather, like a Dog." Although his reply, dated May 1747, likely arrived after the time in which it was needed, it validated the decision Mary Ball had already made.[15]

The men George would have met would have been hard and rough, with no dash of aristocracy thrown in, no softness, and no "femininity." Eighteenth-century sailors, who were covered with tattoos and who had burned and withered skin and often severely mangled limbs, were reckless. As often as not, their morality was dubious. Coming from the lowest ranks of society, they were poor agricultural laborers, former convicts, or individuals variously impressed into service whose primary interest was riches. They seized every opportunity, large and small, with no scruple.[16]

George was not devastated by the aborted plan. Most likely, he had already started to envision himself pursuing his destiny on land rather than at sea.

The Good (and Bad) American Nature

On March 11, 1748, a small surveying party of seven men set out for the south branch of the Potomac River. Their mission was to assess Lord Thomas Fairfax's properties. That day, Ferry Farm and the Rappahannock River ceased to be the grounds where George tested his corporeal mind. Blessed with a sturdy physicality, and precisely because he did not feel he was a little king, young Washington had powerful incentives to move on and move out. At age sixteen, Washington measured himself, physically, against the most palpable background in America, its majestic nature.

When the boy bloomed into a teenager, the relationship with American nature deepened. It was no longer just about exploring the big farm and its environs or about contemplating the bustling river. George started to don the attire of the surveyor. Philip Levy, the scholar and writer who is the most insightful about Washington's early life, writes brilliantly about surveying and surveyors in early America. The surveyor, he notes, "was a unique poet": "It was his art to take the land and its contours, its rises and falls, its turns and trees, and render them in a simple practical terse prose—the poetics of property."[17]

In order to tame nature and outline in words such an American poetics of property, the surveyor had to go into what lay beyond the known limits. He had to confront, and hopefully defeat, a very real lethal force—the wilderness. Of course, Washington is mostly known for all the nature he eventually tamed and owned. He became a substantial landowner, even if not all his land was similarly good, cultivable, and profitable. He would end up controlling about fifty thousand acres, not only in Virginia and what is today West Virginia but also in Maryland, Pennsylvania, Ohio, New York, and Kentucky. A large portion of this tamed nature was fertile, cultivated, and nurturing—thanks to the enslaved persons—in particular the eight thousand acres, distributed in five farms, that made up Mount Vernon. But the nature that teenager Washington first met was much more dangerous. This untamed nature, palpitating beyond the limits of civilization and property, contributed to the creation of his male identity at least as much as his farmland did.

As a rule, going westward boosted one's fortune. In eighteenth-century Virginia, taking measurements and "lay of lots" promised a lucrative career to every young man. George's teachers must have taught him the practical reasons why the art of measuring land had to be pursued, and George had been very responsive. As early as August 1745, he had taken notes in his school exercise books that clearly show his effort to understand the basic principles of the discipline. He studied William Leybourn's *Compleat Surveyor*, first published in 1653, the book he used the most for his school exercises.[18]

School copy book, vol. 1, 1745. Exercise Books, 1745–47, Library of Congress, George Washington Papers, series 1, Exercise Books, Diaries, and Surveys 1745–99, subseries 1A.

Land ownership secured "independency" and made all the difference between a free man and a slave. (In Virginia, land ownership, or "freeholding," remained a requirement for voting and holding office that only disappeared with the Constitution of 1850.) But other motives compelled men to go after the "fat soil" as well. The very act of conquering and converting was perhaps more important than ownership itself. Seen dynamically through the act of conquering, land and soil represented the space where manliness could be successfully tested. Conquering was superior to owning. Men had to prove themselves through their activity, either by going to war or by taking land—or better yet both. Transforming the wilderness into farmland offered an unequivocal demonstration that a man had the physical and mental abilities needed to survive, that he was able to withstand hardship and adversity and recognize opportunity, and reap rewards from it. Only "real" men could thrive in this American nature. Sex-

Surveying

Is the Art of Measuring Land and it consists of 3 Parts
1st the going round and measuring a Piece of Wood Land 2d Platting
the same and 3d To find the Content thereof and first how to
Measure a Piece of Land

First Set your Compass at A of the figure ABCD & direct
the Sights to B and See what Degree is cut by the Needle which Suppose
is North 45 Degrees East and measure the Line AB which let be 120
Poles 2dly Set your Instrument at B and direct the Sights to C and see
what Degree is cut by the Needle which Suppose is South 45 Degrees
East and measure BC 120 Poles 3dly Place your Compass at C & direct
y Sights to D and South ½ Degree west which let be 45 Degrees W and measure
CD 120 Poles and so have you done the Platting

Secondly How to Plat the same or lay it Down on Paper &
Draw the Line AD of the figure aforesaid which represents the Needle
of the Compass. 2 Take the Chord of 60 Degrees in your Dividers and Setting one foot in any convenient place of the North & South Line as at A
describe the arch N on which lay the Chord of 45 Degrees (the given Angle)
then draw the blank Line AN so long as to make Room for AB; 3d at last
take 120 Poles from the Scale of equal Parts of an inch which represents Chains and lay from A to B then draw the Line AB; so have you
finished an Operation

Next take the nearest parallel distance between the Point
at B & NeS Line and Setting one foot at any convenient Place of Said
Line as at the Point b describe the arch xx and draw the Doted Line NS
for a North and South Line then take the Chord of 60 Degrees and Setting
one foot at B describe the Arch yy next take 45 Degrees from the Line
of Chords and Set from y at the Doted NyS to z (the arch yy as will as of
former Arch NN represents an arch of y Compass) then lay a Ruler from
B to z & draw the blank Line Bz on which draw BC Black the Line
of 120 Poles taken from y Scale of equal parts, so have you done the Second
operation

ual undertones are also apparent: wilderness had to be conquered, if necessary raped, and fecundated with the masculine seed of civilization.[19]

The 1748 mission was led by James Genn, the experienced official surveyor of Prince William County. George William Fairfax, the son of William Fairfax, Lord Fairfax's first cousin, and Sarah Walker Fairfax, was propitiously a member of the expedition. Born in 1724, George William had returned from England in 1746. He had grown fond of the other George, the younger half brother of Lawrence Washington, who by this time was a member of his own family, having married George William's sister, Anne Fairfax, in 1743. Despite the eight years' age difference, George William must have cheered up George by establishing a special bond with him, conceivably enhanced by jokes and merriments—what makes every journey a special adventure. The two, obviously, had also to cooperate on practical tasks and share responsibilities. George William was too old to play pirates with his friend, but no doubt these two young up-and-coming explorers shared dreams of riches and personal success. Their futures looked promising owing to their position in Virginia society; their energy and youthful creativity must have added to that promise.

The journey was at once demanding and gratifying. The sheer distance the party had to cover posed a daunting obstacle: "We travell'd this day 40 Miles," Washington wrote in the first entry, March 11, 1758, of his journal detailing his journey over the mountains. The American land—in its materiality of woods, rivers, swamps, fields, and animals—often welcomed human guests and provided many rewards for their efforts: "We went through most beautiful Groves of Sugar Trees & spent the best part of the Day in admiring the Trees & richness of the Land," reads his entry for March 13. America was, indeed, the promised land, forthcoming, seductive. Tired and dirty at the end of each day, the company longed for respite. This peaceful American nature supplied eighteenth-century "tourists" with the pleasure that camping can bring. "Return'd to our Lodgings," Washington noted on March 16, "where we had a good Dinner prepar'd for us Wine & Rum Punch in Plenty & a good Feather Bed with clean Sheets which was a very agreeable regale."[20]

Most of the time, George felt gratified, his perception enhanced by all the specimens of the beautiful and sublime he ran into. But these seven men were no campers trudging along well-known highways. They did not frolic. No matter the beauty, they had to withstand actual miseries, like canoeing all day "in a Continued Rain" or walking along "the Worst Road that ever was trod by Man or Beast." Heavy rains and violent winds were dangerous, hardly a merriment. During "blostering" nights, young Washington awoke to his personal littleness: "We had our Tent Carried Quite of[f] with the Wind and was obliged to Lie the Latter part of the Night without covering." He shivered with cold. George was often reminded of his inexperience. He was not "so good a Woodsman as the rest of my Company." Both unskilled and veterans, however, had to endure appalling hygienic conditions. Not infrequently, the beds they slept on were "nothing but a Little Straw—Matted together without Sheets or any thing else but only one Thread Bear [threadbare] blanket with double its Weight of Vermin." They often preferred to sleep outside, "in the open Air before a fire."[21]

Nature entered George's body. The events he participated in generated both a sense of growing empowerment and a feeling of vulnerability. His responses were not simply based on bookish mock-experiences. He had read travel literature already—and he would keep enjoying this genre. He had studied textbooks. But Washington did not come up with his version of the natural world by simply reading poets or philosophers or by going to Europe to admire English or Italian gardens, as Thomas Jefferson, for example, did. George Washington took his life in his hands from the time he was a fresh teenager.

He did not hate nature, but he never romanticized it because his body had an incomparably wider experience than most human bodies of what nature means concretely. His relationship with the natural world remained one from which a sense of human vulnerability, even personal vulnerability, emerged. Nature, for him, could never be trusted. It was beautiful, at times, but most of the time, the American mountains, forests, rocks, and rivers he encountered took the shape of an adversary with whom it was unwise to strike bargains.

Young Washington got to know that traveling beyond the borders of civilization was dangerous. Taming the untamed entailed risks. Nature's forces could swiftly kill you. And this American nature could also be dangerous for a different reason. Nature could seduce and corrupt. French-born poet Hector St. John de Crèvecoeur, author of the celebrated *Letters from an American Farmer* (1782), raised his voice to warn his fellow settlers. He knew of several people who had reverted to a semibarbarian stage. Moving westward and living on the very threshold of wild nature put one beyond the power of example and the rules of civilized society. Crèvecoeur contended that travelers and frontiersmen could not but degenerate "altogether into the hunting state." They devolved into "savages" or, worse, carnivorous animals. "Eating of wild meat," he surmised, "tends to alter their temper."[22]

In fact, European settlers and colonists had tried to abstain from consuming American foods, including maize, and only succumbed when they were terribly hungry. Decades before Crèvecoeur, travel writers had already made these settlers shiver at the thought of the "seductive," nefarious effects of the "New World," its climate and natural resources. Famous philosophers and naturalists had also written about how easily people could lose the station civilization had provided them—Comte de Buffon, Cornelius De Pauw, and Baron de Montesquieu, among many others. Be wary, they all said, because America could turn you into a corrupt exemplar of the human species.[23]

Washington saw with his own eyes the corruptive power of American nature at work. On March 26, the company traveled to the house of one Solomon Hedges, a justice of the peace for Frederick County and a member of a Quaker family from Maryland. Washington could not overlook the fact that the Hedges's lifestyle showed clear signs of "degeneration," exactly what Crèvecoeur feared: "When we came to Supper," young Washington wrote in his diary, "there was neither a Cloth upon the Table nor a Knife to eat with but as good luck would have it we had Knives of [our] own."[24]

When compared to the irreparable damage nature can inflict, the want of propriety seems an inoffensive foible. But many entries and letters from the days George spent "over the mountains" insisted precisely on the excruciating dualism between civilization and what lay beyond European standards. These documents show that young Washington, in his first real journey into the wilds of America, was impressed by the "barbarism" teeming and pulsing beyond the borders of the society he was familiar with—that of the Fairfaxes, his mother, and his half brother Lawrence. Civilization was soothing, and every fragment of civilization one could retain, no matter how small, was similarly appeasing.

Letters from old friends were also soothing: "Your kind favor . . . afforded Me unspeakable pleasure," George responded to one such missive. It gave him pleasure to receive these signals from home (broadly defined), while he was lost "amongst a parcel of Barbarian's and an uncooth set of People." Civilization versus impending barbarism: this is the existential conundrum that "going out" made visible. The messages he sent back insisted on this dualism. Away from home, we do not lie on proper beds; we are subject to the "coldness of the Weather"; we are compelled to "lay down before the fire"; we are more similar to "a Parcel of Dogs or Catts" than to a human society. There was no doubt, in young Washington's mind, that civilization could get lost easily, too easily: "I have never had my Cloths of[f] but lay and sleep in them like a Negro except the few Nights I have lay'n in Frederick Town."[25]

❧ In Washington's life, landscapes soon yielded to seascapes. At the end of September 1751, he accompanied the sickly Lawrence to the British colony of Barbados. Lawrence was seriously unwell, and Barbados seemed the best place to go to restore his health. Reverend Griffith Hughes had just published *The Natural History of Barbados* (1750) in which he praised the many qualities of the island, including its serenity, health, and the pleasures it offered. *The Natural History's* botanical plates were visually beautiful—another detail that may have enticed readers to take the trip. Both Lord Fairfax and his cousin William were among the thirty-three Virginia subscribers to the publication—which George could have easily consulted ahead of the trip. Another copy was in the home of Honorable James Carter, in Bridgetown, Barbados, where the two brothers stayed briefly upon their arrival on the island.[26]

The allegedly more healthful air of the Caribbean region would restore the equilibrium that Lawrence's body had lost—or so they hoped. Perhaps not the most imposing and energetic man to begin with and quite intellectual in his mien, nature and circumstances had taken a heavy toll on Lawrence's psycho-physical equilibrium. His three children—Janet, Fairfax, and Mildred—had died, and his tuberculosis had worsened. Psychologically, he was devastated. (He would die at his Mount Vernon home in July 1752.)

The short period Washington spent in Barbados, including the passage on the vessel (most likely the brigantine *Success*), broadened his education. He was seasick during part of the long, stormy voyage. But he rationalized his agony by looking at the bigger picture. Aboard the vessel, his mind and body experienced the sublime. The variable and frequently violent weather captured him—it affected him physically. The log he kept, part of the fragmentary diary that remains, shows that he learned the proper mariner's vocabulary: departure, course, distance, difference of latitude, meridian distance, difference of longitude. On board, he talked like a sailor, referring to "right[ing] all the riggan," "croud[ing] all the Sail we cou'd," and "refitting the Riggan." And he behaved like a sailor. He commonly employed the pronoun "we" to describe the tasks mariners were usually performing—which means that he himself must have helped them. He also made observations: "Hard Squals of Wind and rain . . . the Seamen seem'd disheartened confessing they never had seen such weather before." At the end of the long journey, Washington was relieved: "This Morning agreeably arose with assurances of a certain & steady trade Wind which after neer five Weeks buffiting & being toss'd by a fickle & Merciless Ocean was gladening knews." For a short while, Lawrence's aborted plan to turn George into a mariner materialized.[27]

On November 2, the vessel entered Carlisle Bay and landed at Bridgetown. Barbados was expected to provide a refreshing experience, one that might counteract George's fears of the corrupting and harmful powers of nature, a fear he retained from his former trip "over the mountains." A reconciliation with nature's essential beauty and her "maternal" traits seemed more likely to occur here.

As soon as the brothers arrived in Bridgetown, George could see how big the city was. (A 1748 census lists 15,252 white inhabitants versus 47,132 enslaved persons.) The in-town houses of wealthy planters, an English-style church, military installations, and people speaking many languages made Bridgetown a place unlike any other young Washington had been to in his familiar Virginia. The brothers rented a one-story house belonging to one Captain Richard Crofton, built on a rise of land that was one mile from Bridgetown, at the northern end of Carlisle Bay. At £15 a month, "exclusive of Liquors," which included all liquids, not only alcoholic beverages, "& washing," it was rather expensive. But it was a very comfortable abode, commanding the "prospect of Carlisle Bay & all the shipping in such manner that none can go in or out without being open to our view." Lawrence wanted to project an aristocratic, almost fastidious image. The two brothers entered social life right away. Entertained by prominent people from commercial, political, and military circles, the Washingtons went to the balls and to the theater.[28]

In October, the rainiest month of the year, temperatures in Barbados reach daily heights of around 86°F. In November, it cools down slightly, but it is still pleasant and seductive. That November was rainy and stormy, but dank soil and sultry air made the "Avagado," the "Pine Apple," the "Granadella," the "Sappadilla," the "Guaba's," and other tropical fruits exceptionally tasty. George discovered these fruits and liked them, "tho none pleases my taste as do's the Pine." Immersing himself in this alluring, beautiful landscape, he obliterated the bad memories from his former 1748 trip. If one was blind enough to overlook the miserable, seminaked enslaved persons who toiled in the fields, it was easy to be entirely taken in: he was "perfectly rav[ished by] the beautiful prospects wh[ich on] every side presented to our view The fields of Cain [sugarcane], Corn, Fruit Trees, &c. in a delightful Green."[29]

Rapture, unfortunately, didn't last. With its lush vegetation, succulent fruits, and enrapturing landscapes, nature could be nurturing. But young Washington learned at his own expense that nature is not animated by any maternal disposition—and does not abide by human plans. It was November 16 when George was bedridden with smallpox. It was almost a month before he could get on his feet again. Lawrence, meanwhile, didn't show any signs of recovery. In a desperate last try, he went to Bermuda. He hoped that a different island could afford a better therapy. If the Barbados air had not produced the expected relief, as Lawrence wrote his father-in-law, it was because it had no "change of seasons." Nature, there, seemed to have no program, no variation, and no discipline. "Bodily diversions," Lawrence philosophized, were consequently wanting, and "we soon tire of the same prospect." (Eighteenth-century people lived in a totally different world from ours.) In a place like Barbados, he concluded, "our bodies are too much relaxed"—by which he meant unmanned and seduced to an extreme. Furthermore, the hot and sultry climate sapped all the remaining energy: "I am obliged to ride out by the first dawn of the day, for by the time the sun is half an hour high, it is as hot as at any time of the day."[30]

By December 22, after Lawrence had left for Bermuda, George was on board the *Industry*, bound for Virginia. He celebrated Christmas at sea, dining on an "Irish goose" and drinking "a health to our absent friends." He did not reach Virginia until January 29, and so he had that time to mull over his experience in Barbados. Was it positive? Would his dear Lawrence survive? Had he discovered a natural world that was fundamentally better than the one he had known before?[31]

A Soldier, Eventually

For a short period, Washington had become a sailor of sorts. He had talked like a sailor and had perhaps looked like a "jacktar," or simply "tar." When he was on deck helping, young Washington could have easily borrowed a spare pair of the typical loose-fit, ankle-high trousers that eighteenth-century sailors used to waterproof with tar—hence, the name. Like a seaman—but this is pure speculation—Washington might have tied his hair into a ponytail and applied tar to it to prevent it from getting caught in pulleys and hawsers. Whether on or off board, jacktars wobbled around with a characteristic gait that they developed in response to having to try to regain balance as they walked across the deck of a ship rolling and pitching over the waves. Eighteenth-century sailors had a distinctive bow-legged appearance, their feet being far apart; and because the vestibular system of their inner ear had a hard time readjusting to land, when these sailors returned to land, they felt off balance and, as a result, they continued to sway. George may well have walked like them, at least for a short while.[32]

But Washington the sailor was short lived. After his return from Barbados, he forgot about it. He also bid adieu to surveying. Between the ages of seventeen and twenty, George had practiced land surveying with intensity, despite the extreme discomfort and risks. During that time, he had carried out more than 190 surveys, nearly all of them for grants of new lands on the frontiers of Lord Fairfax's Northern Neck Proprietary. During the fall of 1749 alone, for example, he had run at least fifteen surveys on the Lost River. But by the end of 1752, he gave it up and started envisioning himself as a soldier. This transition from surveyor to soldier intensified his physical experience of American nature, mountains, forests, rocks, and rivers.

At the end of January 1752, returning from his journey to Barbados aboard the *Industry*, Washington made landfall in the lower part of the York River. Proceeding by land to Williamsburg, he decided to pay a visit to Governor Robert Dinwiddie in the hope that he might gain an audience and make a persuasive case for why he should be granted a military commission. He presented letters of introduction, and eventually he was invited to stay for dinner. By approaching the governor, Washington, once again, chose to take his life in his hands. Objectively, it was not the most hazardous venture he had embarked on so far or would embark on in the near future. But providing Dinwiddie with the opportunity to evaluate him was risky. Dinwiddie was a powerful man, someone who could censure him or thwart his plans to become a soldier.

Washington was lucky because he and the governor had a point of connection in Barbados. The governor had served as surveyor general of customs for the Southern District of America and so was familiar with the island and loved it. The two no doubt shared experiences of that exotic place. Over a glass (or more) of Madeira, the older man probably talked and talked. The outcome was that the two hit it off immediately. An old, short, chubby, ruddy man, Dinwiddie saw in the young, daring Washington his physical opposite. Not only were they physically different, but they also belonged to different social stations. Regardless, Dinwiddie saw something striking in that aspiring youth, in that physical presence, in that swagger.

The plan worked out. In February 1753, Governor Dinwiddie appointed George adjutant of the Southern District of Virginia with the rank of major. His full title was "Major and Adjutant of the Militia, Horse and Foot, in the counties of Princess Anne, Norfolk, Nansemond, Isle of Wight, Southampton, Surrey, Brunswick, Prince George, Dinwiddie, Chesterfield, Amelia, and Cumberland." (Washington was later reassigned to the Northern Neck, a position much closer to home.) Dinwiddie now needed him. Along with other colonial governors, he had deep concerns about the mounting French presence in the Ohio Valley. Since the seventeenth century, the Ohio Valley had attracted both British and French traders. Occasional skirmishes between the two may have occurred, but that was it. However, by the mid-eighteenth century, the French had intensified their presence, building forts where they should not have, at least according to the British, and installing armed forces at various sites. The threat the French posed was clear: if the British wanted to expand westward, they had to control this important gateway.[33]

Suddenly, twenty-year-old Washington was on a mission. There was a new, very promising career waiting ahead. The British colonial authorities did not want to wage war—at least not yet—and the adjutant's task was limited to delivering a letter from Governor Dinwiddie to the French commandant of Fort Le Boeuf, present-day Waterford in northwest Pennsylvania. Dinwiddie's wishful thinking was that the French would agree to a "peacable Departure." The letter that Washington carried in his hand straightforwardly asked "by whose Authority & Instructions, You have lately marcht [marched] from Canada with an arm'd Force, & invaded the King of Great Britain's Territories." In addition to delivering the letter, Washington had to gather information about French intentions and settlements. On October 31, 1753, Washington headed out. A new journey and a new experience was under way.[34]

The diaries of the narrative of his journey to Fort Le Boeuf repeat themes and topics of previous journals: rain and snow, mires and swamps, frozen rivers, hefty miles to cover, tiredness, risks. Some entries are particularly revealing of the extreme physical discomfort Washington had to endure. We learn, for example, that the passage down the creek on his way back from Fort Le Boeuf to the near village of Venango, from December 16 to December 22, was incredibly "tedious & very fatiguing": "Several Times we had like to have stove against Rocks, & many Times were oblig'd all Hands to get out, & remain in the Water Half an Hour or more." In one place, the ice was too thick for the prow of the canoe to make its way through, and "therefore we were oblig'd to carry our Canoe across a neck Land a quarter of a Mile over." It took Washington and his small crew six days to follow the meandering waterway to Venango.[35]

But this time, beyond the description of physical discomfort and of water freezing to one's clothes, Washington's narrative communicates a sense of doom, of imminent catastrophe, of extreme personal anxiety, sensations that do not appear in his earlier journals. The military context accounts for this: these men knew they could be targeted by other men. Washington's diaries of the trip to the French commandant add more vivid colors to the portrait of a young man meandering through the wilds of America. These diaries also reference certain psychological and anthropological experiences that Washington, now a soldier, would be forced to undergo many times over. Deep in the woods, dirty and tired, frustrated, "with my Pack at my back, with my Papers & Provisions in it, & a Gun," he fitted himself "into an Indian walking Dress" and donned a "Match Coat." A matchcoat was a robe, like a duffel, made of animal skin with the fur turned inward for warmth. It was worn with the traditional leggings and moccasins. One could easily sleep in it. Was Washington Daniel Boone? Was he Davy Crockett?[36]

By December 23, Washington was on his long ride back to Williamsburg. He carried the answer to Dinwiddie's letter, which was noncommittal. The French commandant of Fort Le Boeuf, Jacques Le Gardeur de Saint-Pierre, did not believe himself obliged to obey Dinwiddie's command. The load had become immense; war was on the horizon, and everyone, human and nonhuman, was exhausted. "Our Horses were now so weak & feeble, & the Baggage heavy" that all men had to walk. "The Horses grew less able to travel every Day. The Cold increas'd very fast, & the Roads were geting much worse by a deep Snow continually Freezing."[37]

Although these and similar incidents are no doubt familiar to many readers, I dwell on them because these dense and harrowing natural spaces left an unequivocal imprint that would accompany Washington for the rest of his days. The famous episode of Washington crossing the Allegheny River magnificently serves to conjure the extreme physicality of the surroundings this young soldier had to face. On the morning of December 29, 1753, Washington and Christopher Gist, the experienced guide he had engaged at the beginning of this journey, reached the west bank of the Allegheny River. The Indian town of Shanapins, or Shannopin, near the site of modern-day Pittsburgh, Pennsylvania, was just a few miles downstream on the opposite bank. The river was not entirely frozen, as they had expected and hoped, and the current was dragging big chunks of ice. To cross it, Washington and his guide built a makeshift raft out of loose logs with "but one poor Hatchet." (This is no cherry tree fantasy.) After sunset, they set off using crude poles to steer. Far from shore, the raft jammed against an ice pack and the current twisted them about, sending Washington plunging into the water. The cold nearly killed him. He held on to the side of the raft somehow until his guide dragged him back on. They camped that night on an island, known today as Herr's Island or Washington's Landing. The two were soaked to the skin, suffering from hypothermia, surrounded by enemies and an ominous wilderness. "The Cold was so extream severe, that Mr. Gist got all his Fingers, & some of his Toes Froze."[38]

Only the next morning the frozen water allowed the two men to finally reach the shore. They resumed their march right away, but they did not make it back to Williamsburg until January 16. Reflecting on the undertaking and the inclement human and natural environments he had just traveled into, he concluded it had been worse than surveying and worse than his recent trip to Barbados. He realized he had been exposed to unfathomable forces. Except for one or two days, as Washington wrote in his diary, "it rain'd or snow'd incessantly & throughout the whole Journey." When natural forces prevail with such abandon, even a bivouac, a flimsy tent, may provide both physical and psychological relief. In such circumstances, a layer of plain-weave linen canvas may become a home—and, symbolically, a shelter for the self. He felt vulnerable, "especially after we had left our Tent." The tent was the only "Screen," as he called it, separating him from the "Inclemency" of the immeasurable natural surroundings.[39]

✺ It was in the context of these extreme conditions—shivering with the terrible cold, with sore limbs and frozen toes, and surrounded by invisible enemies—that Washington defined his mind, spirit, and body. As a result of this kind of experience his male identity flourished, but not an identity like that of the cartoonish characters portrayed by John Wayne, and not one like that of a hypermasculine nineteenth-century hero, a boorish figure à la painter Emanuel Leutze. While crossing eighteenth-century waterways, walking under pouring rain, skipping over floating ice, falling into deep snow, trudging along impassable roads, and sleeping in his tent, Washington completed his education. While these events were in one sense accidental and just happened to him, at the same time, they became essential parts of Washington's self: *they were him*. They made Washington's mind and body at once. Additionally, they give us precise coordinates if we want to reclaim this eighteenth-century man for what he really was. Washington could never ever become a dreaming "son of nature," like Thomas Jefferson, the eighteenth-century poet of the American pastoral.

3

❧

A Taste for Cruelty and War

Shocking Scenes

*W*ars bring out the best and the worst of human nature. They trigger heroism and compassion as well as cowardice and wanton recklessness. As a soldier, Washington crossed paths with all types of men: heroes and cowards and plotters, deceivers, and traitors, "ploting every Scheme that the Devil & Man cou'd invent." Surveying was trying, a cornerstone in the development of Washington's sense of masculinity, but it was almost nothing in comparison to soldiering. Unlike a surveyor, at least under normal circumstances, a soldier deals with a human enemy, a person armed with a musket, an arrow, a tomahawk, or a knife.[1]

To an extent, Washington was already prepared for some of the terrible things to come. We must remember that eighteenth-century standards were different. Violence and cruel behaviors, which many of us would readily censure as inhumane, were normal in that long-gone world. And young Washington accepted the most extreme brutalities as a fact of life.

He was perhaps a little too young when he first witnessed the extremes of violence of "man over man." In March 1754, Washington became lieutenant colonel of the Virginia Regiment, and a few months later, he experienced his first real carnage at the Forks of the Ohio (present-day Pittsburgh). It was a "fatal environment," to quote the evocative phrase Richard Slotkin uses to describe the American frontier. On May 24, Washington and his men had arrived at the Great Meadows, what is now Wharton Township, Fayette County, Pennsylvania. He surmised that the Great Meadows was a convenient place to make a stand. "We have, with Natures assistance made a good Intrenchment," Washington informed Dinwiddie, "and by clearing the Bushes out of these Meadows prepar'd a charming field for an Encounter." "An encounter": young Washington had perfectly internalized the vocabulary of soldiery, just as he did when he had adopted the language of surveying and sailing. Words are empowering. They allow us to see ourselves and the world, and they act like a torch enlightening the obscurity. As his behavior evinces, Washington was already a full-fledged soldier.[2]

The night of May 26–27, 1754, sentries at the camp at the Great Meadows noticed something; perhaps it was the French or perhaps just a few escaping deserters. They fired, but no one fired back. On the morning of May 27, Washington sent Gist off with seventy-five men to search for the French intruders. That evening, Washington himself headed out with forty men. Eventually, their reconnaissance effort paid off; they found where the French were encamped. They were about thirty-five men—a tally that included the commander, the Franco-Canadian ensign Joseph Coulon de Villiers de Jumonville. What the French had in mind was not clear. Were they about to attack? Washington, in any case, decided to anticipate them.

On May 28, at what is today Jumonville's Rocks, North Union Township, Fayette County, Pennsylvania, a bloodbath took place. It was very early in the morning, and the French had just woken up. Some were shaving. Some were having breakfast. With the assistance of an Ohio Iroquois leader—Tanacharison or Tanaghrisson, known to the British as Half King—Washington and his men marched "one after the other, in the *Indian* Manner." When they got close to the French, they were discovered, "whereupon," Washington writes, "I ordered my Company to fire."[3]

The action only lasted fifteen minutes, but it was intense. The two fronts exchanged volleys of shots, and casualties ensued. Those who were wounded only slightly, like Lieutenant Thomas Waggener, had some chance to recover. But gunshot wounds were serious stuff. The 0.75 caliber (three-quarters of an inch) flintlock musket (the "Brown Bess") deployed by the British ejected a lead ball that weighed about an ounce. Even if the ideal distance was fifty yards, this musket could stop a man at up to three hundred yards. At the optimal range, in a human body, the shot left an entrance hole about the size of the ball. The exit hole could reach three to five inches across. This ball did not expand, but it shattered every tissue and created an irregular exit wound almost impossible to dress.

The exact chain of events is debatable, and who assumed responsibility for what is also uncertain. Jumonville may have acted as an ambassador and tried to deliver a summons to the British to get them to leave French territory—just what Washington had done a few months earlier on his mission to the French commandant. The British Americans may have opened fire upon the enemy without warning. Likely, on this occasion, Washington did more than just ordering his company to fire.

Legend has it that Washington fired the first shot—the famous shot that ignited a world war, the nearly ten-year-long French and Indian War. But what does "first shot" mean, exactly? Historian David Preston recently discovered a new document entitled "A Treaty with the Indians at Camp Mount Pleasant October 18th 1754" that suggests Washington did not simply discharge his musket as a signal to his men but began shooting at the enemy. In this document, a British scribe recorded word for word some Native Americans' speeches, translated by an interpreter. One "Chief Warrior," whose identity we don't know, delivered a speech in which he claimed that "Col. Washington begun himself and fired

and then his people," hinting that Washington aimed at a particular French soldier in order to kill him.[4]

In all probability, during this first "encounter," Washington killed
a man. There is no indication that he was shocked or that, afterward, he suffered from what we call posttraumatic stress disorder.
Young Washington found himself in the midst of a harrowing scene.
He saw the ten, perhaps twelve, French Canadians who were slain,
including Jumonville, the commander of the party. Washington
saw the French scattered after the initial attack and their escape
blocked by Tanaghrisson's warriors. He saw his Native American
allies rushing to the scene, taking their tomahawks, and splitting
open the heads of the enemies. He saw Tanaghrisson mocking a
wounded Jumonville—"Tu n'es pas encore mort, mon père" ("You
are not yet dead, my father")—then killing him with his tomahawk, taking out his brain and washing his hands in it, and then
scalping him. He saw Indians scalping the dead and taking away,
as Washington wrote, "the most Part of their Arms." He saw the
mountain glen transform into an extraordinarily macabre landscape; unburied and scalped French corpses were strewn about, and
a Frenchman's decapitated head was stuck on a pole.[5]

Cruelty abounded. And yet letters and entries in Washington's
diary indicate that the young soldier wasn't particularly devastated
by those scenes of mangled human bodies. The letters he sent to
Governor Dinwiddie and other recipients in the days immediately
following the battle of May 28 radiate military professionalism and
dispassionate objectivity—he was conspicuously detached, almost
accountant-like in his mien. He didn't flinch, didn't betray emotions, didn't philosophize over the plight of the human condition,
and didn't look for support from religion. With his superiors,
Washington discussed practical matters. He wanted to show he
was mature and reliable and thus gain their approval.

With his younger brother John Augustine, Washington hid
himself still more effectively beneath the persona he had newly

fashioned. The passage is famous and yet worth a fresh analysis: "I can with truth assure you, I heard Bulletts whistle and believe me there was something charming in the sound." One of his most quoted letters, this document extolling the "charming" sound of bullets may be interpreted in many ways: an instance of juvenile bravado; a demonstration that the father of his country was born fearless and more than human, or, more likely, an indication that on occasion Washington could be influenced by his body in action, that, in this case, shaped his psyche. Young Washington knew what a real soldier was expected to say and feel while receiving the enemy's fire. Consequently, in claiming the sound of bullets was charming, he was not quite lying but attempting to fully inhabit the role he had assumed.[6]

The famous eighteenth-century English writer Horace Walpole was likely the first in a long series of interpreters to suggest that Washington's utterance was downright bravado. As Walpole wrote, "this brave braggart learned to blush for his rodomontade." Maybe he did, or maybe he didn't. But my hypothesis is that, in this case, Washington's jesting was not braggadocio. While depicting himself as a soldier and acting as one, young Washington said and felt what he *had to* say and feel.[7]

William James once argued that "we feel sorry because we cry, angry because we strike, afraid because we tremble, and not that we cry, strike, or tremble, because we are sorry, angry, or fearful, as the case may be." So, as James would say on this occasion, Washington acted as a soldier and, as a consequence, he found the sound "charming." Not only did Washington say what he had to say: the sound was, for him, actually charming. For sure, he wouldn't have uttered or written such a sentence—not even in private and to the most trusted confidant—had he envisioned himself dressed up in a garb different from that of a man exercising the profession of arms.[8]

Back at the Great Meadows, Washington and his men tidied up and planned out how they would resist the Franco-Canadian revenge. So-called Fort Necessity was their only abode—a hut, really, rather than a fort, that could not provide any shelter. Perhaps worse, these men had already run short of supplies. Pouring rain began on July 2. Soon trenches turned into ditches. Mosquitoes and mud were everywhere. All this created extreme discomfort and, furthermore, put ammunition in jeopardy. In a desperate attempt, Washington had his men cut down trees to make improvised breastworks.[9]

Military historians have described the battle of July 3, the military defeat, the surrender of Fort Necessity, the negotiations, and the signing of the Articles of Capitulation—which included, at least in theory, the privilege of the "honors of war," plus a controversial admission that the British, under Washington's command, had "assassinated" Jumonville. After Virginia troops abandoned the fort, the French and their Native American allies looted their baggage and supply, a show of disrespect and an act intended to humiliate the adversary. The looting reminds us that wars are always more than what happens while soldiers are "on duty," and that military codes, honor, and signed documents can easily be disregarded.

That ominous summer of 1754 during the battle at Fort Necessity, Washington calculated that thirty British and American soldiers had died on duty, and that seventy had been wounded. The enemy, he claimed, suffered the most, "above three hundred" killed or wounded. (Washington was wrong on this, as no more than a handful of French met their death or suffered severe wounds.) No matter the precise tally, soldiers died on both sides—and that was largely anticipated. But "collateral damage" and the sight of total destruction, of undifferentiated violence, were heavier to bear. Wars are more than striking a military target. Humiliating the adversary and destroying their morale is a nonconventional military strategy that is as effective as shooting them on the battlefield. It would be too much to conclude that Washington was psychologically shattered by all the waste that the battle had left behind, including innocents lying on the ground. But he did, in fact, remark on these unnecessary atrocities: "The Enemy had deprived us of all our Creatures; by killing, in the Beginning of the Engagement, our Horses, Cattle, and every living Thing they could, even to the very Dogs."[10]

❧ After Fort Necessity came the worst catastrophe of this season of Washington's life—Braddock's defeat at the battle of the Monongahela River. British major general Edward Braddock, an experienced military man, had high hopes of beating the Franco-Canadians. In May 1755, Braddock met with Benjamin Franklin in Fredericktown, Maryland. He boasted, as Franklin later wrote in his autobiography, about all the positive circumstances that could lead to a quick victory, concluding that the Marquis Du Quesne, the French governor general of New France, could "hardly detain" him "above three or four days."[11]

Another summer rolled in, bringing another dreadful July. General Braddock marched to capture Fort Duquesne, built by the French in 1754 at the convergence point of the Allegheny and Monongahela rivers, in what is now downtown Pittsburgh. But things didn't go as expected. Braddock overlooked the difficult terrain and underestimated the "savages" fighting, not surprisingly, in a very "savage" manner, hiding beneath trees and shrubs. On July 6, in the morning, Braddock was unaware that these warriors were surreptitiously attacking the baggage train at the end of the flying column. He didn't know that they had already killed and scalped a soldier and a woman. It took the rear guard a while to drive them off. It was already a nightmare, even before the battle itself broke out.

July 9, 1755, was the date of the final carnage. Native Americans allied to the French (the Ottawas and Potawatomis) committed wondrously violent acts. They killed British soldiers with their tomahawks and then nailed their scalps to trees. During the battle, they made a chilling whoop sound that spread panic throughout the British infantry. Projectiles seemed to come unexpectedly from everywhere, not only from the enemy's lines. Washington stormed into battle, not yet fully recovered from a recent bout of the "flux," or dysentery.[12]

Musket balls pierced his coat, but none struck him: "By the all powerful dispensatns [dispensations] of Providence, I have been protected beyond all human probability & expectation for I had 4 Bullets through my Coat, and two Horses shot under me yet although death was levelling my companions on every side of me. escaped unhurt." British and Virginian soldiers lost their temper, their discipline, and consequently their lives. Washington didn't know what to do. Reestablishing discipline was difficult. With the flat of his sword, he hit the cowards who had sought to duck the battle. And yet chaos persisted. As the French gave vent to their muskets, British soldiers fired blindly into the thick woods filled with smoke. Chaos and random events played a role as well. Braddock himself was shot in the lung by one of his men and died four days later.[13]

While in battle death is inevitable, one should nevertheless seek to prevent barbarities and vile exploits. Young Washington was no philosopher, but in the months following Fort Necessity and Braddock's defeat, he witnessed atrocities that forced him to formulate a not-so-cheerful theory of human nature. Too many "melancholy accounts" kept piling up, too many innocents were being slain, preventing Washington from rejoicing in the greatness of the human species.

On April 24, 1756, Washington informed Dinwiddie that while Braddock was dead, the war was far from over: "Three families were murdered the night before last at the distance of less than twelve miles from this place: and every day we have accounts of such cruelties and Barbarities, as are shocking to human nature." Washington did not make this up to buttress preexisting biases against Native Americans. On May 13, the *Pennsylvania Gazette* recounted the atrocities that took place near Winchester: "6 Indians came through the North Mountain . . . and surprized one David Kelly and Family; Kelly they killed and scalped, and carried off his Wife and six Children." One boy managed to escape, reached Winchester, and spread the terrible news. Washington sent thirty men right away to help, but all they could do was bury the poor Kelly. Desolation prevailed among whites and nonwhites alike: "8 Houses were burnt, 6 of which by the Indians, the other two supposed to be set on Fire by some white People, for the Sake of Plunder." Hearing accounts of people butchered was the norm.[14]

Native Americans could be cruel and in a "communal" way. Captain Thomas Morris of His Majesty's Seventeenth Regiment of Infantry was captured and taken to an Indian village. These people, he wrote in his journal, "tied me by the neck to a post, and now every one was preparing to act his part in torturing me." Captain Morris provides a shocking description of what happened. Let me quote extensively from his account: "The usual modes of torturing prisoners are applying hot stones to the soles of the feet, running hot needles into the eyes, which latter cruelty is generally performed by the women, and shooting arrows and running and pulling them out of the sufferer in order to shoot them again and again: this is generally done by the children. The torture is often continued two or three days, if they can contrive to keep the prisoner alive so long." Morris was lucky. Other testimonies told of men captured by the Indians after Braddock's defeat who were taken in triumph to Fort Duquesne, where they underwent a ritual torture with fire, to which death was the inescapable ending.[15]

"Shocking Scenes" like these and many others could never be forgotten. Thirty years after the events at the Monongahela River and the massacres and tortures at the breakout of the French and Indian War, George Washington still remembered perfectly all the horrors: "The dead—the dying—the groans—lamentation—and crys along the Road of the wounded for help." These scenes "were enough to pierce a heart of adamant." Neither the groans of the dying nor the fatal environment itself, "the gloom & horror" that "was not a little encreased by the impervious darkness occasioned by the close shade of thick woods," would ever be erased from his memory.[16]

A Very Masculine Commander in Chief

"*I* am a warrior," Washington bellowed in a 1779 letter to the Delaware Nation. He had gained the title through direct experience, especially after his participation in the other violent affair that was the American Revolution. We may too easily forget the brutality of the War of Independence. As historian Holger Hoock has recently made clear, that war was not an aristocratic undertaking among eighteenth-century coiffed upper classes in which etiquette and mutual respect reigned.[17]

Elected commander in chief by the Congress with a unanimous vote on June 15, 1775, Washington stepped immediately into his role. He had been preparing himself for the culmination of his military career for a very long time. Besides gaining military experience in the field, Washington had also read military books. Julius Caesar's *Commentaries* and Quintus Curtius's *History of the War of Alexander the Great* had long been with him. In 1755, after Braddock's defeat, he had ordered a copy of Humphrey Bland's *Treatise of Military Discipline*, first published in 1727. Most likely, he was already familiar with this book, as Lawrence had a copy because young British aspiring officers typically read Bland before joining the army. Washington kept buying and reading military treatises.[18]

But the Revolution was more than a book and a set of military principles. It was just plain terrible. Both sides slaughtered and mangled their respective enemies. They destroyed property and sexually abused women. "The Enemy like locusts Sweep the Jerseys with the Besom of destruction" and "Ravish the fair Sex, from the Age of Ten to Seventy," Adam Stephen informed Thomas Jefferson at the end of 1776. Washington tried his best to curtail this behavior on the American side. "HIS Excellency General WASHINGTON," the general orders stated, "strictly forbids all the officers and soldiers of the Continental army, of the militia, and all recruiting parties, plundering any person whatsoever, whether Tories or others." The general not only had moral qualms about such behavior but was also mindful of the risk of alienating the local population: "It is expected that humanity and tenderness to women and children will distinguish brave Americans, contending for liberty, from infamous mercenary ravagers, whether British or Hessians."[19]

Left to themselves, both common soldiers and officers, whether British or American, could easily become brutes. Washington wrote to William Livingston, the governor of New Jersey, of a certain "Robert Combs, a Tavernkeeper in Pennytown." Combs "can inform you of a Rape committed on the Wife & Daughter of one Jno. [John] Christopher by the Enemy while they lay there." Washington got news of other similar assaults: "Philip Parmer's [Palmer] daughter was also ravished by six soldiers in that Neighbourhood—Thomas Keynes daughter was treated in the same manner."[20]

On or around the battlefields, so many brutalities took place that a complete list would occupy volumes. For instance, on May 31, 1777, William Martin, lieutenant of the Oliver Spencer's Additional Continental Regiment was ambushed and wounded by a British-Hessian unit near Bound Brook, New Jersey, and he called out for quarter but to no avail. He was "butchered with the greatest cruelty." He was bayonetted about twenty times. His nose was cut off and his eyes yanked out. Washington ordered Martin's body to be brought to his headquarters. He had the body washed and shown as a proof of the enemy's inhumanity. Eventually, he sent the body to General Charles Cornwallis: "I think it my duty to send his mangled body, to your lines, as an undeniable testimony of the fact, should it be doubted, and as the best appeal to your humanity for the justice of our complaint."[21]

Just as in the French and Indian War, cruelty was everywhere. On February 27, 1777, the *Pennsylvania Evening Post* published a letter from an unidentified American "officer of distinction" that recounted the fate of the adjutant William Kelly and five other soldiers of the Fifth Virginia Regiment who, with light wounds only, had been carried off the field. Their lives could have been easily spared, "but the enemy coming on that ground, murdered them by beating out their brains, with barbarity exceeding that of the savages." At the battle of Princeton in early January, Lieutenant Bartholomew Yates of the First Virginia Regiment had been killed in a similarly brutal manner. He had begged for mercy, but his captors had no compassion. Yates was shot in the breast and then stabbed about thirteen times and then clubbed with the musket. The fate of the hapless Yates recalls that of General Hugh Mercer on the same battlefield. A member of Washington's staff, Mercer had been isolated and swarmed by British troops. He was bayoneted at least seven times. When he refused to surrender, he was finished off with musket butts; his body was then displayed at a Philadelphia coffeehouse.[22]

Now acting the part of the supreme commander, Washington could not afford to lose his temper or give in to despair, even though he was living in extreme discomfort. From his quarters, he wrote several letters every day to ensure his officers understood what needed to be done. On the whole, he trusted his chain of command, but to contain the inevitable excesses of human nature, punishment was an effective tool—the general knew he could rely on brutality against his own soldiers. The mystery of George Washington lies here: the civilized man could, on occasion, turn into a very straightforward and reckless male, becoming himself a "barbarian."

From the time of his first experience during the French and Indian War, Washington had proved repeatedly that he was not afraid of flogging traitors, even with perhaps unnecessary cruelty. Exemplary punishment had become both his motto and his practice. Colonel Washington agreed with the harshest sentences handed down by courts-martial: according to his orders for one long-gone day in July 1756, "Andrew Lockhart should receive four hundred lashes: William Pritchard one thousand lashes, and be drummed out of the Regiment with a halter 'round his neck. John Leigh and Thomas Simmons . . . two hundred and fifty lashes each. William Davis being an old offender—a thousand lashes: and John Jenkins, being persuaded off by Davis, five hundred lashes. and Robert Yates for Theft, and assisting in secreting a Deserter, one thousand lashes."[23]

It's unlikely that such a number of lashes was delivered, since Deuteronomy 25:1–3 had established the golden number at thirty-nine, allegedly one short of death. No man would have survived these fantastical numbers. Depending on how lashes are delivered and with which instrument, the skin may tear apart after a few blows, and the probability of irremediably damaging internal organs and even causing heart failure increases with the number. For this precise reason, Washington made sure a surgeon was present: "The above prisoners to receive as much of their punishment as the Surgeon (who must attend upon this occasion) shall judge they are able to bear, this night at retreat-beating." One John Maxfield, tried for desertion, for example, had to be "whipped Thirty-nine Lashes on his naked back for said offence." Another, Nathaniel Stanley, tried for "absenting himself," was similarly "whipped Thirty-nine Lashes on his naked back, and . . . confined seven days upon bread and water." Many others scoundrels were treated the same, with the understanding that "the General approves of the foregoing Sentences, & orders them put in execution at the usual time and place." But even if thirty-nine was the golden number, orders from Washington specifying four hundred or one thousand lashes were common, and they made the soldiers shiver with horror.[24]

On September 20, 1776, the Continental Congress revised the Articles of War and raised the limit on lashes from thirty-nine to one hundred. The general orders Washington sent out before that date show that he had no problems exceeding the biblical limit, and nothing changed after that date. In June 1778, for example, soldier Edward Conolly was found guilty of desertion and worse still of treason, as he had soon thereafter reenlisted in the enemy's army. Consequently, he was "sentenced to receive two hundred lashes, one hundred for each Crime." Of course, the "Commander in Chief approves the sentence."[25]

🐦 Washington took recourse to brutality on a regular basis, whether flogging or worse. Killing was something he could do and did do. Killing animals, to begin with, didn't give him a second thought. When "the number of Dogs that follow the Troops" turned into "a great Neausance in Camp," the young military commander ordered that "all Stray Dogs" that could be found be hanged. Killing these "nuisances" was the obvious solution. In the eighteenth century, violence toward animals—who had not yet become pets—was not taboo. Many years later, Washington felt he had to enjoin his overseers, once again, to hang dogs. The potential loss of some of his sheep sent him into a rage: "I not only approve of your killing those Dogs which have been the occasion of the late loss, & of thinning the Plantations of others," the old plantation master wrote Mr. Whitting in 1792, "but give it as a positive order, that after saying what dog, or dogs shall remain, if any negro presumes under any pretence whatsoever, to preserve, or bring one into the family, that he shall be severely punished, and the dog hanged." On this occasion, he killed dogs to send a clear message to the persons he owned as chattel.[26]

No one among Washington's contemporaries would have seen anything reproachable in the practice of hanging dogs or, similarly, drowning puppies when they were undesirable. Washington loved dogs, as everyone already knows. He bred them and gave them nifty names: Chanter, Forrester, Sancho, Ringwood, Drunkard, Sentwell, Singer, and Busy. Nonetheless, when one of the puppies the bitch Musick gave birth to in 1769 was "thought not true" to the breed, Washington resolved that the hapless one had to be "drownd immediately." The others "were saved." Washington brutalized and killed animals just for fun; he did not just hunt for consumption. In 1770, he wrote in his journal that "we proceeded up the River with the Canoe about 4 Miles more, & then incampd & went a Hunting." There was no military necessity to hunt at that moment, no need to forage in order to supply the troops. It was just play—"game," if you will. Washington's party, on that exploration route in 1770, "killd 5 Buffaloes & wounded some others—three deer &ca." The reason was simply that "this Country abounds in Buffalo & wild game of all kinds."[27]

We shouldn't apply twenty-first-century standards to the eighteenth-century world. But a case can be made that casual lack of compassion and unwarranted cruelty toward sentient beings needs to be judged by a higher, universal standard. We can pit this brutality against what some would call "moral sense." The basic notion of civilization seems to be at issue here.

The unvarnished truth is that Washington was at the same time civilized and humane and, at least occasionally, severely inhumane and violent. Not only did he commit "small" acts of violence toward animals, but he made deliberate decisions to kill other human beings. He had relied on capital punishment since the beginning of his military career. During the French and Indian War, desertion had been a problem. In May 1756, Washington caught Henry Campbell, a "criminal," as he called the man, and the "most atrocious villain" who "richly merits an ignominious Death." Washington, as a twenty-four-year-old colonel, perhaps had to go down this road. But he certainly also wanted to, if for no other reason than to show Governor Dinwiddie he was strong and determined.

Campbell, in his view, had been a bad example to others. For this very reason, he had to be made into a "good" example and a memento: "I hope your Honour will think him as worthy an Example against Desertion." The idea of setting an example became Washington's obsession: "These Examples, and proper encouragement for good Behaviour, will I hope, bring the Soldiers under proper Discipline."[28]

This line of reasoning is no doubt morally problematic. German philosopher Immanuel Kant, a disciple of the Enlightenment, would soon be questioning the practice of treating human beings instrumentally. Kant enjoined people to act "in such a way that you treat humanity, whether in your own person or in the person of another, always at the same time as an end and never simply as a means." This was for him a universal maxim and what he called a "categorical imperative." But Washington considered exemplary punishment the most sensible norm. In the summer of 1757, the court-martial decreed that fourteen soldiers had to be hanged. Washington pardoned twelve of them, but regarding the other two, Ignatius Edwards and William Smith, he was unrelenting: "Our Honor [Dinwiddie] will, I hope excuse my hanging, instead of shooting them." Being shot was more honorable. But hanging Washington believed "conveyed much more terror to others; and it was for example sake, we did it."[29]

Hanging people to deter others was the deepest brutality as was advertising that "I have a gallows near 40 feet high erected (which has terrified the *rest* exceedingly) and I am determined . . . to hang two or three on it as an example to others." Washington was convinced that lenity did not produce the desired effects but triggered more "villainous undertakings." "One of those who were condemned to be hanged, deserted immediately upon receiving his pardon. In short, they tire my patience, & almost weary me to death!" Here, Washington engaged in brutality by deploying language that turned death into a joke and a metaphor ("weary me to death!"); this language had the effect of minimizing the fact that real deaths were taking place everywhere.[30]

Over the two wars, Washington had the last word when it came to the life or death of many American soldiers. When he judged it convenient, he was amenable to abiding by standards of humaneness, happy to pardon criminals and ready to make exceptions to his practice of treating punishment as exemplary: "As your Honor was pleased to leave to my discretion, to punish or pardon the criminals," he wrote to Dinwiddie, "I have resolved on the latter." In this circumstance, Washington may have foregone capital punishment only because these petty criminals represented an "example of so little weight," as he reasoned, or he may have been moved by humanitarian considerations: "Those poor unhappy criminals have undergone no small pain of body and mind, in a dark prison, closely ironed!" Whatever Washington's deep motives, the persona he projected as a young leader was complex; he could live according to more than one standard; he could change depending on the context.[31]

As a more mature commander, Washington came to understand that the norm of military life could not be based on threats of deprivation of life. Punishment was necessary, but the "want of a proper gradation of punishments," as he lamented during the Revolution, was for him a serious bother. "The interval between a hundred lashes and death is too great and requires to be filled by some intermediate stages," he wrote to the Camp Committee at the Continental Congress. To "inflict capital punishment upon every deserter, or other heinous offender" would "incur the imputation of cruelty." Furthermore, there was also the pragmatic consideration that "the familiarity of the example," would "destroy its efficacy." So, for both pragmatic and humanitarian reasons, Washington maintained that other punishments "short of the destruction of life, in some degree adequate to the crime" had to be devised.[32]

Over the years, Washington became much less enthusiastic

about exemplary punishment, considering it often counterproductive: "We do not see the multiplying of executions produce the effects for which they were intended." But here comes a caveat: Washington may have been less enthusiastic in theory about exemplary punishment, but in fact, he deployed the method with regularity. In September 1780, David Hall, a soldier from Colonel Walter Stewart's battalion of light infantry, stole money and silver plates from a local resident. Washington sentenced him to death and forced fifty men from every brigade to watch.[33]

Likewise, the case of Major John André, the British spy and the main coconspirator of traitor Benedict Arnold, became a gaudy public spectacle, a state of affairs for which Washington was largely responsible: "The Commander in Chief directs the execution of the above Sentence in the usual way this afternoon at five o'clock precisely." The sentence was eventually postponed for twenty-four hours, but not because he had second thoughts. It was only that he had devised a way to make it more spectacular: "A Battalion of Eighty files from each wing [has] to attend the Execution." On October 2, 1780, Major André was taken to the gallows. The day before, he had pleaded for a firing squad. But Washington proclaimed that this traitor had to die, ignominiously, by hanging. Most likely, traitor Benedict Arnold would have met the same destiny had Washington succeeded in abducting him: "My aim is to make a public example of him."[34]

❧ George Washington had first met Native American warriors during his 1748 surveying trip along the South Branch of the Potomac River. He was not much of an anthropologist, and so his reaction was that of a biased and patronizing white man. He saw these warriors performing a ritual dance in which they cleared "a Large Circle" and made "a great Fire in the Middle." He then beheld the "best Dauncer" jumping up "as one awaked out of a Sleep." But all that, he concluded, was just "comicle."[35]

By the end of his life, Washington's perspective had changed dramatically. Natives were no longer "ignorant" and "comicle"; they had become neighbors. He nurtured the dream that whites might "live in peace & amity with these borderers." His hope was that all these different peoples, with different cultures and traditions, would *assimilate* under the banner of the United States of America.[36]

Washington also went through a middle phase in relationship with Native Americans. During the years of the Revolution, the commander in chief saw Native Americans for who they were, real women and men who acted and reacted and who often were fierce enemies, even "cruel & blood thirsty" ones. He realized that the condescending belief that the "Indian" was constitutionally weak or "comicle" or already defeated by history was completely false. Eventually, too many Natives ended up being wiped away, though this happened through brute violence, and not because "history" had decreed it or because Native Americans were feeble.[37]

During the Revolution, General Washington lived up to his reputation as a *conotocarious*, a "devourer of villages." Washington inherited this name from his great-grandfather, John Washington. In the late seventeenth century, John Washington had fought to put down an Indian uprising in Virginia and Maryland. When five warrior chiefs sought to negotiate under a truce flag, he and the other colonists murdered them. As a consequence, the Susquehannahs gave John Washington an Iroquoian name that means "town taker." John Washington's reputation was apparently not forgotten, for when Native Americans first saw the young Washington, they called him by the same name. Washington himself was aware of the origins of his name, "registered in their Manner and communicated to other Nations of Indians."[38]

The most striking example of Washington as a *conotocarious* was undoubtedly the year 1779. The Iroquois Confederacy kept attacking the Continental Army, especially in the area that is today upstate New York, and he wanted these attacks to stop by whatever means necessary. He wrote to Major General John Sullivan about what he thought had to be done to maximize the effects of a military expedition he devised "against the hostile tribes of the six nations of Indians, with their associates and adherents." On this occasion, Washington showed hypermasculine determination, recklessness, and blind violence: "The immediate objects are the total destruction and devastation of their settlements and the capture of as many prisoners of every age and sex as possible." There's no context here that can be supplied to exculpate him from what he did. His military strategy entailed starving these people to death: "It will be essential to ruin their crops now in the ground and prevent their planting more." Sullivan's troops must not be timid, Washington insisted; soldiers must "make rather than receive attacks, attended with as much impetuosity, shouting and noise as possible." Fighting during the French and Indian War, Washington had honed the tactics of psychological warfare and was now fully aware of the role fear could play: "It should be previously impressed upon the minds of the men wherever they have an opportunity, to rush on with the war hoop and fixed bayonet— Nothing will disconcert and terrify the Indians more than this."[39]

The campaign was "successful," as the Continental Army destroyed more than forty Iroquois villages and opened the road to new settlements in the Ohio Country, the Great Lakes region, western Pennsylvania, West Virginia, and Kentucky. But curbing the morale and the bodies of these fierce warriors was not an easy task. Many Native Americans remained unwavering, if not openly challenging and boastful in their manly attitude. Like Washington himself, Iroquois leaders had a strong sense of self. Admired in the period for their physical excellence, Native American warriors were also praised for their character, their "activity and indefatigable Sufferings," as Washington had remarked during the French and Indian War. Given their psychological strength and resilience, Colonel Henry Bouquet told Washington it "would be easier to make Indians of our White men, than to cox that damned Tanny Race."[40]

The situation in late eighteenth-century America, nevertheless, was not one of individual against individual, or group against group, as if the participants were on a level playing field. What gave Washington and his men a clear advantage over nonwhite persons was not so much their psychological or physical strength *as individuals*, but an implicit and yet very real set of communal and material resources, transatlantic in their reach, systemic in their constitution. Washington and his soldiers, including the British, could count on advantages such as armies, a navy, superior technology, and effective mercantile connections. Other "others" had no similar assets.

The Slaveowner's Brutality

No chapter on Washington's education in brutality would be complete without an analysis of the gruesome reality of slavery. When he went to Barbados as a young man, he was exposed to horrifying spectacles such as that described by one traveler, John Benson of Rhode Island, in which "the heads of slaves, [were] fixed upon sharp pointed stakes, while their unburied carcases were exposed to be torn by dogs and vultures on the sandy beach." Horrors such as these took place on the continent as well. It was not rare to see executed slaves' heads posted on chimneys at the local courthouses.[41]

Washington didn't invent this "peculiar" and appalling system. However, he got used to it. In all probability, Washington was in his thirties before he heard anything critical about slavery or started to question it. No matter how much Washington's mature intellect may have abhorred slavery as a national scandal, Washington as a person participated physically and emotionally in a brutal system for fifty-six years of his life. In this, he was no different from the other American founders. As historian Lorri Glover writes, "Racial power was *elemental* to their worldview." It was part of their sense of self, a domain that critical thinking could not reach.[42]

In fact, Washington became a slaveowner at age eleven, after his father died and left him the 280-acre farm near Fredericksburg, plus ten slaves. A young adult, he bought eight more human beings. After he married Martha Dandridge Custis in January 1759, Washington added another eighty-four enslaved persons to the family property. By the time of the Revolution, Washington had bought forty more people. In addition, he assumed ownership over the large number of children born to enslaved people on the estate. Reliable estimates suggest that during the course of his life Washington managed or owned nearly 670 enslaved individuals.[43]

That he was a "generous & noble master," as his family members and admirers often claimed, and that he may have repeatedly shown kindness in small ways to "his people" does not change the situation much. Washington was certainly not a sadistic person, but the institution of slavery in which he fully partook is sadistic in itself. So, he earned his first badge of brutality by simply having participated in the game—there was no need for him to do anything else.[44]

But there are many other badges that a slaveowner could and would attain. Because slavery was in itself brutal, even a "generous & noble master" could commit single acts of brutality. These acts vary among themselves, and Washington experimented with them all. A complete catalogue would occupy volumes, but let me provide at least a representative selection of execrable deeds. (The fact that Washington himself wasn't even aware he was perpetrating brutality by his acts adds to the brutality itself.)

Brutality could assume the form of selling slaves and breaking up families. Persons who belonged to debtors, for example, were often sold at tavern lotteries. In 1769, Washington himself cosponsored a lottery for the estate of Bernard Moore of Chelsea in King

William County, who had defaulted on his loans. It was against his inclination, as he wrote in 1786, "to hurt the feelings of those unhappy people by a separation of man and wife, or of families." But a close examination of his financial papers and other documents shows that he made repeated exceptions to this maxim. Unsurprisingly, the people he sold were labeled unrepentant "nuisances," referred to as drunkards, thieves, or idlers. In 1766, Tom, regarded as a formidable troublemaker, was sold in the West Indies, where his destiny would be toiling to death on a sugar plantation. And that was not all: Washington also instructed Captain Thompson to "keep him handcuffd till you get to Sea—or in the Bay." It's very likely that he had kept Tom in shackles before delivering him to the captain.[45]

Violence was also a part of smaller and seemingly less consequential acts, like talking to another person using a specific tone of voice. The Englishman Richard Parkinson was "amazed" by Washington's interaction with his slaves. With them, he "spoke as differently as if he had been quite another man, or had been in anger." While the level of cruelty that inhered in a way of speaking was low, it no doubt helped enforce arbitrary hierarchies and social differences. Parkinson also claimed that Washington treated his slaves "with more severity than any other man."[46]

That way of talking didn't help the slaveowner to empathize with enslaved persons either, or encourage him to rethink his ingrained negative implicit biases. He thought those people were "constitutionally" shirkers and liars and so deserved harsh treatment. Was Doll, to take another example, "really unable to work"? Washington doubted it. The overseer should not be tricked by her "deceitful complaints, of which she is very capable of making," he stated. "Negroes will either idle or slight their work if they are not closely attended to," he insisted on another occasion.[47]

An assistant of sculptor Jean-Antoine Houdon, known as Beglair, was a witness to an episode in which one of Washington's bonded

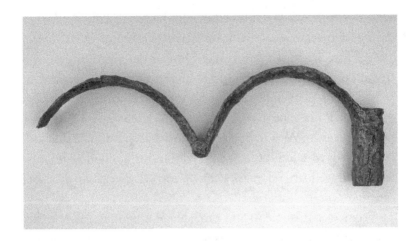

men, whose arm was in a sling, lamented the injury. But Washington didn't buy it. He put one hand in his pocket and mimicked raking with the other: "Since you still have one hand free," he said, "you can guide a rake. See how I do it." How could this intelligent man not grasp that, morally, it didn't make any difference whether in this case the injury was real or just pretended? Deception was not an issue here, as the poor man had the moral right to try to resist the cruel joke and make his burden a little lighter.[48]

Fragment of iron shackles found at Mount Vernon. Courtesy of Mount Vernon Ladies' Association, Mount Vernon, VA.

As a matter of fact, Washington exploited enslaved laborers recklessly, in particular those in the fields. "Every labourer (male or female)," Washington wrote to the new overseer, must do "as much in the 24 hours as their strength without endangering the health, or constitution will allow of." It wasn't easy to work for this detail-oriented man, who continuously looked over the shoulders of those subjected to his iron will, who maintained a close watch on all aspects of the plantation, who constantly pointed out better ways to do a job. "In his govern[men]t of his estates and domestics," one testimony wrote, "he was remarkably particular & exact. . . . A rule once established by him became a law." And when daring "domestics" escaped, a similarly reckless pursuit was inexorable. Historian Erica Armstrong Dunbar described in her wonderful book the relentless, well-planned, and cruel hunt for Ona Judge, Martha's chambermaid, who took off from the President's House in Philadelphia on May 21, 1796. Each time an enslaved person ran away, Washington asked himself a question he shouldn't have asked: why did these people, who in his opinion were privileged and well treated, make such an incomprehensible decision? The question itself is cruel.[49]

Physical punishments are probably the epitome of brutality. Washington wasn't timid in this regard either. Threats were hurled, at first, with the aim of eliciting terror. In one letter to an overseer, he bemoaned the fact that enslaved sewers were making only six shirts a week when they were supposed to make nine: "Tell them therefore from me, that what *has* been done, *shall* be done by fair or foul means." Should sewers fall short of this quota, they would "be sent to the several Plantations, & be placed as common laborers under the Overseers thereat." Similarly, in 1793, Washington warned that one Billy Muclus, an underachieving brick layer, would be "severely punished and placed under one of the Overseers as a common hoe negro" if he did not get up to speed.[50]

Each time Washington said "severely punished," he meant "whipped." With his personal approval, enslaved people were regularly whipped on his farms, at least from 1758 on. The most famous episode is probably the one involving the seamstress Charlotte. In 1793, Anthony Whitting whipped her with a hickory switch. Her fault: being "impudent" and "indolent." After he delivered this first whipping, Whitting told Washington that he expected he would "give her some More of it before She will behave herself." Whitting had no scruples whatsoever: "I am determined to lower her Spirit or Skin her Back." For his part, Washington was in full approval: "Your treatment of Charlotte was very proper."

At least in this circumstance, Washington was oblivious of the difference between "proper" in the sense of habitual and technically legal and "proper" in the sense of what is humane and moral. "If she or any other of the servants will not do their duty by fair means, or are impertinent, correction (as the only alternative) must be administered."[51]

Would Washington stop anywhere? Was there a line he wouldn't cross? It is not known for sure. There are stories that suggest that even with the persons he held in bondage, he had a penchant for inflicting exemplary punishments. An oral tradition passed on through Sall Twine's descendants, for example, relates that Washington was capable of inflicting these types of punishments. During the Revolution, Sall Twine, a young woman, had befriended a British officer who was kept as prisoner of war at or near Mount Vernon. The British had promised freedom to any slave who would support their cause against the American rebels, and Twine's hope was to accompany the officer back to England at the end of the war. Predictably, the plan fell through, and all she got was a "W" that an overseer branded on her cheek, a terrible memento of her insolence.[52]

But Washington not only consented to such atrocities; there's the possibility that he also acted violently, personally and directly, on those bodies he claimed as his property. In 1833, John Gadsby Chapman, the Alexandria-born painter, interviewed Lawrence Lewis, Washington's nephew and manager of Mount Vernon from 1797 to 1802. Besides telling Gadsby the usual stories about Washington's Herculean strength, Lewis also dwelled on Isaac, the skilled head carpenter at Mount Vernon. According to Lewis, on one occasion Isaac did a poor job in following Washington's directions about how some logs had to be cut. When Washington asked who did the poor work, Isaac confessed. Isaac recounted to Lewis that, without saying a word, Washington "gave me such a slap on the side of my head that I whirled round like a top & before I knew where I was Master was gone." Did Washington beat his slaves, full-grown men? There is another story. One morning, a "servant" brought Washington his boots. Washington was in the habit of examining them to make sure they were clean. If they were not, "the servant got them about his head but without the Genl. betraying any excitement beyond the effort of the moment."[53]

❧ Who George Washington was is a question that can never be fully answered; we cannot pretend we know all the facets of this long-gone surveyor, young soldier, Indian hunter, commander in chief during a violent revolution, and slaveowner. Here I have not explored softer sides of Washington's personality but have aimed to demonstrate that he regularly behaved cruelly, that eighteenth-century Euro-Americans were often exposed to horrific scenes, that agony was a daily companion for too many human beings, that life, both human and nonhuman, was way too expendable, that precarity and risk were inescapable, even for the upper classes, and that moral standards were rather imprecise and flexible. Is it different today? Yes and no. But we do know better—or at least we *should* know better. No matter how much we may admire our Washington, the myth, the legend, the familiar symbol, no matter how much we may praise his many achievements and successes, we all must agree that real George Washington is not "one of us." In many ways, he is not relatable.

4

๛

A Body in Pain

By the Skin of His Teeth

Contrary to what many people may assume, Washington did not neglect his teeth. Like other upper-class individuals, he was fastidious about what today we call "oral hygiene." Eighteenth-century men and women, principally those of means, often tampered with their teeth—but they did so with improper tools and harmful dentifrices. They should not have used all those picks and irons that were available to them. Lord Chesterfield, a British diplomat and the eighteenth-century unspoken master of style and bon vivre, underwent the same ordeal as Washington. Chesterfield took care of his teeth thoroughly, exactly as Washington did, with picks, irons, and other odd utensils. The outcome was invariably the same. At a relatively young age, Chesterfield's teeth were almost gone: "My desire to have them look better, made me use sticks, irons, etc., which totally destroyed them; so that I have not now above six or seven left."[1]

George Washington's education in brutality, along with his exploration of the physical limits of the human body, is relevant to the way he approached his teeth. If in Washington's world it was normal to witness violence and see other bodies mangled and butchered, it was likewise normal for individuals to act violently toward themselves or let "doctors" subject them to violent treatments. This is not to hint at masochism or similar aberrations. There was nothing pathological about George Washington. And yet Washington inflicted pain upon his own body, and let many others do the same.

And the most fabulous chapter of Washington in pain and agony concerns his teeth. Popular legend has it that he ended up wearing wooden teeth—at times, they were even wooden teeth he had carved himself. Of course, this is not true; the truth is in fact even more gruesome. (The legend probably originates from the fact that the ivory on Washington's dentures became stained and grained over time, which may have tricked some observers into thinking they were made of wood.) Dentistry, in the period, was not yet a noble art—nor a lucrative one, at that. It was still largely practiced by barbers and reckless practitioners, people often more brutal in their methods than the enemy a soldier could face in battle. Like the enemy, these "experts" could very well kill their patients; not immediately, but certainly in the long run, by administering lethal doses of arsenic or by letting a patient's body get to the point where it responds to an infection with sepsis. Every patient, in the best-case scenario, would have been administered a urine rinse or have been blistered, burned, or mangled.[2]

The story of Washington's teeth can be easily summed up. On November 26, 1755, during Braddock's campaign, he hired his first dentist, Dr. William Baker. At twenty-four, he had his first tooth extracted by one Dr. Watson, paying him five shillings for the job. After that, he lost teeth one by one. When he was sworn in as president, in 1789, only one tooth was still in place, which Dr. John Greenwood pulled in 1796. Washington allowed him to keep the tooth as a talisman. Greenwood had it placed inside a small glass display that he hung to his watch chain. He carried the relic around with him for the rest of his life.[3]

Understandably, Washington's tooth loss embarrassed him a great deal. He did not want his secret to become public: "I would not wish that this matter be made a parade of," he wrote in 1783. To the very end, he tried to ensure that people would not gossip about his less-than-perfect mouth. In 1798, he jotted "For Mr Jno. Greenwood and to be opened

by him only" across the back of a letter to his dentist. Ironically, Henry Clinton, commander of the British forces in North America during the Revolution, had intercepted a letter Washington sent in 1781 to another dentist, John Baker, in which the general discussed dental issues openly. (Coincidentally, Clinton himself had already used a dentist named Jean Pierre Le Mayeur, whom Washington would also use.) Washington's secret was already public. The letter Clinton intercepted was crystal clear, and Clinton must have had a laugh on the subject. Washington had written: "A day or two ago I requested Colo. Harrison to apply to you for a pair of Pincers to fasten the wire of my teeth. I hope you furnished him with them. I now wish you would send me one of your scrapers, as my teeth stand in need of cleaning." The mention of pincers, wire, and cleaning scrapers all point to dentures.[4]

Washington had never been a chatterbox. But what contributed to his legendary silences was also the fact that, by the early 1780s, his teeth were failing him. He was embarrassed. He could no longer speak fluently: "The general converses with great deliberation, & with ease," one testimony noted, "except in pronouncing some few words, in which he has a hesitancy of speech." Senator William Maclay described his speech similarly: "His voice [is] hollow and indistinct, owing, as I believe, to artificial teeth before in his upper jaw." Besides making it difficult to voice sibilant sounds, eighteenth-century dentures could also easily slip off the mouth.[5]

Teeth not only perform mechanical functions, making speaking and chewing possible (good digestion and nutrition are impossible if food is not properly introduced into the stomach). They also carry symbolic, aesthetic, and social value. The mouth is at the center of the human self, our face. In Latin, "os"—from which comes the adjective "oral"—means "mouth." But "os" also means "source," "face," "speech," or "mask." We all know, at least in an instinctive way, that teeth are more than enamel and protruding bones. A missing tooth can affect one's appearance and expression, which can in turn affect the extent to which one is socially successful. Showing good teeth when smiling is a powerful social signifier. But poor Washington couldn't even smile: "I never see that man laugh to show his teeth," an elderly former enslaved man attested. "He done all his laughing inside."[6]

The mouth was central to the individuality of eighteenth-century people. For them, just as it is for us, a perfect mouth was a statement and a status symbol; more than simply a vehicle for verbal language, the mouth was a nonverbal language in itself. As

Auguste Caron's popular book *Lady's Toilette* put it, "Nothing is more pleasing than clean, white teeth, and gums of the colour of the rose." At the opposite extreme, "foul teeth announce vulgar sentiments."[7]

Washington regularly bought tooth brushes as well as picks, irons, pinches, and the like, and he loved dental hygiene sets. He bought tongue scrapers and, of course, dentifrices. Such dentifrices, usually in a powder form but sometime a paste, might be made of ground minerals like pearls, talc, or pumice or might be made of organic material like coral or cuttlefish. They might be mixed with water essences, tree gum, spices, or herbs. They invariably contained acids and were all strong abrasives. Abrasive dentifrices combined with the action of tooth scrapers were detrimental to gums and roots. Scrapers were used by more experienced dentists or by people themselves to remove tartar and stains on dentures or on living teeth. Washington customarily operated on his own teeth.[8]

Washington's dental hygiene traveling set. Courtesy of Mount Vernon Ladies' Association, Mount Vernon, VA.

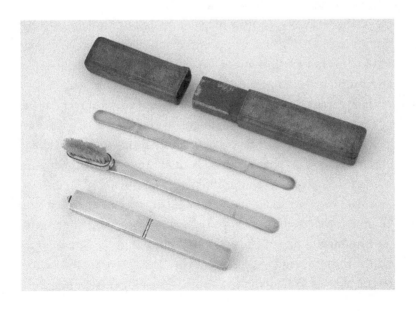

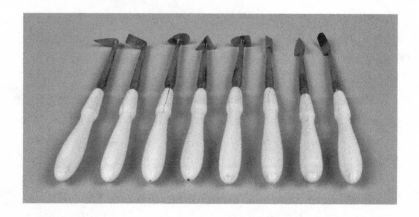

While it is impossible to ascertain the precise circumstances under which Washington lost each and every tooth, the fact that he regularly fiddled with scrapers gives us an essential indication. By scraping the contour of his teeth with nonsterile tools, Washington eased the job of bacteria. Bacteria cause infections, and infections (gingivitis and periodontitis) lead to more serious periodontal diseases. The analysis specialists made of the last tooth—the one that was given to Dr. Greenwood—confirms this hypothesis. Washington lost his last tooth as a result of the destruction of the gum and alveolar bone due to periodontal disease.

Harm was caused not only by a mechanical action of scraping but by the substances that Washington regularly ingested. Eighteenth-century medicines were a concoction of poisons such as lead and other metals. The pharmaceuticals of the period had many unwanted side effects. When in the winter of 1764 John Adams was inoculated against smallpox, he noted that every tooth in his head became "so loose that I believe I could have pulled them all with my Thumb and finger." Adams found himself in the "same Situation with my Friend Washington, who attributed his misfortune to cracking of Walnuts in his Youth." Washington's dental problem did not stem from cracking nuts. Like other individuals from that strange and unfamiliar era, he injured himself with picks, irons, scrapes, and abrasives; he regularly poisoned himself with dentifrices and medications; he rinsed his mouth with tinctures and abused opioids (such as laudanum, an alcoholic extract of opium) to smother the pain.[9]

In 1759, for example, Washington bought "Six Bottles of Greenhows Tincture." Thomas Greenough was a well-respected London apothecary whose shop was at 10 Ludgate Hill, near St Paul. His patented tinctures were used to clean teeth and to cure toothache. They were a mouthwash made from alum (potassium aluminum sulfate), bitter almond (*Prunus dulcis*), logwood (*Haematoxylum campechianum*), orris root (from *Iris germanica* and *Iris pallida*), horse-radish, cochineal, cassia berries (similar to cinnamon), and potassium oxalate (a dicarboxylic acid)—all extracted into alcohol. The typical advertisement promised that Greenough's wondrous tincture "cleanses and takes off all Foulness from the Teeth, renders them white and beautiful, perfectly fastens such as are loose, prevents their decaying, and entirely cures the Scurvy and all other Disorders in the Gums."[10]

Tinctures such as this one remained very popular across the decades. In 1783, for example, Dr. Brown, "lately arrived from Denmark," advertised in the Boston *Gazette* a secret cleansing that rendered teeth "as white as Alabaster; notwithstanding they may be as black as coal." This magical liquid, it was declared, can "also fasten the Teeth . . . and causes the Gums to grow up to the Teeth though ever so much decayed." Brown's medicines, the ad promised, "are at once of an innocent and salutary Nature, and never fail of giving Satisfaction to all who use them."[11]

Neither Greenough's rinse nor any other similar tincture Washington and his contemporaries may have tested on themselves worked particularly well. In the 1760s and 1770s, Washington kept losing teeth, steadily and inescapably. By flipping through his account books, we can get a precise idea of how many dentists he had to employ. He paid for Drs. Baker, Watson, Fendall, Spence, Greenwood, Le Mayeur, Gardette, Peale (Charles Willson, the painter), and Whitlock. From 1772 through 1774, in particular, Washington underwent a period of great difficulty. He paid cash to Dr. Baker on April 6, 1772, March 11, 1773, and October 15, October 26 and 27, November 26, June 14, and August 1, 1774.[12]

Not all of Washington's dentists were created equal. Washington liked some more than others and, more importantly, some were better than others. Dr. John Baker was good enough. Baker relieved Washington of some defective teeth that had long burdened him. And he was the first to build a partial denture, made of ivory, that he fastened to Washington's remaining teeth.

❧ Dentures, alas, soon became Washington's universally acknowledged totem. ("Washington = dentures" is a formula that every American elementary school student knows.) The five sets of dentures he ordered between 1789 and 1798 required constant tinkering and repairs. They also required the utmost care: "I Advice you," Dr. John Greenwood wrote to Washington in December 1798, "to Either take them out After dinner and put them in cleain [clean] water and put in another scett [set] or Cleain them with a brush and som Chalk scraped fine. it will Absorbe the Acid which Collects from the mouth and preserve them longer." In the eighteenth-century world, dentures were time-consuming and expensive items, a true status symbol.[13]

Greenwood, from New York, treated Washington from about 1789 until his death. He prepared and repaired several of Washington's prostheses. His advertisements in the New York *Daily Advertiser* made the process of securing dentures appear much easier than it was: "Persons at any distance may be supplied with artificial teeth, by sending an impression, taken in Wax, of the vacant place where wanted." Greenwood had made a first set of dentures for Washington in 1789. Carved out of a single piece of walrus tusk with real

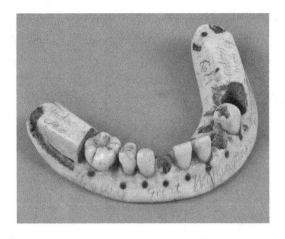

❧
Washington's dentures,
by John Greenwood, 1789.
Courtesy of New York
Academy of Medicine
Library, New York, NY.

human teeth fitted into the base, this set has a hole in it and apparently was fastened to Washington's only remaining tooth. When the capital moved to Philadelphia, it became much more difficult for Greenwood to fit Washington's dentures. No matter what he claimed in his advertisements, Greenwood conceded that in fact "it is dificult to do these things whithout being on the spot."[14]

Greenwood built other sets of full dentures for his famous and now toothless patient. The first relic, a fragment of a mandibular denture from a piece of elephant tusk, is preserved in the (former) Royal London Hospital, now Barts Health Archives and Museums. A second specimen, with the upper (maxillary) part missing, is in the Dr. Samuel D. Harris National Museum of Dentistry, Baltimore. Made in 1795 and greatly altered in 1798, it is carved entirely from hippopotamus teeth, which is harder and denser than elephant tusk and doesn't stain or deteriorate as quickly. It had an impressive maxillary plate of pure gold. The teeth themselves came from elephant, hippopotamus, and walrus ivory. (This set was stolen in 1981 while on display at the Smithsonian, presumably because of the gold rather than for its historic value, and the upper part was never recovered.) A third set of dentures included improvements that Washington had requested. In all probability, this set went into the tomb with Washington. And, finally, there is the grisly exemplar that tourists today can admire in the Museum at Mount Vernon—it's unmarked, and so we don't know if Greenwood built it. Unwearable, it's made of a mix of human teeth and probably horse, cow, and elephant teeth and a plate made of lead tin alloy, silver alloy, and copper alloy.[15]

For all the tampering and constant trimming involved, dentures were technical marvels. Artisanal and artistic abilities were required to assemble such a potpourri of disparate materials into something that looked like human teeth and was wearable. Especially difficult was making the "gums" comfortable enough or at least not too harmful to the mouth. To turn these devices into semioperative instruments allowing for some kind of mastication, springs were attached. Since these dentures lacked a proper palate, the wearer had to apply constant pressure to counteract the springs.

All this was painful, with no guarantee of success, not to mention embarrassing. Dentures would not only move sideways, pop out, inflict injuries, or break down easily; they would also absorb liquids, and food debris would get tangled up in the spiral springs or accumulate in the various crevices they offered. Offensive breath was inescapable, a nightmare for both the wearer and the people coming too close to the wearer.

Despite Greenwood's improvements that aimed to address Washington's grievances, his dentures remained ill-fitting and uncomfortable. Technical marvels though they were, eighteenth-century dentures forced the lips outward, making the mouth bulge.

✿

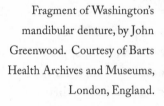

Fragment of Washington's mandibular denture, by John Greenwood. Courtesy of Barts Health Archives and Museums, London, England.

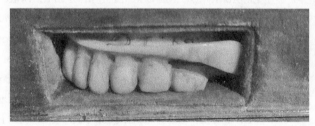

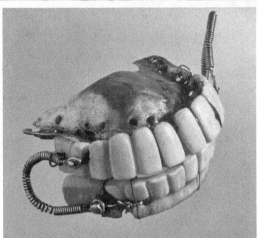

꙳

(*Above* and *left*)
Washington's dentures,
by John Greenwood, ca. 1795.
Courtesy of Dr. Samuel D.
Harris National Museum
of Dentistry, Baltimore, MD.

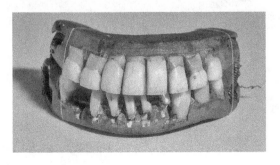

꙳

Washington's dentures,
1790–1799. Courtesy of Mount
Vernon Ladies' Association,
Mount Vernon, VA.

Each time Washington had to dispatch a set back to Greenwood for repairing, he made a point of requesting that whatever solution Greenwood devised did not result in exacerbating this problem: "Nothing must be done to them which will, in the *least* degree force the lips out more than *now* do, as it does this too much already." Dentures caused "a marked change" in Washington's visage, as George Washington Parke Custis wrote, "more especially in the projection of the under lip." Gilbert Stuart's portrait show this deficiency. Because of this very successful portrait, even today many Americans see Washington as an old, cantankerous man with a funny jaw.[16]

While dentures may have been painful and embarrassing, at the same time, the technical aspects of their production were fascinating to Washington. Washington's correspondence with John Greenwood reveals this. "The principal thing you will have to attend to, in the alteration you are about to make," Washington wrote in a letter to the trusted doctor of December 1798 that included sketches detailing what he was asking for, "is to let the upper bar fall back from the lower one thus . . . ; whether the teeth are quite streight, or inclining a little in thus, . . . or a little rounding outwards thus . . . is immaterial, for I find it is the bars alone both above and below that gives the lips the pouting and swelling appearance—of consequence, if this can be remedied, all will be well."[17]

Dentist Jean Pierre Le Mayeur entered Washington's life at an interesting period, in the early 1780s. A younger man, Washington needed someone who might be able to salvage his remaining teeth, and Le Mayeur had all the credentials to succeed in such a heroic feat.

A Frenchman who had passed from the British to the American side of the conflict during the War of Independence, Le Mayeur came originally to America as a naval surgeon with the French forces commanded by the Comte de Rochambeau. This celebrated

Philadelphia 12. Dec. 1798.

Sir,

Your letter of the 8th came safe.—and as I am hurried, in order to leave this City tomorrow, I must be short.—The principal thing you will have to attend to, in the alteration you are about to make, is to let the upper bar fall back from the lower one thus ❭ whether the teeth are quite straight, or inclining a little in thus, ❭ or a little rounding outwards thus ❭ is immaterial, for I find it is the bars alone both above and below that gives the lips the pouting and swelling appearance—of consequence, if this can be remedied all will be well.—

dentist treated patients in New York, Philadelphia, Baltimore, Alexandria, and Richmond. He was preceded by his reputation: he was one of "whose skill much has been said," as Washington wrote to Colonel William Smith. Le Mayeur seemed, Washington continued, to be the man who could offer better options: "Having some Teeth which are very troublesome to me at times, and of wch I wish to be eased . . . and Gums which might be relieved by a Man of skill—I would thank you for making a private Investigation of this Mans Character and knowledge in his profession." Washington hoped that if his credentials passed muster, Le Mayeur would treat him: "I should be glad to see him with his Apparatus."[18]

Le Mayeur's "apparatus" not only included material instruments such as pincers, gum lancets, levers, and the most dreadful of them all, the so-called pelican, a merciless tooth extractor, but also wondrous abilities. Le Mayeur undertook what only a few dentists dared to attempt, the "live tooth transplant." A short-lived technique popular in the 1780s, Le Mayeur had perfected it in Paris before moving to America. Progenitor of today implants, the transplant process involved taking a healthy, living tooth from a donor and inserting it into the empty socket of the recipient and then fastening it to the adjoining tooth by means of a wire. Infections, rejections, diseases such as syphilis, and having the new tooth soon rot in the mouth were more than a probability. Pulp necrosis and root resorption would likely turn the new tooth into a disgusting splotch. However, when the receiver was lucky enough to find a healthy donor with mouth and teeth of comparable size, such an outcome could be postponed for months.[19]

Le Mayeur advertised his abilities in American newspapers. The April, 22, 1784 edition of the *Virginia Journal and Alexandria Advertiser* carried the following announcement: "DR. LAMAYNER, Dentist from New-York, who transplants Teeth, is now in this Town, and may be spoke with by calling at Mr. PERRIN'S Store." Although Washington had expressed hope to Colonel Smith that La Mayeur could help him, he was rather skeptical at first about the transplant approach: "Of this [technique] I have no idea, even with young people, and sure I am it cannot succeed with old."[20]

Le Mayeur tried to persuade Washington, telling him that there was no risk attached to the procedure: "I have had the plaisure of gratifying tow [two] Ladies and tow Gentleman who I believe have the honor of being personally known to your Excellency." Le Mayeur had furnished them "with good living teeth in the Room of those which were broken or otherwise decayed." Washington's close friend, Colonel Richard Varick, had received the same treatment: he "himself has four fronts and one Eye tooth [canine], th[r]ee of which were transplanted in december and are at this day perfectly secure and tow others which have been transplanted some days since are in a promising state and will be perfectly ferm."[21]

Washington remained unconvinced, and in a letter he wrote Varick to compliment him on such a "success," he voiced his skepticism in an ironic manner:

> I received great pleasure from the Acct [account] which you have given me of Doctr La Moyeur's operations on you; and congratulate you very sincerely on the success. I shall claim your promise of relating the Sequel; for I confess I have been staggered in my belief of the efficacy of transplantation— being more disposed to think that, the *Operator* is partial to his own performances, and the *Operatee's*, in general, are inclined to compliment, or having submitted to the *Operations*, are somewhat unwilling to expose the truth.[22]

All in all, the probability that Washington had teeth transplanted in his mouth by Le Mayeur or any other dentists is rather low. There is no indication, not even a clue, in Washington's letters or account books. Correspondingly, Le Mayeur's account books make no mention of whether this daring physician ever performed the operation on his most distinguished patient. Although Washington used to save the teeth he had lost, he did not save them for future transplanting but for denture sets. "In a drawer in the Locker of the Desk which stands in my study," he wrote in 1782 to Mount Vernon supervisor and distant cousin Lund Washington, "you will find two small (fore) teeth; which I beg of you to wrap up carefully, and send inclosed in your next letter to me."[23]

Besides keeping his own teeth, at least on one occasion Washington bought teeth from the mouths of persons who were enslaved at Mount Vernon. In Lund Washington's account book, we read: "pd. Negroes for 9 Teeth, on acct. of the French Dentis—Doctr. Lemay 6. 2. 0." Lund Washington, on behalf of Washington, thus paid some unspecified enslaved persons the sum of six pounds and two shillings for nine teeth and then gave those teeth to Le Mayeur.[24]

The idea that Washington purchased teeth is at once intriguing and morally upsetting. It's upsetting because no one should buy or sell human parts. Persons who agree to selling parts of their own body, especially when such parts are still attached to the body, are evidently in desperate circumstances and thus unable to make a free, deliberate choice. Furthermore, in this case, Washington and Le Mayeur had obtained teeth under their market value. Six pounds and two shillings for nine teeth works out to thirteen and a half shillings a tooth.

And it's intriguing because one wonders whether Washington bought slaves' teeth to use himself. But, although it is possible that some of these teeth ended up in one of Washington's dentures, his ledger books offer evidence that suggests he did not purchase them for himself. There, under the date May 8, 1784, he transcribed Lund Washington's infamous entry: "By Cash pd Negroes for 9 Teeth on Acct of Dr Lemoin 6. 2." Washington's ledger of accounts, mostly in his own hand, organized information on a client-by-client basis, using a system of double entry bookkeeping. So, his ledger entry indicates that he finalized the purchase on behalf of the dentist Le Mayeur, who no doubt was in need of teeth to carry out his transplants, as the larger his stock, the better the chance the doctor would be able to find a good match between donor and recipient. Had Washington bought teeth for personal use, he would have simply entered item and payment. Indeed, he used the item-payment notation each time he bought poultry, fish, or produce from the persons he held in bondage, items he would eventually consume.[25]

Dentists in the period ran advertisements in newspapers in order to recruit individuals willing to sell teeth still intact in their mouths, horrendous as this is. In the July 1785 issue of the New York *Independent Journal,* for example, Dr. John Brown, "surgeon and dentist," asked for "front teeth, for which Two Guineas a piece will be given." In 1782, in the New York *Royal Gazette,* Le Mayeur promised in an advertisement that "Four Guineas will be given for every Tooth." John Greenwood advertised in the New York *Daily Advertiser* for live, healthy teeth, "for which a Guinea each will be given." Every now and then, scruples surfaced. When he made his forays in the South, Le Mayeur himself stated clearly that he would not accept teeth from slaves. In the Charleston *Columbian Herald*, for example, we read that "Any person, white or black, (slaves excepted) willing to part with any of their front teeth, shall receive two guineas for each."[26]

What Le Mayeur and the other dentists did is inexcusable. What Washington did with Le Mayeur is inexcusable as well. But it's unlikely that Le Mayeur ever built dentures for Washington with those incriminated teeth, or that a slave's tooth was ever transplanted in Washington's mouth. In the mid-1780s, Washington's concern was about his remaining teeth. He was in pain. He needed help. At the same time, unfortunately, he was oblivious that he was inflicting pain on other human beings.

Barber Surgeons

*E*ighteenth-century dentists, barbers, and surgeons hammered, pulled, and cut recklessly—they were experts in pain infliction. They possessed questionable techniques and lacked proper physiological and medical knowledge. They had no idea of hygiene, and the only painkiller they administered to their beleaguered patients was laudanum. Everything could go wrong and often did go wrong: "Doctr. Brown was sent for to Frank," Washington wrote in his diary in 1785. Frank Lee was Washington's "waiter," the fair-skinned enslaved man he had trusted with the role of butler and, as Washington recorded, he "had been seized in the Night, with a bleeding of the Mouth from an Orifice made by a Doctr. Dick who some days before attempted in vain to extract a broken tooth."[27]

Examples of operations much worse than the dental one Dr. Dick performed on poor Frank Lee are abundant. In the Philadelphia *Freeman's Journal*, a patient of one Dr. Philip Clumberg published an open rebuke. This patient realized after the fact that Clumberg, rather than a real doctor, was only a tooth drawer or, in the language of the period, a barber surgeon:

> Let me seriously advise you to lay aside the performance (if you so call it) Of tooth drawing, as you have this day done me great injury in your attempt, or I would say barbarous and violent exertion. Indeed the consequences of the fracture you have produced in my jaw and the quantity of Gums and flesh torn away by your instrument and fingers is not and will not be known for some days. Dr. Baker [most likely John, one of Washington's dentists] has just left me, after extracting the splinters of bone you occasioned. I expect every moment to spit out the two sound teeth you have displayed.[28]

Barber surgeons had no formal education. Since the founding of the University of Paris in the thirteenth century, physicians, who prided themselves on being erudite scholars, had kept all surgeons at an arm's length. Physicians disparaged surgeons for their lack of knowledge and their reliance on craftsmanship. But by the end of the seventeenth century, surgery enjoyed an upsurge in prestige. In 1672, Pierre Dionis, a famous surgeon, was appointed demonstrator in anatomy and surgery at the Jardin du Roi, in Paris. Anatomy gained the favor of other important surgeons, like Jean Louis Petit, who had built his reputation by treating battle wounds. Eventually, in 1743, King Louis XV issued a *déclaration* that severed the union between surgeons and barbers. The king stated that surgery deserved a higher status and had been unjustly degraded by its alliance with the guild of barbers.

In England, in January 1745, the surgical members of the Court of Assistants of the Barber-Surgeons' Company petitioned the Parliament for a separation, despite the opposition of the barbers. Royal assent was granted within a few months, and a company of surgeons dedicated to the promotion of science as well as the art of surgery was established. Surgery as a profession, at least in theory, became fully recognized.

Americans played their part in this revolution. In 1750, John Jones, a native of Jamaica, Queens, New York, went to London to attend the celebrated lectures and dissections of Dr. John Hunter and his older brother Dr. William Hunter. Jones was struck not only by the surgical marvels the two could perform but also by the extent of their medical knowledge. The Hunters furnished the proof that a surgeon could possess an enquiring and theoretical mind. Back in America, Jones similarly practiced surgery with an eye to anatomy. In 1775, he published the first American modern surgical textbook, *Plain Concise Practical Remarks on the Treatment of Wounds and Fractures*.

Surgeons, now doctors, realized that pain was a major factor, one that could determine the outcome of any operation. Modern anesthetics like chloroform were only introduced in the late 1840s. But eighteenth-century "modern" surgeons tried to lessen pain either by administering opium or by compressing the nerves that supplied the part to be operated before beginning the surgery. A better understanding of the working of anatomical parts enabled surgeons at this time to rapidly perform a deeper incision of adequate length, hopefully with one sweep of the knife—since a second or a third incision would increase the torment and jeopardize everything.

That is the good part of the story. The bad part is that surgeons kept butchering their patients. The so-called French method of amputating limbs, for example, was widely used in America during Washington's time. It was based to an extent on anatomical knowledge and was considered an improvement over the traditional "saw and knife" procedure because it produced less pain and could be executed rapidly. The amputee's limb was positioned across two vertical boards; with one blow of a narrow sledge or an axe, the surgeon cracked the bone; he then dropped the tool and reached for his knife so that he could cut the soft tissues and make skin and muscle flaps as quickly as possible. A cautery was applied to the stump that was subsequently bandaged. And that was it.

Dr. John Jones—whom we have just met—taught Americans this more "humane" technique. However, he believed sheer luck remained the physician's best ally: "As every operation is necessarily attended with a certain degree of bodily pain, as well as terrible apprehension to the patient's mind," Jones wrote in his celebrated textbook, "a good Surgeon . . . ought to consider, whether the patient will *in all probability* be better for it, or whether he may not be the worse." Washington couldn't agree more. As he wrote in 1777, the "great art" of medicine, not only surgery, was "neither more nor less than a cheat upon the World." He never recanted this opinion.[29]

Personally, Washington never went through the horrors that have just made us shiver—which no doubt explains why he continued to trust the many doctor-surgeons who treated him. A rather sickly person throughout his life, Washington suffered from countless ailments and maladies. Had not nature or chance prevailed, he could have died many times over, not only from lethal infections triggered by his teeth but also from malaria, smallpox, tuberculosis, rheumatoid arthritis, "pleurisie"—which refers to many respiratory issues—dysentery, influenza, or pneumonia. Washington had to spend interminable weeks in bed. He had to abide hazardous therapies and countless assaults on his privacy. Like so many other eighteenth-century patients, he had to ingest poisonous remedies. The topic of this chapter is not eighteenth-century medicine in general, however, but what takes place during surgical interventions—the pulling, yanking, jerking, hammering, and cut-ting, the mechanical infliction of pain. The *hands* of Washington's surgeons interest us.[30]

That he was never chopped and brutalized by his doctors' hands does not, however, mean he got off scot-free. Surgeons or dentists did not chop Washington irremediably, but they cut him nonetheless and inflicted serious pain. He was repeatedly tortured. During the early days of the presidency, for example, a "malignant carbuncle"—which is an inflamed tumor—appeared on his left thigh. In the middle of June 1789, the president was seized by a fever, which was followed by a "tenderness" over the left thigh. By the twentieth, the swelling had turned into a "pointed" abscess. The pain was excruciating—so much so that Cherry Street, the presidential address in New York City, was ordered to be roped off so that the noise of wagons and carts would not disturb Washington's rest. At first wrongly diagnosed as a cutaneous form of anthrax (*Bacillus anthracis*), it was probably a staph infection (*Staphylococcus aureus*) that developed into a fast-growing abscess, a hard and solid mass. Dr. Samuel Bard—a graduate of Edinburgh University and founder of the medical school at King's College, now Columbia University Vagelos College of Physicians and Surgeons—performed the surgery, assisted by his father, Dr. John Bard. Samuel Bard "lanced and drained" the abscess. Needless to say, the whole operation was carried out without anesthesia. Dr. Bard's father, more experienced but with too shaky hands, stood over his son and constantly urged him "cut deeper, cut deeper."[31]

The wound did not heal as everyone hoped. The lancets and knives used by Dr. Bard were not sterilized and an infection occurred. At the beginning of August, President Washington was still "unable to sit yet without (soft) Cushings," as he informed Senator Richard Henry Lee. However, Washington did not lose his poise. In a clumsy attempt to reassure both his friends and himself, he wrote to Lee that he had "assurances from the Doctors that in a few days *more* I may expect to be relieved from this inconvenience."

The days, alas, were many more than anticipated. On September 8, Washington wrote to his trusted friend Dr. Craik to say that "the wound given by the incision is not yet closed." Washington had started to shiver. Was Dr. Bard an ordinary butcher? He had tended to the operation "with skill, and with as much tenderness as the nature of the complaint would admit." Yet Washington confessed to Dr. Craik that he "wished for your inspection." Recovery was very slow and remarkably painful. Only at the beginning of October did Washington start to feel a little better. By then, the incision had begun to heal.[32]

But the same problem resurfaced about two years later, after the president and his family moved to Philadelphia. In the summer of 1791, Washington lamented "a slight indisposition." It was occasioned by a tumor, "not much unlike the one I had in New York in the year 1789." By the end of July, his left thigh presented a bulging spot. Washington, once again, was forced to lie on his side. We learn from Thomas Jefferson that "an incision has been made." Pus was discharged. We do not know who performed the intervention, but we know that for some quasimagical reason, the surgery this time did not elicit lingering consequences—painful as it must have been. "I am now recovered," Washington himself reported enthusiastically to his old comrade, General William Moultrie, on August 9.[33]

The reason why nonsterilized instruments did not cause more serious infections in Washington or trigger a life-threatening septic shock remains shrouded in mystery. Washington's antibodies were sturdy. He was lucky. Also mysterious is the nature of Washington's "tumors." Were they cancerous? And was there a correlation between the neoplastic proliferations on his thigh and another neoplasia that attacked him in June 1794, a "cancer" appearing on Washington's right cheek? Was this last a melanoma?

In August 1794, Dr. James Tate, a surgeon of the Third Pennsylvania Regiment during the War of Independence, was summoned to examine Washington's face. His first line of treatment was medication, possibly a preparation the patient had to ingest or a topical remedy, like a powder, a pomade, or an ointment. But whatever he had administered, it didn't work. "The medicine that is given," we hear from Martha, "has not the last [least] effect that can be perceived except that the spot is a little sore at times." After this failure, Dr. Tate decided to be more aggressive and to make an incision. (In November, Washington recorded a payment of "15 guineas givn to Dr Tate for curing my Cancer.") As Dr. Bard had done when removing the lump from his thigh, Dr. Tate cut very deep. By a stroke of luck, he succeeded. Notwithstanding the pain, the patient was happy with the result—so much so that he recommended Dr. Tate to Thomas Pinckney, former war hero, former governor of South Carolina, and minister to Great Britain: "I have, myself, experienced the fruits of his skill, in this art; being cured by him of an irritable spot on my right cheek which had for years been encreasing in pricking, & disagreeable sensations; and in June last assumed the decided character of a Cancer." When Dr. Tate's expert hand excised the neoplasia, Washington felt "no confinement, or other inconvenience at the time—nor any injury to my constitution since." Martha was similarly relieved. She shared with her niece the good news, that "the spot that was on his face is quite gone[.] There is not the least appearance of it to be seen now."[34]

As a patient, Washington was literally very patient and let scalpels, knives, and lancets nick his body—in this last case as well as in many others. He felt he had to endure such ordeals. They were at one and the same time necessities, vehicles of hope, and tests of masculinity and self-control. Meanwhile, he tempered his body and made it harder. Physical agony was part of the eighteenth-century daily world, a level of bodily pain that we are not subjected to. Stoically, Washington bore this type of pain and discomfort in the same way he withstood the horrors of the battlefield and his travels into the wilderness. It was a lifelong process of education.

5

❧

Checking the Body

The Animal Inside

George Washington Parke Custis tells a story that may well be made up but that nonetheless offers insight into Washington's character and personal challenges. The story goes that Mary Ball Washington, George Washington's mother, had a favorite horse, a sorrel. This horse was dreadfully wild and had such a "fierce and ungovernable nature" that no rider had dared to try break it. The "vicious" sorrel "ranged free in the air," tossing his mane to the winds "and spurning the earth in the pride of his freedom." It was a horse made for hell, should horse hells exist. But twelve- or thirteen-year-old George had a plan. Heedless of the mortal danger, he decided to tame the beast. His friends helped him to decoy the horse into an enclosure, and a bit was forced into the mouth. George was now ready to go. He mounted "bold, vigorous, and young," a "daring youth" springing "to his unenvied seat."[1]

As soon as George managed to get astride, the eternal struggle between wild force and discipline, or between passion and reason, began. Young Washington "clung to the furious steed." The show turned "terrific to the beholders" and the undertaking seemed likely to be fatal to the rider. Everything became so physical, so carnal. The rider himself, Custis swears, soon converted into a centaur-like figure: Washington "appeared to make part of the animal itself." Discipline would eventually win over wild force, and in the most dramatic way—by means of annihilation. The beast tried to resist the formidable rider as long as possible. "Summoning all his powers to one mighty effort," the wild horse "burst his noble heart, and died in an instant." George was apparently already first among men, one who "excelled in all the manly exercises." The day after, the victor of this battle bragged about his quasimetaphysical achievement: "I backed him, I rode him," Washington allegedly proffered, "and in a desperate struggle for the mastery, he fell under me and died upon the spot."

This episode looks by and large like a tall tale. But the battle between the two opposite principles endured by the young Washington that it describes was real. Custis is right as well when he emphasizes that George was a centaur-like figure, at the same time the horse and the rider, the untamed animal and the rational, self-controlled man.

Victory over the "wild horse" wasn't quick, however. George Washington learned to remain in control, but the process was very slow and laborious. His many struggles—over himself and his fears and over his passions and his internal fury—could have easily ended in a long list of defeats. He was not blessed by nature or God with an exceptional character right off the bat, as they say. Washington outlasted the American wilderness, withstood the battlefield, stayed firm in the face of his own fears and physical pain, and curbed his rage, but it took him a huge amount of effort.

In this, his mother and father helped him a great deal. Beyond allowing their son in a cavalier fashion to play outside, explore the environs, and test his physique, they talked to him and taught him the virtues of endurance, exertion, moderation, obedience, and self-effacement. Biographers often contend that Mary Ball Washington, the only remaining parent, was bossy and self-centered, a hindrance and an embarrassment rather than a source of intellectual and moral inspiration to her son. The conclusion is usually drawn from what George Washington's cousin, Lawrence Washington of Chotank, once said. Reminiscing on his juvenile years, Lawrence declared, in the voice of (the less-than-reliable) George Washington Parke Custis, that he was "ten times more afraid" of that woman "than I ever was of my own parents." But Lawrence went on to say that "she awed me in the midst of her kindness, for she was, indeed, truly kind," thus indicating his complex feelings toward her.[2]

Mary was not only kind but also intellectually limber. She read books to her children and grandchildren, and she taught younger generations that religion made life worth living. Religion is not just a system of beliefs and a subject for theological debates. From a practical point of view, it is also a method to enhance discipline for both the mind and the body. It's an existential training and a quasiphysical workout. Through prayers, spiritual exercises, contemplation, and meditation, religion becomes an instrument that may turn a chaotic, passion-ridden life into an ordered one.

Whether Washington as an adult was a religious person and believed in God is hard to say. He went to church, but that may not carry a lot of weight. His letters and public documents are replete with devotional formulae. He also used to celebrate Thanksgiving and Christmas. And he purchased and read books on religion. Even if reading such books and engaging in conversation about providence do not prove he had deep beliefs, there is clear evidence that as a boy he applied himself to his daily chores with religious exertion—the type of exertion he saw in his mother. Apparently, Mary's example, plus her graphic illustrations of hells and the demons awaiting dissolute souls, made an impact. There was still a struggle going on in him, though. George would have preferred to just run outside and act rowdily, as children and teenagers often do, but he also realized the need to work hard to discipline himself.[3]

A religious effort to gain mastery over his passions is clearly visible in the early stages of Washington's life. George's extant school copybooks show that the energetic boy who liked to play outside was at the same time trying to curb the untamable "horse" in him. George's handwriting, mathematical diagrams, sketches, and drawings communicate artistry and care, effort and discipline. Those early signs on paper reveal a young mind and a young body already invested in order and application.

Lord Fairfax understood the danger that Washington faced in his early years. Just like Washington's mother, he suggested that if the boy were to attain success, he would first have to learn how to win control over his passions. In a 1748 letter to Mary Ball Washington, he told her up front that he did not think sending the youth to England to complete his education was a good idea. England, Fairfax wrote, is "a country for which I myself have no inclination," and he believed it would end up spoiling the boy. Although "method and exactness," Fairfax continued, seemed "to be natural to George," in England he would be exposed to countless temptations—including women. His lust would be roused. "He is, I suspect, beginning to feel the sap rising, being in the spring of life, and is getting ready to be the prey of your sex, wherefore may the Lord help him, and deliver him from the nets those spiders, called women, will cast for his ruin." Fairfax concluded: "I wish I could say that he governs his temper." While everyone could lose their temper, of course, this provincial boy, an orphan who didn't have the chance to complete his formal education, seemed especially hotheaded. "He is subject to attacks of anger on provocation, and sometimes without just cause." Character, Fairfax trusted, would eventually prevail, or so he hoped: "Time will cure him of this vice of nature."[4]

Without excusing Lord Fairfax for his misogyny, we can say that he got young Washington's personal challenge totally right. For many eighteenth-century European and American upper-class boys, growing into truly accomplished and virile adults was a laborious process of gaining command over anger, passions, and urges. The body was, to an extent, the enemy. Teach the boy "to get a Mastery over his Inclinations," the famous philosopher John Locke had similarly advised, "and *submit his Appetite to Reason.*" Only in this way will you produce virile gentlemen.[5]

❧ Upper-class virility wasn't a status or a title easy to achieve and maintain. For men like Washington, virility was definitely about the body and its physical strength, about daring feats and ventures, like outlasting battles and surviving the wilderness; it was about recklessness, including enduring personal pain; and it was about a certain lack of empathy, demonstrated by dominating, brutalizing, or killing other living beings. More important, however, virility was about control and self-control. The eighteenth-century formula was very simple: when a man lost control of his body through self-indulgence, lust, passion, excessive cruelty, or rage, his virility was lost.

No Virginia gentleman tried to become a saint. No one sought to get rid of the body, renounce appetites, jettison passions, thus killing "the horse" once and for all. Rather, the manly man sought to enjoy pleasures regularly while remaining at the helm, to curb passions while venting them, but only in a controlled environment, as we would say today. The mastery of self, in short, was the goal.[6]

Such eighteenth-century masculine men were expected to act with prudence—especially during times of crisis. After the War of Independence broke out, Washington's calls for this type of virility, unsurprisingly, intensified. The entire country's honor, he believed, depended on the proper manly behavior of its soldiers and commandants: "The fate of unborn Millions will now depend, under God, on the Courage and Conduct of this army." Manly behaviors, in this case, were acts of self-possession and self-discipline; they were the exact opposite of what the "cruel and unrelenting Enemy" was doing. Let us remind our soldiers, Washington wrote on September 4, 1776, of the importance of "subordination and Discipline," including the "just and true sense of their duty."[7]

Each time his officers exchanged insults or fomented a brawl, the general felt "real Pain." The "indecency of the behaviour and language which passed between the Gentlemen concerned" was "utterly inconsistent with that delicacy of character, which an officer ought under every circumstance to preserve." "Delicacy," here, referred to the modest, self-aware, tactful, and considerate deportment setting upper-class men apart.[8]

Ordered bodies produced ordered minds and vice versa. Virility as a fine balance between mind and body, in turn, increased the chances of both personal and collective success. Washington was convinced that effort, method, and regularity—and above all self-control—were liberating and gave meaning to one's life. A man who gave free rein to his appetites and fury could only be a weak man, able to wreak havoc, but nothing more. In his capacity as a commander, Washington made sure all his men cultivated self-control. He believed that "keeping up a Strict discipline among both Officers and Soldiers" was essential not only for the single individual but for "the Salvation of the Province" as a whole. Unmanly behaviors "should be severely punished."[9]

Washington wanted to see only certain types of men around him. (As philosophers would say, he favored a particular process of embodiment in others.) He reinforced specific habits and punished contrary ones. He sought men who succeeded in thinking, feeling, desiring, and acting orderly and with "delicacy." And for Washington, even the most seemingly trivial behavior could betray a want of delicacy: "All Officers, non-commissioned Officers and Soldiers are positively forbid playing at Cards, and other Games of Chance." Washington's concern may look like moralism or conformism: "At this time of public distress, men may find enough to do in the service of their God, and their Country, without abandoning themselves to vice and immorality." But Washington's "moralism" did not have at its root the fear of God's wrath or the disapprobation of his peers; instead, it was based on pragmatic concerns about the best ways of enhancing effectiveness and advancing the common cause. Washington did not fear social nonconformity. He did not dread what we call multiculturalism or cultural relativism or divergences among ideas, beliefs, and traditions.[10]

There were worse types of immorality besides gambling, obviously, that undermined effectiveness. "The General is sorry to be informed that the foolish, and wicked practice, of profane cursing and swearing . . . is growing into fashion." Cursing and swearing have always been obvious examples of bravado. They are features of an annoying caricature of real manliness, the clearest example of "masculine overcompensation" through which men try to ward off their feelings of powerlessness and inferiority. Consequently, the general ordered his officers to check this and similar wild behaviors, and on occasion would assume the role of a preacher delivering an edifying sermon. Everyone should "reflect, that we can have little hopes of the blessing of Heaven on our Arms, if we insult it by our impiety, and folly; added to this, it is a vice so mean and low, without any temptation, that every man of sense, and character, detests and despises it."[11]

Men of sense, delicate character, and proper form, particularly in time of war, should not vent their frustration in such a wanton and foolish way. They should resist and control their urges and inclinations. They should not discharge their physical and psychological energy by becoming wild and unruly. More importantly, they should avoid the many grey areas of human behavior. Semisexual, ambiguous, or simply indecent practices should always be avoided:

> The General does not mean to discourage the practice of bathing, whilst the weather is warm enough to continue it;

but he expressly forbids, any persons doing it, at or near the Bridge in Cambridge, where it has been observed and complained of, that many Men, lost to all sense of decency and common modesty, are running about naked upon the Bridge, whilst Passengers, and even Ladies of the first fashion in the neighbourhood, are passing over it, as if they meant to glory in their shame: The Guards and Centries at the Bridge, are to put a stop to this practice for the future.[12]

The "honest" man, Washington philosophized, "feels something within him, that tells him, that the first measure is dictated by that prudence wch ought to govern all men who commits a trust to another." Only prudent people are social, ethical, useful, and effective and therefore worthy of the trust society places in them. On the other hand, the "dishonest man," Washington explained, is "indolent, inattentive & careless; fond of company, pleasure & perhaps liquor." The unmanly man is intolerant of every norm, always "uneasy under restraints, and averse to a[ll] checks," and this rejection of norms shows "how unworthy he is to be entrusted." Prudence and acceptance of norms, order and self-sacrifice, effort and endurance: these qualities, according to Washington, had to be learned at school or, more often, by examples and orders. These "virtues"—a term that connotes strength—had to become automatic habits.[13]

In the eighteenth century, the soldier was a good example of a manly man, forbearing and self-controlled, but only provided he kept acting "soldierly." If he became wild or openly violent, if he did not govern his temper, he lost his station and dignity. Look at our enemies, Washington fumed; look at the spectacle they offer. The British only bring about "devastation," whether on "defenceless towns," or "helpless Women & Children." "Resentment, & unsoldiery practices in them, now seems to have taken place of all the Manly virtues." Washington's assessment of what happened during the Revolution may not be impartial or historically accurate. But the dualism between cruel and "manly" men allows us to grasp the essentials of his vision of masculinity. That eighteenth-century version of masculinity thrived on uprightness, prudence, control over the body, and exemplarity.[14]

Benjamin Franklin had already said the same, almost word for word, in a pamphlet he published in which he denounced the flawed logic of the massacre of Native Americans by the Paxton Boys, a central Pennsylvania vigilante group: "If an Indian injures me, does it follow that I may revenge that Injury on all Indians?" The Paxton Boys, criminals who styled themselves as Christians, were precisely immature boys, as their name suggests, not real men: "Unmanly Men! who are not ashamed to come with Weapons against the Unarmed, to use the Sword against Women, and the Bayonet against young Children."[15]

Rage was also considered an unmanly feeling. Like cursing and swearing or running about naked, anger is a form of overcompensation, betraying fragility, anxiety, and immaturity. Considered one of the seven "cardinal sins" in Christianity, wrath has been customarily construed as the typical emotion of debased people—a weakness, by all accounts. Ancient Greeks and Romans also castigated anger as childish and maintained that it set a bad example and led to bad decisions. For them, it was a personal flaw conducive to a greater harm in the entire community. In eighteenth-century Euro-America, anger was seen as similarly outrageous, childish, and even primitive.

The manly man did not give in to rage. It was typical during the period for gentlemen competitors seeking to discredit each other by means of the accusation that the other party was angry, furious, unable to abide by prudence and execute restraint. Criminals, lower classes, and enslaved people, by contrast, were understood to be subject to such fits. In fact, the lower classes did not have many emotional options at their disposal. As historian Nicole Eustace writes,

"They wanted their anger to be regarded as a source of masculine strength, rather than as a source of servile shame." But the elites were different and luckier in so many ways. Men of sense, delicate character, and proper form could well show resentment, regarded as rational and honorable, but displaying rage was an embarrassment. Mastery over anger signaled that one was fit to be a master of men.[16]

A Modern Cato

*T*he reason why Washington ended up a soldier was not that he was perpetually hotheaded. It was not because he had an instinct for soldiery or was a warrior anxious to prove himself on the battlefield. This characterization is based on a problematic interpretation of what a soldier should be. It relies on an incomplete understanding of the kernel of eighteenth-century upper-class masculinity. Prudence is missing from the account; there is no self-mastery. The quick-tempered type, anxious to prove himself, a person with tunnel vision who is always only in the moment and loses track of the big picture, was not the template for the ideal of a manly man and a soldier in the eighteenth century—nor is it today. This type is rather a caricature of a soldier. The eighteenth-century soldier, especially the commander and the master of men, emerged as valiant and brave not if he was instinctive, impulsive, passionate, and furious, ever eager to face off his opponent, but only if and when he succeeded in quelling his passions and his fears. A soldier always needs to stay coolheaded. For any soldier, conquering inner feelings is as important as vanquishing the outer enemy.[17]

As Washington matured, he gained control over his body. His manners became very placid and serene. As Lord Fairfax had hoped, time had cured him "of this vice of nature," anger. But it didn't come easily. The boy grew into a manly man and a real soldier but, as historian Mary Thompson notes, Washington's "fierce temper" kept "lurking just beneath a generally calm surface."[18]

Washington controlled his passions, so much so that he projected a bright Catonic image. Marcus Porcius Cato Uticensis, the Roman aristocrat who countered the rise of Julius Caesar and sought to steer Rome back to republican virtues, struck a chord with many white upper-class Euro-Americans of Washington's generation. As a character, Cato was not only an example of patriotism and self-sacrifice, the opposite of Caesar's "ambition," but also, and perhaps more important, the embodiment of a fully-fledged virility. Like a perfect soldier, he stayed balanced. As a perfect male, he mastered his force but without killing it. He was not meek, as women were thought to be, but a powerful and yet tamed horse or, if you prefer, a bomb that does not explode.[19]

Joseph Addison's 1712 play *Cato, a Tragedy*, first performed at the Theatre-Royal in Drury Lane, London, on April 14, 1713, rendered Cato a universal source of inspiration. The virile words Addison put in Cato's mouth were repeated over and over again, both in Europe and America. As historian David McCullough remarks, Washington's 1775 praise for Benedict Arnold ("It is not in the power of any man to command success; but you have done more— you have deserved it") was directly lifted from act 1, scene 2, of the tragedy: "'Tis not in mortals to command success; but we'll do more, Sempronius, we'll deserve it."[20]

Washington was captivated by the masculine figure of Cato. He had read Addison's play as a young man and could quote by heart from it, and he often made references to it in his correspondence: "I shoud th[ink] my time more agreable spent believe me," he wrote to Sarah Cary Fairfax in 1758, "in playing a part in Cato with the Company you mention, & myself doubly happy in being the Juba to such a Marcia as you must make."[21]

Those who provided a "physiognomical" analysis of Washington as a mature man noticed the enduring tension between wild force and discipline that recalled Cato. Washington's face, one testimony noted, is "full of noble audacity," an ebullient primeval energy that, however, "never yields to the heat of passions, but always remains self-possessed because it is conscious of its strength." Isaac Weld, the Irish explorer, writer, and artist and a member of the Royal Dublin Society, also read in Washington's face the signs of a Catonic conflict between fury and self-restraint, passion and reason. Weld provided a fascinating account of painter Gilbert Stuart practicing physiognomy: Stuart told him that there were "features in [Washington's] face totally different from what he ever observed in that of any other human being," features that were "indicative of the strongest and most ungovernable passions." Had Washington been "born in the forests," Stuart and Weld agreed, "he would have been the fiercest man amongst the savage tribes." But like Cato, while Washington was familiar with forests and wilderness, he did not belong to them; he was not a "savage" who was all passion and no reason.[22]

"Ardent, and impetuous by nature," he "subjected his passions to his reason; and could with facility, by his habitual self-control, repress his inclinations whenever his judgment forbade their indulgence," according to Henry "Light-Horse Harry" Lee. But the precise amount of "facility" plus how consistent Washington was in maintaining his Catonic virility have yet to be determined. "He was, *naturally*, of a warm temper," another observer noted. And his fury showed itself "in smaller vexations, suddenly occurring; but rarely (though it appeared sometimes) in great matters." (Which is to say that, on occasion, Washington was a typical violent slaveowner.) Exerting self-control was hard for Washington, so much so that it was seen as a principal achievement: "I have considered his victory over his natural temperament, as one of the greatest he had obtained."[23]

"His temper was naturally irritable and high toned," Thomas Jefferson wrote in a letter, "but reflection & resolution had obtained a firm and habitual ascendancy over it." However, on occasion, Washington the savage broke free, thus appearing, in Jefferson's words, "most tremendous in his wrath." Henrietta Liston, the wife of the British minister to the United States during the final year of Washington's presidency, recounts that "in private & particularly with his Servants, its violence sometimes broke out," the brand of violence I explored in chapter 3.[24]

Even in public, Washington "occasionally gave way to almost ungovernable fits of anger, from which he would, however, rapidly recover." He would chide senators and break the etiquette of civility, as happened on August 22, 1789, for example, when the president appeared before the Senate, and the senators failed to agree on a treaty with Native Americans in the prompt manner the president had expected. Washington withdrew from the room with a visibly discontented air.[25]

Washington lashed out in letters as well: "Your impertinent Letter of the 24th ulto, was delivered to me yesterday," a younger Washington wrote to George Muse, lieutenant colonel (major) in the Virginia Regiment, on January 29, 1774. (Muse's letter to which Washington refers is unfortunately lost.) Muse was advancing claims about shares of land he felt he had been unjustly deprived of, and Washington was unyielding, to say the least:

> As I am not accustomed to receive such from any Man, nor would have taken the same language from you personally, without letting you feel some marks of my resentment; I would advise you to be cautious in writing me a second of the same tenour; for though I understand you were drunk when you did it, yet give me leave to tell you, that drunkeness is no excuse for rudeness; & that, but for your stupidity & sottishness you might have known, . . . that you had your full quantity of ten thousand acres of Land allow'd you; . . . But suppose you had really fallen short 73 acres of your

10,000, do you think your superlative merit entitles you to greater indulgences than others?[26]

Washington's calling this man a drunkard, stupid, sottish, "ungrateful & dirty a fellow" was hardly edifying. (Incidentally, Muse was ten years older than Washington.) In this case, Washington did not appear a wise and virile man, one who was in control of his "horse." He could have been more sympathetic to Muse, an old comrade, his next in command during the early stages of the French and Indian War. There is a backstory, however. Muse was notoriously a peculiar man, one with a tarnished military reputation, accused of cowardice in the wake of the debacle at Fort Necessity. During that battle, Muse had led his troops back into the fort, leaving Washington's men exposed to a French attack. Everyone was flabbergasted. Washington, apparently, had been holding a grudge against this man for a long time—and for good reasons. But through this letter, Washington had nonetheless shown weakness. Not always was he a perfect Cato.

  Mishaps and embarrassing episodes notwithstanding, the conclusion of this chapter is that Washington managed to control his body; he retained substantial mastery over his passions and the "horse" within; he also devised what we may call "Washington's formula." Most of the time, he succeeded in curbing his appetites, passions, or inclinations, but, simultaneously, he let people know that he could unleash his terrible wrath without warning. Washington's real genius consisted in making his wild force visible—either through his face, which could suddenly freeze, or by his tone of voice, or by writing violent letters fraught with violent language, or via "little" acts of brutality against the persons who happened to be his property. By and large, he learned to control himself, but everybody was aware that he could explode at any moment. Washington had the unique ability to convey the message, with his entire body and mien, that he was *barely* in control, that he was *scarcely* able to hold back his temper, and that he was poised to act. Furthermore, he often stayed silent.

John Adams wrote that Washington "possessed the gift of silence," probably "one of the most precious talents." Silence was Washington's most exceptional quality—the best part of his "formula." Testimonies have described him as "much given to silence." He was in fact given to silence even before he started developing issues with his teeth. Lord Fairfax described the young Washington as "reserved in his intercourse; not a great talker at any time." Washington himself agreed with this characterization. A "monitor," to borrow from a juvenile letter he wrote, "faithful in my own Breast," always told him that he would be better off by keeping his mouth shut. From very early on, young Washington characterized himself as taciturn. "In silence," as he said, he could better "express" himself. We cannot tell whether he truly believed silence is golden, as they say, or whether he heard the adults around him remarking that fatherless George did not attend college and could not compete against better-educated pupils with strokes of eloquence and thus came to rely on the idea that reticence was a virtue. Whatever the case, he trusted that "silence . . . in some cases . . . speaks more Intelligably than the sweetest Eloquence." His mastery of the art of silence did not go unnoticed: "He is feared even when silent," as another witness put it. *Especially* when he was silent, we must add.[27]

There is a direct relationship between silence, violence, and virility. Silence increases the mystery. With one single stroke, he who is silent shows his self-control and reveals what lies beyond silence's border. Beholders suddenly become aware that they don't know what is about to happen. In the temple, the statue of the god has sealed lips. The silent god is self-possessed because he is conscious of his strength—this god may answer one's prayers or, just as likely, expectedly unleash his anger; silence is integral to the space of the sacred. Silence reveals as much as it conceals.[28]

PART II ❧
Emotional

6

The Love Letters

Loving Sally

*W*e are all familiar with the claim: George Washington pined for Sally—Sarah Cary Fairfax—his entire life. In Washington's heart, there was no room for the woman he ended up marrying. Sally, not Martha, was his secret paramour and true love. The passage of time simply "failed to obliterate the traces of that passion which still slumbered in his heart till almost the day of his death for the woman who had first stirred his soul to its depths." Sally remained an "unfulfilled and unrequited love." It's that simple: if Washington eventually became a stiff and cold man, a marble statue bereft of feelings, it was because he wasn't capable of developing an "emotional attachment to another woman."[1]

We have been told multiple times that George may have loved his wife, Martha, but not as much as he loved Sally. As Ron Chernow writes, "Martha had become his life's standard prose" while Sally, on the other hand, "may have introduced some forbidden spice of poetry." Washington, in essence, no doubt loved Sally because she was precisely what "good" women are supposed to be, "a coquette," as another biographer openly says, "full of charming vanities, laughingly yet truly annoyed when other women got more attention from the men than she." Sally was "the power behind his lifelong total

123

sense of reality"; she taught young Washington "the ability to curb his emotions, to restrain his passions, to quietly accept facts instead of dreams." He continued to love her even after marrying Martha, and he must have been consequently "guilty about that feeling."[2]

Assertions such as these, first of all, ooze misogynist biases. They tell us about how men, on average, saw and still see women; how they expect them to be and behave; under which conditions they become "lovable"; and how men, in turn, are expected to behave in women's presence.

Through these accounts, women like Martha Washington and Sarah Cary Fairfax are presented as powerless and lacking their own agency; they are either too old, too fat, or too stupid; they resemble bad characters in a movie. Invariably, they remain an appendage to the only real protagonist, the "seductive" male.

Second, these assertions lack credible evidence. Washington's heart did not belong to Sally. Not only was she married; she was the wife of his best friend, George William. True, there's an "infamous" letter. On September 12, 1758, Washington wrote a letter to Sally in which he expressed his "true feelings," a letter that many have taken as proof that the two must have felt intense romantic passion for each other. "'Tis true," Washington confessed, "I profess myself a Votary to love. I acknowledge that a Lady is in the Case—and further I confess, that this Lady is known to you." But was that lady the same Sally he addressed, as many suppose?[3]

Let us begin with some facts. Sarah Cary came from an aristocratic family in Bristol, England, that migrated to the colony of Virginia in the mid-seventeenth century, where they became rich and influential. Sally, the eldest of four girls, was considered the most attractive and appealing of her sisters. Her first biographer emphasizes her "clever sprightliness," and swears she was "a woman of unusually fine mind," having "been enriched with the best literature of the day," which challenges the suggestion she was a coquette. Faced with many suitors, she was ultimately promised to George William Fairfax via an arrangement between the families.[4]

Sarah and George William got married in 1748. The bride was eighteen and the groom twenty-four. Because the marriage was arranged by the families, it's easy to infer that it was bereft of love and happiness and thus vulnerable not only to an affair but to a truer and deeper love. The implicit assumption is that only a "spontaneous" romantic love match can produce a successful marriage. Although among the higher classes marriage was a public contract that had to benefit both families, this pragmatic approach to the institution may well have encouraged the couple in question to try to love each other even more deeply and remain committed and faithful to each other. The idea that love is a simple emotion in which reasoning or self-interest play no part is debatable. Some psychologists, in fact, consider love to be a system of decisions, motivated by biological and cultural pressures and unconscious biases, that evolves over time. Sally may have decided that George William was the best choice she could make and then come to appreciate him more and more, and vice versa.[5]

George William, furthermore, was a decent man, at least by eighteenth-century standards. He had been born in the Bahamas, where his father held a prized position as customs agent for the British Crown and was also the chief justice and governor. George William's father was then assigned to Virginia, where he also became influential and prestigious. The boy grew up in privilege and received a good education. He was not violent or a drunkard, so far as we can tell from extant records, or in any way unfit to act his role.

Young Washington and George William had become friends years before he married Sarah. Washington's half brother Lawrence had introduced Washington to the Fairfax family when he married George William's sister, Anne Fairfax, in 1743. Washington was George William's junior by eight years, but the two spent a lot of time together. After George William married Sarah, the three developed a strong bond. They read to one other, danced, played cards and, in typical eighteenth-century fashion, spent hours in conversation.

That this friendship was innocent is suggested by the fact that it continued after Washington married Martha. The two couples often visited each other at their respective homes, Mount Vernon and Belvoir, and went on holidays together. In August 1767, for example, the four of them took a trip to Warm Springs (now Berkeley Springs, West Virginia). They had a great time. Besides "taking the waters"—which means both drinking the mineral water and immersing themselves, loosely dressed, in the springs—the four strolled about, played cards, indulged in hours-long conversations, and enjoyed lavish meals, prepared by their own cook, whom they had brought with them.[6]

Now, let's go back to the letter of September 12, 1758. Sarah and George William had been married for ten years by this point, and in a few months, Washington would marry Martha. Indeed, at the beginning of his letter, Washington alluded to his recent engagement to the young widow Martha Custis. He declared himself enthused by "the annimating prospect of possessing Mrs Custis." At this time the engagement was apparently still a secret shared only among the closest friends, a fact that invites us to read many of his "illicit" gallantries in the letter as directed to Martha.

This, however, is not to deny that the letter is flirtatious and ambiguous. Washington's "recollection of a thousand tender passages that I coud wish to obliterate" clearly refers to Sally. Furthermore, the letter alludes to a secret that Washington confesses and that the world has no right to know: "You have drawn me my dear Madam, or rather have I drawn myself, into an honest confession of a Simple Fact—misconstrue not my meaning—'tis obvious—doubt it not, nor expose it,—the World has no business to know the object of my Love, declard in this manner to—you when I want to conceal it." The remark that "the World has no business to know the object of my Love" is a masterpiece of ambiguity. It is possible that Sally, in a previous letter, had asked Washington "Are you engaged?" or "Did Martha say 'yes' already?" This would explain Washington's abrupt allusions to his secret love and his noting that "this Lady is known to you." But if he was referring to Martha, why treat it as a secret to be kept hidden from the world? People in the eighteenth century not only were masters of ambiguity but in fact delighted in it.[7]

Washington was twenty-six when he penned the letter and leading a contingent of Virginians in the Forbes Expedition, another attempt to recapture the French stronghold at Fort Duquesne, in modern-day Pittsburgh, after General Braddock's expedition had failed in 1755. He could not know the outcome of the mission yet and feared for his life—especially because he was highly critical of Lieutenant Colonel Henry Bouquet and Brigadier General John Forbes and how they were managing the campaign. In the letter, Washington clearly refers to this military context and the load of uncertainty it put on his shoulders: "The hours at present" were "melancholy dull"; "the rugged Toils of War" were not "in my choice"; the "Fate of the Expedition" was still to be determined. Washington consequently longed for the "happier times, if I ever shall see them."

Young Washington missed his friends, George William and Sarah. He missed his little world, Belvoir and Mount Vernon. For him, keeping alive the correspondence was in itself soothing—no ulterior motives need be ascribed. The affairs of war in which he was immersed embroiled him, consumed him. On his way to join General Braddock, on April 30, 1755, George had already written Sarah a letter in which he had asked her to carry on a personal, "private" correspondence. More important, the young man had already explained everything we need to know—an open warning to all biographers and readers who look for a scandal. *Communication*, not love, was the object of Washington's pleasure: "A correspondence with my Friends is the greatest satisfaction I expect to enjoy, in the course of the Campaigne." (And take notice of the phrase "my Friends.") Furthermore, Sarah was special; from no other friend "shall I derive such satisfaction as from yours." (Washington had also written, and then scrubbed out, that "none of my Friends are able to convey more real delight than you are.") Sarah was George's favorite companion and coconspirator—because she was clever, sensible, tender, and willing to play ball, someone with whom he knew it was safe even to play romantic.[8]

These mundane details throw doubt on the idea that Washington experienced a melancholic, life-long pining for Sally. He was far from home, exhausted from clearing roads, and anxious about supply lines and attack plans. In his tent, at night, he must have pondered all he had left behind, not only George William and Sarah, but also Martha, whom he had met not long before. Writing a flirtatious letter to his friend Sally offered the perfect distraction from his worries and melancholy. Amusing himself for an hour or so by acting as a sentimental character "confessing his love" to a sympathetic friend was a typical diversion in the eighteenth century. No deeper explanation is called for: George must have written Martha similar letters, perhaps even on the same night.

The chain of correspondence surrounding this letter supplies more evidence that Washington was not declaring his secret love for Sally in it. On September 12, 1758, Washington wrote not just the well-known letter to Sally but also one, which has unfortunately been lost, to her husband, George William.[9]

Washington was answering letters George William and Sally had written to him on September 1. Sally, whose letter is also lost, wrote to George in response to yet another lost letter of August 22, 1758, that Washington had sent her through George William and not to her directly. In his letter to Washington, George William discussed daily business—corn, tobacco, a long overdue rain, trees that had died, but also, importantly, informed Washington that Sarah was undertaking to answer the letter of August 22 that Washington had sent Sarah through him. So, it is as a sequel to this lost letter of August 22 that George Washington wrote the infamous letter to her. What this tells us is that letters circulated openly between husband, wife, and friend. Sarah was used to enclosing her letters to Washington in other letters she knew would reach him quickly.[10]

After the letter of September 12, 1758, the two "lovers" exchanged other missives. (In reality, they had been flirting regularly, at least since 1755, when Washington chided Sarah for what he claimed was her decision, "forbidding my corresponding with you.") On September 25, Washington wrote to Sarah again. She must have replied to Washington's infamous letter right away, but this letter does not survive. In the lost letter, she could have pretended to be in doubt about the true meaning of George's confession, or could have kept flirting playfully, or could have chided her "suitor" openly. Whatever the case, in the next letter, George wrote: "Do we still misunderstand the true meaning of each others Letters? I think it must appear so, tho I would feign hope the contrary as I cannot speak plainer without—but I'll say no more, and leave you to guess the rest."[11]

There was love in that moment in Washington's life, and perhaps for Sally as well as for Martha. But his letters were also typical eighteenth-century *representations* of love. So, there is love and "love"—the first is *experienced* as a variation in the cycles of testosterone, dopamine, norepinephrine, serotonin, oxytocin, and vasopressin; the second is *represented* in theater, literature, or, as in this case, in personal letters. Represented love is a fiction, a spectacle appealing to the taste of a given historical period and place that does not necessarily exist in a physical body.

Washington was flirtatious, deliberately ambiguous, and highly sentimental. The letter to Sally indicates delight in witty and frivolous engagement—in "love." But it was mostly literature and theater—and such a show needed an audience. That fact that, as I noted, Sally enclosed her letters and notes in her husband's correspondence makes it clear that such letters were not regarded as private. Not only could any correspondence be easily intercepted, in particular in time of war, but in high-class society letters conveying ardent romantic sentiments were typically read aloud to friends, wives, and husbands. When the author was gifted, such letters might even be published. Indeed, it may sound strange, but the phenomenon of the public love letter was common. Public declarations of affection were made not only during courtship and illicit trysts but also in the negotiation of associations and contracts of many kinds. Such expressions of sentiment both revealed and concealed—they were a plot, a play.[12]

Individuals who were in a position to parade love, especially by means of the letters they sent to their friends and paramours, knew they would not be misunderstood; they were aware they had cracked the code of the game and drew pleasure and self-satisfaction from this fact. Through such performances, young people like George Washington and the Fairfaxes received confirmation that they belonged to an exclusive circle, a circle that was up-to-date on the latest in literature and theater. Coming from a different era, we may easily skew such letters, by ascribing them an immediacy and literalness they didn't possess. The sender wasn't saying, "Listen, I love you, I'm serious."

Jonathan Swift wrote Mrs. Henrietta Howard passionate letters, stating in one, for example, that "I wish I were a young Lord, and you were unmarried. I should make you the best husband in the world." But he was not in love with her. The game consisted in both players exchanging volleys and coming to a quick understanding, after which it ended. Henrietta Howard promptly replied to "her" Jonathan as she was expected to, with playfulness: "I did desire you to write me a love letter; but I never did desire you to talk of marrying me."[13]

Women were made sparring partners for countless men in "love." In many cases, these men allowed themselves to be more forward and initiating than a woman might have preferred. Bantering as Washington did with Sarah Cary Fairfax was also a mechanism for the dominating male to show and assert control. Women acted and reacted. They could turn flirtatious and playful, but oftentimes they must have felt a little cornered. James Lovell, the Massachusetts delegate to the Continental Congress and a married man, for example, made Abigail Adams the target of his attentions.

Over a period of five years, from 1777 to 1782, the two exchanged letters in which Lovell assumed the role of the seducer. Obviously, Abigail Adams had not solicited such attention from him.[14]

Lovell referred to Adams by her familiar pen name "Portia" and would even address her as "lovely Portia," though he was not an intimate acquaintance. At times, he was inappropriate and almost vile. When John Adams was away in France for eleven months, for example, Lovell congratulated Abigail on not becoming pregnant. He goaded her in other letters with the twisted logic that we would describe today as that of a stalker, remarking that "your having given your heart to such a man [as John Adams] is what, most of all makes me yours, in the manner I have above sincerely professed myself to be."[15]

This is certainly gross. But when both parties agreed on the game, it could be very entertaining. The drama of courtship and marriage or courtship and seduction became the focus of the novel from the early eighteenth century onward. More interestingly, the eighteenth-century novel took a characteristic epistolary shape. Such novels started to appear at the end of the seventeenth century with works such as Aphra Behn's *Love-Letters between a Noble-Man and His Sister* (1684–87). It reached a peak of popularity in the eighteenth century with Samuel Richardson's *Pamela* (1740) and *Clarissa* (1747–48) and Frances Burney's *Evelina* (1778).

Simultaneously, manuals designed to helping lovers express themselves with fluency were printed and reprinted. These manuals had become an essential part of the education of young gentlemen, and young women also spent several hours each day practicing at their desk. Like the epistolary novel, manuals started to become popular in the late seventeenth century. In 1678, an early practitioner, identified only by the initials W. P., published *A Flying Post with a Packet of Choice New Letters and Compliments: Containing Variety of Examples of Witty and Delightful Letters upon All*

Occasions both of Love and Business. It was only the beginning of a sweeping transatlantic trend. Daniel Defoe's 1726 *Complete English Tradesman, in Familiar Letters* explained how to write proper "delightful" romantic letters.

Samuel Richardson, the author of *Pamela* and *Clarissa*, also published a collection called *Letters Written to and for Particular Friends on the Most Important Occasions* (1741). These 173 letters provided eloquent examples intended to teach letter writers how to adhere to proper style and form, how to express thoughts and feelings appropriately, and even how to exaggerate slightly for effect. The titles of the letters are amusing in their mischievousness: "From a Father to a Daughter against a Frothy French Lover"; "To a Young Fellow Who Makes Love in a Romantic Manner"; "A Gentleman to a Lady Who Humorously Resents His Mistress's Fondness of a Monkey, and Indifference to Himself"; "A Lady to a Gentleman of Superior Fortune, Who, after a Long Address in an Honourable Way, Proposes to Live with Her as a Gallant." We could easily include among them another letter, the letter we already know all too well: "From a Young Virginia Colonel to the Woman Who Is Already Married to His Best Friend."

Many other manuals, pamphlets, and books, for both women and men, were readily available in American bookstores in Boston, Philadelphia, and New York. These publications all had something in common. While letter manuals had long existed—basically to teach ceremony, formality, rhetorical elegance, and the daunting art of living at court to pupils of the European aristocracy—this new genre of "familiar letter manuals," as they are called, insisted on the "true" picture of the heart, on "love," on the "naturalness" of conversation, on "intimacy" and "emotional honesty," on "spontaneous" feelings, and on social complaisance. Of course, since eighteenth-century society remained fundamentally hierarchical and deferential, the goal of these modern manuals that touted "sincerity" was not to erase social distinctions; it was not intended to foster social mobility by inviting the lower sort to mingle with the elite via a democratic playfulness. The goal was simply to create a "modern" atmosphere, a sophisticated style.[16]

The authors of familiar letter manuals invited men and women alike to practice an "easy sentimentality," because that was seen as the basis of personal success and cultural refinement. Men as well as women were urged to experiment with ornate sentences, philosophical questions, and most of all with high sentiments. This type of emotion was largely confined to the page. Possible next steps could well be taken, but none of these manuals suggested going down that road.[17]

Washington did not in fact need to read such manuals and books to absorb their lessons and perfect the art. That style and approach were the gist of a new culture emerging across Europe and the American colonies that regulated normal courtesies between men and women in conversation, gesture, manner, and behavior. Extravagant behaviors, such as flirting, maintaining a coy ambiguity, and confessing prohibited "love," were both admissible and encouraged.

☙ Letters of long-gone people allow us to gain a better grasp of them and their inner world of emotions. Represented emotions help us to unlock the secrets of experienced emotions. Our ways of talking or writing about our loves, desires, hopes, and other emotions contribute to the shaping of such emotions—letter writing can thus be seen as a laboratory. Men like Washington could be reckless and wrathful, violent in the extreme, as we have seen. But letters and other written documents demonstrate that these very individuals could also be playful and "feminine." For all its posturing and exaggeration, the eighteenth century was indeed a period of strong, complex feelings and strong passions. Political revolutions would have never taken place otherwise.

With his male friends, Washington could flaunt tumultuous "romantic" feelings—as he did with Sarah Cary Fairfax. Writing to "Dear Friend Robin," possibly his cousin Robert Washington, George opened up entirely: "As its the greatest mark of friendship and esteem absent Friends can shew each other in Writing and often communicating their thoughts to his fellow companions mak[es] me endeavour to signalize myself in acquainting you from time to time and at all times my situation and employments of Life and could Wish you would take half the Pains of contriving me a Letter by any oppertunity as you may be well assured of its meeting with a very welcome reception."[18]

Especially through their letters, scions of well-off families made their hearts visible not only to female friends or women they were courting but also to their male friends. The flood of their bursting inner feelings was in part real and in part the literary fashion of the day. Historian Richard Bushman argues that participating in such a literary culture—half romantic and natural and half sophisticated and artful—spoke to an individual's refinement. Letter writing such as this, suspended between immediacy and performance, between an uncontainable inner life and a restrained outer one, afforded young genteel Americans the opportunity to display their status. Gushing out with tumultuous passions was not shocking or beyond the mark—even among men. And, of course, we do not have to overinterpret their scorching declarations, treating them as if they were factually true or as if they contained homosexual innuendos.[19]

With "Dear Friend John," possibly one of his cousins, Washington could be very romantic, an erupting volcano, not just emotionally but also stylistically. Washington's spelling was very poor in one particular letter, a clear sign that his heart was about to burst: "As its the greatest mark of friendship and esteem you can shew to an absent Friend In often Writing to him so hope youl not deny me that Favour as its so ardently wish'd and Desired by me its the greatest pleasure I can yet forsee of having in fairfax to hear from my friends Particularly yourself."[20]

But young Washington did not exceed the proper limit. He didn't try to shock the recipient, thus breaking the rules of civility and propriety. Had he engaged in a complete, honest self-revelation, he would have insulted the other person. A polite man does not bare his soul. The man who shows himself naked would simply be a bore.[21]

Washington never attained a degree, nor even completed his formal education. But he was not a man of instinct either. His letters were in part a means through which he could flirt and share with his young friends his most ardent wishes and in part an exercise through which he could hone his "epistolary self." Youthful letters such as these can thus be categorized as "entertainment." Young men as well were playful with each other, and their letters to each other were intended to display an artfulness that at its best would represent the triumph of wit and humor and imagination. There was a dose of courtier-like elegance also. The underlying code was mutually understood, which was possible only among "civilized" men and women.[22]

Young Washington let loose his passions to his friends, either John or Robin, exactly in the way a more mature John Arbuthnot, the famous Scottish physician, polymath, and satirist, did to Jonathan Swift: "Dear Friend, the last sentence of your letter quite kills me. Never repeat that melancholy tender word, that you will endeavour to forget me. I am sure I never can forget you, till I meet with, what is impossible, another, whose conversation I can delight so much in as Dr. Swift's, and yet that is the smallest thing I ought to value you for. That hearty sincere friendship, that plain and open ingenuity in all your commerce, is what I am sure I never can find in another man. . . . God knows I write this with tears in my eyes." In the eighteenth century, male friendship was at once spontaneous and constructed, liberating and empowering, and yet it adhered to the prevalent codes of behavior.[23]

A Playful, Mature Man

"My time is so much taken up at my desk," General Washington grumbled in January 1776, "that I am obliged to neglect many other essential parts of my duty." Without the help of his secretaries and aides, Washington could not have signed the circa twelve thousand missives he churned out during his years in service as a commander in chief, from 1775 to 1783, when he resigned. He produced more letters than any other American officer produced.[24]

And yet, despite the just complaint about an activity that siphoned off energy that could have been directed toward other duties, at least during that delicate period, the truth is that Washington loved writing letters. He wrote thousands on thousands of letters during his lifetime, not only out of necessity and to make sure his officers, his cabinet, his subordinates, or those who helped him in his official duties got his orders right, but also to deliver private, far-from-urgent messages to his family, tailors, purveyors, friends, and acquaintances.

Washington complained every now and then, but it's apparent that letter writing gave him an intimate satisfaction. Letters provided Washington and his peers with a sense of freedom, of new possibilities; through letters, he and his acquaintances experimented, pushed their personal boundaries by donning a new costume and acting out a new drama. It was like exploring, traveling in time and space. In the eighteenth century, writing letters was at once a distraction, an amusement, and an act of empowerment. "Washington was at his best when he was writing letters," one biographer rightly concludes, and "like any good letter writer, he shaped his tone and persona to suit individual readers."[25]

Anyone who closely examines Washington's correspondence will come to realize that he evolved in this difficult art. By the eve of the Revolution, he had become a self-aware writer—one who was in command of a direct, simple, mature prose and who used more correct spelling and syntax. Washington's style when he was younger had been much more convoluted and immature. Florid phrasing and baroque composition can be found in many of his letters, and he vented strong passions, without too much self-control.[26]

But Washington did not only write sentimental letters when he was young. He reveals deep emotions in letters he sent later in life to those whom we ought to consider his real friends: the Scotch-Irish Presbyterian Dr. James Craik, the Reverend Lord Bryan Fairfax, the Comte de Rochambeau, the Marquis de Chastellux, Baron Von Steuben, the Comte de Grasse, General Henry Knox, David Humphreys, and Alexander Hamilton.[27]

The language of Washington's romantic and youthful heart reached the highest peaks in his correspondence with Lafayette. The many letters the two exchanged suggest that Washington the general was again in "love." The two had met at a dinner, on August 5, 1777, right after the Continental Congress had appointed the young French marquis volunteer major general in the Continental Army and placed him under Washington's direct command.

Washington and Lafayette hit it off immediately, despite the twenty-five years' difference in age. They soon were living under the same roof, and they shared meals and had countless discussions. Every separation was sorely felt, and the moment of a future reunion much anticipated. Washington dreamed about a cheerful future when Lafayette would eventually become family: "After our Swords & Spears have given place to the plough share & pruning-hook, I see you as a private Gentleman—a friend & Companion—I shall welcome you in all the warmth of friendship to Columbias shore; & in the latter case, to my rural Cottage, where homely fare & a cordial reception shall be substituted for delicacies & costly living." "Love" always loomed large between the two: "I love every body that is dear to you."[28]

After Lafayette went home to France on leave in January 1779, Washington began writing his friend the most romantic letters one can imagine—which unfortunately, due to adverse circumstances, didn't reach their destination: "To hear that not one of the many letters which I have written to you since you left this Continent had arrived safe was not only surprizing but mortifying," he wrote in March 1780. The feeling he expressed in this letter was definitely more than a generic gesture of civility. Washington wrote many sincere, playful, sassy, and romantic letters to his friend. Not much had changed since young Washington first developed the literary persona we have met in the letters to Sarah Fairfax: "I have been thus particular My dear friend that in case there should be the least suspicion of my want of friendship or want of attention, it may be totally removed; as it is my earnest wish to convince you by every testimony that an affectionate regard can dictate, of my sincere attachment to your person—and fortunes," he wrote on one occasion. "When my dear Marquis, shall I embrace you again? Shall I ever do it?," he asked on another. And on yet another, he complained, "Often, since you left this Country have I written *to you*, but have not been favoured with a single line *from you* . . . this I shall ascribe to any cause rather than a decline of friendship."[29]

On April 11, 1774, before he first met Washington, Lafayette had married Adrienne de Noailles, now the Marquise de Lafayette. Washington's retrospective "jealousy," which was accompanied by tender jokes and many proclamations of "love," exploded every time Lafayette happened to mention his wife. At the end of an already impossibly long letter the general wrote to his friend on September 30, 1779—courtesy dictated that letters should stay within a one-page limit—the jealous lover burst out. Letters such as these are a wonderful window into a long-gone society, in which it was not always clear who was the lover and who was the beloved, who was younger and who was older. In Washington's eighteenth-century world, one could easily assume a role that defied convention, at least within the space of the literary imagination. Sassiness and exaggeration were a matter of course. And when a man happened to lavish his "most respectful compliments" to the wife of his dearest friend, the plot could suddenly turn into an intricate love game.

Everyone must have laughed at the coquetry and the game that Washington played in his September 30 letter—because it's obvious that the passage you are about to read was meant to be read out loud:

> Tell her (if you have not made a mistake, & offered your *own love* instead of *hers* to me) that I have a heart susceptable of the tenderest passion, & that it is already so strongly impressed with the most favourable ideas of her, that she must be cautious of putting loves torch to it; as you must be in fanning the flame. But here again methinks I hear you say, I am not apprehensive of danger—My wife is young—you are growing old & the atlantic is between you—All this is true, but know my good friend that no distance can keep *anxious* lovers long asunder, and that the Wonders of former ages may be revived in this—But alas! will you not remark that amidst all the wonders recorded in holy writ no instance can be produced where a young Woman from *real inclination* has prefered an old Man—This is so much against me that I shall not be able *I fear* to contest the prize with you—yet, under the encouragement you have given me I shall enter the list for so inestimable a jewell.[30]

When his leave of absence was over, Lafayette returned to America, entering Boston harbor on April 27, 1780. That very same day, Lafayette wrote to the general. He could assume the role of lover as well: "Here I am, My dear General, and in the Mist of the joy I feel in finding Myself again one of your loving Soldiers." Impatient, Washington wrote back to Lafayette immediately: "Your welcome favour of the 27th of April came to my hands yesterday—I received it with all the joy that the sincerest friendship could dictate—and with that impatience which an ardent desire to see you could not fail to inspire. . . . I most sincerely congratulate with you on your safe arrival in America & shall embrace you with all the warmth of an Affectionate friend when you come to head Qrs—where a bed is prepared for you." Lafayette reached Washington's Morristown quarters on May 10, where he spent too few days with his "lover" before leaving for Philadelphia on May 13.[31]

Maybe Washington saw in Lafayette the son he never had—many biographers have made this claim. Or perhaps, more simply, the two were playful and yet, at the same time, sincere friends in the most typical eighteenth-century fashion—both in reality and within the realm of literary imagination.

After the rebels won the Revolution, Lafayette's time in America came to an end—for good, this time. Victory was at once a blessing for the country and a curse for many personal friendships. On a gloomy winter day, December 8, 1784, Washington had to bid Lafayette adieu. He accompanied his friend up the road, and then the two parted company. When "our Carriages distended," it was awful for Washington in particular: "In the moment of our separation upon the road as I traveled, & every hour since—I felt all that love, respect & attachment for you, with which length of years, close connexion & your merits, have inspired me."[32]

Is there anything more quintessentially sentimental than the image of the two carriages "distending"? Or anything more emotional than asking, as Washington did via the romantic letter he quickly penned that same ominous day, "whether that was the last sight, I ever should have of you"? With Lafayette, this allegedly peculiarly cold man let his imagination soar. Washington was again young and in "love." Answering his own question as to whether that would be the last time he saw his friend, he remarked, "And tho' I wished to say no—my fears answered yes" (and he was right).

⁊❧ So, love letters such as these help us to weave together a psychological portrait of George Washington that flies in the face of not only the hypothesis that eighteenth-century letters must always be taken literally, as if they were legal documents, but also the myth that Washington had a peculiarly cold, stern, distant, and glacial personality. No matter what Thomas Paine claimed—a man who, ideologically speaking, was miles apart from Washington—Washington was not emotionless and "incapable of forming" friendships. He had no "constitutional indifference" and in no way was he dominated by a "cold, hermaphrodite faculty," whatever Paine meant by that. Unquestionably, Washington was no stranger to his friends, male or female. He was not outlandish and idiosyncratic. The truth is that he fully participated in the emotional openness and the complexities characterizing eighteenth-century sensibility.[33]

Eighteenth-century letter writing was not only a complex and time-consuming activity; it was a highly constructed ceremonial ritual. Through letters—and the excesses they contained—well-educated, upper-class society performed the ritual of mutual recognition. But while these letters could be overblown, they typically didn't embarrass the recipient by suddenly revealing prohibited, extramarital love or by hinting at homosexual inclinations, although obviously that could happen. People used letter writing as a means of preening themselves and reassuring their associates that they belonged. By means of these clearly "feminine" letters, men like Washington could furthermore style themselves as modern. Being modern meant that they defined themselves in opposition to less-educated and less-refined people. *We* are these less-educated people each time we take eighteenth-century "revelations" literally. Washington and friends could go playful or sassy or just be openly "romantic"—with no strings attached.

7

※

The Meaning of Love (and Marriage)

Happy with Martha

Enter Martha Dandridge Custis Washington, the woman George Washington married. Countless biographers and historians have suggested that he could not have possibly loved her and have trotted out the same motive for why he married her: while she may have been physically and intellectually unremarkable, she was rich. Washington was shrewd and far-sighted enough to see he could use her, but that was it. Martha, for her part, succeeded in catching a man far superior to her. He was the living symbol of timeless masculinity; she was merely a plush elderly lady. According to (male) biographers, she wasn't "pretty, certainly not beautiful," nor was she "the least bit flirtatious" or "flamboyant in any way." The attraction she elicited was near zero. And a man could only "feel comfortable with her." It goes on and on.[1]

Interestingly, these rather dismissive characterizations of Martha only came about in the twentieth century. Nineteenth-century biographers, at the opposite extreme, had crafted a quasi-saintly Martha, again a purely fictional creature, all spirit and no body. This older version of Washington's wife was modeled on the Virgin Mary, the icon of moral perfection, the only option in a Victorian weltan-schauung that framed women as either virgins or whores.[2]

There is no evidence for most of these characterizations; they are instead the product of biases and misogynist preconceptions. By analyzing the extant evidence (family letters and contemporary descriptions), a strong case can be made that Martha was deep and real, personable, often sweet and loving, but also complex, and, like George, she had a darker side. Martha was indeed real and fully alive, successful and active, likely desirable to many eighteenth-century suitors. Physically, she was a pretty young woman, an at-tractive "petite"—a "pocket Venus," as she has been called—and defi-nitely a "cuddlesome armful." "With dark brown hair and strongly marked eyebrows," biographer Patricia Brady writes, "smooth white shoulders sloping down to full breasts, bright hazel eyes, and a ready smile displaying beautiful white teeth (a rarity for the time), she epitomized the feminine ideal for many Virginians." She was not only lovely but had sexual appeal.[3]

Martha was educated in the typical Virginian fashion; like many other girls of comparable social status, she was taught reli-gion, housekeeping, conversation, good manners, dancing, and mu-sic (the spinet was her instrument of choice). Her teachers were the adult women in her household plus itinerant tutors Martha's fa-ther hired. She was raised on the Chestnut Grove plantation in New Kent County, east of Richmond, which was a place of "rural simplicity" comprising five hundred acres of land and nearly twenty enslaved workers. The setting was very earthy: they kept cows and pigs, which they slaughtered in the fall, and they bred horses; heaps of steaming manure covered the ground, the odor of chamber pots and privies rose through the air, and the silence of the night was

Martha Dandridge Custis,
by John Wollaston, 1756.
Courtesy of Museums
at Washington and Lee
University, Lexington, VA.

broken by babies just born or by people about to die. Against this background, Martha grew into a proactive, down-to-earth, and powerful individual. She was warm and talkative, sure of herself and aware of her potential. Like George, she had a personality with many colors.[4]

On May 15, 1750, after a two-year courtship, Martha married the wealthy Daniel Parke Custis. At eighteen, she was slightly younger than average. Daniel was twenty years her senior. The couple had four children, two of whom (Jacky and Patsy) survived infancy. But on July 8, 1757, Daniel died, age forty-six, probably of a heart attack. While Martha had a lot of experience by this point; she had grown up quickly, jumping from childhood to womanhood within the span of a few years. As I have noted, this was not atypical; eighteenth-century individuals did not have the luxury of adolescence.[5]

In her mid-twenties, Martha had suffered much already: pregnancies, the deaths of her first two children, Daniel and Frances, and the sudden passing of her husband. The unexpected widowhood left Martha with a nearly eighteen-thousand-acre estate to manage, two very young children to raise, and about three hundred enslaved individuals to supervise. But she was self-aware and understood the privileged position she occupied in a complex, hierarchical and brutal society. She knew her responsibilities.

Her situation as a slaveowner didn't concern her terribly or make her morally uncomfortable. Especially as a younger woman, she accepted the institution of slavery as one from which she would benefit; it was the price that had to be paid for her social status. But the assertion made by biographers that in her approach to the people she held in bondage she was much harsher than George Washington, even positively cruel and verbally abusive, relies on scanty evidence and on snippets lifted from unhappy letters: "Blacks," Martha once wrote, "are so bad in thair nature that they have not the least gratatude for the kindness that may be shewed to them." Martha's blindness is inexcusable. But just like the claim that she was unattractive, the allegation that she was a worse slaveowner than George has been contrived as a means of aggrandizing him even further—she has to be worse in all respects because he has to be better. History cannot exonerate her or George, but she was also a woman of her times—an alibi that is usually reserved for men.[6]

As a single parent of a three-year-old son and one-year-old daughter, she decided she had to remarry. Enter George Washington. How Martha and her soon-to-be husband met is shrouded in mystery. There's the official story, told by George Washington Parke Custis. It goes as follows. At the beginning of 1758, Martha and the two little children paid a visit to some friends, the Chamberlaynes. Unexpectedly, a young army officer and his body servant, Thomas Bishop, on their way to Williamsburg to see the governor, stopped by for a short visit. Upon entering the house, the young officer met the young widow. The two were thunderstruck. The Chamberlaynes convinced Washington to stay for dinner, and then he ended up spending the night as well. Only the next day, very late in the morning, did he make the tough decision to leave the company. It's the typical nineteenth-century romantic plot, spontaneity and love at first sight.[7]

But Martha and George must have been on familiar terms already. In the 1750s, Washington was a military hero, well known in Europe as well as the American colonies. More importantly, he made frequent trips to Williamsburg. The Custises' White House estate in New Kent County, not far from Chestnut Grove, Martha's birthplace, was on the way, a pit stop he could hardly miss. Washington must have attended the same social affairs as Martha and Daniel. Martha, for her part, was the wife of one of the wealthiest men in the colony, which meant everyone knew who she was. The two also had mutual friends. Daniel Parke Custis's lawyer, Robert Carter Nicholas, was married to Anne Cary, whose sisters, Sally and Elizabeth, had married two of George Washington's best friends, the brothers George William and Bryan Fairfax, of Belvoir and Towlston Grange, respectively. Robert Carter Nicholas, furthermore, used to do legal work for George Washington.[8]

Ten days after they got married, Robert Stewart, an officer who knew Washington well, wrote his friend a revealing letter. Stewart alluded to the fact that the young colonel of the Virginia Regiment had long been attracted to Mrs. Custis—but she was already married, and George had no other option than to snuff out his pique. Stewart congratulated Washington "on your happy union with the Lady that all agree has long been the just object of your affections—may you long enjoy all the Felicity you propos'd by it, or that Matrimony can possibly afford."[9]

So, it's very likely that Martha and George had already met. Indubitably, they had heard of each other. As a matter of fact, they were cut from the same cloth. The Washingtons were closer to the Dandridges in status than were the Custises, who had initially looked down on Martha, regarding her as too "lower class." She had to win over John Custis IV, Daniel's father, a leading member of Virginia's Governor's Council. The Custises belonged to the top echelon of Virginia's aristocracy. Martha's family, on the other hand, was merely wealthy and established.[10]

In 1758, Martha must have felt relieved at the prospect of getting closer to George and his family. George was an up-and-coming youth, at once trustworthy and full of potential. (George had been elected to the Virginia House of Burgesses, for example, the summer after he began courting Martha.) George was also Martha's age, with no particular emotional baggage, such as a dead wife he was grieving or children that could divert his attention away from Martha's small son and daughter. They married on January 6, 1759, at her White House estate. Washington's financial records show that he had visited Martha there the year before, on March 16, April 25, and June 5. Maybe George proposed to her during one of these visits, in person.[11]

By any standard, that Saturday, the day of the wedding, the bride was beautiful. She wore a petticoat of white silk interwoven with silver. Her overdress, a deep yellow brocade with rich lace in the neck and sleeves, was open in front. Her shoes were purple satin with silver trimmings. She wore pearls. The groom himself had spent time and money preparing for the wedding. He wanted to make sure Martha got the message that her new husband cared for her and that the occasion was deeply important to him. For it, he wore civilian dress, an homage to delicacy and an augury of a soon-to-be happy "retirement." The blue coat lined in red silk and trimmed with silver was impressive. His breeches were fastened at the knees with gold buckles. He had a dress sword at his side, and his hair was powdered white. On his hands he wore white gloves of exquisite manufacture. George Washington Parke Custis was probably right in his assessment that George, on that day, surpassed in elegance all the other gentlemen "in their gold lace." It was his act of love. "None looked like the man himself."[12]

It would be wonderful to know more about their relationship, but unfortunately, when George died Martha destroyed their personal correspondence. (Other letters had been already destroyed by Washington himself.) Five documents survive: a note Martha wrote at the bottom of a letter Lund Washington sent to George Washington on March 30, 1767; another even shorter note she scribbled on the reverse of a letter sent to Washington by John Parke Custis on September 11, 1777 (Martha was then visiting her sister, Anna Maria Dandridge Bassett, and her family at Eltham in New Kent County, Virginia); two letters George sent to Martha, dated June 18 and 23, 1775, respectively—found in a drawer of a writing table that Martha gave to her granddaughter Martha Parke Custis Peter of Tudor Place; and a short letter of introduction that George wrote, dated October 1, 1782, from Verplanck's Point, Westchester County, New York, for one Mr. Brown who wanted to visit Virginia, although this letter never reached Martha.[13]

In her first note, Martha calls George "my dearest" and expresses her regret at the fact that George will get back to her only in May and not April as she had hoped: "I am sorry you will not be at home soon as I expe[ct]ed you." The second note reads: "My love the silver cup I mentioned to you in my letter by the last post—Wt 113 ouz." Martha calls George "my love."[14]

George, similarly, is loving and warm. On June 18, 1775, a freshly appointed commandant of the Continental Army about to start off on a dangerous campaign against the British addresses his wife with tenderness. "My dear Patcy," he calls her. Martha was then at home, alone, and no doubt was fretting about what was going to happen. She must have felt miserable, not least because her daughter Patsy had died exactly two years before. George told Martha that he tried everything "in my power" to eschew the new appointment, adding, "I should enjoy more real happiness and felicity in one month with you, at home, than I have the most distant prospect of reaping abroad, if my stay was to be Seven times Seven years." He understood how she would "feel at being left alone." He relayed that he had drafted a will, "in case of my death," concluding with a post scriptum that lets us peep into a cozy daily life: "Since writing the above I have receivd your Letter of the 15th and have got two suits of what I was told was the prettiest Muslin. I wish it may please you—it cost 50/. a suit that is 20/. a yard." On June 23, as he was wrapping up things and about to leave Philadelphia for Boston, he couldn't help "dropping you a line." He was fully confident in a "happy meeting with you sometime in the Fall," and told Martha he loved her and belonged to her entirely: "I retain an unalterable affection for you, which neither time or distance can change."[15]

The two exchanged many more letters—there's no doubt about this fact. We know because after Elizabeth Willing Powel, the famous Philadelphia salonnière, bought a writing desk from Washington in early March 1797, she discovered a bundle of letters Martha had sent to her husband hidden in a drawer. Washington had forgotten about these documents. But Powel did not forget to chide her friend about "the love Letters of a Lady addressed to you under the most solemn Sanction; & a large Packet too." While the president may have made very few blunders in his political life, he was off to a poor start as a private gentleman, leaving intimate correspondence from his wife for anyone to find.[16]

Powel wasn't just intelligent and amusing; she was a real friend and did not read those letters but sealed them up with the intention to return them to Washington: "Tho' I know that your Nerves are not as irritable as a fine Ladies, yet I will with the Generosity of my Sex relieve you." But she couldn't help teasing her friend over his negligence. Powel concluded with a recitation on the nature versus nurture theme: "Tho' Curiosity is supposed to be a prominent feature of the female Mind, yet it will ever be powerfully counteracted when opposed by native Delicacy, or sense of Honor, and I trust a pious Education."

❧ Martha and George were a happy couple. They were accomplices and gladly shared responsibilities and burdens. The two must have laughed about those damn letters George forgot in that damn drawer. Martha, like Elizabeth Powel, must have scolded her absentminded "pappa," as she used to call him. Martha also deployed the more dignified "general" after George became president—but this last title was probably tongue-in-cheek, an affectionate way for a wife to chide her husband. Martha made fun of her "pappa," her "general," and her "old man," and would yank his coattail unapologetically each time she needed to get his attention. Friendliness, affection, and repartee abounded. The two understood each other. Their relationship went very deep, embracing their entire being. And Washington remained "your entire George Washington" to his wife. It was love—but not the Hollywood-type of romantic love, all passion and sensuality.[17]

Eighteenth-century love hinged on happiness more than romantic desire. And Martha and George were happy together. Happiness in this period was associated with rural simplicity and self-containment, or "independence," and it made a man complete and healthy, especially if he happened to have been born on the right side of the social fence. Even though happiness was an "unalienable right," according to the Declaration of Independence, achieving and maintaining that status was not possible for everyone. But Washington thought he had achieved it, thanks to his wife.[18]

On April 6 or 7, 1759, Martha, the bride, arrived at Mount Vernon with her two children, John Parke Custis (Jacky) and Martha Parke Custis (Patsy). Colonel George Washington, the groom, accompanied them. From that moment on, Washington repeated the same mantra, which was that "fixd at this Seat with an agreeable Consort for Life," he expected "to find more happiness" than he had "ever experienced amidst a wide and bustling World." Happiness, concretely, was a pleasant routine: getting up at or before dawn, work, a light breakfast, work, playing with the children, work, dinner at 3 p.m., perhaps a walk, work, tea, and, after the "servants" had lit the candles, card playing, backgammon, newspapers, dancing, and singing—and more work, naturally. Martha had a copy of *The Bull-Finch*, a collection of more or less popular songs, which she might have sung from. George had inscribed the copy with "Martha Washington. 1759." It was the first time he would write her new name.[19]

In Washington's world, love didn't happen in a void. It was not a magic, exclusive link between two persons. It was inextricably tied to marriage and social conventions, not independent from them. ("I love you tenderly *because* we are married," George and Martha would have said.) It was a situation, a set of circumstances one could or could not choose. In this sense, marriage, as Washington insisted, was "the most interesting event of ones life"; it was "the foundation of happiness or misery," the social institution in which love could test itself. Love was happiness for him precisely because, in his and Martha's case, it was based not upon a flimsy, presocial emotion, as romantics would prefer, but on sensible choices and suitable circumstances. Love had to be approved by both reason and society: passions, feelings, and emotions were an asset, Washington would have concurred, but they only thrived when they had roots in the proper terrain.[20]

At the end of the century, romanticism took hold in Europe and the entire Anglo-American world. Increasingly, a new generation of poets, novelists, and philosophers would celebrate love as an emotion worth pursuing independently of all other material and social factors. They would laud individualism and the newest discovery, "subjectivity," in an attempt to curtail all the "objective" canons of neoclassical culture. Romantics rejected constraints such as the institution of marriage or pragmatic considerations because the "heart" had to be set free. Romantic love, eventually, took the place of eighteenth-century happiness.

But George and Martha Washington didn't belong to this romantic universe. For them, happiness was more important. In 1794, for example, George Washington warned young Elizabeth Parke Custis, his step-grandchild, about the deceptions of romantic love. Do not trust, he told her, "the fine tales [that] the Poets & lovers of old have told us, of the transports of mutual love, that heaven has taken its abode on earth." And he continued:

Nor do not deceive yourself in supposing, that the only mean by which these [blessings?] are to be obtained, is to drink deep of the cup, & revel in an ocean of love. Love is a mighty pretty thing; but like all other delicious things, it is cloying; and when the first transports of the passion begins to subside, which it assuredly will do, and yield—often-times too late—to more sober reflections, it serves to evince, that love is too dainty a food to live upon *alone*, and ought not to be considered farther, than as a necessary ingredient for that matrimonial happiness which results from a combination of causes; none of which are of greater importance, than that the object on whom it is placed, should possess good sense—good dispositions—and the means of supporting you in the way you have been brought up. Such qualifications cannot fail to attract (after marriage) your esteem & regard, into wch or into disgust, sooner or later, love naturally resolves itself; and who at the sametime, has a claim to the respect, & esteem of the circle he moves in. Without these, whatever may be your first impressions of the man, they will end in disappointment; for be assured, and experience will convince you, that there is no truth more certain, than that all our enjoyments fall short of our expectations; and to none does it apply with more force, than to the gratification of the passions.[21]

Was George describing his personal experience with Martha? Maybe. Undoubtedly, he was voicing once again his theory that happiness does not depend on romantic love alone but on "a combination of causes." Happiness, more important, takes place "after marriage." "Love" is an "ingredient" of "matrimonial happiness," but not its heart and soul.

Marriage was for Washington superior to love in the same way society at large, in the eyes of the American founders, was superior to discrete individuals and their "unalienable" rights—which tells a lot about why slavery was such a difficult problem for them to tackle. (Slavery was not as much a moral dilemma for the single subject as a social, political, economic, and communitarian issue.) The eighteenth century was a communitarian period. It was not yet an age when "subjects" were free to seek acknowledgment of what we would call their "intrinsic value." The pivotal tenet of modern moral thinking, that there is an intrinsic, irreducible value in each individual, no matter his or her circumstances, was inconceivable to Washington's generation.[22]

Sex without Sexuality

*L*egend has it that George Washington was known as "the stallion of the Potomac" and that he used a secret code to rank the enslaved women he slept with. As with other "real" men, sex and carnal pleasures were never enough for him, or so it is claimed. Washington's sexuality was as gigantic as his stature. But these stories reflect present-day obsessions. In the same way the eighteenth century was not ready for romantic love yet, for pushing all individuals to become who they wanted to be, or for acknowledging dignity in every human person, the period was not ready for sexuality as we understand it either.[23]

Sexuality, the half-sinful galaxy made up of desires, behaviors, and cultural symbols aimed at pursuing and increasing pleasures, is our field, not theirs. Our world is in love with a certain idea of sexuality as an arena of human experience that lies beyond the social and that is an end in itself. But not all societies, not all individuals have engaged in seduction, cultivated prohibited fantasies, sought pleasures for their own sake, and maximized libido. (The ancient Romans probably did.) Moreover, while human beings have been having sex since the beginning of the world, the reasons why are various—including a desire to indulge in libidinous pleasures, to procreate, to express love and intimacy, to experience momentary tenderness. Or to exert power.[24]

Sexual intercourse can be a rather direct way to attain domination over someone else—over whomever happens to be the "prey"— and European aristocrats were notoriously experts in exploiting the power of rank when it came to sex. There was nothing instinctive or biological about that. Kings had countless lovers because being entitled, they could. Many noblemen and noblewomen enjoyed wide sexual license. Among those aristocrats, gender could be fluid as well. A French gentleman who fought in the French and Indian War, the Chevalier d'Éon (Charles-Geneviève-Louis-Auguste-André-Timothée d'Éon de Beaumont), switched his identity from masculine to feminine without experiencing any social discrimination in turn. Because they were powerful and firmly ensconced in the highest echelons of society, such individuals could largely do whatever they wanted. Their actions and experiments affirmed their own identity and class. It was a luxury they had the freedom to exploit. It was power.

For the slaveholding class in America—elites such as the Washingtons and the Jeffersons—slave communities represented another likely venue for sexual domination and power. Washington certainly didn't rank enslaved women, but many slaveowners abused these women recklessly. (This is not to say that pleasure didn't play any part; it's just that it was mostly about the affirmation of privilege.) Enslaved men too were often abused by both women and men who were in a position of control.[25]

Power plus control was more of a back and forth, however. It could be asserted by anyone, male or female, upper class or lower class, who just happened to be in the right circumstances to use it. Eighteenth-century women and girls might accept an offer of sex as a means of mitigating male control. These women were not strictly passive nor were the men completely dominant. Enslaved people, similarly, could offer or agree to have sex to gain advantages.[26]

Power is and was a factor explaining sex, which goes beyond the search for pleasure and what we call sexuality. But pleasure and sexuality, at some point, became dominant. Nearly 150 years ago, sexuality became a specific domain, an end in itself, a goal individuals wanted to achieve, no matter other considerations. Within the world of sexuality one can find seduction, prohibited fantasies, perversion, voyeuristic tendencies, a compulsion with "scoring new prey," occasional partners telling each other "you turn me on," and many other elements that are rather common today. None of these elements, however, are univocally linked to an instinct. They cannot be deployed as tools to explain people's behaviors or to describe human cultures in general, including the cultures of the past.[27]

To put it bluntly, sex existed before it started to be seen through the lens of sexuality. Washington's biographers may be excused for not immediately grasping the difference between the reality of sex and the cultural pattern of sexuality. Immersed in sexuality and the maximization of personal pleasure as an obvious, "natural" mode of being for a "real" man, they depict their hero as a reckless ladies' man. Washington is sexualized, often hypersexualized. Whenever he showed up, women started drooling, at least according to some biographers. Women were aroused, and some even swooned at his presence. He was seductive.[28]

But George Washington was not seductive because he did not belong to a world of sexuality. What we mean by seductiveness, for him, would have been an anachronistic feat or at least a juvenile embarrassment. He wasn't even blinded by power—there is no indication that he ever abused the women he held in shackles. We should talk the eighteenth-century idiom instead: George had sex with his wife Martha, whom he married and, hence, loved. He was sincere and happy. Another way of putting this is that his "sexuality," should we gauge it by our criteria, was rather low.

People of Washington's class made love in a different way than we do today and perhaps for different reasons. Washington didn't just want to "have fun." Not all men in all cultures crave sex for its own sake. While sexual desire is often presented today as a biological given and a fundamental drive, philosophers, historians, and anthropologists point out that it must be understood in the context of specific human experiences. The so-called universal human need for sex can't easily be separated from a cultural construction of desire and the exercise of power. The "natural" libido may not be so natural, after all, but rather the product of the behaviors and mores of a particular culture.[29]

Washington had no incentive to sexualize, let alone hypersexualize, his male identity. For men like him, taking advantage of an enslaved person or a social inferior would have been tantamount to giving into unmanly conduct—tolerated in a bachelor but unworthy of a man of propriety. Being perceived as rough, ungracious, brutal, rude, libidinous, or seductive would have hampered his reputation. Among the eighteenth-century upper classes, honor, education, and the many rules of "good society" contributed to make sexual behavior more regimented. Abuse still took place, but it had to be kept secret.[30]

Boys had to learn quickly how to become men. A teenaged Washington already recognized the danger of "adding Fuel" to the "fire" of unrestrained passions. He was aware he had to take precautionary measures. Living "retired from young Women" was the best method if one had to bury that "troublesome Passion in the grave of oblivion or etarnall forgetfulness." Another precautionary measure was to rely on the services of an experienced lady of pleasure. In fact, Washington may have lost his virginity with a "Ciprian dame," as a prostitute was also known. There's a letter that William La Péronie, a fellow officer who was eventually killed during Braddock's defeat, wrote to young Washington in early September 1754. It's a revealing document in which this hapless friend imagines George wandering the "metropolises" of Williamsburg and Alexandria, "plung'd in the midst of dellight heaven can af[f] ord: & enchanted By Charms even stranger to the Ciprian Dame." The person La Péronie alluded to, as he wrote in a note to that letter, was one "M's Nel." Although "M's Nel" need not have been a prostitute, she could have been.[31]

An older and wiser man, Washington cautioned his nephew George Steptoe Washington that maturity and manliness were not about licentious behaviors or stockpiling pleasures; they were about emerging victorious from "scenes of vice & dissipation which too often present themselves to youth in every place, & particularly in towns." Washington's counsel didn't sprout from moralism, as we may hastily conclude, but from his understanding that "real" men were expected to control themselves and downplay sexual exploits as stand-alone activities.[32]

❧ In the eighteenth century, American republican elites believed that sexual pleasures, like other wild passions and pleasures, should be harnessed and controlled. (We do remember the wild "horse," don't we?) The rituals of courtship represented an important first step in social maturation, supporting bachelors in their entrance into proper manhood. Courtship guided the young disorderly man to his place in society, while giving that society a means of closely watching over his conduct. When these rituals were followed, the young man would likely wed and become a householder. Once married, he could expand his identity through additional means. He could now practice orderly sex and hence prove his masculinity. Exercising self-control over his own urges and emotions reinforced his control over his wife, children, and enslaved persons.[33]

No young man could be indifferent to this gilded pathway that made sexual intercourse safe to engage in. "I could wish to know," Washington wrote to his friend John, "how my friend Lawrence drives on in his art of courtship." As to the frequency and intensity of sex, habits obviously varied from couple to couple. However, two general considerations need to be taken into account. The first is that the eighteenth century was not moralistic about sex. The Victorian era, with a dose of hypocrisy, may have saluted chastity and abstinence on moral grounds as conducive to more spiritual pleasures, turning sex into something people should be very curious about yet not talk about; but the world the Washingtons inhabited had not yet turned sex into a taboo. A quick read of Jonathan Swift's *Gulliver's Travels* (1726) or Laurence Sterne's *Tristram Shandy* (1759), the "dirtiest novel in English," reveals how uninhibited eighteenth-century society could be. Sex was a topic of conversation and of countless jokes, including gross ones. The library Washington inherited from Martha's previous marriage contained Daniel Defoe's *Conjugal Lewdness or, Matrimonial Whoredom* (1727) and Aphra Behn's *The Lover's Watch: Or the Art of Making Love* (1686). We can't know if or how often Martha and George consulted these "handbooks," but practical sexual guides, rather explicit in content, such as Nicholas de Venette's *Mysteries of Conjugal Love* (1712) and the anonymous *Aristoteles Master-piece: or, the Secrets of Generation Displayed in All the Parts Thereof* (1684), were easy to get hold of.[34]

The more important question is why George and Martha made love. Was it for lust and pleasure or to procreate? Or was it to achieve something else? Did they engage out of spousal duty or in pursuit of a shared and romantic intimacy? It is impossible to know for sure, but we can make some educated guesses.

Washington had no apparent sexual problems. He and Martha certainly had sex. A vigorous man, Washington was also a farmer and an expert mule breeder—which means that he was very familiar with the mechanics of procreation. There is no way to ascertain if or when sex between the two dwindled or stopped, if or when one of the two ever cheated on the other. Martha and George spent periods apart, but their intimacy doesn't seem to have suffered. During the early stages of their marriage, Washington had ordered four ounces of Spanish fly, a popular, almost legendary aphrodisiac from a dried insect, cantharis (*Cantharis vesicatoria* or *Lytta vesicatoria*). This aphrodisiac, made from the remains of such dried beetles, contains a substance, cantharidin, that in high concentrations can be toxic. Used since ancient times, the concoction created a rush of blood to the sexual organs.[35]

During the initial years of their marriage at least, Martha and George must have had sex in part because they did want children. But, no less important, they no doubt also had sex because it was considered healthy to do so. Sex, in the eighteenth century, was much more medicalized than it is today. Medical theories about sex and about how the sexual body worked circulated widely in the period and were absorbed by eighteenth-century cultured classes. As historian Andrew Burstein writes, sex was "seen much as diet was, part of a regimen of self-control, and important to understand if one was to enjoy a productive life." In other words, it was viewed not just as pleasurable and psychologically beneficial in fostering spiritual harmony between the couple but also as physiologically beneficial—something that was "good" for you.[36]

Sex was a method for maintaining the correct balance of bodily fluids, or humors—an idea derived from Galen, the father of humoral medicine. Briefly put, sex provided nourishment. By means of sexual intercourse, male and female bodies would help each other to preserve and, if necessary, to restore equilibrium. The "cold and wet" humors of female bodies balanced the excessively "hot and dry" humors of male bodies. Conversely, when a woman's body became too wet and cold, the male body offered warmth and dryness through the "dry heat" of semen. Sexual desire, in the eighteenth century, was understood in these very physiological terms. The logical corollary was that masturbation, or onanism, had to be prevented. Self-pleasuring did not help the "dry" body become "wet," or the "wet" become "dry." It would only shatter the equilibrium and halt desire. Fluids would simply be wasted. Such popular works as *Onania, or the Heinous Sin of Self-Pollution* (1712) and Samuel Auguste Tissot's *Onanism: or a Treatise upon the Disorders Produced by Masturbation* (1760) provided pseudomedical details about the "horrible" consequences of masturbation.[37]

Though he was no academic or theoretician, Washington nonetheless embraced the Galenic vision of a natural complementarity between the two sexes. For him, the male needed the female and vice versa. Eleanor Parke Custis confessed in a letter to her stepgrandfather her "apathy" toward the young men who were present at a ball she attended at Georgetown, and in his reply to her letter, Washington seized the opportunity to give her a short lecture about the secrets of the physiology of love. "Men and Women feel the same inclinations towards each other *now* that they always have done," he wrote. Love was for him almost a mechanical desire, a physiological force: "Do not therefore boast too soon, nor too strongly, of your insensibility to, or resistance of its powers." The "inflaminable matter" that is part of the "composition of the human frame" would unavoidably, "however dormant it may be for a while," set Nelly in motion.[38]

One of the most fascinating aspects of this discourse, though prescientific, is the emphasis on the complementarity rather than the duality between male and female bodies. Men's and women's "composition" was fundamentally identical; the only difference in anatomical terms was that male sexual organs were more externally distended than female organs. The vagina and uterus were believed to be an inverted penis and scrotum—although some preferred to associate the clitoris with the penis and the ovaries with the testicles.[39]

The notion that women and men were bearers of qualitatively different natures was a nineteenth-century one that would be accompanied by the bourgeois myth of "separate spheres," the idea that women were "naturally" made to stay at home while men were "naturally" meant to go out into the world. Eighteenth-century physiological discourse, by contrast, held that women were quantitatively rather than qualitatively different from men. Women, for instance, were believed to have less of the faculty of reason and less of the capacity to develop their sexual organs externally. They were seen as incomplete and inferior examples of the same essence, comparable variants of one common kind. (It was a vertical rather than a horizontal difference.)[40]

Women were repeatedly described as weaker and softer. Dr. Benjamin Rush, the eminent Philadelphian and signer of the Declaration of Independence, for one, characterized women as "more susceptible of impressions of mind and body, more subject to nervous diseases than men." But women's "natural softness" had advantages. They were "more long-lived than men," Rush maintained, because their "natural softness" required "more time to become solid, and then to decay." Also, on a different score, the "fairer Sex," as Washington claimed, had a better knack for delicate feelings, for gracefulness, for providing moral examples, and even for poetry. Femininity, for Washington, was an asset: "I know not by what fatality it happens that even Philosophical sentiments come so much more gracefully (forcibly I might add) from your Sex, than my own." Rush's and Washington's ideas were certainly highly patronizing, but they were not predicated on the fantasy of a female essential passivity and biological "otherness."[41]

With respect to physiology, the eighteenth century was relatively democratic. When sexual intercourse took place, it was believed that both the man and the woman had to reach orgasm, better if simultaneously, for pregnancy to ensue. Medical treatises and popular literature, such as Venette's *Mysteries of Conjugal Love*, affirmed the connection between female orgasm and pregnancy. Aristotelian medicine had claimed that women did not produce seed and thus that female orgasm was not required—conception occurred when the active male substance worked on the passive female substance contained in her menstrual blood. But more modern Galenic theories stated that both the male and the female emitted seeds and that the two seeds were required to work on the matter provided by the female. The violent pleasure both sexes experienced during intercourse was the signal that successful generation had taken place.[42]

This made several eighteenth-century men attentive to the satisfaction of their female partners, though for utilitarian reasons. Especially when sex was aimed at procreation, the woman had to be as active as the male partner. No man would have questioned the natural right of the woman's body to have the procedure fulfilled through orgasm.

At the turn of the nineteenth century, this understanding of sex and reproductive biology began to change, effecting a shift from a "one body" model to a "two body" model, that is, a shift from the idea that men and women represented two forms of the same sex to the idea that they were two different sexes. Whether this evolution in the scientific view occurred because of the discovery of new anatomical facts or because there was a mounting social need to redefine women as fundamentally different from men, the two began to be seen as embodying distinctly different natures. Suddenly, women were not only weaker or softer than men but inherently passive, too. Instead of being encouraged to take part in the "procedure," actively and with vigor, they were increasingly expected to be sexually withdrawn.[43]

While women were being recast this way, men were increasingly presented as naturally sexually aggressive. To prove their masculinity, men were expected to seduce. They had to score high in the game of sexual performances—and in other "competitive" performances as well. Medicalized and naturalized though it was, the Galenic sexual world of the eighteenth century, including the sexual world of the Washingtons, did not regard seduction and penetration as discrete activities men should obsessively keep score of—which suggests that these activities and "drives," far from being natural, have a history of their own.[44]

Women were recategorized as "loving," "lovable," "chaste," or "maternal" and were expected to repress their sexual needs. They were encouraged to embrace a middle-class image of respectable and asexual femininity. Their whole sexual being was reduced to the act of losing their virginity. (Washington did not care that Martha was not a vestal virgin.) The new men, the "real" men, for their part, abided by an extreme, phallocentric culture and were subjected to an increasingly restrictive form of masculinity.[45]

❧ To conclude: Martha Washington is often ridiculed because she was allegedly too short, too fat, and too unattractive; but she was a strong, fulfilled, and multidimensional eighteenth-century upper-class woman who participated fully in her husband's life. She was capable of tenderness. She was also tough, and able to reprimand her George and seize him by the button of his coat when she had something to say. This woman also knew how to satisfy her appetites, including her sexual appetites. Martha and George were comfortable and happy; they had sex, exchanged tender words, scolded each other, and shared projects. Their first encounter was probably not a coup de foudre, romanticism likely did not define their relationship, Washington may not have been a "real" man, but the two were in love.[46]

She wasn't a "virgin." And she wasn't a caricature either. Attractive when young, Martha retained "strong remains of considerable beauty" even in her mid-sixties, as one guest who visited Mount Vernon commented. More important, she retained control over her body. Having grown up on a small Virginia plantation, she knew what sex and other bodily events looked and sounded like. Familiar with Galenic principles, she could claim her due. "Patsy never fell into the chilly, tight-lipped clutches of prudishness," biographer Patricia Brady writes. "Good humoured and laughing, she enjoyed all the pleasures life offered."[47]

8

≈

A Sentimental Male

Washington Was No "Real" Man

*W*e may expect "real" men, whether of today or two thousand years ago, to have certain attitudes and behave in certain ways. We may believe, for example, that the biological constitution of men makes them naturally predatory and that they lack the lighter, softer colors of the emotional palette. In particular, from eighteenth-century upper-class white Virginians, we may expect not much besides a "culture of honor": hypermasculine public displays of prowess, a passion for cockfights, horses, and racetracks, indulgence in balls and taverns, and a penchant for drinking, fornicating, and even gratuitous litigious behavior, including duels.[1]

Those who got to know George Washington well spotted traits and characteristics that don't quite square with this allegedly universal masculine identity. "He was a man of great sensibility— amiable—kind—benevolent," they swore. There was "a small mixture of timidity in his general demeanor, lest he might commit an error." Firsthand testimonies remarked a "modesty" that was "exceedingly prepossessing," giving "a mildness and kindness to his manner." Washington was an eighteenth-century Virginian, certainly, but, like other real people of his milieu, he could easily step out of stereotypes and turn into a tender, amiable, emotional person, "as capable of giving attention as of expecting them, & never failing to reciprocate a kindness." He "never failed to express pleasure." He was "generous" as well as "kind-hearted," and "most sincere Friend." He was empathic and capable of laughter. And he was by no means pretending.[2]

The Virginia gentleman and brutal slaveowner was the same thoughtful person who made sure his step-grandson was punctual for breakfast so as to not to force "servants" to do extra work: "It is not only disagreeable, but it is also very inconvenient, for servants to be running here, & there, and they know not where." Etiquette manuals, including rule 36 of the famous "Rules of Civility" which he copied as a boy, insisted that persons of "high Degree" should treat those "of low Degree" with "affability and Courtesy, without Arrogancy." But a consideration deeper and more genuine than what etiquette called for seems to be at stake here.[3]

Samuel "Sambo" Anderson, an enslaved carpenter at Mount Vernon, remembered Washington as "the most correct man that ever lived." Anderson had a small boat and, occasionally, Washington would borrow it, but never "without asking me if he could use it." When Washington was done, Anderson continued, "he was so particular to place the boat just where he took it from. If it happened to be high tide when he took it, and low tide on his return, I have known him to drag the boat twenty yards, so as to place it exactly where he took it from." It may be only a small act, but little attentions can carry much weight. Another example is when Washington approached a servant of Benjamin Latrobe as they were leaving Mount Vernon after a visit and asked if he had had breakfast.[4]

It might strike us as an apparent contradiction or blatant hypocrisy that eighteenth-century gentlemen could at once be delicate souls, lovable friends, tender companions, amiable letter writers and brutal slaveowners, enraged patriarchs, and bloodthirsty warriors. But there is nothing strange in this, and hypocrisy is not the right interpretive grid. Only a naive psychology supports the view that "men will always be men" and, more generally, that one's personality is a monochromatic solid. In human lives, situation follows situation, role follows role, performance follows performance, and gender traits and personalities are never permanent kernels and fixed essences. Each human being is many colors *at once*—which means that George Washington was not a hypocrite for trying to be generous and kindhearted, tender like a "woman," and even compassionate. We are variable and change over the course of our lives, and from one situation to another, more profoundly than common sense allows.[5]

Likewise, masculinity can't be reduced to a hard kernel. The lone wolf, the predator, the "rough and tough" variety, the "Virginia type" are neither universal, nor do they define the essence of masculinity. A man has variable, multiple masculinities at once, just like a woman has multiple femininities. Washington's male personality was as complex and multilayered as are our personalities and identities today.[6]

Those who saw Washington firsthand almost invariably wanted to relate their experience to their friends and family. The man stood out, and it was not because he was tall, muscular, or hard. Other qualities that were perhaps more important attended "his tall and noble stature and just proportions," in the words of Dr. James Thacher, a surgeon in the Continental army. It was not Washington's testosterone-driven personality but rather his "fine, cheerful open countenance, simple and modest deportment" that made him "beloved even while we are unconscious of the motive."[7]

Washington appeared often lovable rather than threatening. When, in 1779, the Marquis de Barbé-Marbois was sent to America as secretary of the French legation, he was lucky to meet the general. He was impressed, to say the least. Washington was "masculine looking" but, as Barbé-Marbois emphasized, "without his features' being less gentle on that account." Serene amid his staff, simple and unpretentious in his habits, Washington cast his blue eyes, "rather large," on those in his presence with benignity. He conquered everyone. It was "the character of humanity," in Barbé-Marbois's words, that made him "so dear to his soldiers in camp."[8]

Washington controlled the aura surrounding his person. He was "sensible, composed, and thoughtful" rather than loud, histrionic, or hypermasculine, the archetypal alpha male. Washington's face projected "a remarkable air of dignity . . . with a striking degree of gracefulness. . . . Gentle in his manners, in temper rather reserved, no man ever united in his own person a more perfect alliance of the virtues of a philosopher with the talents of a general."[9]

"His exterior disclosed, as it were, the history of his life," Louis-Philippe, Comte de Ségur, a French nobleman who served during the War of Independence, wrote felicitously. "Simplicity, grandeur, dignity, calmness, goodness, firmness, the attributes of his character, were also stamped upon his features, and in all his person." The Comte de Ségur was right: the placid harmony and general softness of Washington's physical presence were signs of how he understood his masculine identity. Had a public display of anger and litigious behavior taken the place of gracefulness and calmness, Washington would have not been as noticeable and praiseworthy as he was, especially among the upper classes.[10]

Washington didn't fear that his appearing graceful and his being a true "philosopher"—a term that would translate today as "liberal"—would trigger exclusion from male company. Washington didn't worry he would be called a "faggot," or a "snowflake," or a hypocrite for seeking to act in ways that did not trample on what he referred to as "delicacy of my feelings." He lived in an age when, for men of his status, a lack of tender feelings and an inability to express them could easily be detrimental to achieving recognition in society. Softness was part of Washington's ideal masculinity.[11]

❧ Eighteenth-century philosophers pronounced the period they lived in an age of refinement and civilization—it was an aspiration, of course, and not the depiction of reality. Several well-off men, including Washington, responded to such new intellectual, moral, cultural, and social ambitions by trying to elevate themselves to the rank of a modern gentleman. Not only did they want to improve their souls, but they also avoided the rough-and-ready self-image, homely corporeal styles, brash or defiant behaviors, and crude masculine identities. Similarly, they discarded aristocratic pomp and courtly self-indulgence. And they took repeated exception to the code of southern honor.[12]

In their quest for refinement and civilization, they embraced the expression of feelings, adopting a Quaker-like understanding of masculinity and emotionality as being mutually compatible. As Nicole Eustace writes, "Nothing marked a gentleman like an easy sensibility, nor was the allure of emotion applicable only to men moving in the polite culture of ballroom and drawing room. On the contrary, emotional sensitivity was valued even in military camps."[13]

The most eloquent way of expressing such an easy sensibility was through tears. Rather than an embarrassment, it could be good and even socially appropriate to weep. The death of a loved person was an obvious circumstance under which both men and women could openly express their emotions. While the mourning style of nineteenth-century Virginians was much more emotional and "romantic" than that of their eighteenth-century counterparts, the latter did cry loudly and conspicuously for their dead as well.[14]

The death of "near relations," Washington acknowledged, "always produces awful and affecting emotions." The absence of specific references in Washington's documents to weeping and grieving does not mean that he didn't engage in it, and no doubt young George cried when his father and his half brother Lawrence died. "The death of a Parent," Washington once wrote, is always "Awful, and affecting," and "the separation from our nearest relatives is a heart rending circumstance." In 1773, Jacky Custis confessed to his stepfather that upon hearing that his seventeen-year-old sister Patsy had died, he acted "like a woman." He said he gave himself "up entirely to melancholy for several Days."That ominous day, June 19, Washington entered a few words only in his diary: "At home all day. About five oclock poor Patcy Custis Died Suddenly." But testimonies swear that Washington himself fell into the deepest anguish for the loss of the "Sweet Innocent Girl." He also acted "like a woman."The few family members who were at the scene recalled the mother frantically seeking help and George Washington kneeling beside Patsy's deathbed, with tears streaming down his face, praying for her impossible recovery.[15]

Jacky excused himself for behaving "like a woman." However, eighteenth-century civilized men, including Virginians, held that weeping was not just for wimpy cowards and women. When Washington died in 1799, the Senate of the United States issued an address to convey condolences to President John Adams, remarking that "on this occasion, it is manly to weep." It was indeed manly to cry, even in less dire public circumstances. At a refreshment in the Long Room of Fraunces Tavern on December 4, 1783, after the remaining British troops had left New York, the general bid adieu to his officers: "With a heart full of love and gratitude, I now take leave of you," he said. According to witnesses, those words produced extreme emotions: "tears of deep sensibility filled every eye— and the heart seemed so full, that it was ready to burst from its wonted abode." Washington was also in tears.[16]

A couple of weeks later, on December 23, in Annapolis, Washington resigned his commission as commander in chief of the Continental Army. The congressmen all cried. The general made a deposit of his commission and, "in a very pathetic manner," took leave of Congress: "It was a solemn and affecting spectacle," James McHenry noted, "such an one as history does not present. The spectators all wept, and there was hardly a member of Congress who did not drop tears. The General's hand which held the address shook as he read it."[17]

For upper-class men, emotional display, including crying "like a woman," was a way to demonstrate they were civilized. The elite man cried, whether ensconced in the bosom of his family or in public; he displayed tender feelings for others or indulged in more self-centered emotional exhibits by merely pretending to. This upper-class civilized man wept to vent his emotions or, alternatively, when he wanted to show that he belonged to the group that laid exclusive claim to refined emotions. In all cases, weeping was empowering.[18]

Like A Real Christian

Washington and his peers could be strong even when emotional to the extreme, masculine when "feminine," and still formidable when humble, amiable, and caring. Their easy sensibility helped them to project the image of someone who, like a "real Christian, and in the language of Scripture, walked humbly before God."[19]

This reference to the "real Christian" is pivotal to the whole discussion so far. Between 1660 and 1830 across the entire transatlantic world, Christianity was probably the most important component of ideal masculinity—more important than honor. Piety, humility, service, and restraint exemplified a higher level of manliness that was much more challenging and much more difficult to attain than that channeled by aggressiveness, physical strength, copious drinking, bragging, gambling, racing, ball-going, dancing, fornicating, frolicking, and singing. Practicing Presbyterians, Baptists, Methodists together with a colorful cohort of not particularly devout elite white men aspired to become perfect Christians.[20]

One did not have to be extraordinarily religious to fit into the category of a "real Christian"—although Washington went to church regularly. A "Christian" in this sense was not necessarily a man who believed, or who was versed in the knowledge of the Scripture, or who was able to crack the mysteries of theology. He was one who mastered the most tender sensibility, the most powerful emotions, and the most "feminine" qualities: moderation, tranquility, humbleness, charitableness, magnanimity, benevolence, and patience.[21]

At Mount Vernon, Washington could be very "Christian," caring, and compassionate, even with strangers. Elkanah Watson, traveler and writer, visited Washington in January 1785. They dined together, had a deep conversation, and remained seated at the table after the rest of the family had retired. But Watson didn't feel well, "oppressed by a severe cold and excessive coughing, contracted by the exposure of a harsh winter journey," as he later wrote in his memoirs. Washington offered him remedies, but the guest declined. After retiring in his room on the third floor, the coughing increased. Washington heard him and, after a little while, he gently opened the door of Watson's room: "On drawing my bed-curtains, to my utter astonishment, I beheld Washington himself, standing at my bedside, with a bowl of hot tea in his hand." Washington holding a bowl of hot tea was just a "little incident," as Watson himself labeled it. But it is one that discloses "a trait of the benevolence" that is not commonly associated with the idea of a "real" man.[22]

Washington's way of eating and, more specifically, the types of foods he ate are also not typically connected with "real" men, who have often made shows not only of their toughness, strength, and lack of empathy but also of their vast appetite for "real" food—especially for animal, blood-soaked flesh. An appetite for the roasted meat of large animals still signals power and success because "real" men eat a lot, and they do not eat vegetables, nuts, berries, or ingredients that can be easily foraged. Traditionally, such foods almost invariably have been seen as second class, more likely to be consumed by women or by the lower tiers of society, above all enslaved people. Europeans have long believed that foods of a "light" substance—the flesh of young animals, bread made of pure wheat, fresh eggs, light soups, boiled ingredients, milk, vegetables, berries, and nuts—produced refined and feminine bodies.[23]

But George Washington was a "Christian," a modern upper-class man of the eighteenth century. His personal version of manliness, in matters of food as well as in many other issues, did not embrace "fullness," recklessness, or a brazen appetite. He largely adhered to "a vegitable and milk diet," eating only small amounts of red meat. Washington's alimentary philosophy was to avoid "as much as possible animal food." Consequently, he never turned his meals into occasions during which he would promote his masculinity by eating roast beef in the English way, *à la* Henry VIII. A hunger for animal flesh consumed in large quantity was not a facet of his self-representation as a man.[24]

At home, either at the President's House or at Mount Vernon, Washington usually woke up before dawn. By 7 or 7:30 a.m. in the winter, his enslaved house servants had already served breakfast. On hunting mornings, he had breakfast before dawn, by candlelight. He enjoyed tea—three cups without cream—and coffee, chocolate, a small helping of cold or broiled meats, and a cornmeal pancake (also known as Indian hoe cake), with butter and honey. After breakfast, he would retire to his room—if he was alone. If he had company, he would go to the drawing room. At 9 a.m., he would take a long ride around his estate, usually until 2 p.m.[25]

Dinner, the main three-course meal, which lasted two hours or more, was usually served at 3 p.m. Habitually, dinners were public gatherings, a way to enhance connections and to publicize political visions. Vegetables, or pickled vegetables if the fresh were not in season, were presented to the Washingtons and their guests together with some red meat, fish, and poultry. Dessert, which included pastries and cheeses, followed shortly afterward. Once the table was cleared of the main course, fruits and nuts were served—which gave the company and Washington personally an excuse to continue the conversation. In the early evening, a "tea" (a light meal) was also served, and at 9 p.m. a light supper might be served as well. Washington was fond of fish. On Saturday during his time as president, he usually had what was called a "salt fish dinner," boiled beets, potatoes, and onion mixed with boiled fish, fried pork scraps, and egg sauce.[26]

Washington always aimed for moderation and to remain "temperate" in his dietary habits—even if, by today's standards, he does not appear ascetic. The cornmeal pancakes with butter and honey he often enjoyed during breakfasts and the nuts he nibbled on during the day, his passion and weakness, don't seem to square with the common idea of frugality. The Marquis de Chastellux noted that the general consumed "a great quantity of nuts," which he "usually continues eating for two hours." However, his love of pancakes and nuts are not sufficient to place Washington among legendary immoderate eaters and crapulent males. By eighteenth-century standards, these aliments, while caloric, were not considered the best food for the best among men. By regularly eating vegetables, fish, cornmeal pancakes, nuts, and similar "second-class" aliments, Washington was not only embracing a different model of virility but was also offering other men a lesson in Christianity (to avoid self-indulgence) and encouraging them to repudiate an essential English privilege.[27]

While Washington eschewed red meat as much as possible, he was fully aware that many men, including his soldiers, did not. Washington was adamant about the benefits of vegetables and "second-class" food: "The health of the army is certainly an object of the last moment, and it is equally certain, that it cannot be preserved without a due portion of vegetable diet. This must be procured whatever may be the expence." His officers were expected not only to supervise the "cleanliness of the camp" but above all "to inspect the food of the men, both as to the quaility and the manner of dressing it, obliging the men to accustom themselves more to boiled meats and soups, and less to broiled and roasted, which as a constant diet, is destructive to their health."[28]

It was not only "destructive to their health"; it was a bad example for the new nation. Many people saw the general and later the president eating moderately, consistently avoiding roasted meat, and telling his soldiers and fellow citizens about the advantages of consuming "feminine" food. Those who did not witness him eating sparingly could have encountered descriptions of the famous man's "unvarying habits of regularity, temperance, & industry." By refusing blood-oozing meat as his primary nutrient, Washington established a clear-cut difference between himself, a civilized, modern, Christian man, humble and calm, and those hapless creatures who were trapped at an inferior, almost grotesque stage.[29]

"I fancy it must be the quantity of animal food eaten by the English," Thomas Jefferson wrote playfully to Abigail Adams, "which renders their character insusceptible of civilisation. I suspect it is in their kitchens and not in their churches that their reformation must be worked." It was 1785, the war had been won, and Jefferson was a merry Parisian. Playful though he may have been on this occasion, he was serious about the link between aliment and character and about how aristocratic and outdated foods produced outdated men. Washington would have agreed.[30]

The same principles applied to drinking. Although David Ackerson, in 1811, claimed that it was Washington's custom "to take a drink of rum or whiskey on awakening in the morning," sound evidence suggests that Washington was a "Christian" even in his relationship to the glass and to the bottle. During dinners, he "only" drank "from half a pint to a pint of Madeira wine," accompanied by "one small glass of punch" and "a draught of beer." At the table, a silver pint cup of beer usually sat in front of him, and he drank from it freely. In the period, beer, porter, and cider were not considered real drinks, like wine or strong spirits, and they were consumed like water and regarded as safer than water. Moreover, there was a difference between drinks *at* dinner and *before* or *after* dinner. Madeira, claret, punch, and a variety of beers were consumed in large quantity at dinner. After dinner, a stronger beverage was served, which is when temperance became relevant.[31]

"He is very temperate in his Diet," a witness reported, and "the only Luxury he indulges himself in is a few Glasses of Punch after Supper." Washington certainly was very sociable, if not a downright socialite. The household as a whole consumed a great amount of liquor and wine. Though not disproportionate for an elite household of this period, the expenditures for these items were significant, especially when Washington was president. But he retained a strong grip on himself and always drew a clear line between cheerfulness—which he didn't despise—and drunkenness. Washington reviled strong liqueurs. "Rum," he wrote in 1788, "is, in my opinion, the bane of morals & the parent of idleness." He stayed away from these powerful enhancers of manly prowess.[32]

❧ Any number of witnesses maintained that George Washington was unwelcoming and bristly, rather "un-Christian" in his general demeanor. "The President is a cold, formal man," averred Senator William Maclay from Pennsylvania, who was not a fan of the administration, truth be told. Likewise, Reverend Jonathan Boucher, who was a resolute loyalist, affirmed that there was "nothing generous or affectionate in his nature."[33]

Biographers have also contended that Washington was not only cold, formal, and ungenerous but also touchy and untouchable. Nineteenth-century Jefferson biographer James Parton reported that during the Constitutional Convention in Philadelphia a trick of sorts was played on Washington that allegedly exposed his hypermasculine emotional dreariness. The preamble was that Alexander Hamilton apparently asserted that Washington, in the words of Parton himself, was "reserved and aristocratic even to his intimate friends, and allowed no one to be familiar with him." Gouverneur Morris, Parton went on, wanted to disprove Hamilton's statement. Morris was confident he could be very familiar with Washington, as if with a close friend. Should he succeed in slapping Washington on his shoulder and say, "My dear General, how happy I am to see you look so well!," Hamilton would supply him with dinner and wine. Although Morris was able to slap Washington and utter the prescribed words, after he did so, "Washington withdrew his hand, stepped suddenly back, fixed his eye on Morris for several minutes with an angry frown, until the latter retreated abashed, and sought refuge in the crowd. The company looked on in silence."[34]

This story is not very credible. First of all, Morris belonged to the club of Washington's close acquaintances; he was a high-profile founder himself, a patriot, a wealthy landowner, and a fellow Federalist. On that occasion, there would have been no reason for Washington to react that way. The episode makes sense only if we buy into the postulate that Washington must have been a "real" man constitutionally averse to the Christian virtues of humility, forgiveness, and magnanimity. (Parton, by the way, doesn't provide any specific source.) The man in Parton's sketch seems to be a supercilious aristocrat and a patriarch of old obsessed by hierarchies. The real Washington was different. His body and persona were not off limits, a private space others were not supposed to enter. He habitually greeted his soldiers or saluted them: "Officers all pay their respect to the Commander-in-Chief," Lieutenant Ebenezer Denny from Pennsylvania noted. They "go in a body." And Washington did not cringe or show coldness, hauteur, or grumpiness. He was not the imposing, intimidating man. "He stands in the door, takes every man by the hand."[35]

No matter what Senator Maclay, Reverend Boucher, or biographer James Parton might have said, Washington was accessible and touchable. After the Battle of the Chesapeake on September 5, 1781, magisterially won by the Comte de Grasse, the admiral in command of the French fleet, Washington realized the War of

Independence could be won. He was ecstatic. On September 14, arriving in Williamsburg, he became even more jubilant at the prospect of being reunited with his friend, Lafayette. When Lafayette got the news of Washington's arrival, he rushed to meet him. The two saw each other, and Lafayette "caught the General round his body," in the words of St. George Tucker, and "hugged him as close as it was possible, and absolutely kissed him from ear to ear once or twice . . . with as much ardor as ever an absent lover kissed his mistress on his return."[36]

A military man, Washington had known camaraderie; he had known friendship. Hugging and kissing were a part of his repertoire. There is no indication that he had ever been uncomfortable or embarrassed about being approached and touched in the way Morris did; that he wasn't can be explained not only by his "Christianity" but also by an "emotional security" that characterized his masculinity. Insecure personalities, according to the classic description of psychologist Abraham Maslow, see the world as fundamentally threatening and other persons as essentially dangerous. But Washington was decidedly secure in the way he dealt with his own feelings and emotions and, most important, with the world and the people around him.[37]

During a trip from Philadelphia to Mount Vernon that Washington took during the spring of 1784, a sudden rain shower prompted him to dismount his horse and find a seat in a common stage wagon. The wagon eventually stopped at a tavern. Knowing the rank of his illustrious guest, the innkeeper wanted to immediately show Washington into a private room where he and his aides could dine undisturbed. "No—no," said Washington. "It is customary for the people who travel in this stage always to eat together. I will not desert my companions." He thus dined with a large and noisy company in a common room in a country inn.[38]

In the eighteenth century a need for privacy was not keenly felt. If prominent nineteenth-century men would have experienced a middle-class embarrassment or irritation at the idea of having their personal space invaded or their body touched, their counterparts in the eighteenth century had a much larger comfort zone. Their "self," in a way, was much more communal than the psychoanalytic self is, and less vulnerable to "trauma." In this regard, George Washington's world was much closer to the medieval world—with its heavy smells, lack of hygiene, promiscuous habits—than to our germ-concerned, virus-obsessed, identity-theft-preoccupied regimens.

One night in late summer 1776, on their way to negotiate a possible peace with Great Britain, John Adams and Benjamin Franklin had also stopped at an inn in New Brunswick, New Jersey. The inn was already full, and so they had to share a bed. The chamber where the two founders slept was, in the words of John Adams, "little larger than the bed, without a Chimney and with only one small Window." They weren't concerned at all about the fact that they had to spoon under the same duvet, but they did have a disagreement about the window. Adams wanted the window closed, fearing the cold air would make him sick. Franklin, the author of a piece on how stagnant air in closed rooms was the cause of sickness, insisted it stay open. Eventually Adams caved in, stood up, opened the window, and jumped into the bed to hear Franklin's thoughts "upon air and cold and respiration and perspiration, with which I was so much amused that I soon fell asleep."[39]

What befell Franklin and Adams was not unusual. Adults and strangers had always shared rooms and beds in country inns and taverns. When women and men needed to be accommodated, they were separated by a flimsy sheet or an improvised curtain. (We, by contrast, may cringe at the mere thought of sharing a table at a restaurant.) Eighteenth-century women and men didn't fear that their bodies would be contaminated by being so close together. The middle-class body—with its load of germs and Victorian taboos—had not been invented yet.

The word "privacy," in Washington's world, had a quite different sound. Not only would strangers spending the night in inns likely share beds; they had to share chamber pots. Roommates, like Franklin and Adams, needing to take a leak or excrete their "night soil," couldn't run to the bathroom, because there was no bathroom in the house, tavern, inn. They had to stay in the bedroom and do their business, discreetly and yet publicly. In addition, when a man was wealthy enough, a *valet de chambre*, often an enslaved person, would have access to the intimate space of the bedchamber. (Washington relied on William Osborn, among others.) The valet was expected to lay out clothes, dress the hair, and shave the face. Private parts were visible, and the valet would touch the body of his master repeatedly. If a man could not afford a valet, a barber would come in to assist him in making his toilet. The barber might also put his hands into the client's mouth to fix a tooth and use lancets to get rid of an annoying pimple or to cure an abscess. A human body was far from sacred and untouchable—Morris's legendary slap on the shoulder wouldn't have disrupted Washington's emotional world.

Mount Vernon tourists cannot help noticing a small outbuilding—a privy or "necessary"—standing near the big house—a faithful replica of what originally stood there. Many, I suspect, have glanced inside and wondered why there are three holes with no partition. While there is no evidence that George Washington ever invited his friends or Martha to what we may call a "poo party," multiseat latrines have been the norm in many cultures. Romans, for example, pooed together while discussing politics. At Mount Vernon, multiple holes in privies may have just been a designed feature intended to prevent feces from piling up. But standards of privacy were much different back then, and we cannot rule out that a second or third person could have used this facility while Washington was already "in session." The other person would have just uttered a "good morning" in the most polite manner before entering.[40]

Privy. Courtesy of Mount
Vernon Ladies' Association,
Mount Vernon, VA.

❧ I mentioned barbers, or valets, coming in to shave the man of the house: the beard, or lack thereof, was also a tool for conveying a precise idea of masculinity. Washington preferred smoothness and tenderness over bristliness, just as he did in the matter of character. He didn't want to look prickly and hard, and he wished his face to remain open. He opted for a welcoming and maternal appearance.

Washington's face was indeed smooth, except for a few pock marks, the remnant of the smallpox he contracted at the end of 1751 during his trip to Barbados. In his prime, Washington developed a habit of buying and using razors. Cash accounts and invoices list razors, razor strops, and traveling razor cases regularly, at least from 1763 on. This manly male shaved his face, and he did so all his life—although at the end of August 1786, he was seized by a severe episode of "ague & fever" that "made such havock of my mouth, nose & chin that I am unable to put a razor to my face," and he had to use scissors instead. Similarly, he bought and used many

❧

Washington's razor kit. Courtesy of Mount Vernon Ladies' Association, Mount Vernon, VA.

personal grooming instruments, such as tweezers and nippers, to prevent his face from becoming "uncultivated."[41]

Washington no doubt decided to shave his face for a number of reasons. Most likely, it was not even a deliberate *decision*, but a semiconscious and yet obvious habit that came to him via education and example. Razors, to begin with, were beautiful objects in their own right, part of the broader and growing trade in men's "toys." Consequently, it comes as no surprise that men, provincial and urban alike, might gratify themselves by purchasing various kinds of technical instruments. In this sense, razors had become a nonverbal language of show and display, although more for the elites than the middling and lower sorts. These instruments were status symbols, and presenting a shaved face was a status symbol too. It indicated refined emotions and Christian masculinity.[42]

More significant, perhaps, was the fact that the smooth, clean-shaven face had become a masculine ideal across the English-speaking world. A dramatic change in culture had taken place; after centuries, beard and moustaches had at last become undesirable. These models of roughness and rugged masculinity did not disappear entirely but were increasingly confined to the army. Certain French regiments insisted that recruits wear moustaches, going so far as to require recruits to paint them on or don make-shift ones made from horsehair if they couldn't grow their own. The belief was that tall men with beards or moustaches made the enemy cringe, and so these men were often placed at the head of a column. But successful civilians and modern men of tender feelings flaunted a smooth, open face.[43]

Washington did not like beards either on himself or on others—including his soldiers. For him, the beard made a man look unkempt and slovenly and prevented him from conveying higher emotions; beards were out of step with civilization and juvenile rather than virile. Facial hair made a man, as Washington said, "unsoldierlike." Every man, the general made sure, must appear in public as "decent as his circumstances will permit." For every soldier, it was mandatory to have "his beard shaved—hair combed—face washed—and cloaths put on in the best manner in his power." The soldier, he remarked on yet another occasion, "may always shave his beard, appear with clean hands and face & in general have an air of neatness."[44]

Ethnic considerations must have played a role as well. The cultivation of a more delicate male appearance and of a soft, kind-hearted, empathic, approachable, "feminine," maternal, and "Christian" character was perhaps also a strategy to enhance Anglo-American distinctiveness at the expense of many other cultures. European eighteenth-century society—the society Washington identified with—had a growing "scientific" interest in distant populations. But this very anthropological or ethnographic curiosity contributed to enlarging a gap between "us" and "them." It was a process of orientalization, or orientalism, signaling an increasingly patronizing attitude toward Middle Eastern and Muslim male cultures, where beards were often the norm. The beard thus began to seem exotic and "un-Christian," especially among civilians. Oriental men were backward looking. They were unsentimental. They had no tender emotions to express. They didn't partake in the march of civilization. They were untouchable. They were prisoners to the brutal, rugged, testosterone-driven masculinity that had become increasingly unfashionable among the eighteenth-century elites.[45]

9

〜

A Maternal Father

Infertility

By 1787, Washington had made clear that he had had enough of serving the country, or so he jested. He wanted to retire and spend more time attending to his farms, his family, and his personal interests. In the spring, as the Constitutional Convention was about to meet in Philadelphia, Henry Knox, the three-hundred-pound, six-foot-three secretary of war, wrote Washington a letter in which he tried to persuade Washington to reconsider. He invoked his "paternal" role and pointed out that chairing the Constitutional Convention would be "highly honorable to your fame." "In the judgement of the present and future ages," Washington would be entitled to "the glorious republican epithet—The Father of Your Country."[1]

Washington had not fathered children. Everyone knew. (The wildest among the wild legends posit that he was a eunuch or a woman in disguise, though some proclaim him the father of West Ford, whose mother, Venus, was an enslaved house servant at the Bushfield plantation owned by Washington's brother and his wife.) Everyone kept reminding Washington that he was a father in a higher, metaphorical sense. The reluctant, soon-to-be president would become "the Father to more than three Millions of

Children," Gouverneur Morris offered as a consolation (and would not expose the nation to a hereditary monarchy).[2]

Intentions were good: Washington's friends wanted to console him and to awaken him to the laurels of his future glory. Washington was already a quasireligious figure; people worshipped the man who in their opinion dwelled above the fray of the human lot. But such a maimed fatherhood bothered Washington precisely because it was only symbolic, political, perhaps metaphysical, and certainly metaphorical. The issue of not having "issue" returns in Washington's correspondence, the more so when he started aging and realized that the prospect was irremediably beyond his reach. "There is a moral certainty of my dying without issue," he wrote in 1786 to George Augustine Washington, the oldest son of his brother Charles. He was a little embittered. At fifty-four, he believed his time had already passed.[3]

Washington put up with this reality, just as he had always resigned himself to all the unpleasant and trying circumstances in his life. People around him told him that "it didn't matter." But young couples often tell themselves a different story. They had no idea why Martha did not get pregnant. Washington did not think he had a problem—the letter Washington wrote to George Augustine Washington in 1786 is revealing in this regard. Should Martha die, he fantasized, he could remarry. But "while I retain the faculty of reasoning, I shall never marry a girl," he wrote. Washington was joking, of course, depicting a purely hypothetical scenario. He did not want his wife to suddenly die. At the same time, however, Washington flattered himself with the idea that "a girl" might give him the offspring he so sorely lacked. In reality, should his wife die, as Washington admitted, he would pick someone just like Martha, and "it is not probable that I should have children by a woman of an age suitable to my own."

This letter is not enough to conclude that Washington blamed his wife—it is simply a display of bad taste. But was Martha the problem? While Martha was married to Daniel Parke Custis, she had given birth four times. Her last pregnancy does not seem to have been complicated by postpartum infection or a hemorrhage triggering a uterine fibrosis or even Asherman's syndrome, although historian Mary Thompson notes that former Mount Vernon Ladies' Association curator Christine Meadows told her there was an age-old story passed down by members of the Masonic Lodge in Alexandria, to which several of the Washington family's doctors belonged, that Martha was so severely injured after she gave birth to her last child in 1757 that she was no longer able to get pregnant. We also cannot rule out that she might have contracted an ovary infection along the way or some other disease.[4]

Thompson also suggests that in her late twenties and thirties Martha might have developed an endocrine or hormonal problem. Disorders such as these would square with the fact that she gained substantial weight during her lifetime, even if she always had a pretty active lifestyle. (She had a strong appetite, however, which may be a sufficient explanation.) A problem affecting the thyroid would have had an impact on her fertility. She may have developed polycystic ovarian syndrome, or PCOS as it is more commonly known, which also can affect one's ability to conceive. It's also possible that after having given birth to her fourth child during her first marriage, Martha used an abortifacient as a form of birth control—a practice much widespread in the period. Such a substance might have triggered permanent damage. Eighteenth-century attitudes toward procreation were much more complex than we might expect. Using abortifacients to postpone parenthood was admissible. (These people gulped so many improbable substances that an abortifacient would make perfect sense.) But we are here in the realm of pure speculation.[5]

There is a higher probability that George was the obstacle. In 2004, John Amory, a professor of Medicine at the University of Washington Medical Center, published an article that is to date the most reliable source of information on this delicate issue. An expert on male infertility, testosterone deficiency, Klinefelter syndrome, and new approaches to the treatment of men with infertility, Dr. Amory discusses the probable causes of Washington's difficulty by taking into consideration the six major categories of male infertility.[6]

The first is germ-cell failure caused either by Klinefelter syndrome, a genetic condition in which the male is born with an extra copy of the X chromosome, or by a microdeletion in the Y chromosome. Washington might have also been born with the XYY syndrome, as others have suggested, in which the son inherits from his father two Y chromosomes instead of just the usual one.[7]

People who suffer from Klinefelter syndrome tend to be tall and to have dental problems (taurodontism, an enlargement of the tooth pulp)—elements that, in theory, square with Washington as we know him. But Klinefelter syndrome also begets mild to severe cognitive deficits, speech impairments, and diminished visual and spatial capabilities—and we know that Washington did not suffer from any of these conditions. Washington was normally muscled and very smart. So, Klinefelter syndrome must be ruled out, though XYY syndrome is still a possibility.

The second is endocrine disease often caused either by testosterone or gonadotropin deficiency. (Gonadotropins are hormones secreted by the pituitary gland, which in turn stimulate the activity of the gonads.) Congenital gonadotropin deficiency, also called Kallmann syndrome, would explain Washington's height. However, endocrine dysfunction also causes gynecomastia, osteoporosis, pronounced fatigue, problems with peripheral vision, and depression—and Washington had none of these symptoms.

The third is anatomical factors. Cryptorchidism, a condition in which one or both testes fail to descend from the abdomen into the scrotum, can cause infertility. Other anatomic causes, such as the absence of the vas deferens or a varicocele, can similarly explain the issue. Congenital absence of the vas deferens—the duct conveying sperm from the testicle to the urethra—can either occur spontaneously or be caused by diseases such as cystic fibrosis. The hypothesis that Washington suffered from cystic fibrosis seems improbable, although he could have been missing the vas deferens. Varicocele—an enlargement of the veins in the scrotum—is also possible. Cryptorchidism and varicocele have an impact on sperm production, both in terms of quantity and quality, but these conditions need to be severe to cause infertility.

The fourth is sexual dysfunction such as retrograde ejaculation, which is, however, unlikely in the absence of a trauma to the spinal cord, neuropathy, or urologic surgery. Similarly, there is no indication that Washington suffered from erectile dysfunction due to vascular disease or diabetes, especially when he was a young and stronger man.

The fifth is toxic exposure, which cannot be entirely ruled out. Eighteenth-century people abused weird "medications," as we have seen apropos abortifacients. Washington used calomel (mercurous chloride) regularly to treat his chronic diarrhea and abdominal pain, but the effect of mercury on the sperm count is transient. He might have used other substances as well, but their effect as inhibitors would only have been momentary.

The sixth is infections, the most likely culprit. Washington may have suffered from an infection of the testis, the epididymis (the duct behind the testis along which sperm passes to the vas deferens), or the prostate. Infections such as these could have been caused by mumps (a common viral disease) or by sexually transmitted maladies such as gonorrhea or chlamydia, which Washington may have had.

The argument that sexually transmitted infections are incompatible with Washington's character and moral standards is weak. I'm not calling into question Washington's morality and the standards he could have set for himself as a mature (and married) man.

But there was a George Washington who was young, curious, and willing to experiment. (I have already mentioned "M's Nel," perhaps a prostitute, and the fact that young Washington may have lost his virginity to her.) That "our" George did stay away from mercenary sex does not discount the fact that the man who took part in the French and Indian War could have done what many other young soldiers of that period did when they found themselves in that context. He may have paid one of the many women who tagged along with the marching troops. The silence of Washington's account books and ledgers on such topics—no expenses recorded, no memos—does not prove anything, obviously.[8]

Another possibility is that he had tuberculosis and that this affected his ability to have children, as there is a direct link between the disease and male infertility. We know that George's half brother, Lawrence, died of tuberculosis in 1752. George's bout of smallpox, which he contracted in Barbados, considerably weakened his immune system. This immunodeficiency prevented Washington's body from forestalling the effect of the contagious droplets his brother spewed all around. Weakened by smallpox, he "breathed" a much worse illness. Upon his return to the mainland, at the end of January 1752, young Washington started a months-long fight against what he called a "violent pleurise." Almost certainly, it was an initial pulmonary infection with tuberculosis, which also affected the pleura, the two membranes surrounding the lungs. The Mycobacterium tuberculosis bacteria, the cause of the disease, spreads from the lungs to the pleura and from there to other organs. By the end of May 1752, Washington felt better, but he could have died. He realized that he had been lucky and that his organism had been put to test: "Pleurise," he wrote, "has reduced me very low."[9]

There is more than a 70 percent probability that individuals with untreated pulmonary tuberculosis will end up developing gastrointestinal tuberculosis as well from swallowing the infectious secretions. In fact, during the years of the French and Indian War,

Washington could not get rid of his annoying abdominal pains, diarrhea, and fevers. Dr. Amory notes that these recurrent episodes are inconsistent with bacterial dysentery and are better explained by gastrointestinal tuberculosis. Dr. Amory also provides evidence that patients who suffer from gastrointestinal tuberculosis have a nearly 20 percent probability of developing genitourinary tuberculosis, which affects the epididymis or testes and has a high incidence of infertility.[10]

Fatherhood

As tourists and visitors walk into the Ford Orientation Center at Mount Vernon, opened in October 2006, they cannot fail to stop at the bronze sculpture groupings of Martha and George holding hands with grandson Washy, age four, and granddaughter Nelly, age six. The scene conjures a moment of intimacy, even tenderness. Unlike the family in Edward Savage's famous *The Washington Family*, which is actually a depiction of a political act—the nation's first family planning the nation's ultimate capital—the family that greets visitors at the Ford Orientation Center is private, informal, and engaging. These people are not stiff and distant but personal and personable, touchable and close. They seem to smile. They seem alive and warm.

Gay Hart Gaines, the former regent of the Mount Vernon Ladies' Association, remarks that this version of the Washingtons is meant to "be welcoming other American families." "It's a way of saying at the very start of the tour that the experience at Mount Vernon will be a warm and personal one. We want our visitors to think of Mount Vernon as a family's home, not just a historic house." Mount Vernon would in fact be an almost regular home— were it not for the elephant in the room.[11]

We can forgive unapprised visitors who think that Martha and George are the parents—the ambiguity of the scene is intentional. This George Washington is erect and light, and the sprightly steps of the four communicate youth and life. They smile gently. They are serene. They are happy. In 2005, the actor and impersonator who helped the sculptors to capture Washington correctly—William A. Sommerfield—was much older (he was seventy-five) than the real Washington would have been. In 1785, the year this scene supposedly took place, George Washington was fifty-three, but the specimen the artists of the StudioEIS conjure is an even younger man. The bronze sculpture groupings at the Ford Orientation Center suggest that while Washington was never a biological father, he was nonetheless a father in a sentimental, emotional sense.

≈

Bronze sculpture groupings of the Washington family. Courtesy of Mount Vernon Ladies' Association, Mount Vernon, VA.

Washington, as we know, took good care
of the two surviving children from Martha's
first marriage, four-year-old John Parke Custis, called Jacky ("Jack" as he got older), and
Martha Parke Custis, known as Patsy, who
was about two years old. Martha's children
were fond of their new father and very grate-
ful to him: "He best deserves the name of father who acts the part
of one," Jack would write in 1776. Washington in turn adored them.[12]

They both died prematurely. Patsy had suffered from seizures
since she was three or four, most likely epilepsy. She died in the
summer of 1773, when she was about seventeen years old. Jack died
unexpectedly in 1781, during the final stages of the Revolution. Fe-

ver struck him after he decided to follow General Washington to Yorktown as a volunteer aide. Martha and George brought the youngest two of Jack's four children, Nelly and Washy, into their own home and raised them—the two older girls, Elizabeth (Eliza or Betsey) and Martha (Patty), stayed with their mother, Eleanor Calvert Custis, who eventually remarried and gave birth to sixteen more children. These two girls also ended up spending a lot of time with their grandparents.

Washington never fell short in his responsibilities as a de facto father. In his will, he wrote that "it has always been my intention, since my expectation of having Issue has ceased, to consider the Grand children of my wife in the same light as I do my own relations, and to act a friendly part by them; more especially by the two whom we have reared from their earliest infancy," by which he meant Nelly and Washy. But there were many other children roaming about Mount Vernon and the other temporary residences Martha and George occupied during their forty-year marriage. There were the children of Washington's deceased younger brother Samuel, little Harriot, in particular, and there were the children of ill-starred Tobias Lear, whose first two wives died far too soon, among others.[13]

Although Washington aimed "to act a friendly part," it is worth noting that John Parke Custis, Jacky, gave him trouble, that Washy drove him crazy, and that George Steptoe Washington and Lawrence Augustine Washington, the children of his brother Samuel, the one who died in 1781, annoyed him a great deal. To a greater or lesser extent, they all were slackers—as boys, they, unlike the girls, had to scramble up the steep hill of a college education. These young men were aware of their wealth and at times acted like brats.

Take Jacky, for example. In 1773, he went off to King's College (today Columbia University) and bragged to his mother about the apartment he had found waiting for him. It had a large parlor, two studies, two tables, six chairs, and a separate room to accommodate

Joe, his personal "servant." In his correspondence home, Jacky skipped over his studies entirely and preferred to emphasize the special treatment he and he alone received from the faculty: "There is as much distinction made between me & the other students as can be expected." In effect, he could dine regularly with his teachers.[14]

All the boys kept asking for money and often overspent. It's clear Lawrence Augustine Washington, to take another example, had asked Washington for money before, as in one letter he remarked that he knew that George Washington would not send him any more, "having often learnt fro your own mouth that your expenses here vastly exceed the compensation [that is] allowed [to a] President." The girls were not too different in this regard. Harriot Washington repeatedly sent letters to her uncle asking or thanking for money: "You may rely on it that I will not purchase any thing I am not in want of." Harriot was grateful for the silk jacket and shoes she had requested; she made a case for a sum to buy new summer dresses; she explained she needed fresh petticoats and a new great coat, as her former great coat was so small she couldn't get it on; and she begged for a loan to repay Aunt Betty for the twenty-four shillings she had borrowed from her. While her requests were not outrageous, Harriot was herself a nuisance. "I hope my dear Uncle will not think from this I am extravagant for believe me I am as careful and attentive to my clothes as I possibly can be."[15]

For his part, Washington could only do what was within his limited power. Technically, he did not adopt any of these children, as adoption came to America only in the mid-nineteenth century. He couldn't do much, other than giving advice or bellowing out reproaches: "It is better to offer no excuse than a bad one," he once chided Harriot after she didn't write to him the longer letter he expected. Not having full legal paternal authority, Washington knew that sooner or later he had to surrender. "I have yielded," he once conceded, "contrary to my judgment, & much against my Wishes."[16]

Washington was successful in managing his family, despite the war, an astounding political career that dragged him away from home for years on end, and more or less rebellious youngsters. But his success is often inappropriately viewed through the lens of a nineteenth-century ideology of family and fatherhood that obscures the eighteenth-century family Washington belonged to and conceals the type of father he was.

By the mid-nineteenth century, ideas about fatherhood had shifted as a new masculine ideal emerged. Both in America and Europe, many fathers distanced themselves emotionally from the lives of their children. Urbanization and industrialization separated the workplace from the home and carried fathers away from their children's daily lives. Fathers thus became positively detached. Because they thrived elsewhere, their main role at home and in the family was to inspire productive work habits and "healthy" competitiveness. Mothers, who stayed home and negotiated the complex experience of domesticity, were the sentimentally involved ones. They were identified as the primary emotional caregivers for the younger generation—their bodies were the ones children were allowed to hug, the haven where they could find solace. Mothers were the ones youths confided in and to whom they sent long, affectionate letters.[17]

In eighteenth-century Virginia, though, family life was different and, in many ways, more complex. On the one hand, family meant the total sum of estates, land, and enslaved persons—it was *the* workplace. Families were hubs of economic activities where various men and women, free and unfree, exerted their public functions, each according to his and her station—and Washington's family was no exception. But, on the other hand, Washington's family was also an intimate, informal space where parents and children loved each other and found compensation for the torments of life. Washington may have been the patriarch of his family conceived as an *oikos*, which means an economic unit, but at the same time he was a father in a much different sense, which should encourage us to appreciate a fact that is often overlooked in highlighting Washington's success in managing his family, namely, that he was not emotionally distanced from the family members whose lives he oversaw. He was, for example, more than a bit aggrieved by the unruly behavior of his "children"—and not simply because he feared they could compromise economic stability or because they disobeyed and dared to question his authority, thus harming his reputation as an alpha male and a patriarch. He sincerely wished they were more affectionate than they apparently were.[18]

Within his family, Washington himself could freely express his emotions. He could love, mourn, play, and speak his mind—domesticity was for him a badge of masculinity, allowing him to be tender and loving, just like a "Christian," just like a mother. More consequential, this was the place where he could also help others—at least some others—fulfil their dreams and nurture their emotions.[19]

A desire to cuddle and "dry nurse" may not come immediately to mind when we think about the life of a patriarch and a Founding Father—certainly not Washington's life. Cuddling seems almost blasphemous, something too trivial, too apolitical, and too "feminine." And yet, eighteenth-century Virginia fathers derived intense joy from touching their children, no matter if they were grownups. Like mothers, fathers embraced daughters and sons, nephews, nieces, and grandchildren with hugs and kisses. Eighteenth-century fathers took charge of child rearing, even feeding babies, cleaning them, administering them medicines, and putting them to bed. Fathers encouraged intimate connections, chatted freely about daily concerns, and provided not only mentorship but also companionship—it was "Christian" to do so. Far from being perceived as detrimental to the dignity of the father, activities such as these were part and parcel of a white elite ideal of manhood.[20]

The domestic devotion I'm pointing at is more real than the stale image of Washington as the "perfect" father we find in one of the most notable descriptions ever, Henry "Light-Horse Harry" Lee's "First in war, first in peace, and first in the hearts of his countrymen." Lee conjured a loving father and dedicated husband. But he did not enter Washington's real world, nor his psyche. He did not broach the topic of Washington loving "maternally." In his depiction of Washington as a family man, Lee postulated a private Washington who was once again heroic and unmatched, "second to none in the humble and endearing scenes of private life." And yet such "humble and endearing scenes" were very concrete and real for him, an essential outlet for Washington's and other people's emotional life. In the family, he not only acted his part; he was entirely himself, and often happier than he was in the arena of politics.[21]

❧ A widespread myth holds that Martha tended to be much more lenient with children than George. Eleanor Calvert Custis Stuart, Jack's widow and the mother of Eliza, Patty, Nelly, and Washy, for example, voiced her concern about what she perceived as Martha Washington's easygoing attitude. "My good Mama," Eleanor wrote, referencing the way she was raising Washy and Nelly, didn't seem to recognize the value "of making the D[ea]r Children respect as well as love her." Grandma's "improper indulgence to them" would, she added, be their ruin. "Dear Grandmama," she wrote nine months later, "is too much pleased with the attentions paid to Nelly to judge of their impropriety."[22]

Whereas Martha was too soft, at least according to this narrative, the president remained the embodiment of authority, a person the children dreaded. One nineteenth-century testimony documented a confession obtained from George Washington Parke Custis, the same Washy of old. Custis declared that although Washington "was kind in his manner" to all children, "they felt they were in the presence of one, who was not to be trifled with." Allegedly, Custis also admitted that his grandmother was "overindulgent."[23]

That Martha Washington, on occasion, may have fallen into an excess of indulgence doesn't mean that she couldn't also be severe. Touted for her "admirable management of her servants and household," Martha knew how to be stern. After all, she had survived Valley Forge. She had managed the family estate. And she had Nelly, for example, practice on the harpsichord for hours on end. As Custis writes in his recollections, the "poor girl would play and cry, and cry and play, for long hours, under the immediate eye of her grandmother, a rigid disciplinarian in all things."[24]

Just as Martha could be both overindulgent and an adroit manager and a severe educator—a "rigid disciplinarian"—so Washington could be both stern and lenient. A father or grandfather, like a mother or grandmother, can be at once severe and tender, authoritarian and extremely welcoming, and Washington was no exception. He didn't see being indulgent as incompatible with his roles of patriarch, educator, guide, manager of an economic venture, and slaveowner.

Nelly unleashed Washington's "maternal" drives. For her, Washington's hearth was an intimate space bustling with intimacy and a private lexicon, with kindness and deep emotions. The two spent time together; they were tender companions. Nelly was singularly able to help her step-grandfather shake off the stiff formality he had to assume in so many of his public performances. Washington enjoyed Nelly's jokes and laughed heartily when in her presence. A gay child, Nelly would give him one of her sassy descriptions of a scene in which she had taken part or tell him about one of her pranks. She made him melt: "He liked to see us gay and happy," she later confided to her friend, "I have often made him laugh heartily at the relation of my frolics and difficulties." And she concluded: "I never felt that awe of him which others did—I was too thoughtless perhaps or considered him as a father, I did not admit so cold a sentiment."[25]

In October 1795, Nelly had to leave Grandma and Grandpa for the first time since she was two. George and Martha took off for Philadelphia, and she was sent to her mother's house, ten miles west of Alexandria, to spend the winter. These two figures seemed distant and cold to some, but they were very affectionate and warm toward her. Parting with them was "the greatest trial, I ever experienced." She loved them: "This is the first separation for any time, since I was two years old." Grandma "has been ever more than a Mother to me, and the President the most affectionate of Fathers. I love them more than any one."[26]

Virginia fathers could be tender and loving. It was not too difficult for Jacky, Patsy, Nelly, Washy, and many other little ones to cajole Washington into revealing a different side—and each time he was quite comfortable being cajoled that way. When in 1798 Washington met sixteen-month-old Elizabeth, daughter of Elizabeth Parke Custis Law, the eldest daughter of poor Jack and Eleanor Calvert Custis, he called to her. Then he took from his pocket a roll of so-called peach cheese, a molded paste of fruit and water that is sliced after it hardens, and said, "Here is something for you." He gave her a piece and embraced her. He then gave the whole roll to her mother: "Take it, Mme for your little Law." It is a scene fraught with tenderness, one quite at odds with the image of the patriarch we behold in Edward Savage's painting. In this cameo, Washington is not seated, his long, statuesque thigh at the forefront; instead, he moves, crouches, and gives hugs. He is not the unmovable center of his household, surrounded by minor characters. He touches and is touched. He gives love rather than commandeers it.[27]

The seemingly formal "take it, Mme for your little Law" also reveals a secret world of companionship and playful tenderness. Eliza, or Betsey, was no stranger to George Washington. She was not "Mme" at all. The sister of Patty, Nelly, and Washy and herself a constant presence at Mount Vernon, Betsey was the one to whom Washington confessed his tender, paternal love. When in 1796 Betsey was about to marry the wealthy Thomas Law, twenty years her senior, both Grandma and Grandpa were at first shocked. But then Washington gave his approval and wrote her a wonderful letter: "If Mr Law is the man of your choice . . . your alliance with him meets my approbation." And the tender father goes on:

> *Yes*, Betsey, and this approbation is accompanied with my fervent wishes that you may be as happy in this important event as your most sanguine imagination has ever presented to your view. Along with these wishes, I bestow on you my choicest blessings. . . . Nothing contained in your letter—in Mr Laws—or in any other from our friends intimate *when* you are to taste the sweets of Matrimony—I therefore call upon *you*, who have more honesty than disguise, to give me the details. Nay more, that you will relate all your feelings to *me* on this occasion: or as a Quaker would say "all the workings of the spirit within." . . . You know how much I love you—how much I have been gratified by your attentions to those things which you had reason to believe were grateful to my feelings.[28]

Other young men and women got to experience the softer, loving, playful Washington—including the adolescent son of the Marquis de Lafayette and namesake of George Washington, Georges Washington Louis Gilbert de La Fayette. In September 1795, the boy had arrived in America. His father was languishing in an Austrian prison, and he hoped that the president could do something, at least send a word to the Austrians—which he eventually did. Washington, obviously, was afraid that if he intervened he would offend the French government. However, though circumspect in public, in private, he was a *"father—friend—protector—*and *supporter"* of his best friend's son. Washington's concern about the boy, his "visible distress," weighed more than his diplomatic worries, and he decided to take him into his household. Washington grew rapidly fond of this "modest, Sensible, & deserving youth; deserving of the parents who gave him being." When architect Benjamin Latrobe dined at Mount Vernon, he saw the real affection between the two: "A few jokes passed between the President and young La Fayette," Latrobe wrote in his journal, "whom he treats more as his child than as a guest." As biographer Ron Chernow comments on the episode, "The situation was further testimony to Washington's hidden emotional nature."[29]

It's nearly impossible not to marvel at the tension between the public and the private father, between the Founding Father of patriotic lore, the mythical leader and the nation's educator, and the more emotional and "maternal" father. In the early 1790s, Howell Lewis briefly served as Washington's personal secretary and manager of Mount Vernon. Lewis was George Washington's nephew, the son of his younger sister Betty Washington Lewis, and second cousin to Meriwether Lewis. Unsurprisingly, Washington took Howell under his protective wing. He treated him with respect and with tender affection: "I was in no *real* want even of Howell Lewis," Washington admitted, "but understanding that he was spending his time rather idly, and at the same time very slenderly provided for by his father, I thought . . . by taking him under my care, I might impress him with ideas, and give him a turn to some pursuit or other that might be serviceable to him hereafter." Washington sought to educate Howell and give him advice. Simultaneously, he doted on the young man. And Howell marveled, as we all do: "I could hardly realize that he was the same Washington whose dignity awed all who approached him."[30]

PART III 🐦
Social

10

❧

A Person of Fine Manners

The Art of Pleasing

George Washington acted politely throughout his life. "In every movement," one historian and early biographer wrote, "there was a polite gracefulness equal to any met with in the most polished individuals in Europe." "Politeness" means "the art of pleasing," which is the art of gaining approval from society by means of good manners. A by-product of the Enlightenment era, politeness was a goal for many eighteenth-century individuals, both in Europe and in America.[1]

Every society has its etiquette—its code of appropriate behaviors and right apparel. While etiquette traditionally applied only to an exclusive elite comprising aristocrats, courtiers, and high priests, the form of etiquette that fell under the label of "politeness" in the eighteenth century speaks to a growing heterogeneous class—well-off merchants, artisans, traders, professionals, intellectuals, and *philosophes*, and, in America, planters and many commoners.

While etiquette manuals published during the Renaissance such as Baldassare Castiglione's *The Book of the Courtier* (1528) and Giovanni Della Casa's *Galateo* (1558) were intended for aristocrats, the

Earl of Shaftesbury's *Characteristics of Men, Manners, Opinion and Times* (1711), together with the ubiquitous *Spectator* (published in England from 1711 to 1712 by Joseph Addison and Richard Steele), had turned politeness into a quasimoral obligation for everyone. Many books and manuals—so-called conduct literature—appeared that took their cue from Shaftesbury and Addison and Steele. Men were now expected to talk a with a lower voice, dress with less pomp, less splurge, less flashy colors, and assume less affected postures. In short, naturalness and simplicity became fashionable.[2]

Shaftesbury and Addison and Steele sparked a plethora of new manuals of style that democratized good manners and electrified a large portion of the transatlantic world. Their message captivated people who had traditionally not only been excluded from the *beau monde*, but who had also been regarded as the sort that did not require an education in style. Readers were guided on a journey to self-awareness; they were invited to look at their bodies more closely and take stock of what these bodies could do and should not do. Society put pressure on everyone, enjoining them to curtail behaviors and habits that were once commendable, normal, or simply tolerated. The modern, polite body had to be more thoroughly regulated. Bodily noises, smells, fluids, and filth created serious embarrassment. (All this was an ideal, clearly, because in reality, the eighteenth-century world was still relatively medieval.)[3]

In 1774, Philip Dormer Stanhope, Fourth Earl of Chesterfield, a British diplomat, published a series of letters he had written for his son that became the bible of style, from dressing to talking to moving to eating. The letters forcefully conveyed that individuals should work to appear a certain way, regardless of their true character, natural endowments, and inheritance. People were invited to cultivate appearances—even, if necessary, to dissimulate. In this sense, Chesterfield's *Letters* have aptly been described as "a manual for strivers." While Washington nurtured noble inner sentiments and could abandon himself to maternal feelings and the tender, sincere emotions that fostered Christian compassion, he also laid emphasis on public presentation in the way Chesterfield advocated. Like other eighteenth-century fops and swindlers, he put on personal shows and pirouetted in the hope of gaining approval.[4]

Young George entered the world of politeness when he was between ten and thirteen years old, decades before Chesterfield's letters were published. In his school book, he copied 110 maxims, which came to be known as Washington's "Rules of Civility & Decent Behaviour in Company and Conversation." He did not author these rules. They were taken from Francis Hawkins's *Youths Behaviour, Or, Decency in Conversation amongst Men* (ca. 1640) and republished over again in no fewer than eleven editions through 1672. Francis Hawkins was a precocious boy from London who, at the age of eight or ten, had translated a book written in French in 1595, the *Bienséance de la conversation entre les hommes* (*Propriety of Conversation among Men*). This late-sixteenth-century courtesy book was prepared by the *pensionnaires* of the prestigious French Jesuit College of La Flèche and passed on to their brothers at Pont-à-Mousson, another French Jesuit College. In turn—and with this we go full circle—the *Bienséance* was based on Castiglione's and Della Casa's etiquette books.[5]

The reason why young Washington copied these maxims is unclear. One of his tutors might have wanted to familiarize George with politeness, or, alternatively, it might have been a mere exercise in calligraphy and penmanship. George also might have just come across on his own one of the editions of Hawkins's book that his father or his half brother Lawrence could have brought back from England (no copy survives). George himself might have decided to write the maxims out to perfect his calligraphy or, on the other hand, he might have wanted to commit them to paper because they touched him deep inside, psychologically.[6]

Even if Washington didn't write these rules down because he was deeply impressed by them, they can nonetheless be assumed to have shaped his mind and body because they resonated with the polite culture of eighteenth-century society of which he aspired to become a member. The gist of guides like "Rules of Civility" was that polite men should regulate, control, and contain their bodies. Seemingly laughable precepts from the "Rules of Civility" teach us precisely that the grotesque and precivilized body was a major concern: "When in Company, put not your Hands to any Part of the Body, not usualy Discovered" (rule 2), "Spit not in the Fire, nor Stoop low before it neither Put your Hands into the Flames to warm them, nor Set your Feet upon the Fire especially if there be meat before it" (rule 9), "Kill no Vermin as Fleas, lice ticks &c in the Sight of Others, if you See any filth or thick Spittle put your foot Dexteriously upon it if it be upon the Cloths of your Companions, Put it off privately, and if it be upon your own Cloths return Thanks to him who puts it off" (rule 13), and "Do not Puff up the Cheeks, Loll not out the tongue rub the Hands, or beard, thrust out the lips, or bite them or keep the Lips too open or too Close" (rule 16).

While these self-imposed limits represented the ground zero of politeness or its necessary conditions, the eighteenth-century gentleman aimed at simplicity, a much loftier goal. "Candour, sincerity, affability, and simplicity, seem to be the striking features of his character," as one John Bell wrote of Washington. Simplicity wasn't simple at all, however. It was easy to make the mistake of thinking as Robert-Guillaume Dillon, the Frenchman who served as *mestre de camp* in Lauzun's Legion during the last years of Revolutionary War, did, that "la nature," not training and application, had "given him an appearance that seduces as we simply look at him" ("elle lui a donné un ensemble qui séduit à mésure qu'on le regarde"). By "seduction" Dillon didn't imply anything sexual, obviously. But Dillon was plain wrong, as no one could be born with that type of simplicity of manners "with no hint of affectation" ("point d'affectation"). Washington was not "naturally and spontaneously polite," as the Marquis de Barbé-Marbois also believed. Washington's simplicity and hence his politeness were hard-won.[7]

Eloquent simplicity was the secret of eighteenth-century manners, as reflected in architect Benjamin Henry Latrobe's description of Washington. Latrobe had arrived in the United States in the spring of 1796, and as soon as he could, he went to Mount Vernon to pay a visit to the famous old man, not just because he wanted to see Washington but also because he had befriended Bushrod Washington, George Washington's nephew. "In about ten minutes the President came to me," Latrobe wrote in his journal. "There was a reserve but no hauteur in his manner. He shook me by the hand, said he was glad to see a friend of his nephew's, drew a chair, and desired me to sit down." The gesture of drawing of the chair perfectly captures the understated easiness that defined the ideal of politeness during the period.[8]

"The Graces, the Graces! remember the Graces!" Lord Chesterfield had warned his son, coining one of the most famous eighteenth-century mottos about understated manners and unostentatious refinement. Gracefulness was the epitome of an updated version of gentility—one that trod the fine line between showiness and austerity. The challenge was all about making gracefulness appear simple, unconstructed, effortless, and natural. Castiglione had already directed courtiers to practice in all things "a certain sprezzatura, so as to conceal all art and make whatever is done or said appear to be without effort and almost without any thought about it." Over time, sprezzatura gained international currency.[9]

Simplicity was similarly visible in small details characterizing Washington's persona. In his journal, Latrobe also wrote that he wore "a plain blue coat, his hair dressed and powdered." When at home, at Mount Vernon, a single enslaved person prepared his clothes. That same person combed and tied his hair. Powder was applied—giving Washington's hair a frosted appearance. While some eighteenth-century gentlemen wore wigs, like aristocrats of old, in the name of simplicity Washington did not. Modern fashion dictated the use of a thick coat of pomatum and white powder. Pomatums were made of starch (either from potato or rice flour), coloring pigments, and fragrant oils. For a man, pomatum was not meant to maximize volume, as it was for the ladies. Washington wanted his pomatum to hold his hair out of the way, sleeked back from his forehead, which made it easier to then tie it up in a long bunch with a black silk bow, or a "queue." For formal occasions, the queue was encased in a black silk bag. With this simple and polite hairstyle, he set a powerful example, as his officers continued to wear a variation of the style long after the War of Independence.[10]

Washington's hair bag. Courtesy of Mount Vernon Ladies' Association, Mount Vernon, VA.

⁑ Washington believed that simplicity was gaining momentum internationally. There were encouraging signals of what he called a "progressive Refinement of manners, the growing liberality of sentiment." Manners were improving, he trusted, and the entire world was undergoing a process of "melioration." Particularly during the immediate aftermath of the War of Independence, Washington "endulge[d]" in a cheerful philosophy of history, a "fond, perhaps an enthusiastic idea" that the world was "evidently much less barbarous than it has been, its melioration must still be progressive—that nations are becoming more humanized in their policy—that the subjects of ambition & causes for hostility are daily diminishing—and in fine, that the period is not very remote when the benefits of a liberal & free commerce will, pretty generally, succeed to the devastations & horrors of war."[11]

But he also feared that not all individuals, and not all nations, were ready to embrace civility, refined manners, and simplicity. The British, primarily, were still ensnared in semibarbaric habits. So, while celebrating such a universal "melioration," Washington also expressed the sneaking suspicion that the "Nations of Europe" weren't ready to get rid of the hindrances to "melioration," including a "thirst after riches" and a "promptitude to luxury." Optimism and pessimism were, in him, blended together.[12]

Like many other American "provincials," Washington looked to Europe, especially the former mother country, for both ominous examples of corruption, depravity, or barbarism and guidance and inspiration. The attitude was typical. Even after the Revolution, America remained an integral part of the European social and cultural world. Americans might have despised their British foes—for all the roasted meat they ate. But the desire for the approval of the high arbiters in England was embedded in American Britishness, no matter the hard-earned independence. Americans remained British through and through in their taste and manners. They were British because of the language they spoke and because of the poets, rhetoricians, and jurists they read. But Americans also became French.[13]

Even though it is impossible to tell if American patriots were more British or more French, the general trend shows that Frenchness gained momentum from the 1770s to the late 1780s and early 1790s. Chesterfield himself advised his son to cultivate a French style: "The French . . . attend very minutely to the purity, the correctness and the elegancy of their style, in conversation, and in their letters. . . . Observe them, and form your French style upon theirs." Washington couldn't have agreed more, and by the end of the war, it seemed to him that well-off Americans were at least on their way to acquiring a refined material French sensibility: "The consumption of French wines is," he remarked in 1788, "much greater than it has formerly been." What tilted Americans toward the French was not only wine but more favorable commercial policies at the end of the war. Washington's lists of articles of importation "directly from France" are fascinating. They reveal the very tangible world of things well-off Americans surrounded themselves with: "Superfine Broad Cloth's (particularly blue, which can be afforded cheaper and better than from England) Glass, Gloves, Ribbons, Silks, Cambricks, plain Lawns, Linens, Printed Goods, Wine, Brandy, Oyl, Frute." That the French had supported the patriotic cause also explains this trend: "The change of taste in favor of articles, pro-duced or manufactured in France," Washington reasoned, owed "in a great degree" to "the affection and gratitude still felt for her generous interposition in our favor."[14]

Washington esteemed the French, and not just for their political ideas but also because they were "a people who study civility and politeness more than any other nation." (It's not true that Democratic/Republicans, or Jeffersonians, were attracted to France while Federalists, or Hamiltonians, favored England.) In the eyes of many patriots, France was the best venue for perfecting one's education in politeness. Addressing the topic of the education of his unruly stepson John Parke Custis, he advised that Jacky's tutor, Jonathan Boucher, provide an intensive course in Frenchness. "To be acquainted with the French Tongue," he wrote, "is become a part of polite Education; and to a Man who has an[y idea] of mixing in a large Circle, absolute[ly] necessary." In theory at least, the stepfather was not "averse to his Travelling for the completion of his Education." Washington was convinced that the best way "to form the manners, and encrease the knowledge of observant youth" was to send them to Europe.[15]

Jacky, however, did not live up to his stepfather's expectations. By 1771, Washington was writing to Jacky's tutor that he did not care much that Jacky was "ignorant of the Greek, (which the advantages of understanding I do not pretend to judge)," but he did worry that he knew "nothing of French, which is absolutely necessary to him as a traveler." Further, Jacky had begun to turn to "Dogs Horses & Guns," symbols of a decadent aristocratic taste— British, on the whole. Similarly, Washington was concerned that Jacky's fascination with "Dress & equipage, which till of late, he has discoverd little Inclination of giving into," would turn him into a molly, a fop, a dandy. Boucher, whose school Jacky had been attending for some years, made Washington still more anxious about Jacky: "I never did in my Life know a Youth so exceedingly indolent, or so surprizingly voluptuous," Boucher wrote. "One w[oul]d suppose Nature had intended Him for some Asiatic Prince."[16]

Maybe it was too much to invoke the "Asiatic Prince," but Jacky's voluptuousness could well have prompted him to embrace the latest in European decadence—not the French style that so many Americans admired but the excesses of a macaroni. Popular in England in the mid-eighteenth century and in the big cities of America a few decades later, macaronis were style-conscious individuals who made a spectacular show of their love of fashion, going beyond the ideals of politeness. But it was only affectation, the goal being to make bold statements and shock common feelings. Macaronis provoked.

They acted out their fastidiousness and bragged about the Italian grand tour they took, which often they had taken only in their imagination. They were self-preening individuals, very provincial in their flaunted cosmopolitanism. They lacked civility and American republican simplicity. They were the new barbarians.[17]

The Power of Politeness

Good manners and simplicity were a statement of power, a show of self-possession and self-awareness. Men who knew how to behave gained respect from their peers, and they also increased their chances of getting better wives, securing business connections, and becoming politically relevant.[18]

Washington seemed to have treated everyone "with great politeness," as Claude-Victor, Prince de Broglie, testified. He was not a snob or a passive-aggressive individual, to use our vocabulary. "He had nothing chilling or repulsive in his manner, or countenance," Richard Peters, another witness, remarked. "On the contrary, his demeanor was polite and inviting." And yet, with his demeanor perfectly Chesterfieldian, "like a gentleman," Washington affirmed his power. No one would ever know if his manners were the expression of sincere Christian sentiments or just aristocratic affectation. Was he pretending? Every eighteenth-century individual was aware that politeness could be treacherous, inclusive and exclusive at once. "It is incompatible with the propensities of a candid mind," Peters continued, "to practice the hypocrisy and insincerity of politeness, by affecting emotions not felt." "What is called *graciousness*, if it be indiscriminately exercised" justified suspicion that the person in question possessed a "general coldness of character."[19]

Politeness may have been virtually for everyone, but as a code prescribing social norms, it also created distinctions. Enslaved persons, poor whites, many types of women, and recent immigrants could not play the game called "simplicity" or "Frenchness." They could not invent themselves as Chesterfield and Washington did. Washington would have perhaps denied it, but polite society was mostly made of, and for, "Persons of Distinction, as Noblemen, Justices, Churchmen," as per rule 26, defined by nonnegotiable hierarchies, as rule 29 indicates: "When you meet with one of Greater Quality than yourself, Stop, and retire especially if it be at a Door or any Straight place to give way for him to Pass." Overall, politeness excluded. The harmony effected by polite society was predicated on deference to superiors; order was preserved when inferiors respected superiors and, just as important, when superiors did not trample over the sensibility of inferiors. The elite were not expected to humiliate the nonelite. As Washington's rule 28, for example, puts it, "If any one come to Speak to you while you are Sitting Stand up though he be your Inferior."

As to class and hierarchies, the early American republic was Janus-faced. The promise of opportunity and equality proclaimed by the Declaration of Independence and supported by enlightened elites who had faith in "melioration" was counteracted by a society that reinforced distinction. The founders themselves, through their words and ideas as well as through their bodies, expressed a conflicting message. Treat the people "civilly," Washington wrote in a letter to William Pearce, because this is "what all men are entitled to." But his complete "advice" was "to keep them [the people] at a proper distance; for they will grow upon familiarity, in proportion as you will sink in authority, if you do not." As a show, politeness was indeed a culture of condescension, hierarchical and patronizing.[20]

Washington himself had to work his way up. He wasn't born into one of the first families of Virginia, the Byrds, the Randolphs, the Carters, the Fairfaxes. "Not even retroactively," historian Clifford Dowdey wrote long ago, "not even after George became the absolute number one citizen of Virginia and the new nation, were the Washingtons ever included in the aristocracy." That family hadn't inserted themselves "soon enough into the dominant group." Washington enjoyed the favors of the Fairfax family, but while their attention was objectively a blessing, it was also subjectively a tremendous responsibility and a psychological burden he had to carry: "To that family I am under many obligations," he soon acknowledged. George couldn't help comparing himself, unfavorably, to the Fairfax family, the elite of the elites. They were examples of persons of "Greater Quality"; they were extremely rich and very well educated; they had the appropriate social connections; they were exceedingly polite.[21]

Washington made it eventually, though, by hook or by crook. He also became very polite, himself the number one. Without fear of being laughed out of doors, he could play the general, the president, the planter, the exquisite host, and many other characters. These personae were endowed with propriety and social standing, manners and civility, elegance and style, republican simplicity and "Frenchness." People lower down on the social ladder could peep into his famous residences—whether in New York, Philadelphia, or Mount Vernon. They could make mental lists of all the things this man possessed and they didn't, of his belongings and amazing assets, and all the proxies he could rely on. They could praise him for his triumph. The American Cincinnatus had won by relinquishing power. The lower sorts would have immediately felt intimidated, seized by a sense of inferiority, almost annihilated.

Like other members of the elite, Washington didn't need to act with brashness. To intimidate and maintain social hierarchies, he could simply gesture toward his uncontested financial success, his exquisite "simplicity," his elegant house, and chiefly his land. For apparent reasons, the possession of land has always been a key indicator of status. During Washington's time, land provided crops and economic "independence" as well as afforded political visibility and social influence.

Washington loved land also because he believed it facilitated "melioration." If society were made up entirely of landowners, wars among states and individuals would no longer break out. The "manly employment of agriculture," as he wrote to Chastellux, could bring "the age of Knight-Errantry and Mad-heroism" to an end. Land ownership produced men who were better looking, less violent, less unruffled, more gentle and genteel, more civilized and polite, and he so wished for a time when "the manly employment of agriculture and the humanizing benefits of commerce would supersede the waste of war and the rage of conquest."[22]

But of course these land-controlling men could only thrive thanks to a system of hierarchies that pushed other men and women down the ladder. In concrete terms, without the enslavement of many people and the displacement of native populations, ownership of massive tracts of land and their management would not have been possible. Neither Washington's peers nor Washington himself looked like knights or madmen. They were calm and self-possessed, simple and modern, and also sincerely tender and emotionally rich, like real Christians. But this was because they had waged and won an internal war against lesser men and women for the control of the most important asset, land. Washington would not be Washington without the land he owned and controlled— nearly fifty thousand acres. Washington needed his land. He had responsibilities and could not afford to give this main resource away. Without it, his family would no longer be able to support itself. He would be ruined, and the country would suffer. The land system and the social system would collapse. Washington did not, and maybe could not, call the entire system into question.

As a "landed man," Washington moved with ease within the perimeters of the system, sometimes falling into the most archetypal habits of the gentry. It is very interesting to behold his reactions to minor acts of noncompliance, when people broke the rules of civility and didn't keep the proper distance. He could not tolerate it when another man literally trespassed into his exclusive "field for manhood"—even if he did so only for fun, such as in order to hunt on his land. In that case, he turned into an American eighteenth-century medieval knight: "My fixed determination is, that no person whatever shall hunt upon my grounds or waters." The land was his private property, but Washington in his remonstrance came off as rather aristocratic as well: "Besides, as I have not lost my relish for this sport when I can find time to indulge myself in it, and Gentlemen who come to the House are pleased with it, it is my wish not to have the game within my jurisdiction disturbed."[23]

In point of fact, very few dared to question Washington's authority and face him off. And even when they did, he didn't need to raise his voice. To defend his polite masculinity and "my Land," he didn't need to bellow a war cry. He didn't need to remind people about who he was. His mansion, Mount Vernon, intimidated enough already. His "simple" and yet elegant way of life also bespoke his dominant position within the system. He was not a Fairfax or a British squire. But his achievements and his total acreage were more than sufficient to cudgel other males.

❧ Robert Cary, the head of a famous merchant house in London, did not always treat his American special customer the way he treated his habitués. He would send substandard articles overseas—for Cary, Americans remained provincials to the bone. Each time Cary did so, Washington became furious—politely furious: "It is needless for me to particularise the sorts, quality, or taste I woud choose to have them in unless it is observd." Washington could not tolerate the idea that he might be considered uncouth: "You may believe me when I tell you that instead of getting things good and fashionable in their several kind we often have Articles sent Us that could only have been usd by our Forefathers in the days of yore." Washington deplored the trick that the British often played on American provincials: "'Tis a custom, I have some Reason to believe, with many Shop keepers, and Tradesmen in London when they know Goods are bespoke for Exportation to palm sometimes old, and sometimes very slight and indifferent Goods."[24]

Seeking to make himself ever more refined, Washington amassed a huge collection of objects. The invoices to the London firm are a privileged window that allows us to peep into that long-gone world. Washington consigned the harvests of his farms to Robert Cary & Company in exchange for manufactured goods. Washington began his relationship with Cary in 1759, right after he married Martha, and kept it through the 1770s. Cary had also been the preferred merchant of Martha's deceased first husband, Daniel Parke Custis. Washington saw no reason why the estate should not continue to use the services of the firm.

Invoices for "Sundry Goods to be Shipd by Robt Cary Esq. and Company for the use of George Washington" are many, each and every one replete with details that reveal Washington's expertise about materials and objects. This man not only spent money but also time to gather information about the objects he needed or simply wanted. His research put him in the know about those items that better exemplified the latest, the most genteel, the most adequate ideals of politeness. He always made sure he was well understood regarding his desiderata, providing detailed instructions, as suggested by his requests for a "Bedstead 7½ feet pitch, with fashionable blew [blue] or blew and white Curtains," a "Fashionable Sett of Desert Glasses," a "Half a dozn pair of Men's neatest Shoes and Pumps," and "One neat Pocket Book, capable of receiving Memorandoms & small Cash Accts to be made of Ivory." Not yet thirty, Washington knew perfectly what he wanted; he wanted "this" and not "that."[25]

His priorities never changed. In his mid-thirties, for example, Washington wrote to Cary about his new "need," this time a chariot to be "made in the newest taste, handsome, genteel, & light."

This chariot would be more than a utilitarian means of transportation. "Made of the best Seasond Wood, & by a celebrated Workman," it would convey an appropriate image of gracious elegance. As to the color, Washington wanted green, "being a colour little apt, as I apprehend, to fade, & grateful to the Eye," unless, he added, "any other colour more in vogue & equally lasting is entitled to precedency." In that case, "I woud be governd by fashion." While eschewing flashy details, "a light gilding on the mouldings (that is round the Pannels) & any other Ornaments that may not have a heavy & tawdry look" would add to the general "impression." If a secondhand chariot for much less could be found, Washington would take it. "But if I am obligd to go to near the origl cost I wd e'en have one made." Eventually, he paid a hefty £133.4 pound sterling for a brand-new one.[26]

Unfortunately, however, the chariot proved to be second-rate. The mythic chariot, "which I begd might be made of well Seasond Materials, and by a Masterly workman" was actually made of cheap wood, "so exceedingly Green that the Pannels slipd out of the Mouldings before it was two Months in use." Rather than "meliorating" Washington's status, the chariot turned out to be a piece of junk, even though "every possible care was taken of it."[27]

Chariots, swords ("with Chain & swivels"), gold watches ("*well* executed in point of Workmanship"), cutlery, plates, glasses, brushes, scissors, chimney pieces, axes, hinges, fancy furniture, shoes, and so many other items adorned Washington's life—even during straitened times. After the War of Independence broke out, for example, the commander in chief surrounded himself with camp furniture that emphasized his gentility and, at the same time, preserved rank distinctions. Still mindful of the ordeal he had undergone when he fought in the French and Indian War and, even worse, when he was a surveyor, this time the general did not renounce luxuries and comforts. The pieces he bought were similar to the furniture one would find in a typical southern mansion, but they

could be assembled and disassembled quickly
and stored in cases for transportation.[28]

He also availed himself of real lodgings on
occasion during the war, including Colonel
Stephen Moore's House, also known as the
Red House, on the site of what is today the
US Military Academy at West Point, where
he resided for part of the summer of 1779. He was able to relax and
enjoy time in a real house, with proper furniture, a cook, and friends
eager to visit him, such as John Cochran, his old friend and husband of Gertrude, the sister of General Philip Schuyler, whom he
invited for a visit in August. The general was in a good mood. He
was even playful and promised his pals decent food—though not
in great quantity: "Since our arrival at this happy spot, we have had
a Ham (sometimes a shoulder) of Bacon, to grace the head of the

table—a piece of roast Beef adorns the foot—and, a small dish of Greens or Beans (almost imperceptible) decorates the center." The cook, occasionally, tried "to cut a figure (and this I presume he will attempt to do to morrow)." So, he jocularly warned his guests, "two Beef-stake Pyes, or dishes of Crabs in addition, one on each side the center dish" would be presented. The layout of the table, Washington joked, would be craftily contrived, "dividing the space, & reducing the distance between dish & dish to about Six feet, which without them, would be near twelve a part." Though the banquet was less than Lucullan, Washington was happy to entertain his guests as they deserved: "If the ladies can put up with such entertainment, and will submit to partake of it on plates—once tin but now Iron—(not become so by the labor of scowering) I shall be happy to see them."[29]

❧ In Washington's personal world, objects were not nuisances or necessities, artefacts cluttering his self and a life that otherwise would have been purer, happier, and more natural. Owning certain things was more than a willy-nilly concession to social conventions. Objects had a paramount importance for Washington, as they helped him to become the refined and polite person he wanted to become.

Whether he was fully aware of this dynamic we cannot be sure, but his reaction as a young man to being deprived of things suggests he was. As we recall, the young traveler "over the mountains" felt disempowered and disenfranchised when he first realized that things were scarce and could be easily taken away from him. "When we came to Supper," he wrote on one occasion, "there was neither a Cloth upon the Table nor a Knife to eat with but as good luck would have it we had Knives of [our] own." "Our Spits," he wrote on another, "was Forked Sticks our Plates was a Large Chip as for Dishes we had none." Washington was terrorized. Objects recorded, shaped, and constituted his experiences. Objects boosted his imagination and transported him into a narrative space where his persona was stronger, better, more successful, more republican, more "French." Without his things, he not only lost rank in polite society but became like a barbarian or, worse, "like a Negro."[30]

Washington located himself amid a rich universe of material things. He was a "thing-man" rather than an "idea-man," to use catchy phrases that author William Woodward invented about a century ago, "a man who loves material possessions with a passionate intensity." Washington was not unique in his craving for things, of course. No individual is ever just herself or himself—a naked body, a pure physicality, an abstract individuality. What we call "our self" or, in an alternative phrase, our persona, is the sum of our thoughts, emotions, our inner life—the so-called spirit—plus our body (which is always located within a social context), plus the innumerable things that surround us or that are laid on us. Some of these things we label "ours." Things make us more visible, and they root us more deeply in the world—which becomes our world. As enhancers of the self, things carry out three functions: they convey personal power; they speak to the type of individual we think we are; and they situate our private self within the social network.[31]

Historically speaking, the eighteenth century was the century of the industrial revolution. New efficient ways to mass-produce a quantity of new objects like tools, domestic appliances, furniture, and fabrics created new types of material desires. Consumption became à la mode, even in America, and principally within polite society. Newly available manufactured goods helped people in the construction of a new type of "polite" self. Eighteenth-century individuals wanted to appear a certain way, and to achieve that goal, they felt they had to demonstrate good manners, attend the right social events, wear the right clothes, and acquire goods.[32]

II

❧

The Message of His Clothing

The Cowl Makes the Monk

*N*athaniel Hawthorne once proclaimed that George Washington naked was "inconceivable." To behold him exposed, his vulnerability made into a public spectacle, was one small step short of blasphemy. Washington "had no nakedness," Hawthorne stated, "but, I imagine, was born with his clothes on and his hair powdered, and made a stately bow on his first appearance in the world." That is, Washington was not quite human, for Hawthorne, but was rather the eternal hero, a stiff, emotionless, unapproachable demigod.[1]

Washington, of course, was not born with his clothes on. But Hawthorne was partially right: Washington would not be Washington without his clothes. Dress, it has been written, "can be considered a form of performance in everyday life." In other words, we use our apparel to effect a certain self-image, which is to say that, contra the old adage, perhaps the cowl does in fact make the monk. Washington became visible by means of his clothes, and through the many types of clothes he wore, he became more than one person. He chose his apparel to convey specific messages and to reach specific audiences. He dressed up to indicate that he belonged, for example; or, conversely, he dressed down to show that he was an

American to the core rather than a "corrupt" or "aristocratic" European. Washington practiced what is usually called the art of self-presentation.[2]

But in addition to choosing his own style of clothing, he was chosen by his clothing. Washington was reared in a set of norms and stylistic types that he considered desirable and appropriate and that thus dictated his choices. Styles were passed down to him. He must have implicitly said to himself, "This is not masculine enough," "not white-bread enough," "not Virginian enough," "not modern enough," "not martial enough," and so on. He gauged himself using models that were part of his instinctive sense of self— he knew, preconsciously, that the freeman had to look different from the bondman, the freewoman different from the bondwoman, the American different from the Briton, the upper classes different from the lower classes.

Washington put a lot of effort into educating himself in the matter of clothing. A teenager, he began familiarizing himself with the types of fabrics, styles, quality, and colors. He thus soon became very knowledgeable, allowing him to exert a large amount of control throughout his life over the unconscious mechanisms that contributed to setting styles. He no doubt also picked up sartorial notions by looking at his male models—Lawrence, first and foremost. There is a note in his 1748 diary, one of the earliest of his writings that we have, perfectly revealing young George's interest in clothing. When he jotted down this note, he was about to set out for Belvoir, William Fairfax's elegant new home, about four miles downstream from Mount Vernon. He had just come back from his successful surveying trip over the mountains. Because the young man didn't want to make a meager figure, he planned well in advance. Just in case, he took with himself, among other things, seven shirts, six linen waistcoats, six bands (a type of shirt collar), four neck cloths, and seven caps.[3]

Our attention is immediately drawn by the seven caps, which

sounds excessive. But in the eighteenth century, both women and men wore caps at night, and they often did so during the day as well. Bedrooms were either not heated at all or were heated only just before the occupants went to bed. Also, during the day, a cap made reading, writing, and conversing more comfortable. (Washington did not wear a wig, but the men who did shaved their head, making the cap all the more important.) So the seven caps perfectly balance the seven shirts. Most likely, Washington had planned to put on a clean shirt and a clean cap every day or every other day. (Bathing, for obvious reasons, was not easy, and "cleanliness" was conveyed by crisp shirts and the other "smalls"—underwear and socks and the like—of the laundry.)

The four neck cloths are more interesting. As a sign of distinction, upper-class people used to wear a neck cloth—a kind of scarf—often made of fine white cambric, folded appropriately and wrapped twice around the neck. Again, it signified "cleanliness." Young Washington wanted to send a message. He wanted his patrons, the Fairfaxes, to know that he was dependable and belonged to the world of politeness.

As early as 1749–50, George was already sending out incredibly detailed orders. He desired the most up-to-date apparel. In the following example, he was on the lookout for a frock "with a Lapel Breast," a very modern garment indeed:

> The Lapel to Contain on each side six Button Holes and to
> be about 5 or 6 Inches wide all the way equal and to turn as
> the Breast on the Coat does to have it made very Long
> Waisted and in Length to come down to or below the Bent
> of the knee the Waist from the armpit to the Fold to be ex-
> actly as long or Longer than from thence to the Bottom not
> to have more than one fold in the Skirt and the top to be
> made just to turn in and three Button Holes the Lapel at the
> top to turn as the Cape of the Coat and Bottom to Come

Parrallel with the Button Holes the Last Button hole in the Breast to be right opposite to the Button on the Hip.[4]

The frock, often untrimmed, was a type of coat open-minded British gentlemen began wearing in the 1730s and embraced by the French about twenty years later. The design of the frock was modeled on coats worn by the working classes; it had a turned-down collar that could be buttoned up during inclement weather and so was quite practical. At first used for informal wear only, the frock gained popularity among polite society. As Thomas Jefferson, long a resident of Paris, explained to David Humphreys, "the *habit habillé*," the evening dress coat, "is almost banished, and they begin to go even to great suppers in frock."[5]

For men, as already pointed out, the line between style and ostentation was always rather thin. But Washington had learned to approach this dangerous line without ever trespassing it, and he did so sartorially as well. As an experienced man, he would direct others to make sure they avoided mistakes: "I shall always wish to see you clothed decently and becoming your stations," Washington wrote to his nephews, George Steptoe Washington and the younger Lawrence Augustine Washington, adding "but I shall ever discountenance extravagance or foppishness in your dress."[6]

Washington had a fine sense of balance: while "conformity to the prevailing fashion" was necessary, at least "in a certain degree," economy and frugality were also important because embracing them conveyed a message. In another letter to the two nephews, he laid out sound principles: "It does not follow from thence that a man should always get a new Coat, or other clothes, upon every trifling change in the mode, when, perhaps, he has two or three very good ones by him. A person who is anxious to be a leader of the fashion, or one of the first to follow it, will certainly appear, in the eyes of judicious men, to have nothing better than a frequent change of dress to recommend him to notice." In other words, macaronis, fops, mollies, and "corrupt" Europeans were unmanly and un-American.[7]

Washington had taught himself these principles when he was in his prime. Overcoming the self-doubts of a provincial, one who understood he did not belong to the top echelon of the colonial gentry, took a lot of work. In 1758, for example, George sent out an order to a merchant in Bristol for "two pair of Workd Ruffles," the typical curled white fabric that trimmed the end of shirts' sleeves. Bur he wasn't sure whether this style was too ostentatious or perhaps too obsolete. "If workd Ruffles shoud be out of fashion," he specified, "send such as are not."[8]

Worked ruffles were neither out of fashion nor excessive—and they remained so for many more years to come. In his late 1780s depiction of John Adams and Thomas Jefferson as modern American patriots and "simple" republican idols, painter Mather Brown spruced them up with frocks, neckwear, and rather elaborate ruffles. (Brown's Jefferson, furthermore, had a goddess of liberty beneath his shoulders, with a lance and a Frisian cap.) George Washington himself, in Gilbert Stuart's famous 1796 *Lansdowne Portrait*, has fine ruffles that are very visible.

Washington ventured daringly into the maze of sartorial choices, no matter the self-doubts he might have had in specific circumstances. By any objective standard he was an expert. He stood clear of overindulgence and, more important, he never settled for average and tawdry outfits. Washington knew precisely what he wanted: "Be pleased to send me," he wrote his tailor in 1763, "a genteel sute of Cloaths made of superfine broad Cloth handsomely chosen." On another occasion, he asked for two pairs of breeches, one to be made of "Crimson Velvet" and the other of "black knit silk." Washington could name fabrics, including "Irish Holland," "Cambrick," "Irish Linnen," "Muslin," "fine white Gauze," "Canting," "Callico," "Bird Eye," "Nankeen," "Mohair," and many other types.[9]

For Washington it was self-empowering to be able to give

proper names to things. It made him feel like he was in control. And it must have given him pleasure to tell Robert Cary and other purveyors that he desired only the "best Oznabrigs," "black Sewing Silk," or a "Black Russel Quilted Coat."[10]

☙ When a certain fastidiousness meets expertise, the outcome is often disappointment. As a rule, Washington was not happy with his tailors. They caused him to waste too much time; they misunderstood him; or they just did not listen to him attentively. Probably worse, they also failed miserably with measurements.

Charles Lawrence, a tailor on Old Fish Street in London, had been making suits for Washington since 1759. Lawrence had a talent for disappointing his client. It was like that from the beginning of their relationship. A "suit of Cloaths of your making," Washington complained as early as 1760, "dont fit me so well as I coud wish—this I attribute to some error in the measure that was sent." Maybe the measurements were wrong or maybe Lawrence was just unheedful: "Be so good therefore," Washington added, "to keep the Measure." But Lawrence did not keep the measure, and Washington kept complaining: "I have hitherto had my Cloaths made by one Charles Lawrence in old Fish Street but whether it be the fault of the Taylor, or the Measure sent I can't say but certain it is my Cloaths have never fitted me well."[11]

The testy letter Washington sent to one of his tailors, perhaps Lawrence, exemplifies his general feelings about all the annoying to and fro that his tailors subjected him to: "I desire you to make me a pair of breeches, of the same cloth as my former pair, but more accurately fitting." Washington knew he could not trust these people fully: "These breeches must be made exactly to these measurements, not to those to which you imagine that they may stretch after a period of use."[12]

Washington switched tailors frequently and often relied on more than one at the same time. He used one Alexander in 1768 and 1769 and a Bryant Allison (or Alliston) through 1772. He also employed Thomas Gibson, whose shop was on 5 Laurence Lane, London, in the 1770s, and at least one indentured tailor, Andrew Judge, the father of the enslaved Ona Judge, a white Englishman, from 1772 to 1784.

Washington spent a lot of time with tailors, whether he was writing letters to them or having them over to take measurements. "At home all day," he entered in his diary in the winter of 1770. "Carlin the Taylor came here in the afternoon and stayed all Night." William Carlin, from Alexandria, was an artisan Washington trusted, as he also made clothes for Jacky, Patsy, and some of the Mount Vernon house "servants" between 1764 and 1772.[13]

His tailors rarely got the garments they made him exactly right. In part this was because in many cases their shops were located beyond the ocean and so Washington had to enclose self-taken measurements in his letters. Not only was communication difficult, but fashion, by definition, is a flimsy matter. To get the garment just right, neither too short nor too long, was exceedingly difficult. The Londoner Thomas Gibson, whom Washington trusted well enough, had to listen closely: "If it ever shd be the taste of the prest [present] times to wear short Cloaths I shd not like to have mine made in the extreame of it." Short coats, frocks, and breeches, were "a fashion I nevr admird." Gibson was apparently not that bad, as Washington placed several orders with him. But Gibson wasn't perfect either: "The Coat and Waistcoat which you sent me last year," Washington wrote again, "fitted very well." But they were too long, and "I was obliged to cut of[f] near three Inches from the length." Furthermore, they were "a little too tight in the Sleeves." One year later Gibson made the opposite mistake and sent Washington a coat which was "rather too short in the Sleeve, from the Elbow downwards."[14]

Having tailors nearby helped. James McAlpin, who served him and his family during the presidency, had a shop conveniently located in Philadelphia, on 3 South Fourth Street. McAlpin could easily assess his client in person. He delivered a huge array of apparel to Washington: full regimentals and half regimentals made of "Spanish Cloth," of "olive colour," of "dark brown," of "light [brown]," of "Raven grey," of "Black," of "Velvet," and of "Uncut [velvet]." McAlpin continued to make clothes for the family until shortly before Washington's death.[15]

While there is a widespread belief that Washington distanced himself from fashion and clothing as he matured, the evidence shows that he retained a vivid interest in this subject. He kept buying apparel. He kept giving precise directions to his tailors. And he kept being rather fastidious about *every* detail. In Washington's orders, words such as "fashionable," "handsome," "superfine," "proper," and so on, regularly appear.

He wanted to present himself as a "gentleman of taste," one who avoided extremes or impropriety. "I want neither Lace nor Embroidery," he wrote to the London merchant Richard Washington (unrelated). "Plain Cloaths with a gold or Silver Button (if worn in genteel Dress) is all I desire." Plainness and simplicity in the late eighteenth century could assume several forms, depending on the circumstance. It could take the shape of the plain cloth with a gold or silver button or an appropriate mourning dress. "This Letter," Washington wrote to Thomas Gibson in the immediate aftermath of poor Martha Parke Custis's death, "is intended to desire you to make me a genteel Suit of Second Mourning, such as is worn by Gentlemen of taste, not those who are for running into the extreame of every fashion." The second mourning followed the almost ascetic first three months of full mourning—sometimes called deep mourning. During deep mourning, men were expected to abstain from any item even remotely ostentatious and to wear only plain black cloth. Buttons on sleeves and pockets were not allowed. Second mourning, on the other hand, was the time when minimal concessions to fashion could be made again. In fact, as a complement to this second mourning dress, Washington also ordered "A Genteel Mourng Sword—with Belt Swivels &ca." (The whereabouts of this sword are unknown; it may not have survived.)[16]

Washington cultivated style and distinction but not in the mode of a haughty aristocrat. The old world with its stiff aristocracy and its circles of high clerics—the court—had a different etiquette. Those upper-class individuals were fond of fabric made of bright colors, such as red and scarlet, that were heavy gilded with embroidery. They wore flashy clothes for the sake of public display—the flashier, the better. But "modern" individuals like Washington sought to be elegant in a much more subdued way. While they did "quote" from the aristocratic chic (incorporating the golden or silver button into their clothing, for instance), they did away with elaborate apparatuses, often choosing "workwear," such as the frock. They embraced practicality and sprezzatura.

Furthermore, by the mid-eighteenth century, garments in general and stockings and breeches in particular were increasingly made of smoother fibers that encouraged a feeling of movement and liberty. They would move with the body rather than rigidly fix it in place. Aristocrats were hefty and rigid, in both their bearing and attitude and in their garments. Most of the time, European aristocrats wore ceremonial costumes. Their coats and breeches constricted the body. The bodies of the king and queen, for example, were considered perfect because they were highly constricted, positioned, and regulated. Washington and his peers were practical men and aimed at a simpler, more practical elegance.

≈ Washington was not a would-be aristocrat looking back nostalgically to previous sartorial codes nor a fashionista, a fop who loved excesses. But his garments were powerful statements nonetheless. His sartorial choices could be at once playful and sophisticated. A silk and linen waistcoat he likely had made between 1775 and 1785 sports a false double-breasted front, which was very fashionable during the 1780s, a standing collar, superb embroidery with polychrome feathers and flora, and buttonholes edged in green silk thread.

Another silk satin waistcoat that dates to the same period was made of handsome English fabric in a more subdued cream color that was cut, assembled, and lined by an American tailor. It has similar precious details and a front entirely quilted in chain stich. The silk threads were originally shades of green, pink, and lavender. A floral vine interlacing a linked chain in green, lavender, mauve, and cream goes through the center front and reaches the front skirt edges and the lower edges of each pocket flap.

Another silk velvet waistcoat, from 1780–90, has similarly exquisite details. A striped voided velvet of fine quality, originally lavender, black, and cream, this waistcoat could easily go along with many types of breeches and coats—especially the typical black velvet suit that Washington wore during his presidency. The

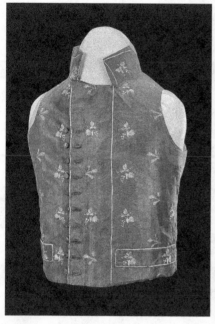

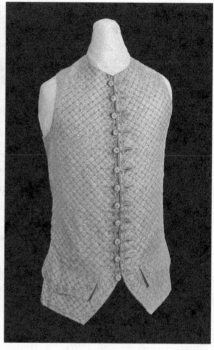

Washington's waistcoat,
ca. 1775–85; altered ca. 1795.
Courtesy of Mount Vernon
Ladies' Association, Mount
Vernon, VA.

Washington's waistcoat,
ca. 1775–85. Courtesy of Mount
Vernon Ladies' Association,
Mount Vernon, VA.

visual effect this waistcoat elicits is quite unique, almost tridimensional, and he liked it a lot. (The many repairs on the waistcoat prove it.)

The celebrated blue and buff (from buffskin, a pale yellow) uniform that he wore regularly from the War of Independence until his death is the closest we can get to a ceremonial costume. It is General Washington at his most recognizable. The uniform is on display at the National Museum of American History, in Washington, DC (the coat was made in 1789, while breeches and waist-

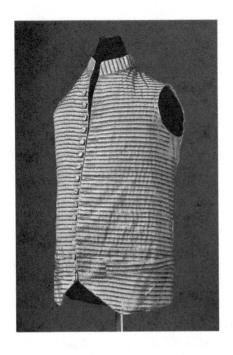

☙

Washington's waistcoat,
ca. 1770–90. Courtesy of
Mount Vernon Ladies'
Association, Mount Vernon,
VA.

coat are from the Revolutionary War period.) Blue and buff were
the colors of the British Whig Party, which stood against the Tories. Ever since the Glorious Revolution of 1688, the Whig Party
had represented the "freedom of the people"—or, more accurately,
constitutional monarchism. Thousands of men identified with this
symbol of rebellion against absolutism. After the publication in
1774 of Johann Wolfgang Goethe's *Sorrows of the Young Werther*,
the blue and buff became universal, an icon that circulated within
polite and fashionable circles, in Germany and everywhere else.

Goethe did not take his cue from George Washington or vice
versa. But by making blue and buff his colors of choice, Washington contributed to the international success of this outfit. "If Blew
and Buff can be had," the general wrote in requesting garments for
his officers, "I should prefer that uniform, as it is the one I wear
myself." "The Buff of the very best sort," as he also declared many
years later, "fine, & not inclining to yellow or Orange," was pre-

cisely "what I have been accustomed to wear." He cut a distinctive figure in his signature uniform. And he knew it.[17]

Although Washington never reverted to embroidered scarlet coats, like an aristocrat, on occasion he would become rather stiff. A cape made of superfine blue cloth that he wore during his presidency with one corner thrown back over his shoulder, exposing the scarlet lining, can also be considered a ceremonial costume of sorts, and one he knew would make an impression. William Sullivan, an acquaintance from Massachusetts, describes this Washington during his public receptions (or levees) as "clad in black velvet; his hair in full dress, powdered and gathered behind in a large silk bag; yellow gloves on his hands; holding a cocked hat with cockade in it, and the edges adorned with a black feather about an inch deep. He wore knee and shoe buckles; and a long sword, with a finely wrought and polished steel hilt, which appeared at the left hip; the coat worn over the sword, so that the hilt, and the part below the coat behind, were in view. The scabbard was white polished leather."[18]

At the other end of the spectrum was the Washington who had donned the hunting shirt, also called an Indian shirt, during his military days. This generously fitting shirt, made of rough "tow cloth"—the lowest quality of osnaburg, made of tow, which are the broken fibers remaining when flax, hemp, or jute is processed— with long breeches of the same material, was cheap to produce and easy to maintain. It was cool during the summer and could be worn over layers of underclothes in the winter. More important, it carried "no small terror to the enemy, who think every such person a complete marksman."[19]

The rugged outfit added an element of surprise, as the enemy could not be sure if this combatant was a savage or a well-trained rifleman. Washington had first grasped the symbolic power expressed by this garment during the French and Indian War. Both officers and common soldiers, he advised during the Forbes Expedition of 1758, should "adopt the Indian dress." Washington had

Washington's uniform, 1789.
Courtesy of Division of
Political and Military History,
National Museum of American
History, Smithsonian
Institution, Washington, DC.

"set the example" himself. A rather "unbecoming dress I confess for an Officer," the hunting shirt would leave room for movement, allowing men to proceed "as light as any Indian in the Woods." "Convenience rather than shew I think shoud be consulted"—but Washington was being disingenuous, as he knew the outfit would make a powerful show on its own. During the Revolution, Washington again ordered his officers to rely on this type of disguise: "If you were to dress a Company or two of true Woods men in the right Indian style," he passed the word down through his chain of command, "and let them make the Attack accompanied with screaming and yelling as the Indians do it would have very good consequences especially if as little as possible was said, or known of the matter before hand."[20]

Washington directed not only his soldiers to dress a certain way but also nephews and nieces, and, alas, his "negroes." The infamous South Carolina Slave Code of 1740 had mandated "that no owner or proprietor of any negro slave, or other slave, (except livery men and boys,) shall permit or suffer such negro or other slave, to have or wear any sort of apparel whatsoever, finer, other, or of greater value than negro cloth, duffils, kerseys, osnabrigs, blue linen, check linen or coarse garlix, or calicoes, checked cottons, or Scotch plaids, under the pain of forfeiting all and every such apparel and garment." Washington followed the mandate, only buying cheap textiles for the persons he held in bondage—except for liveries for his house "servants." These brownish and yellowish fabrics trapped these hapless individuals in a social cage. Rather than adding power as the hunting shirt did, such fabrics subtracted it, immediately distinguishing enslaved people from free people. By being forced to wear such clothing, persons in bondage were taught to believe that their diminished self-representation was logical and natural, that they were born coarse, dirty, and cheap.[21]

As president, Washington also had a vision for clothing the

nation, an idea that was based on the style that the rebellious colonists adopted during the late 1760s after they boycotted British goods, especially luxuries. Ideologically, the Americans had justified the boycott by imagining a mythical republican simplicity, the exact opposite of European "promptitude to luxury" and its inlays of corruption. They had convinced themselves that life must be turned simple, unfashionable, American, and that they must dress in nothing other than coarse homespun. Notable individuals had kept buying British sundries yet publicly frowned on ostentation of elegance not only as unpatriotic but as a moral evil. Washington himself had been a staunch advocate of nonimportation and had taken care to ensure that purveyors did not send him prohibited items. "You will please," he had written to Robert Cary, "to be careful that none of the glass, Paper, &ca contain in my Invoices are of those kinds which are subject to the duty Imposed by Parliament for the purpose of raising a Revenue in America."[22]

When Washington became president, he immediately conceived an idea to bring homespun back. He saw himself dressed down in a rugged American style. He imagined his fellow citizens dressed like him. His homespun-clad body, as he must have been aware, could be turned into a visible symbol of American citizenship, rendering the daring philosophical ideas contained in the Declaration—"all men are created equal"—visible and accessible to everyone: "all men are dressed equal."

Washington did not advocate a national costume, as the new French republic would—painter Jacques-Louis David was commissioned to design a national uniform, and the Committee of Public Safety distributed twenty thousand engraved copies of David's template from which tailors could take their cue. But Washington assumed that American rough fabrics would empower citizens and help them to visualize themselves as different from Europeans.[23]

Dressing the President

"I have been writing to our friend Genl Knox this day," Washington informed Lafayette at the end of January 1789, "to procure me homespun broad cloth, of the Hartford fabric, to make a suit of cloaths for myself." Washington was curious about this new "Hartford fabric" and had sent Knox to investigate. Having learned from an advertisement in the New York *Daily Advertiser* "that there were superfine American Broad Cloths to be sold at No. 44 in Water Street," he appointed Knox "with the Commission of purchasing enough to make me a suit of Cloaths. As to the colour, I shall leave it altogether to your taste." A former comrade and trusted friend, Knox took his mission very seriously.[24]

Washington's imagination was electrified. Founded in 1788 by Colonel Jeremiah Wadsworth, the former commissary general of the Continental Army, and Peter Colt, with £2,150, the Hartford Woolen Manufactory was envisioned as a patriotic enterprise. Washington immediately recognized its importance. The Revolution had cut ties with Britain, the major supplier of textiles, and Americans had to make do. Thirty subscribers contributed to the creation of the company that also received considerable encouragement from the state of Connecticut in the form of tax exemptions and bounties. To spread the word, Wadsworth had launched an advertising campaign in major newspapers—the New York *Daily Advertiser*, where Washington got the information, was one of those. The factory could churn out different types of fabrics, more or less refined. Its staple was the broadcloth, "Congress Brown," "Hartford Grey," and "London Smoke."

These fabrics caught the imagination of many Americans. In the *Federal Gazette*, a "Philadelphia Mechanic" wrote that a "PASSION for encouraging American manufactures has, at last, become fashionable in some parts of our country." To promote the Hartford Woolen Manufactory, as the "Mechanic" also suggested, "the gentlemen who are, or who shall be, elected to serve in the senate or house of representatives of the United States; as also the president and vice-president, should all be clothed in complete suits of American manufactured cloth, on the approaching *fourth* of March," which was the opening day of Congress.[25]

Knox was now on a mission—a no less important one than organizing the government. "I immediately sent to the store where the american cloths were advertised for sale," he informed his friend at Mount Vernon, "and to all other stores where it was probable there were any." But nothing was available. "Four peices are however expected hourly": light grey, Hartford grey, bottle green, and dark brown.[26]

One week later, Knox was ready to make his first shipment. By stage, Knox forwarded to Mount Vernon the bottle green cloth, enough for a coat and a waistcoat "for you and for Mrs Washingtons riding dress." As to the greys and the dark browns, unfortunately, they "were too mean and coarse." Washington was happy with the green he received—or at least said so. "Thanks," he wrote back. The cloth, he admitted, "exceeds my expectation." The green was fine—and, after all, he had said to his friend that he would trust him completely with the choice of the color. At the same time, the green wasn't the best hue for the type of show the soon-to-be president had in mind.[27]

Washington in fact appears to have settled on the color brown from very early on. He had planned on making brown the trademark of his presidency through his inaugural suit, which indeed quickly became legendary. At the beginning of March, Washington told Knox that he was happy with the green but by mid-February he had already pulled strings in order to get hold of the brown. He had sent Tobias Lear, his secretary, on a parallel mission. On February 15, 1789, Colonel Jeremiah Wadsworth wrote Lear that he was ready to forward "patterns" (i.e., samples) of the Hartford fabrics. One was "a dark Brown and of ye best Wool—it will be superior in quallity to any yet made." Wadsworth had a suit made of precisely this fabric and had enough left for one more: "If you wish to have it, direct where it shall be sent." Wadsworth hoped that "it will be worn by one whose example will be worth more than any other encouragement that can be given to our infant Manufactures."[28]

Lear must have told Washington right away about Wadsworth's plan. And Washington agreed—enthusiastically. Lear also pulled his own strings. Whatever the to and fro, on March 5, Knox apprised Washington that a batch of "superfine brown Hartford cloth," was on its way. Knox had completed his task. By the end of the month, he informed Washington that the Hartford Woolen Manufactory's agent Daniel Hinsdale had sent the cloth.[29]

When Washington received the brown cloth, he was truly elated. "I am extremely pleased," he wrote to the manufactory's agent. What he received, he admitted, exceeded "in fineness and goodness whatever the most sanguine expectation could have looked for at this period." Whether it was the quality of the brown fabric per se or the patriotism with which he was infused, the fact is that Washington had an inspiring vision: "We shall very soon be able to furnish ourselves at least with every necessary and useful fabrick upon better terms than they can be imported."[30]

Washington received the brown cloth on April 8. There was no time to waste, as the inauguration was April 30 and Washington had planned to leave home for New York on April 16. His tailor at Mount Vernon, or other tailors we don't know of, set to work on the suit immediately. We can easily picture the flurry of excitement seizing the entire household: Washington donned and doffed first cuts; Martha assisted and gave advice; tailors cut and seamstresses stitched tirelessly; and the "servants," indubitably, ran many errands. Together with the cloth, Washington had also received "some federal buttons," but not enough. "To trim the Coat in the manner I wish it to be," he wrote Knox, he needed more. "I would thank you, my good Sir" for procuring "six more of the large (engraved) button" and "retaining them in your hands until my arrival at New York." Knox obeyed. Upon his arrival in New York, the gilt buttons engraved with the arms of the United States by William Rollinson were presented to him and sewn on the coat. Washington was now ready to roll.[31]

For the great performance in the brown Hartford suit, Washington appeared on the balcony on the second floor of Federal Hall, on the corner of Wall and Nassau Streets, and Robert R. Livingston, the chancellor, administered the oath. A huge crowd had gathered underneath to assist in the historic event. The *Gazette of the United States* wrote that "the Cloth was of so FINE A FABRIC, AND SO HANDSOMELY FINISHED, that it was universally mistaken for a foreign manufactured superfine-Cloth." In reality, the fabric looked "superfine" only from afar. Up close it was rather "slubby"; Washington, however, had chosen it not for its intrinsic qualities but as a means to an end—the end being to boost Americanism. The brown color was itself American, an antiaristocratic hue that was a gesture toward the working people. Dull whites, greens, and browns obtained by vegetable dyes were cheaper and had thus been the only choice lesser people could make, while enslaved persons remained caged by the browns. At the same time, it was an homage Washington paid to the natural world he had championed ever since he took the first trip over the mountains of America. Brown was American because it conjured the American land.[32]

We cannot say for sure whether the heirloom admired by tourists when they take a tour of Mount Vernon today is, as many claim, the original. This heirloom (*on next page*) is double breasted, which was a more informal option than the single-breasted jacket, although it is possible Washington requested a double-breasted jacket to make a statement. Acceptable for daytime events, the double-breasted jacket was normally worn by military men or sail-

Washington's suit, ca. 1790–1800. Courtesy of Mount Vernon Ladies' Association, Mount Vernon, VA.

ors (in the form of the peacoat) and for riding or sports. It was practical in that one could sit on the saddle or crouch without having to unbutton it. While the fact that the coat currently at Mount Vernon is double breasted does not rule out the possibility that it is the original, the fact that it has only five buttons on the

front raises doubts. Washington had made an explicit reference to "six more of the large (engraved) button." Did the inauguration suit have six buttons on the front? On that historic day, he could well have worn another brown coat (*above*) or another suit entirely

that does not survive. Unfortunately, accounts of the 1789 inauguration do not comment on the cut or style. They only mention the color, the most American among all the possible browns.

Washington bought fabric from the Hartford factory again and again. Another man's double-breasted jacket made of blue wool with a turned-down collar, for example, still exists. According to Washington's step-grandchild, Elizabeth Parke Custis, this garment was "made of the first American cloth sent to General Washington and much worn by him." The item in question is an American homespun that, originally, was also bound with braid—which would have made it a little more fashionable. Washington publicly performed with American simplicity and rusticity, but when he was left free to follow his personal taste, he fancied more refined items.[33]

On certain public occasions, President Washington gave into his enthusiasm for elegance. On Friday, January 8, 1790, he delivered his first annual message (what is now called the State of the Union Address) to a joint session of Congress in the Senate chamber of Federal Hall in New York City. Less under the pressure of public scrutiny than a few months earlier, he was once again clad "in a suit of Clothes made at the Woolen Manufactory at Hartford," as Washington himself wrote in his diary, "as the Buttons also were." But Washington's suit, this time, was very elegant, the fabric magnificent. Washington was at his best. No one failed to notice his "crow-coloured suit of clothes." The *Pennsylvania Packet* wrote about "this elegant fabric." The cloth "appeared to be of the finest texture—the colour of that beautiful changeable blue, remarked in shades not quite black." Mary Ball Washington had recently died of breast cancer at her home in Fredericksburg, Virginia, on August 25, 1789. Washington was in second mourning.[34]

This changeable crow-colored dark blue, by any standard, is indeed beautiful, but Washington had in fact played a trick on his onlookers. The quality of the Hartford fabric was tawdry, but from afar, it duped all the people in the room. He had visited the factory himself at the end of October 1789, and while it was a "place which seems to be going on with Spirit," the fabrics themselves left something to be desired: "Broadcloths are not of the first quality,

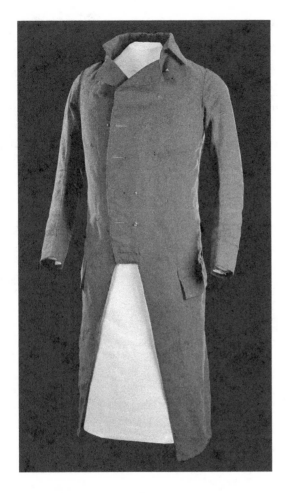

as yet, but they are good; as are their Coatings, Cassimers, Serges and everlastings."[35]

The Hartford Woolen Manufactory had many problems and faced constant struggles. In 1794, Henry Wansey, a British clothier, antiquarian, and traveler, visited Hartford. He did not like the way the production was managed: "None of the partners understand any thing about it, and all depends on an Englishman, who is the sorter of the wool." Wansey was perceptive; the manufactory closed later that year.[36]

≈ Washington may have bought many cuts of the less-than-perfect Hartford broadcloth, but the mass of the American clientele didn't follow his example. His fellow Americans, apparently, were choosier. Furthermore, they no doubt thought that taste and style, dressing up and dressing down, were matters of private concerns only. Flaws in the Hartford textiles didn't matter to Washington because he picked this fabric for two precise political reasons and not out of personal sartorial preferences: to pitch the message about the need to buttress American manufacturing in general and to stress that he also was a homespun American. However, this chapter has shown that Washington was more than a rough piece of homespun. His education and expertise were amazing—he was a self-aware cosmopolitan, with touches of "Frenchness" and sprezzatura, who could appreciate quality, good taste, and really superfine fabrics.

12

❧

Astride the Great Stage

A Theatrical Age

On October 19, 1781, the British general Charles Cornwallis surrendered at Yorktown, Virginia. The war was over. But while everything seemed to be going well, the Continental Army found itself entangled in a second war, perhaps a still worse ordeal. Under the Articles of Confederation, the first American Constitution, Congress could not raise taxes to provide salaries for the military. It could only make "requisitions," a tricky term that reveals the weakness of the new political organization. Congress could only ask states to provide voluntarily for the needed funds. Unsurprisingly, as the British started to withdraw, states were less willing to satisfy Congress's requests, leaving both American officers and soldiers in distress.

By early 1783, Continental Army officers could not take it anymore. Out of desperation rather than animated by unpatriotic feelings, they challenged Congress on open ground. The Newburgh Conspiracy, as it is known, made clear that these men were ready to mutiny. On March 10, Major John Armstrong, an aide-de-camp to General Gates, circulated an address that sounded like an ultimatum: should the officers' requests not be met entirely (and the back pay be delayed), the army would either disband immediately, thus leaving civilians unprotected, or, worse, refuse to disband after the peace treaty was signed. It was a threat of a military coup.

Washington was faced with a conundrum. On the one hand, he sympathized with these officers—he had written so many letters on his soldiers' behalf during the Revolution. On the other hand, he grasped that the supreme political authority of Congress could not be confronted in this way by any subordinate, no matter the legitimate complaint. Doing so would dissolve the most sacred bond and precipitate the polity into a dangerous state of internal unrest—civil war.

Washington had made his decision: he could not approve, but, with his general orders dated March 11, he called for a meeting with officers so that the question be properly discussed; he also let them believe that he would not be present. The date was set: March 15, 1783. The place was decided as well: the "Newbuilding"—a low-ceilinged room about seventy by forty feet with a small stage and lectern at one end in Newburgh, New York.

As soon as General Gates stepped forward to chair the meeting on the set day, Washington suddenly entered the room. It was a coup de théâtre—the first one, on that day. Washington took to the stage and in his Newburgh Address said what he was supposed to say. He expressed patriotic feelings and, with the help of expected rhetorical formulae, he rehearsed the principles these soldiers had fought for. By using his own persona, he set out to persuade the rebels to stand down. "Give one more distinguished proof of unexampled patriotism & patient virtue," he harangued. Do not lose your temper but retain your "full confidence in the purity of the intentions of Congress." He had the audience's full attention. As he wrapped up his address—which lacked any literary distinction and was only passable because he delivered it—he executed a second, incomparably more powerful and cunning coup de théâtre.[1]

Joseph Jones, congressman from Virginia, had sent Washington a supportive patriotic letter, and Washington now declared he wanted to read it to his officers as proof of Congress's good intentions. He took the letter from his pocket and started to read it, but he stumbled through the very first paragraph. He reached in his pocket again, and this time he pulled out a pair of spectacles. He put on his spectacles and remarked: "Gentlemen, you will permit me to put on my spectacles, for, I have grown not only gray, but almost blind in the service of my country."[2]

With his spectacles on, Washington donned a proper theatrical mask. While he truly needed this medical prosthetic, as his sight had recently begun to fail ("The Spectacles suit my Eyes extremely well," he had written to astronomer and genial inventor David Rittenhouse, "as I am perswaded the reading glasses also will when I get more accustomed to the use of them"), they also conveyed a cultural meaning and theatrical energy. For a contemporary of Washington, they represented the Enlightenment's fascination with sight and were a metaphor for undaunted intellectual enquiry.[3]

Spectacles have existed since antiquity. But after the 1720s, they were no longer perceived as an external item, meant to be held up to the eyes only occasionally and in private, when exceptional circumstances dictated. Increasingly, they were meant to be "worn." They enhanced sight, but they also enhanced the appearance of the wearer. Rather than merely utilitarian tools that a person had to put up with, spectacles were more and more about the self, an element of style, a statement of fashion. They signified that the bearer was an open-minded, modern man aware of new technologies and a cosmopolitan Enlightenment devotee.[4]

Everyone was moved to tears. Washington's audience was conquered by his theatrical persona. He contrived a deliberate show that had all the appearance of being natural and unplanned: "There was something so natural, so unaffected, in this appeal," one witness remarked, "as rendered it superior to the most studied oratory; it forced its way to the heart, and you might see sensibility moisten every eye." When Washington finished his act, he took leave of the stage, as expected. It was a feat of studied oratory, but one performed with the body rather than through words.[5]

❧ The eighteenth century was the age of theater. John Gay, in London, Carlo Goldoni, in Venice, and so many other authors and playwrights contributed to the epochal transformation of the genre from an exclusive pastime appealing to aristocrats and courtiers to an inclusive and democratic amusement.

Eighteenth-century women and men were highly theatrical; they believed they were constantly on stage—and Washington was no exception. Marie Antoinette, queen of France and wife to Louis XVI, who loved to dress as a milkmaid, was not the only one to don costumes. Eighteenth-century people, no matter their social origins, put on costumes whenever they could. It was exhilarating but also nerve wracking, and authenticity emerged as the problem of the period. Did the surface reveal or conceal interiority? Was life only a big shadow, an appearance without an essence, a fruit with an enticing peel but without the nutritious pulp?[6]

Washington, for one, was uneasy about dissimulation and inauthenticity—the peel without the pulp. "Appearances are deceiving," he wrote to John Augustine Washington in 1777, when he was seven miles from the enemy's principal post at Brunswick, not sure whether the British would move toward Philadelphia or more eastward. "False colours are often thrown out to mislead or bewilder." But even if separating appearances from reality was tough, he accepted masks and costumes as *the* fact of modern life. Theater, for him, was inescapable.[7]

Washington attended the theater, to begin with, and he loved it. Whether he attended it because it was entertaining, because it provided a means of escapism, or perhaps because he knew he could learn moral lessons and take cues from it, theater was a big part of his life. From diaries and his cash accounts, historians have estimated that he attended no fewer than 108 plays—some of them more than once. *The London Merchant, or the History of George Barnwell*, by George Lillo, a tragedy, was the first production he saw, on November 15, 1751, when he was in Barbados with Lawrence. *Dermot and Kathleen*, a pantomime ballet based on William Shield's *Poor Soldier*, was the last show he enjoyed, on February 27, 1797, in Philadelphia.[8]

He attended almost everything, including plays that clearly sound cheap and corny, such as *The Way to Get Married*; *Animal Magnetism*; *The Clandestine Marriage*; *The Duenna, or, The Double Elopement*; *The Wonder! A Woman Keeps a Secret*; *The Shipwreck or the Aerial Travellers*; and *The Romp, or A Cure for the Spleen*. And he had his favorites: *The School for Scandal*, a comedy of manners by Richard Brinsley Sheridan, which he attended in New York on May 11, 1789, and again in Philadelphia in January 1791 and in November of 1792; *The Poor Soldier*, which he saw in New York on May 11, 1789, and again in Philadelphia in January 1791; and *Cato*, of course, a piece we have already met in a previous chapter.

In the eighteenth century, going to the theater was not what we might expect. An evening program could go on for up to five hours. More than one show was typically performed and, as a perk, there were always many extras. Typically, the evening started off with a long piece followed by a shorter one, the latter of which might be a comic opera or masque. Musical numbers came next, and in between, there were dances as interludes. An evening at the theater was a potpourri of disparate genres—perhaps mind boggling to us. After this long evening of listening and spectating, the audience would often end up moving to a nearby ball. Going to the theater was a rather over-the-top affair.

The fact that theatrical metaphors were part of Washington's daily language also attests to his love of the theater. There is the "stage of human action," the "stage of public affairs," the "American stage," the "theatre of public life," "I have once more consented to become an Actor in the great Drama," and so many others. At the end of the Revolutionary War, he had deployed the most theatrical of theatrical metaphors: "Nothing now remains, but for the actors of this mighty Scene to preserve a perfect unvarying consistency of character, through the very last act to close the Dramma with applause, and retire from the Military Theatre, with the same approbation of Angels and men, which have crowned, all their former actions."[9]

But not only did Washington love theater and use theatrical metaphors; like many other men and women of his time, he was theatrical, as the scene that took place on March 15, 1783, indicates. Other such scenes punctuated his presidency. On Wednesday, December 7, 1796, for example, in his eighth and last annual message to Congress, he advocated the creation of a national university and a military academy for the reason that "a flourishing state of the arts and sciences contributes to national prosperity and reputation." But in addition to hearing the words he uttered, congressmen saw him dramatically garbed in a black velvet suit, with a long sword at the side. That costume also made a lasting impression.

More than twenty years earlier, he had done something even more theatrical. Before being unanimously selected commander in chief of the Continental Army, on June 15, 1775, he had already entered the chambers of the Continental Congress wearing full military regalia, the blue-and-buff uniform of the Fairfax Independent Company. As a delegate from Virginia, Washington should have simply dressed as a civilian, but his decision to present himself in military garb undoubtedly sent a clear signal to Congress, forcefully conveying that he was a man with experience who was willing to serve again. He was being a little disingenuous, therefore, when right after his acceptance he told his wife he had "used every endeavor" in his power to avoid the commission. Judging from this performance, he very much wanted the appointment.[10]

We pitch messages. We do this by means of the words we say and by means of the performances we put on the public stage—a well-cut suit, the right tie, the proper shoes, an ironic facial expression. (By the same token, we can compromise our ability to effectively convey our message through the inappropriate words or a tasteless suit, mismatched tied, or the wrong shoes.) Washington, by common consent, was not a powerful patriot-orator, like Patrick Henry or John Randolph of Roanoke. However, what the traditional judgment of his oratorical skills misses is that words are not the only aspect of oratory. Washington was a superb orator, but his best performances came from his whole body rather than from speech alone.

Upper-class masculinity in the eighteenth century required the mastery of oratorical skills. Confident public speaking was a prime indicator of refinement and manliness. For a man to prepare for political office—which was the traditional path to power for the southern gentry—oratory was a necessity. Studying law was a common method of reaching oratorical proficiency. Instructors would advise their pupils to exercise by speaking aloud before a mirror. Cicero was the male ideal during the period, a man who deserved public honor because he had attained the most sublime eloquence in both letter writing and public speaking. But Washington's own personal version of genteel masculinity was grounded in a mastery of the "theater of public life." He controlled nonverbal languages better than verbal ones. He had successfully walked away from clumsiness and self-doubt. He could now dominate the room—in silence. He learned how to behave, which detail could make a difference, which impression could convince his audience.[11]

Washington did not have an instinctive sense of the theatrical. Rather, he became a consummate actor along the way through much training and self-observation. His experience as a theatergoer, similarly, helped him to take stock of the strategies he could deploy. As one historian has observed, "he may have learned something of the relationship between a performer and his audience by watching professional actors practice their art." Never flamboyant, Washington's performances were nonetheless successful.[12]

Acting Out the President

*T*he office of the presidency brought Washington's acting to a new level. Having reached the summit, he realized he had no other choice but to put on the costume of the central character of the play. It was risky: "The eyes of Argus are upon me," he wrote to Bushrod Washington in July 1789. Argus Panoptes, the many-eyed giant of Greek mythology, was spying on Washington the president, "and no slip will pass unnoticed."[13]

Washington was very clear that there was a precise script and a choreography he would follow. He had to act out with prudence, conciliation, and firmness, not an easy task: "Few, who are not philosophical Spectators," Washington wrote to Catharine Sawbridge Macaulay Graham, an English historian and an enthusiast for the American cause, "can realise the difficult and delicate part which a man in my situation had to act":

> All see, and most admire, the glare which hovers round the external trappings of elevated Office. To me, there is nothing in it, beyond the lustre which may be reflected from its connection with a power of promoting human felicity. In our progress towards political happiness my station is new; and, if I may use the expression, I walk on untrodden ground. There is scarcely any action, whose motives may not be subject to a double interpretation. There is scarcely any part of my conduct wch may not hereafter be drawn into precedent.[14]

The official residences of the president set the stage for his receiving guests and was adorned with furniture, carpets, draperies, mirrors, paintings, and china that befitted his station. While he owned many average pieces that were easily sourced from the local market, guests could also marvel at some fancier items that were imported. Nothing was splendid, extravagant, or markedly aristocratic. Washington had arrived in New York a few days before his inauguration, and Congress had taken care to polish up the Samuel Osgood House at 3 Cherry Street, his first residence, where he lived from April 23, 1789, to February 23, 1790. The house "was then in a state of the greatest confusion," Tobias Lear writes, "pulling down—putting up—making better & making worse." The outcome was not bad, however. "By spirited exertions, it was got into good order by the arrival of the President."[15]

Samuel Fraunces, the former owner of the eponymous tavern in New York City, was hired as steward and superintendent of the kitchen. Fraunces could count on a staff of about twenty people, that included wage workers, indentured servants, and seven enslaved persons whom Washington had brought with him from Mount Vernon: Billy Lee, Giles, Paris, Christopher Sheels, Austin, Moll, and Ona Judge.[16]

Thanks to Fraunces, Washington and his friends Lear and David Humphreys spent a pleasant time among themselves. We can easily picture these former soldiers enjoying soothing moments of rest. Fraunces, Lear writes, was able to produce "such a number of fine dishes that we are distracted in our choice when we set down to table, and obliged to hold a long consultation upon the subject before we can determine what to attack. Oysters & Lobsters make a very conspicuous figure upon the ta[ble] and never go off untouched." Washington held Thursday dinners, to which he invited a large audience made of foreign diplomats, ministers, congressmen, and political allies—including his foes. Martha was usually there, the only woman. A fresh president, Washington could claim he was not "desirous of being placed *early* in a Situation for entertaining," but in fact he entertained. He realized he had to abide by "the public desire and expectation, with respect to the style proper for the Chief Magistrate to live in." Consequently, he capitulated to public demand.[17]

Samuel Osgood House soon became too small for the purpose of impressing others—it could accommodate only fourteen guests, plus the family and the five secretaries, at the table. Furthermore, this five-window-wide and three-story-high building facing what was then Saint George's Square (now Franklin Square, on a site covered by the foundations of the Brooklyn Bridge) was too close to the East River and the port, a very busy and noisy part of town. Alexander Macomb House, on 39–41 Broadway, on the west side of the street, just north of the Bowling Green, was larger and quieter. Martha and George could receive people with ease. The superior dining room was big enough to allow for parties of up to twenty-seven persons.[18]

Washington did not get to enjoy Macomb House for very long, only staying there from February 23, 1790, to August 30, 1790. On July 16, 1790, Congress passed and the president signed "An Act for Establishing the Temporary and Permanent Seat of the Government of the United States." The Residence Act, as it is commonly called, mandated that a site on the Potomac River become the permanent capital, to be built in ten years' time. The act also mandated the immediate relocation of the capital from New York to Philadelphia. Washington would live there from November 27, 1790, to March 10, 1797 (in between New York and Philadelphia he was at Mount Vernon).

It was a good bargain, all things considered. Morris House, by Washington's own admission, was "the best *single House* in the City." It was selected on the president's behalf by a committee of the Corporation of the City of Philadelphia. Washington liked it but also insisted that "without additions it is inadequate to the *commodious* accomodation of my family." The want of public spaces bothered the president more than the lack of quarters for private purposes. "The first floor contains only two public Rooms." Hence the need for an overhaul: "The second floor will have two public (drawing) Rooms," and the third story will have "a public Office (for there is no place below for one)." Public rooms were paramount as they served as his public stage.[19]

Washington kept saying he had no spare time for style and domestic economy: "The multiplicity of my public duties leaves me but little leisure to suggest domestic arrangements." But these disclaimers notwithstanding, when James Germain succeeded Samuel Fraunces as steward for Washington's household at Philadelphia in June 1794, the president made sure the new employee understood that he had to help Washington reach a specific goal. Washington never missed a chance to stress that his residence was a theater and a space for entertainment, "that my table [s]hall be handsomely but not extravagantly furnished on the days that company is en[t]ertained." Washington sought the paraphernalia and the right stratagems with which he might impress his guests. He hoped to strike them with the proper balance of "a handsome style, but without waste or extravagence."[20]

It was clear to everyone that the president had to be a persona, a character other than a real individual. But which type of character had to be determined. Even before his historic inauguration on April 30, 1789, Congress had already taken up the question of what titles and what measure of pomp should be bestowed on the president. The titles given to the president needed to conjure a certain national vision, a vision that conveyed what the president expected of his citizens and that motivated them to act in line with those expectations. On April 23, the Senate had appointed a committee to tackle the question of titles. Both the Senate and the House dedicated time to the issue. The debate dragged on. Senator William Maclay wrote in his diary what happened in the Senate on May 8:

"Excellency" was moved for as a title by Mr. [Ralph] Izard. It was withdrawn by Mr. Izard, and "highness" with some prefatory word, proposed by Mr. [Richard Henry] Lee. Now long harangues were made in favor of this title. "Elective" was placed before. It was insisted that such a dignified title would add greatly to the weight and authority of the Government both at home and abroad. I declared myself totally of a different opinion; that at present it was impossible to add to the respect entertained for General Washington; that if you gave him the title of any foreign prince or potentate, a belief would follow that the manners of that prince and his modes of government would be adopted by the President. (Mr. Lee had, just before I got up, read over a list of the titles of all the princes and potentates of the earth, marking where the word "highness" occurred. The Grand Turk had it, all the princes of Germany had [it], sons and daughters of crown heads, etc.) That particularly "elective highness," which sounded nearly like "electoral highness," would have a most ungrateful sound to many thousands of industrious citizens who had fled from German oppression.[21]

On May 14, after days of wearing discussion, the committee delivered its recommendation, which was that the president should be addressed as "His Highness the President of the United States of America, and Protector of their Liberties." But the House disagreed. This formula was still too aristocratic and deemed tainted by "an appearance of singularity." Republicanism had to be simple, free from titles and hauteur. The Senate eventually surrendered: "The Senate, Desirous of Preserving Harmony with the House of Representatives, where the practice lately observed in presenting an address to the President was without the addition of Titles, think it proper for the present to act in conformity with the practice of that House:—Therefore Resolved, that the present address be—'To the President of the United States'—without addition of Title."[22]

It was now up to Washington to turn such a theory into practice. He was a little bemused, understandably. On May 10, he wrote to John Adams to ask for his "candid and undisguised opinions" in matter of etiquette and behavior. "The President," Washington sensed, "in all matters of business & etiquette, can have no object but to demean himself in his public character, in such a manner as to maintain the dignity of Office, without subjecting himself to the imputation of superciliousness or unnecessary reserve."[23]

The concept was clear: republics, based as they were on the notion of the equality of the people, abhorred titles and aristocratic privileges—"singularity," in the language used by the House. Unnecessary reserve and superciliousness did not appeal to Washington. He didn't want to present himself as an aristocrat—a king. But the eighteenth century was different from the mass society of the nineteenth and the twentieth centuries. Republics, in the eyes of Washington's peers, should be nothing less and nothing more than what Montesquieu had clearly described. Republics, including the new American republic, had to be a government *for* the people and *with* the people. But "the lower class," as Montesquieu averred, "ought to be directed by those of higher rank, and restrained within bounds by the gravity of eminent personages." The people, "whose nature is to act through passion," Montesquieu concluded, should be mediated by their "ministers," that is, their magistrates. In a republic, people could certainly elect their magistrates—and the whole eighteenth century agreed. But they shouldn't do more than that: "The people are extremely well qualified for chusing those whom they are to intrust with part of their authority." People are good at choosing because the choice is determined "by facts that are obvious to sense." Many observers in the eighteenth century embraced this myth.[24]

Washington wasn't sure what type of public figure he should embody. However, he knew that he was expected to convey the gravity of an eminent personage, as per Montesquieu. Also, deep in his heart, he saw what he had to avoid. He realized that he must never court the people but rather always maintain a safe distance. To inspire the people and lead them and even to intimidate them, if necessary, were admissible goals, but a leader should never follow people's passions.

❧ Without unnecessary superciliousness, Washington let people know that his persona had become the embodiment of the American republic. The president had to be approached through a ceremony—whether he personally liked this or not. Visitors were calling on the president of the United States and not on him personally.

Washington settled on the levee. The French term, meaning "rising," originally indicated the most intimate and yet spectacular moment of life at court, when a selected group of dignitaries entered the monarch's bedchamber and attended the rituals that accompanied the king's awakening and dressing. Many kings and emperors had adopted the custom, from Charlemagne to Louis XIV. During a levee, the most private became temporarily the most public—only the king's body had the power to accomplish such a wonder. Nonetheless, by the eighteenth century, the levee had lost its former mystical allure and had come to signify a formal reception held by the king, the governor, the prime minister—in short, by the man in charge. Levees turned into regulated public gatherings, usually by invitation only, during which the leader made his persona momentarily accessible to the public within the limits defined by the ritual, which enabled him to remain in control and project a dignified public image.

Washington entertained his selected guests, all men, at levees, that is, during official receptions—John Adams also did it, but Thomas Jefferson did away with the ceremony in 1801. At the beginning of his presidency, Washington held levees twice a week, on Tuesdays and Fridays. A symbolic gesture was attached to these ceremonies. The levee, as Tobias Lear wrote, "gives a dignity to the

President." Through levees, the president presented himself as at once approachable and aloof. In Washington's own words, levees allowed him to strike "a just medium between much state and too great familiarity." The president did not return visits. His persona occupied a different plane that exempted him from reciprocity.[25]

The levees isolated the chief magistrate, although persons who had official business to transact could make their appearance at any time by appointment. When visits were "of a public nature" and the guest "was acting in a public character," then Washington agreed to "let them come to me," he wrote in his diary. Otherwise, the guest, in particular if he was a foreigner, should attend a levee, "when he might be received & treated agreeably." Etiquette of this sort, Washington realized, was essential "to give respect to the Chief Majestrate and the dignity of the Government, which would be lessened if every person who could procure a letter of introduction should be presented otherwise than at Levee hours in a formal manner."[26]

A month or so into his presidency, Washington had already reduced levees from two to one a week, on Tuesday afternoon; at first he began at two o'clock but then, after reconsidering, he moved it to three, and it lasted one hour exactly. While he understood the importance of levees, he nevertheless complained about these "idle and ceremonious visits." He would have preferred to be at Mount Vernon, obviously, "with a friend or two about me, than to be attended at the Seat of Government by the Officers of State and the Representatives of every Power in Europe." He would have preferred to be himself rather than the persona that he, momentarily, had to be.[27]

But despite all his complaints, Washington liked to act his part. A "porter"—an enslaved person dressed in a red-and-white livery, the colors of the Washington family—would show the guest into the room, and Colonel David Humphreys would then loudly announce his name. The visitor would make a bow that was returned by Washington, who stood by the fireplace (the president did not shake hands during levees), and Humphreys would place each guest in a circle around the room. Fifteen minutes after the scheduled time for the levee, doors would close, and the president would begin his tour of the room, from right to left, chatting briefly with each visitor. When finished, the president would go back to the fireplace, where each guest was expected to quickly approach him again, take a bow, and leave. The levee was over forty-five minutes later. No one sat, which made the ceremony more formal—but it was also the case that the room was not large enough to contain chairs for all the guests.[28]

By the fireplace, Washington cut a very distinctive figure. At first, he wore his brown inaugural suit—homespun and antiaristocratic. But he then switched to the black velvet suit—a change he likely in part made because his mother passed away at the end of August 1789 but perhaps also in part because he recognized that the outfit was very dramatic. The deep contrast between the black of the fabric and the white of ruffles and neckwear gave off an ecclesiastical aura.[29]

Washington appeared regal, hieratic, stiff, and less-than-sympathetic witnesses mistook his behavior for an attitude, and a very dangerous one, at that. William Maclay, from rural Pennsylvania, had strong preexisting biases (terming the president, as we recall, "a cold, formal man"). Elected to the United States Senate on March 4, 1789, Maclay soon became a radical member of an antiadministration faction. He didn't like Washington (or Adams, for that matter). In addition, he considered levees "a feature of royalty" and "certainly anti-republican." He could not square rituals such as these with a sterner vision of civic duties within a republican institution. The Boston *Independent Chronicle* echoed Maclay: "Ideas of *foreign pomp*, *parade* and *luxury* are rather to be *spurned*, than *courted* and *fostered* by a young republic, whose simplicity, and purity of manners, should be combined to resist the advances of extravagance and dissipation." The *National Gazette* expressed the same idea, describing Washington's levees as "the legitimate offspring of inequality, begotten by aristocracy and monarchy upon corruption."[30]

They were all mistaken, unable to grasp that it was just a performance designed to impress an audience. In crafting a proper republican style at his "court," Washington had no precedent to draw on. The image of an American republicanism had to be invented. He acted as a ceremonial officer and not on his own personal behalf. The simple fact that he also attended less formal gatherings, such as his wife's receptions, shows that he could relax and enjoy himself.[31]

Martha Washington held these more sociable receptions on Friday evenings, from seven to ten o'clock, which both women and men of social standing attended, even without special invitation—they only had to wear full dress. At Martha's receptions, George presented himself as a "private gentleman." He dressed plainly, without his sword, and mingled with the company. The president and his secretaries made sure each guest received proper attention. He spoke freely, especially with women—because of his situation, it was one of the few opportunities he had to talk to ladies. Martha usually remained seated with one or two close friends. Upon entering, guests approached her, bowed, and exchanged a word or two. They then moved to the next room where food and drinks were offered, including hot tea, coffee, cakes, and candies as well as ice cream and lemonade during the hot months. Guests were merry, moved about freely, and conversations flowed unhampered. Frequently, Martha's "drawing-rooms," as these receptions were also called, were "as much crowded as a Birth Night at St James," Abigail Adams wrote to a friend, "and with company as Briliantly drest, diamonds & great Hoops excepted." Upon leaving, each lady was escorted to the carriage, Washington himself performing this courtesy for Mrs. Greene and Mrs. Montgomery, the widows of the celebrated Revolutionary generals.[32]

Outings

*W*ashington let people see him. Between 1789 and 1791, he took several trips that were political and in a sense promotional—the first was an overland tour in 1789 from Mount Vernon to New York City for his inauguration, the second was a trip through New England in the fall of that year, the third was a visit to Rhode Island in the summer of 1790 right after that state had joined the union, and the fourth was a four-month-log tour of the South in the spring and summer of 1791. He felt he had to take the federal government directly to Americans.

Washington had an uncommon talent for bringing the most diverse people together. By showing himself to the citizens of the country, he could persuade them that, no matter their differences, they shared a common vision. Women, Jewish leaders and textile workers in New England, and many enslaved people in the South greeted the president at his stops. Washington had perfected a ritual for attracting this kind of attention. He would ride through the countryside in an open carriage, with "servants" in their red-and-white liveries and jockey caps. A wagon with the luggage would follow along behind, while one of his trusted men—possibly Giles or Paris—would accompany his white charger at the end of the caravan. The most theatrical part of the performance was when the company approached a town. Washington would get off his carriage, mount the white steed, and then enter with gravity.[33]

The local reception committee usually greeted the president, who, in turn, delivered a short patriotic speech. But more powerful than the speech itself was the image of Washington on his white horse, the saddle set in leopard skin edged with gold braiding. The man's riding skills were already legendary: "Those who have seen *Washington on horseback*," George Washington Parke Custis wrote, "will admit that he was one of the most accomplished of cavaliers in the true sense and perfection of the character." People had been hearing about the miracle of Washington on horseback ever since the end of the French and Indian War, and, therefore, they loved to see that miracle in person. The sight of this public figure validated their faith in the hero and national symbol. (It's common psychology that human beings always look for evidence that confirms their preexisting convictions.)[34]

But Washington made other political outings that were not directed to the masses. He also performed for smaller, more select audiences. These performances were no less studied, no less choreographed than his grand promotional tours. He went to the theater, as we already know, not only to see but to be seen. Similarly, he attended sport events, dinners, clubs, and balls.

At balls, Washington danced—and this, in particular, is revealing of his masculinity. He was not a born dancer, any more than he was a born rider, and we lose track of the real eighteenth-century man if we insist that God or nature gave Washington a unique talent and that he didn't have to do anything else other than exerting that talent. Washington couldn't be a born dancer because in the eighteenth century, for the elite, dancing was hardly an amusement or a pastime. It was an activity requiring study and application, and every rookie could easily end up being laughed out the door. We do not know if Mary Ball Washington paid for dance lessons for her son. In 1748, she paid for lessons with a "musick master," and this same teacher might have taught dance as well. George might have learned the difficult art by watching his brother Lawrence. A more mature and successful man, Washington paid for dance lessons for his nieces, his nephews, and even for his neighbors.[35]

Eighteenth-century doctors recommended dancing as healthy, and everyone agreed that it was a useful expedient for improving posture and good manners. Being able to dance was also seen as a fundamental social asset. From the elite's point of view, balls served the function of bringing together dignitaries, officials, diplomats, and in general people of means—they are the equivalent of today's government receptions, embassy cocktail parties, or military clubs. Learning the rules was painful, however, and certainly time-consuming and expensive. In 1773, one Francis Christian, for instance, held dancing classes in Westmoreland County, Virginia. These classes lasted several days, and the days were long. The newbies began soon after breakfast with minuets. After the minuets, the whole class joined in so-called country dances, which were easier to execute. In both cases, as a witness writes, "it was indeed beautiful to admiration, to see such a number of young persons, set off by dress to the best Advantage, moving easily, to the sound of well performed Music, and with perfect regularity, tho' apparently in the utmost Disorder." The class continued until 7:30 p.m., with breaks for dinner at 3:30 and candle lighting. As a dance teacher, Christian was "punctual, and rigid in his discipline, so strict indeed that he struck two of the young Misses for a fault in the course of their performance, even in the presence of the Mother of one of them!"[36]

James Tilton, a physician and revolutionary war soldier from Delaware, confessed candidly that the ballroom could be scarier than the battlefield, even for a mature man. At the end of 1783, at the State House in Annapolis, Maryland, the governor organized a ball. "Every window was illuminated," and ladies and gentlemen had honed their repertoires. But Tilton didn't dare: "Such was my villainous awkwardness, that I could not venture to dance on this occasion."[37]

Ladies and gentlemen from the top echelon of the local society, together with many strivers, stepped onto the dance floor to flaunt their real or pretended station, prepared to intimidate and to challenge opponents. It was not a friendly, inclusive atmosphere. It was war. As Eliza Bowen Ward wrote of a dancing soiree in Charleston, balls could become the scene of the most reckless competition: "I never desire to be at [this ball] again." She felt she was "*crowded—jamed*—and *mashed* to *pieces*—my head is still in confusion . . . there were upwards of four hundred people in the room." The dancing party described by Eliza Bowen Ward may have been a little unsophisticated and extreme. But the "Dancing Gentry," as Washington in 1769 labeled the people at the top, were there precisely to outdo all other competitors by strokes of elegance rather than by force.[38]

We don't know how or when, but Washington cracked the code of the eighteenth-century dance floor. He succeeded in moving his body with grace and propriety in the framework of a complex choreography, as was expected from any member of the elite. Descriptions of Washington at balls record that "the General danced every set" and that all the ladies had "the pleasure of dancing with him." As president, he opened many balls, "dancing a minuet with some lady" and then dancing "cotillions and country dances." On each occasion, Washington "was very gallant, and always attached himself, by his attentions, to some one or more of the most beautiful and attractive ladies at the balls." Let's not interpret this sexually and romantically, as all this was part of a choreographed social code.[39]

In March 1779, the Philadelphia *Pennsylvania Packet* applauded the graceful way Washington danced a minuet—again, it was a celebration of a social rather than an erotic feat: "When this man unbends from his station, and its weighty functions, he is even then like a philosopher, who mixes with the amusements of the world, that he may teach it what is right, or turn trifles into instruction." Analogously, George Washington Parke Custis describes a ball held in Fredericksburg, about a month after the victory at Yorktown, during which the general danced a minuet with a lady: "The minuet was much in vogue at that period, and was peculiarly calculated for the display of the splendid figure of the chief, and his natural grace and elegance of air and manners."[40]

An intense, slow-moving dance performed by a man and a woman alone on the floor with the rest of the company watching, minuets opened the soiree. The first minuet was performed by the leading man and the most important lady present, and then other couples followed along a descending hierarchical order. The minuets, thus, reminded everyone of his or her position within the group.

In a real eighteenth-century minuet—unlike the fictionalized version we see in movies—no stilted, toe-tapping movement was performed, and no bow or deep curtsey took place. It was all about contained and elegant movements, the distinctive sign of the true elite. Enthusiasm and excitement were not on display; feelings were entirely suppressed. By suppressing and hiding rather than revealing, the minuet aimed at creating an intensity, the promise of a buoyant force, the poised athletic gesture that might explode but never does. Movements were straight or in clear curves, apparently made without effort, and the body did not weave or sway. Should dancers wobble, tilt, or put the other toe on the floor to regain their balance, bystanders would crack up. Reputation would be lost.[41]

Dancers kept their backs as straight as possible and their shoulders down and back. Hands and arms moved without affectation in a seemingly natural and graceful motion. The man hung his arms comfortably at his side, elbows slightly bent to form an attractive curve and palms forward. He also moved his hands delicately throughout the dance. To begin, he gently pressed his thumbs and index fingers together and then separated them about an inch. The other fingers would be kept curved, in line with the index finger. Eye contact with the partner was consistently maintained, except when the couple took two steps forward, a demi-coupé followed by a pas de bourrée, and looked at their audience. Meanwhile, the music was played in three-quarter time in units of six beats or two measures—so it was not like a waltz tempo.

In his account of the ball in Fredericksburg, Custis also describe how "as the evening advanced, the commander-in-chief yielding to the general gayety of the scene, went down some dozen couple in the contre dance with great spirit and satisfaction." Generic country dances were relatively easy to perform, and, for this reason, they were saved for the end of the evening. These dances were democratic rather than hierarchical. Danced by many dancers, partner facing partner, the country dance was contrived in a way that each couple in the line took a turn in the leading position. But even this type of dance was far from an undisciplined romp. It was formal and presentational—quite different, for instance, from the Scottish reel, an impromptu dance for three or four people in a line who sought to display their personal dance skills. (There is no trace in the primary sources that Washington ever danced a reel.)[42]

The cotillion—also called "contredanse," again meaning "country dance"—was a little more complex but not impossible to perform. French dancing masters took the "country dance" to the court of Louis XIV and made it more palatable and refined than its English precedent. Usually performed in a square of four couples, it consisted of a number of standard verses labeled "changes" that were followed by a chorus characteristic of that particular dance. The changes were circles, hand turns, hands across, allemande turns, or rights and lefts. The chorus was repeated after each change. Eight to ten changes could take place. (The cotillion was later replaced by the quadrille or, in the United States, the square dance, but the two dances have a lot in common.)[43]

We cannot presume that Washington ever mastered all the subtleties of eighteenth-century dance, but he learned how to live in a society where an inch in either posture or gesture, in the way one held his hands, or in the way the toe reached the floor, could make a world of difference. And he was brave enough to dance a minuet.

Washington secretly rejoiced when, in 1799, his advancing age provided him with an excuse to turn down an invitation from the Dancing Assembly in Alexandria. This time, he would not partake in the ball at Gadsby's Tavern—he had fought too many battles and risked his reputation on too many occasions already. This time, he could state out loud and without nostalgia that he was done with dancing: "Mrs Washington and myself have been honoured with your polite invitation to the Assemblies in Alexandria, this Winter; and thank you for this mark of your attention. But alas! our dancing days are no more; we wish, however, all those whose relish for so agreeable, & innocent an amusement, all the pleasure the Season will afford them."[44]

13

❧

Consummation

An American Moses

Old Washington didn't sport a white beard and long white hair, but even so he could impersonate authoritative characters, including Nathan the Wise, the Prophet Isaiah, Zeus, and Moses. Washington was conscious of his symbolic strength. He didn't need to move a muscle. In life, he had already become a classic.[1]

Washington worked hard not only on his final persona but also on the stage on which he played it. His temporary residences in New York and Philadelphia were his personal theaters and a space for entertainment. The furniture, the style, the understated elegance constituted a language at once inspiring and intimidating. But Mount Vernon was beyond comparison.

His last stage, Mount Vernon, allowed the American Moses to reach out very effectively. Mount Vernon was not a "private" abode. It was more than a retreat, a sanctuary, a tranquil island in a bitter sea. It was a public venue where scores of people, both free and in chains, worked to keep it up. In 1754, Washington began running the estate built in 1734 by his father Augustine. Over the next forty-five years, he worked diligently to improve it, delivering to the public the twenty-one-room mansion we can still visit today.

Washington supervised every renovation, big and small, from design and construction to decorations and colors, down to every detail. He realized this was the stage posterity would mostly remember.

Mount Vernon was paradoxical in a very material sense. The house near the Potomac was a masterpiece of trompe l'oeil. The rusticated boards, the use of "graining" (cheap local wood turned into mock expensive mahogany), the seeming symmetry, the ha-ha walls, the amazing view from the river, and the equally amazing surprise effect any visitor got when approaching the estate from the old road that ran west to east—all these factors communicated a studied stagecraft.

Mount Vernon was a theater or "a well resorted tavern," as Washington said with a dash of wit, "as scarcely any strangers who are going from north to south, or from south to north do not spend a day or two at it." "So many come here without *proper* introductions," he remarked on another occasion. But despite all the grumbles, he accepted the public nature of the place he lived in and understood that it enabled him to project a certain image. "I have no objection to any sober, & orderly person's gratifying their curiosity in viewing the buildings, Gardens &ca about Mount Vernon," he wrote in 1794. (Obviously, uncouth or rough interlopers beyond the pale of "common civility & hospitality" were not welcome.) Visitors, neighbors, friends, and strangers alike flocked there. Between 1768 and 1775, for example, Mount Vernon entertained about two thousand guests. And for many of them it was not a quick visit. They lingered for days, were fed, and accommodated at the expense of the master of the house. Many visited repeatedly.[2]

The thousands of visitors must have reacted in the same way Winthrop Sargent and Richard Platt did. Sargent and Platt arrived at Mount Vernon on Saturday, October 12, 1793, and departed two days later. They treated themselves to a long weekend, surely one of the most memorable of their lives. The "elegant and Courtly appearance" of the house with its bowling green and sheep grazing the lawn, as Sargent recorded in his diary, was a spectacle in itself. It was further magnified by the spectacular road that led to the mansion. "Immediately upon our Arrival," Sargent wrote, "the President . . . came in and was pleased to shew us much Civility." The whole setting, the furniture, and the dinner "served up in a plain frugal Style" left a lasting impression of understated elegance and republican simplicity. "The glass," of course, "circulated . . . in sufficient Freedom," which always helps to elevate the spirits.[3]

By the 1790s, Washington had perfected one of his most successful roles. At home, he was the old man "worn out" by the "toils" of his "past labour" and "again seated" under his "Vine & Fig tree." There was no escapism, pessimism, or cynicism in those sentiments. Washington did not renounce acting "manly" and being politically relevant. Not only was he ready to fight again, as we will see in a moment, but he was also willing to broadcast enticing national visions of biblical scale: "A Century hence, if this Country keep united . . . will produce a City—though not as large as London—yet of a magnitude inferior to few others in Europe, on the Banks of the Potomack; . . . A situation not excelled for commanding prospect, good water, salubrious air, and safe harbour by any in the world; & where elegant buildings are erecting & in forwardness, for the reception of Congress in the year 1800."[4]

Washington claimed that he wished "to spend the remainder of my days (which cannot be many) in rural amusements—free from those cares which public responsibility is never exempt," but this was not literally true; rather, he was performing the role of old man seated under his vine and fig trees at Mount Vernon. It was an extreme version of republican self-effacement. By strategically emphasizing the fact that he was old—which he certainly was—he hoped to remain relevant and in control. He retained his authority and masculinity in the very act of declaring his lack of physical strength. He was still masculine, if not so muscular.[5]

The theme of the old man has both real and symbolic aspects to it; it is suspended between history and mythology. Washington had started practicing for this role in his early fifties—an indication that he had long been emotionally attracted the idea of a nonmuscular masculinity. At the beginning of 1784, for example, he had written to Lafayette about how happy he was, "a private citizen on the banks of the Potomac, & under the shadow of my own Vine & my own Fig tree, free from the bustle of a camp & the busy scenes of public life." He was posing, a little prematurely, as the old man, a Cincinnatus, a Stoic sage, a blind seer, a Moses. He pretended he was solacing himself "with those tranquil enjoyments," but he was actually networking, planning the destiny of the new nation, and considering further action. Indeed, his presidency was yet to come. However, the tunic he was symbolically donning pitched the diametrically opposite message: "I am not only retired from all public employments, but I am retireing within myself; & shall be able to view the solitary walk, & tread the paths of private life with heartfelt satisfaction—Envious of none, I am determined to be pleased with all. & this my dear friend, being the order for my march, I will move gently down the stream of life, until I sleep with my Fathers."[6]

Because of its many seeds, figs have always stood for fertility and life as well as for peace and prosperity, rootedness, and a strong sense of community—and both vines and fig trees bear fruit only after a long and undisturbed time. Accordingly, the house where the vine and the fig tree grow was an abode of hospitality and good neighborliness. Washington hoped that every man would eventually sit safely "under his vine and under his fig tree." The metaphor came to Washington from Micah 4:4, 1 Kings 4:25, and Zechariah 3:10. No doubt, this was one of his favorite scriptural phrases; he employed it on nearly fifty occasions during the second half of his life. The metaphor not only anticipated or celebrated his personal retirement to Mount Vernon but spoke of utopian national visions and ideals of masculinity.[7]

Whether through references to the vine and fig tree or the sword turned plowshare (another biblical phrase he often deployed), Washington presented himself as the old sage. Nations "shall beat their swords into ploughshares, and their spears into pruninghooks: nation shall not lift up sword against nation, neither shall they learn war any more," we read in Isaiah 2:4. Washington agreed completely: "Your young military men, who want to reap the ha[r]vest of laurels," he wrote to the Marquis de Chastellux, "dont care (I suppose) how many seeds of war are sown." Washington, assuming the opposite posture, cared for all of humanity: "For the sake of humanity it is devoutly to be wished that the manly employment of agriculture and the humanizing benefits of commerce would supersede the waste of war and the rage of conquest." It was not self-deception, because a wish can trigger momentous transformations: "the swords might be turned into plough-shares, the spears into pruning hooks—and, as the Scripture expresses it, the nations learn war no more."[8]

The metaphors of the vine and fig tree and the sword turned plowshare helped Washington to highlight the opposition between old age and young, experience and immaturity, wisdom and foolishness, reason and passion. He emphasized that while the old sage may be blind and physically weak, he sees beyond self-interest; he prefers to give rather than receive. Whereas the hyperactive, muscular young man spends his "watchful days & sleepless Nights," as Washington wrote to Lafayette, "in devising schemes to promote the welfare of his own—perhaps the ruin of other countries, as if this Globe was insufficient for us all," the old man has grasped a superior truth. He sits under his vine and fig tree; his gaze encompasses the whole planet; he is no longer hindered by his egotism and petty subjectivity.[9]

Perhaps the most successful among the famous old sages was Moses. When Washington is described as Moses, it is almost always with a facile and meaningless celebratory intention that overlooks the excellent coup de théâtre that Washington as Moses constituted. This American Moses, just like the Moses of the Hebrews, had also served his nation ably in both military and civilian capacities. They had both offered their people sagacious counsel. Washington, however, was not a modern Moses. He should not be decontextualized and turned into a biblical type—or into any type, for that matter. Washington was not Moses, but he keenly played the role of Moses. Intentionally and with considerable shrewdness, Washington used his persona to promote his political ideas. Washington worked hard to be seen by his fellow Americans as old, wise, and above the fray. But he remained more than ready to jump into the arena again.[10]

~ In 1798, as the winds of war intensified, Washington decided to don, once again, the costume of the general, putting his Moses temporarily on hold. This time, it was more than acting and pretending. In 1797, President John Adams had dispatched three ministers to Paris to negotiate a commercial agreement to protect American shipping. Unexpectedly, three French agents approached the American ministers and suggested a bribe and a loan of $10,000,000 to be paid to France as a prelude to negotiations. By April 1798, the machinations of the three French agents (called X, Y, and Z in the diplomatic correspondence) were made public in the United States. The outcry was vast, although President Adams managed to avert war—one of his greatest achievements. Nevertheless, he at the same time prepared for an invasion and asked old Washington to serve once again in a military capacity.[11]

Washington was at once thrilled and puzzled. On the Fourth of July, 1798, with the consent of the Senate, President Adams had issued a proclamation appointing him "*Lieutenant General and Commander in Chief of all the Armies raised or to be raised for* the service of the United States." Washington replied directly to John Adams with a letter of acceptance. "I cannot express how greatly affected I am at this New proof of public confidence," he wrote. He was old—not only playing the old man—and declared that he would have much preferred if "the choice had fallen upon a man less declined in years and better qualified to encounter the usual vicissitudes of War." At first, Washington didn't know what to do. He was at Mount Vernon, retired for good, and wearing his Moses getup. From his "present peaceful abode," Washington experienced "Sensations"—which means mixed feelings—at the prospect of entering, "at so late a period of life," the "boundless field of public action—incessant trouble—and high responsibility." And yet he accepted.[12]

Washington was cognizant of the strenuous efforts President Adams had made to prevent war. So he may have accepted the commission only because he was betting on the improbability of another war on American soil. However, he did start right away to prepare for his last public role. He had to hone his military persona, revive his role as an active general and put that of the biblical Moses aside.

There was the bigger picture, naturally—the army, its organization, the logistics, the chain of command, recruitment, officers, soldiers, supplies. But there were also "smaller matters," as he labeled them, "meriting consideration." What should be "the clothing of the Regiments, and the fashion of that clothing" and how should "distinctions between one Regiment and another" be preserved? "Would not cotton, or (still more so) Flannel be advisable for shirting, and linings for the Soldiery?" "What had best be the distinctions in dress, in the badges—and other peculiarities, between the Commander in Chief and his Suit, and the Majors General & their Aids?" Should soldiers, or at least officers of superior rank, wear a cockade? That might be smart: "I have seen, and it appeared to have no bad effect, a small Eagle (of Pewter, tin, & in some instances silver) fixed by way of Button in the center of a rose cockade; which was not only very distinguishable, but somewhat characteristic."[13]

The figure of the supreme commander occupied most of Washington's attention. He knew that this was likely to be his last public role. Washington mulled over his uniform as if it were a question of life and death. How to deal with embroidery? "On re-considering the Uniform for the Commander in Chief," he wrote to Secretary of War James McHenry, "it has become a matter of doubt with me—(although, as it respected myself, *personally*, I was against *all* Embroidery)—whether embroidery on the Cape, Cuffs and Pockets of the Coat—and none on the *Buff* waistcoat, would not have a disjointed, and aukward appearance." And he could not decide whether the coat should "have slash Cuffs (with blue flaps passing through them) and slash pockets." Washington had not turned into a molly and a fop. But self-presentation was a critical issue for the old man—particularly so as his physique was inexorably dwindling. He maintained a clear mind: "These, apparently, are trifling matters to trouble you with; but, as it is the commencement of a New Scene, it is desirable that the thing should take a right direction."[14]

Washington duly sent precise instructions to James McAlpin, his tailor in Philadelphia. At that critical moment for the country, the aging Washington felt he had to transform himself by donning a new uniform. It was pure theater once more: "Let your blue cloth be of the best & softest French or Spanish; and the finest you can procure, of a deep colour. And the Buff of the very best sort, fine, & not inclining to yellow or Orange. . . . The buttons are to be plain, flat, and of the best double gilt." The buff waistcoat had to be "straight breasted, that is without lapels. and the Cuffs of the Coat neither large, nor tight; observing a just medium between the two."[15]

Washington realized he would be remembered and undoubtedly memorialized by painters as the general who became an American Moses and then a general again, a peculiar Cincinnatus who could wield and relinquish power at pleasure. War didn't come, fortunately, but Washington couldn't know this at the time. He wrote again to the secretary of war in February, underscoring the historic importance of the uniform: "Being the commencement of a distinguishing dress for the Commander in Chief of the armies of the United States . . . and probably will be a permanent one— my wish . . . is, that it may be correctly executed." Dozens of letters were exchanged among Washington, McHenry, and McAlpin regarding Washington's uniform. On May 12 he wrote to his tailor to ask him to "send on my Uniform Suit so soon as the gold thread, which you informed me was expected in the Spring shipping, should have arrived," while on June 7, he informed the secretary of war that "the Stars for my Epaulets have stood suspended & I would thank you for sending them to me." It would be wonderful, he concluded, to get hold of the uniform "by the Anniversary of our Independence," July 4, 1799.[16]

The last uniform was what Washington thought he would bequeath to future generations, his last impression. Ironically, he would die too soon preparing for a war that was not meant to be. No one would ever see old Washington-Moses in his gilded uniform. On September 30, 1800, the French and the Americans signed the Treaty of Mortefontaine. Hostilities between France and the United States ceased and trade ties between the two nations resumed. And the commander in chief, an American Moses resplendent in his hypothetical last uniform, was already dead.

The Fragility and Regrets of an Old Man

Washington was not a "beautiful soul" and never tried to disguise himself as a saint—he knew he was a slaveowner, at that. But he cared for his reputation or "character," in the language of the period. While for us, character is a disposition, a psychological makeup, the final label stitched on our personality, the sum of moral and mental qualities defining an individual, the capacity to control one's urges, or the ability to withstand adverse circumstances, for Washington's contemporaries, character was how one looked through other people's eyes. Character was thus a public performance, an aspect of the self that was always actualized in society.

Eighteenth-century men and women, principally of higher rank, watched themselves constantly through the eyes of others. When a person was brought into society, as Adam Smith famously wrote, he or she was "immediately provided with the mirror." Every person was "placed in the countenance and behaviour of those he lives with." A decision, a choice, or a gesture gone bad could ruin a person's character forever.[17]

Washington feared for his character. Since July 16, 1775, the day he accepted his appointment as commander in chief of the Continental Army, Washington had grave misgivings about being equal to the task. He worried "that my abilities & Military experience may not be equal to the extensive & important Trust." But he was perhaps even more concerned about losing his character. "Remember," he told Patrick Henry, "what I now tell you: From the day I enter upon the command of the American armies, I date my fall, and the ruin of my reputation." From that moment on, he risked his reputation on countless other adventures, from literal battles— Long Island, Kip's Bay, Harlem Heights, White Plains, Fort Washington, Fort Lee, Trenton, Princeton, Brandywine, Germantown, White Marsh, Monmouth, Yorktown—to the no less dangerous metaphorical battles of his presidency. Washington didn't win all his battles, for sure, but he never fell. He saved his character.[18]

He saved his reputation because he acted sensibly. He took care of his "papers," his bulky correspondence and countless other documents. In part, he did it himself over the course of his lifetime, purging what he thought might compromise his reputation. He also hired clerks, secretaries, and copyists. He gave his wife Martha directions to destroy documents they thought were too personal. He also planned to build a repository at Mount Vernon, "for the accommodation & security of my Military, Civil & private Papers, which are voluminous and may be interesting." (The building was not constructed by the time of his death.) Washington's papers were constantly on his mind. On his deathbed, his breath departing, he instructed Tobias Lear to "arrange & record all my late Military letters & papers—arrange my accounts & settle my books."[19]

However, Washington couldn't edit out the fact that he owned other human beings. That he was born into a system he did not contrive, that he couldn't abolish it singlehandedly, and that he changed his general attitude as he matured—from silent acceptance to a more vocal criticism of the "peculiar institution"—don't make the blot on his character less noticeable. Washington knew that slavery was wrong and, consequently, that history would not absolve him. He owned and read books about slavery and emancipation—he was an informed participant who did his due diligence, although no eighteenth-century individual needed to be a genius or even to peruse books on the subject to be able to see that slavery was a scandal in every respect. In 1774, commenting on the so-called Intolerable Acts legislated by the British Parliament after the Boston Tea Party, Washington had warned Bryan Fairfax that the British were about to "make us as tame, & abject Slaves, as the Blacks we Rule over with such arbitrary Sway."[20]

Slavery's weight was not great enough to cause a shift in his personal balance once and for all and prompt him to act, without regard for the consequences. Fears for his long-term reputation notwithstanding, in February 1793, when the House of Representatives passed the Fugitive Slave Act (by a vote of forty-eight to seven, with fourteen abstaining), President Washington signed it right away. The act defined any assistance given to "fugitives" seeking to escape the horrors of slavery as a federal crime, thus making it possible for slaveowners to reclaim their "property" across state lines. Washington knew that this law dehumanized enslaved persons even further by making the one method by which they might realize their "unalienable rights" to life, liberty, and the pursuit of happiness illegal. National concerns were more important than his reputation and his personal inclinations, apparently.

From a strictly economic point of view, furthermore, slavery didn't work: "Half the workers," Washington eventually realized, "would render me a greater *nett* profit" if they were paid for their labors. He told friends and correspondents about his plan to get rid of slavery at Mount Vernon. (He took the first step in this direction in the 1760s, when he decided to shift from tobacco to wheat, a less labor-consuming staple.) Upon hearing of the project to "get rid of all your Negroes," correspondents complimented him on a course of action that would "give the finishing stroke & the last polish to your political characters." But not much came of this ambitious project. The citizen-master kept the inefficient economic organization rolling, right through to the end.[21]

Slavery was a dilemma for the nation at large, and Washington thus reasoned that it could only be tackled by politicians, not by private citizens: "I hope it will not be conceived from these observations, that it is my wish to hold the unhappy people, who are the subject of this letter, in slavery," he wrote Robert Morris in 1786. "There is not a man living who wishes more sincerely than I do, to see a plan adopted for the abolition of it—but there is only one proper and effectual mode by which it can be accomplished, & that is by Legislative authority."[22]

Morally, Washington was uncomfortable. That his owning slaves was at odds with the "justice of the Creator" bothered him. "The unfortunate condition of the persons, whose labour in part I employed, has been the only unavoidable subject of regret," Washington told David Humphreys while taking stock of his achievements and failures. He thought he had made the life of enslaved persons less terrible, and that "afforded some satisfaction to my mind." He believed he had made "the Adults among them [the enslaved persons] as easy & as comfortable in their circumstances

as their actual state of ignorance & improvidence would admit."
He also believed he had changed the minds of enough legislators
and politicians that "a foundation to prepare the rising generation
for a destiny different from that in which they were born" had been
laid.[23]

Washington had undeniably made a difference. He launched a
powerful signal, for example, when he wrote in his will that, upon
Martha's death, the 123 individuals he personally owned, out of a
population of 317, had to be set free—"manumitted" was the term.
But whether he entirely believed he had done enough to save his
reputation and to appease his conscience and the wrath of God
remains an open question.[24]

In his heart, George Washington understood that the people
he and his peers had put in shackles were not generic "slaves," vari-
ables within the national political layout, economic units to be used
to maximize profitability. As the one in charge of Mount Vernon
for more than forty years, he had known as many as three generations of the same enslaved families. He grasped that these people
were just like him—just like you and me. Had Washington really
believed that his chattel were subhuman, he wouldn't have bothered about maintaining a minimum level of humanity, by, for instance, not separating enslaved families: "It is much against my
inclination as it can be against your's," he had written to John Mercer, "to hurt the feelings of those unhappy people by a separation
of man and wife, or of families." (We have seen already that Washington did not always remain faithful to the principle.)[25]

All slaveowners knew, in the deep of their souls, that these people had personalities, hopes and dreams, and plans for their lives;
that these persons could experience love, joy, shame, fear. In the
words of Patrick Henry, slaveholding was an "abominable practice"
that Christians should feel ashamed of: "I will not, I cannot justify
it," Henry declared. Such a "species of violence and tyranny" was
antithetical to the teachings of the Bible and to basic humanity.

No valid excuse could ever be crafted; no slaveowner could ever become an example for others to imitate.[26]

❧ One morning, at the end of February 1785, Washington went to Belvoir, on the west bank of the Potomac. Belvoir had been the theater of so many "pleasing scenes." It was there that he had spent the "happiest moments" of his life. But Belvoir was no more. "I took a ride there the other day to visit the ruins—& ruins indeed they are," he wrote to his distant friends, Sarah Cary Fairfax and her husband George William, who had fled America before the turmoil of the War of Independence. Time wreaks havoc and devours buildings as well as human beings and everything in its path. It takes no prisoners.[27]

Old Washington, with his well-motivated concerns for his "character," didn't become a heap of rubble and ruins like Belvoir, but he didn't escape the effects of time. The Moses seated under his vine and fig tree and the general resplendent in his hypothetical last uniform had a much less heroic flipside, the actual frail old man.

Washington never tried to hide from the public view the less-than-enticing spectacle of his aging body and his diminished figure. As the years went by, his strength and vigor dwindled. His body abandoned him. But Washington did not lose his manly self-confidence and his virility—an indication that perhaps he had never wanted to build his masculine persona around an explosive physicality in the way many Washington enthusiasts seem to think.

As he grew older, Washington did not become cantankerous and cynical, frustrated and desperate, a counterexample to himself. Old Washington remained entirely Washington, upright and inspired, attentive and orderly. The way he dealt with himself as an old man was in line with the eighteenth-century canon. He kept up the artful mastery over one's manners and conduct, relying on self-control and self-discipline as the classical legacy of republicanism and stoicism dictated.

But Washington's body betrayed him rather prematurely—and it wasn't just his teeth that gave him trouble. We can set the "official" date when George Washington became old with nearly scientific precision. In late August 1786, he was hit by "fever and ague"—malaria. Aches and pain seized his body for more than six months, almost continuously. At the end of March 1787, he still lamented that he could not even "raise my hand to my head or turn myself in bed." It was a severe blow to his physique, a condition from which he never fully recovered. It was *the* point of no return. Upon seeing Washington after he had apparently recovered from this bout, one Fredericksburg resident observed that "the Gen[era]l is much altered in his person one arm swung with Rheumatism."[28]

Washington came out of his 1786–87 encounter with malaria with a new self-awareness. In early January 1787, his brother John Augustine had died suddenly from "a fit of the Gout in the head." This provided confirmation of a theory Washington had been mulling over for a few years: "Though I was blessed with a good constitution," he had written Lafayette in 1784, "I was of a short lived family." Indeed, his father and two of his half brothers didn't make it to fifty. Accordingly, Washington expected to die soon, "entombed in the dreary mansions of my father's."[29]

From there, to borrow the words he used in his letter to Lafayette, he began "descending the hill." On April 30, 1789, at Federal Hall in New York, he was sworn in as president. He had worked with David Humphreys to draft the inaugural address. Washington, at first, had planned to jest about his situation as an old man. He wanted to rehearse, verbatim, the same theme of his 1783 speech ("I have grown not only gray, but almost blind"). He intended to say the following: "I have prematurely grown old in the Service of my Country." But he realized that bystanders were about to behold an actual old man. So, Washington didn't crack the joke—because, this time, it would not be a joke. Congressman Fisher Ames of Massachusetts was there on that historic last day of April. And he couldn't help but notice that "time" had "made havoc" on Washington's face and entire persona.[30]

Medically, Washington was not doing well. Those who saw him at close range or who tried to strike a conversation noticed a sweeping physical decline. One year into his presidency, he may have been "in more good humor than I ever saw him," as Senator Maclay wrote. But Washington was "so deaf that I believe he heard little of the conversation." At times, Washington rationalized and minimized his decline. He thought that his physical setbacks were only temporary and owed to the great difference between his previous life as a farmer or a military commander and his life as president: "My late change from active scenes, to which I had been accustomed, and in which the mind has been agreeably amused, to the one of inactivity which I now lead, and where the thoughts are continually on the stretch, has been the cause of more illness and severe attacks of my constitution, within the last twelve months, than I had undergone in 30 years preceding put together." It was an enduring change, however, and an irreversible one.[31]

The June 1789 tumor on his left thigh was only the beginning. In the spring of 1790, he was struck by a bout of influenza and pneumonia that permanently affected both his hearing and eyesight—hence, Maclay's comment on the president's deafness. Washington could have died, of course. But he recovered, although it took time: "I still feel the remains of the violent affection of my lungs," he confided to Dr. David Stuart in mid-June, "the cough, pain in my breast, and shortness in breathing not having entirely left me." In early September, during Congress's recess, Washington set off for Mount Vernon, the place he yearned for, where he and Martha remained for about two months. Frances Bassett, Martha Washington's niece, was there to greet the presidential couple, her beloved ones. She was happy to see them, but she had a painful feeling of premonition, a sense that the arrow of time could not be reversed. She wrote to her father: "the President looks better than I expected to see him, but still there be traces in his countenance of His two last severe illnesses, which I fear will never wear off."[32]

In 1791, Maclay again dined with the president. He couldn't help noticing Washington's "lax appearance": "His motions rather slow than lively. . . . His complexion pale, nay, almost cadaverous. His voice hollow and indistinct." Moreover, Washington had lost weight: "His frame would seem to want filling up."[33]

His "sedentary" presidential life in New York and, later, in Philadelphia didn't help. James Madison confirms that "the fatigues & disagreeableness of his situation were in fact scarcely tolerably to him." Washington would have much preferred to rush to Mount Vernon, "take his spade in his hand, and work for his bread." It was not a disingenuous exercise in self-effacement. The scenario of a second term in office scared him. He feared that four more years of such a life would deliver the coup de grace.[34]

But Washington kept going, even taking up the much-dreaded second term. Contemporaries realized there was something patently wrong. He "seemed considerably older." At sixty-four, Washington revealed an unmistakable and disquieting "aged appearance." It was likely due to the "innumerable vexations he has met with in his different public capacities"—two wars and the many public offices. These experiences "very sensibly impaired the vigour of his constitution." When he was fully dressed, he looked younger; "the hand of art" could compensate for "the ravages of time." But this was a theatrical illusion only.[35]

In March 1797, he retired. It was long overdue. He rushed back to his vine and fig tree. By the time Washington resettled at Mount Vernon, he was almost totally deaf. Deafness did not affect his spirit, however. At the end of 1797, from Mount Vernon, Martha Washington sent a letter to Elizabeth Willing Powel, their trusted friend in Philadelphia, that has the merit of making visible the most delicate phase of Washington's life and that reveals how he could make light of his old age and joke about his ailments:

I am now, by desire of the general, to add a few words on his behalf; which he desires may be expressed in the terms following, that is to say,—that despairing of hearing what may be said of him, if he should really go off in an apoplectic or any other fit (for he thinks all fits that issue in death are worse than a love fit, a fit of laughter, and many other kinds which he could name) he is glad to hear *beforehand,* what will be said of him on that occasion; conceiving that nothing extra: will happen between *this* and *then,* to make a change in his character for better, or for worse—and besides, as he has entered into an engagement with Mr. Morris and several other gentlemen not to quit the theatre of this world before the year 1800, it may be *relied upon,* that no breach of contract shall be laid to him on that account; unless dire necessity should bring it about maugre [malgré, despite] all his exertions to the contrary. In that case, he shall hope they would do by him, as he would by them, excuse it:—at present there seems to be no danger of his giving them the slip, as neither his health, nor spirits, were ever in greater flow, notwithstanding he adds, he is descending, and has almost reached the bottom of the hill;— or in other words, the shades below.[36]

Unfortunately, Washington would bid adieu to the theater of this world before 1800—he would miss the goal by only a handful of days. At the dawn of 1798, his humor and playfulness about his personal condition also faltered. In February, Washington for the first time conceded he had difficulty in riding his horse: "Impracticable to use the exercise (on horseback) which my health, business & inclination requires." Since the horse, in the Virginia mentality, was what made a man a man, it was a blow for him. He felt a little emasculated. Of course, he didn't quit riding. (In less than two years, he would meet his fate right after dismounting his horse.)[37]

By the end of 1798, Washington realized that the end was near. Friends and doctors issued warnings and guidelines. He thanked them: "I thank you for the trouble you have taken in delivering your thoughts on the means of preserving health." But there was little he could or would do: "Against the effect of time, and age, no remedy has ever yet been discovered; and like the rest of my fellow mortals, I must (if life is prolonged) submit, & be reconciled, to a gradual decline."[38]

Dust to dust: time is never a friend to individual lives, no matter whether they are patriots or loyalists, tall or short, villains or heroes.

14

❧

Giants Die as Well

He Found He Was Going

Among the relics of George Washington preserved in the Museum at Mount Vernon, there is a banyan. The banyan, also known as morning gown, India gown, or dressing gown, is a loose-fitting robe based on the Japanese kimono. Back in the day, it could be used as nightwear—that is, before going to bed, rarely for sleeping. More often, one wore it as an informal garment during the day—over the shirt, waistcoat, and breeches—while studying, casually entertaining guests, or at the gambling table. It could be paired with slippers and a cap. In sultry climates, such as Virginia's, it could also become summer wear to be sported outdoors.

But this gown is stained with brownish/reddish spots. It is said to be Washington's blood, the upshot of a reckless bloodletting right before he died. While it is certain that during the hours before he died Washington was put in and taken out of bed, dressed and undressed, there is no decisive evidence that he wore this very banyan on his deathbed. Perhaps no witness thought it worth mentioning what he was wearing, it being such a mundane detail. The garment shows significant wear, which tells us that it was one of Washington's favorites. So, even though we can't know whether he wore this

Washington's banyan,
ca. 1780–99. Courtesy of
Mount Vernon Ladies'
Association, Mount Vernon,
VA.

exact banyan, we may picture the dying Washington dressed—or rather undressed—in such homely apparel. This was the last way this complex man was seen. During his last moments, Washington asked for solace. His hand was held and kissed. And he held hands. He didn't resemble a titan or even an American Moses.

Tobias Lear, who had been Washington's trusted secretary since 1786, was at the scene. He wrote a detailed account of what happened during those two fateful days, December 12 to 14, 1799. Lear's

"Last Illness and Death of General Washington," the standard text on the subject, is not a comprehensive report. Certainly, Lear played down the most agonizing elements, the less-than-heroic aspects that go along with dying a painful death. But the text vibrates with the sense that those events were unexpected and that everyone was just trying to cope with something big and ominous. Lear also sent a letter to his mother that faithfully repeats the account—and he asked her to keep that letter private.[1]

But let's start from the beginning, the beginning of the end. Thursday, December 12, 1799: after a horse ride in sleet and snow, the sixty-seven-year-old Washington went home for dinner but made the wrong decision to not change out of his damp clothes. It was about 3 p.m. already and his family and friends had been waiting for him. He did not want to appear impolite. As a consequence, he dined as he was and then retired to his room.

The next morning, Friday, December 13, Washington showed signs of a cold. He complained of a sore throat. Despite the bad weather, he again went out in the afternoon to mark some trees he wanted to cut down. By the evening, he was very hoarse but still in relatively good spirits, and he insisted on reading out loud to Martha and Tobias Lear, cherry-picking from the newspapers and sharing amusing pieces. He was cheerful, lingering in the cozy parlor well after 9 p.m., the chimney in full blaze. When he was preparing to go to his room, Lear advised him to take a medication, but Washington refused, treating his illness as if it were a passing ailment: "You know I never take anything for a cold," he said. "Let it go as it came," Washington decreed.[2]

Saturday, December 14, at 2 or 3 a.m., he woke Martha and said he was very unwell. Washington breathed with difficulty. Early in the morning, almost unable to make a sound, he sent for Lear. Lear rushed in and called on Albin Rawlins, an overseer, because Washington wanted to be bled before the doctors arrived. Meanwhile, a mixture of molasses, vinegar, and butter arrived from the kitchen.

The concoction was meant to ease the burning in his throat, but, unsurprisingly, Washington could not swallow a single drop.

After sunrise, Rawlins arrived. Out of the blue, he was informed he was the one expected to bleed the patient—a task he was not eager to perform. Washington realized Rawlins was nervous. With his croaky, flimsy voice, he managed to say: "Don't be afraid." But Rawlins was definitely afraid, and the way he cut the arm seemed substandard. Washington chided him: "The orifice is not large enough." The blood, however, ran freely. Martha was not positive that drawing blood was the best thing to do in such a circumstance and called for a stop. But Washington disagreed: "More, more!," he said. We know that Martha was objectively right and that all the measures that had been taken so far—such as wrapping Washington's neck with a damp piece of flannel, plus bathing his feet in warm water—could not have been very helpful. But those experts, Washington included, thought otherwise. And they persevered.[3]

Rawlins's incision let out a half a pint of blood, perhaps twelve ounces. When Dr. Craik arrived, at 9 or 9:30 a.m., he took more, another eighteen ounces or so. But Dr. Craik also performed a vesiculation, which means that he blistered Washington by applying a blistering agent. Since the problem was located somewhere in the throat, he put the vesicant directly on the part. The substance Dr. Craik used was cantharides, a popular remedy at the time, believed to forestall many maladies, from hysteria to gout, inflammation, malignant fevers, and insanity, and as we recall, Washington had already used it in lower concentration as an aphrodisiac. Obtained from the Spanish Fly, the powder, mixed with some gloopy paste and then spread with a brush, raised a watery blister on the skin that was subsequently cut open and eventually dressed with muslin and oil or some other substance. The blister was meant to drain bad fluids, or humors. However, cantharidin, the active component of cantharides, is highly toxic—an inhibitor of the protein phosphatase 2A. It can easily trigger unwelcome side effects, such as ulcers, the bleeding of mucosa, gastrointestinal bleeding, acute tubular necrosis, and organ failure. Affecting the airways and easily absorbed through the skin and lungs, cantharidin commonly produces respiratory distress. No further comment is necessary.[4]

As if the blister was not enough, Dr. Craik administered a "gargle of Vinegar, & sage tea" to Washington. He also had him inhale the vapors of vinegar and hot water. The patient obeyed, but the gargle almost suffocated him. When Washington spat it back, some "phlegm" was in it—the thick mucus produced in the throat and lungs that can show traces of blood, or hemoptysis. It was seen as a very good sign. Washington wanted to cough and expel some more phlegm, but he wasn't able to do it.[5]

Breathing had become difficult. At about 11 a.m., Dr. Craik bled Washington again. One hour later, he was given a "glister"—an old term for enema—and evacuation followed, which only served to worsen his dehydration. Dr. Elisha Dick and Dr. Gustavus Brown arrived between 3 and 4 p.m. The three doctors consulted and decided to bleed him again. Nearly thirty-two ounces were taken, and this time, "the blood came very slow, was thick"—a probable indication of dehydration and hypovolemia. At about 4:30 p.m., George called Martha to his bedside and gave her instructions about the last will—which copy she should keep and which one she should destroy. Lear took Washington's hand. The dying man said: "I find I am going."[6]

Lying in his bed, Washington couldn't find respite. Since the early morning, he had been uneasy and restless and yet grateful for the attention he received. At 8 a.m., he had wanted to get up. He was dressed and seated by the fireplace. By 10 a.m., he was undressed and put again in bed. At 5 p.m., he was helped up one more time. Half an hour later, he was once more undressed and put in bed. Meanwhile, Washington kept asking what hour it was. At about 8 p.m., the doctors applied blisters and cataplasms to his legs and feet. But they had lost hope. Between 10 and 11 p.m., his breathing had become easier. Washington seemed calmer. His countenance suddenly changed. He died. Seated at the foot of the bed, Martha asked, "Is he gone?" Lear couldn't speak but only moved his hand to signal. Martha wilted a little and said, "'Tis well."[7]

᠊᠍᠊᠍᠊ Washington's body was not made of steel. It could not withstand the medical ordeal of the last two days. Washington's doctors didn't think they were doing harm. They regarded bleeding, vesiculation, and enema as necessary treatments. The eighteenth-century view of how the body functioned is much different from the way we now understand our bodies. That body was not defined as an organism, a closed, self-sufficient, and self-governing system. It was rather seen as porous and permeable, open in all its parts to the environment. The body was an element in a cosmological network of sympathetic linkages and dependencies that went far beyond its own borders. Diseases, in turn, were not specific, as we consider them today—symptoms *were* the illness. They were disturbances among the four humors (blood, phlegm, black bile, and yellow bile). Therefore, logically, eighteenth-century physicians simply tried to restore the "harmony." To achieve harmony, they deployed generous doses of purgatives, vomitives, blistering agents, and a lot of bloodletting.[8]

In about twelve hours, Washington's body had been bled at least four times—decidedly too many. He lost approximately five pints of blood, nearly half of a human body's capacity. Horrific though this "therapy" appears to us, it made sense at the time. Across the globe, bloodletting has remained an established medical treatment for more than two millennia. The theoretical justification for bloodletting was intuitive and simple—too simple. Bleeding was the most expeditious way to remove diseased matter from the body. Bloodletting evacuated "poisonous" elements and reestablished harmony.[9]

Besides Martha, only Dr. Dick was against the excessive bloodletting. He also advised a tracheostomy—making an opening in the throat to bypass the obstruction and allow Washington to breathe. But Dr. Craik and Dr. Brown, who knew better, overruled him. Physicians did perform tracheostomy in the eighteenth century, but the procedure carried a high level of risk.[10]

When Dr. William Thornton, a friend and the architect of the new Capitol building in the city of Washington, heard about Washington's dire condition, he rushed to Mount Vernon. He had the "fullest confidence of being able to relieve him, by tracheotomy." He arrived on Sunday, too late. "The best friend I had on Earth" was already lying in the freezing drawing room, better known as New Room. But Thornton didn't want to surrender. Resurrecting Wash-

The "New Room." Courtesy of Mount Vernon Ladies' Association, Mount Vernon, VA.

ington didn't seem a quaint idea to him. Thornton had studied sleep, stupor, and resuscitation. And he was familiar with persons and animals reviving from (apparent) death. He knew of people breathing again after drowning, of fishes thawing out after freezing, of frogs waking up again after being sealed in trees. Thornton had a plan: "First to thaw him in cold water, then to lay him in blankets, and by degrees and by friction to give him warmth, and to put into activity the minute blood vessels, at the same time to open a passage to the lungs by the trachea, and to inflate them with air, to produce an artificial respiration, and to transfuse blood into him from a lamb." Unsurprisingly, Thornton's proposals for Washington's "restoration," as he called the sorcery, left everyone flummoxed. He was not seconded.[11]

Washington had died and there was nothing anyone could do. But the discussion about the causes of his death had only begun—and this topic still lives on. Thornton says that Washington died "by the loss of blood and the want of air," which is not a diagnosis at all. At the end of December, newspapers published Dr. Craik's and Dr. Dick's account of what had happened—and this is more interesting, "particularly so to the professors and practitioners of medicine throughout America." The two doctors stated that Washington was "attacked with an inflammatory affection of the upper part of the wind pipe, called in technical language, *cynanche trachealis*." The onset was sudden and violent, they remarked: "The disease commenced with a violent ague, accompanied with some pain in the upper and fore part of the throat, a sense of stricture in the same part, a cough and a difficult rather than a painful deglutition, which were soon succeeded by fever and a quick and laborious respiration."[12]

The inflammation of the glottis, larynx, and upper trachea, which Dr. Craik and Dr. Dick called "cynanche trachealis," vulgarly "quinsy"—the words "cynanche" and "quinsy" both come from the Greek "kunankhē" meaning "dog's collar," from "kun," "dog," and "ankhein," "to squeeze"—had been described by Dr. William Cullen, the famous professor of medicine at the equally famous University of Edinburgh in Scotland. (Dr. Craik and Dr. Brown had studied at Edinburgh, while Dr. Dick was a graduate of the University of Pennsylvania.) To treat quinsy, Dr. Cullen had in fact prescribed bleeding, both topical and general, blistering, laxatives, and vomitives. So, Washington's doctors only did what Dr. Cullen would have done in a similar circumstance.[13]

It's not wrong to say that Washington died of quinsy, but it is far from specific enough. In the eighteenth century, "quinsy" was a rather imprecise medical term. It could indicate any "inflammation"—any infection, viral or bacterial—disturbing any structure of the throat, whether pharynx, larynx, or trachea. Was the infection located in the larynx, glottis, epiglottis, trachea, tonsils, soft palate, vocal cords, or where, more precisely? Yes, Washington died of quinsy, but only in an eighteenth-century sense—which does not satisfy our higher medical standards. Doctors, today, still use "quinsy," but by it they mean something more specific: peritonsillar abscess, or PTA. Washington, certainly, did not die of PTA, which has a much longer onset. The abscess begins to appear two to eight days *after* the patient shows symptoms. Pain and swelling are either right sided or left sided. Furthermore, a peritonsillar abscess would not have produced total obstruction of the airway.[14]

Without virological or bacteriological tests or without a postmortem anatomopathological examination, there's no way to arrive at any diagnostic certainty. But there are two major clinical hypotheses. The first posits an acute edema (swelling) of the larynx (or "voice box," the two-inch structure located between the pharynx and the trachea) caused by a bacterium of the genus streptococcus. (The presence of bacteria would explain the rapid progression.) Also, an infection of the larynx could have easily attacked the adjoining tissues above, including the epiglottis, causing great difficulty and pain in swallowing. Just as easily, it could have involved the glottis, the narrow passage to the lungs, and obstructed the entrance of air.[15]

The second hypothesis suggests that Washington died from acute epiglottitis (the epiglottis is the thin flexible cartilage that covers the larynx, the "lid" that prevents us from choking on food) caused by a virulent bacterium, likely haemophilus influenzae type b. Epiglottitis in adults has a higher mortality rate than acute laryngitis, but given Washington's already difficult clinical picture acute laryngitis, without antibiotics, could have been sufficient to kill him.[16]

Patients with either acute epiglottitis or acute laryngitis show precisely Washington's symptoms: the rapid onset of the condition, severe sore throat, difficulty in swallowing, difficulty in speaking, increased airway obstruction—in particular when leaning backward—a desire to assume a sitting position in spite of weakness, persistent restlessness, and an apparent improvement shortly before death. When these pathologies strike, it is hard to inhale air and thus to set in motion the mechanism that transfers oxygen to the blood, leading to hypoxemia, a condition in which there is insufficient oxygen in the blood. In Washington's case, not having enough blood further reduced his oxygen supply (hemoglobin in the blood carries oxygen). While bleeding per se didn't kill Washington, it exacerbated hypoxemia and triggered preterminal anemia and hypotension. (The fact that, shortly before his death, Washington stopped struggling and appeared calm may have been due to grave hypotension.) The use of purgatives worsened the situation even further by significantly reducing his body fluids. And other complications, such as a septic shock (the immune system's abnormal reaction to an infection) could have been factors.[17]

The supreme, tragic irony is that George Washington could have survived had Dr. Thornton arrived in time. This forerunner of Dr. Frankenstein was crazy enough to attempt a tracheostomy.

Postmortem

George Washington died in his bed, a massive piece of furniture made of mahogany, poplar and yellow poplar, sycamore, and white pine, which probably arrived at Mount Vernon at the beginning of 1797. The bedstead is seven and a half feet tall, six and a half feet long, and six feet wide—an example of the elegant, simple style that Washington liked. Its size is generous. A myth goes that Martha had this bed made to accommodate Washington's "gigantic" height. However, comparison of this bed's dimensions with other similar examples reveals that the length is far from unusual. The width of the bedstead is more atypical. The couple settled on a wider-than-usual bed for their comfort, perhaps because of Martha's

 Washington's bed, ca. 1797. Courtesy of Mount Vernon Ladies' Association, Mount Vernon, VA.

size, or because he was an early riser, or because one of the two was a restless sleeper.[18]

At some point, probably late in the night on Saturday, three or four enslaved men hoisted Washington's body from the deathbed, carried it away from the bedchamber, and placed it in the cold New Room, where it rested for three days. Mourners came to bid adieu. They saw the dead Washington, the empty vessel left behind by the "grim King." In the eighteenth century, death was domestic. Yes, it was scary—and only a few shared Washington's stoic attitude in the face of the prospect of death. But the dying body was not hospitalized and thus surgically removed from survivors' daily lives.[19]

Death was not a cultural taboo. It was a common topic of conversation. More important, the dead body was subject to precise rituals that took place in the family. For example, locks of hair were cut off the dead person's head and given to friends and relatives (although Martha had already presented Washington's hair to friends as a "memorial to the General" when her husband was still alive). Hair was often braided and placed in a locket, in a mourning ring, or in the back of a miniature. Upon George's departure, Martha gave a framed miniature with a lock of hair to Tobias Lear. She also sent some hair to Lear's mother, Mary Lear, together with a lock of her own hair.[20]

Alleged specimens of Washington's hair still circulate—about sixty in all. They are found in books, kept in museums, and often sold at auctions to gullible buyers who want to "own" a piece of the general. Ultimately, however, there's no way of knowing if these specimens really are his hair. The FBI did test a few, but even with testing it's impossible to go beyond assumptions and suppositions. Diane Dunkley, former director of the Museum of the Daughters of the American Revolution, once wryly noted that any lock of hair on display today is "kinda sorta probably maybe" George Washington's.[21]

The dead body was not pushed aside as if it were cursed, a contagious debris to be consigned to professional undertakers. It was still part of the family. It lingered with the family for days—at least three—before it was buried. Further, people feared apparent death leading to *premature burial*—eighteenth-century doctors were not infallible when they pronounced their diagnoses. To prevent any mistake, Washington himself had given clear directions to Tobias Lear: "Do not let my body be put into the vault in less than three days after I am dead." The dying Washington didn't want there to be any confusion: "Do you understand me?," he asked. He wasn't calm until Lear replied with a firm "Yes!"[22]

The body was washed and prepared—a few enslaved persons probably attended to the task. They dressed the remains. Bodies in the eighteenth century were not just wrapped up in a rectangular winding sheet like the shroud of Turin, for example; eighteenth-century taste dictated more elaborate grave garments. In the age of civilization and politeness, "Frenchness" and "simplicity," winding sheets had gone out of style. They were superseded by open-backed, long-sleeved, loosely-fitting shirts (chemises) with draw-strings at the wrist and neck. These grave clothes often had an integral hood and were emblazoned with more or less elaborate flounces and pleats running down the length with optional appli-qued horizontal bows. Additional mittens, stockings, and slippers would complete the outfit. Ankles were tied together and the arms were bound to the body by using the waistband of the shirt itself.[23]

In life, Washington didn't like overly elaborate garments and embroidery. So in death, the chemise that accompanied him to the afterlife must have been equally tasteful and yet plain enough. Margaret Gretter of Alexandria was the tailor who made Washington's last shirt. (While male tailors usually cut garments for living people, interestingly, female tailors often made apparel for the dead.) Gretter charged Washington's family $6.00 for the chemise and a like amount for the black pall cloth that was placed over the coffin.[24]

In his will, Washington had made clear that it was his "express desire" that his body "may be Interred in a private manner, without parade, or funeral Oration." But that's not how it went. The day of the funeral, December 18, 1799, mourners gathered at Mount Vernon. It was a large procession organized by the Masonic Lodge of Alexandria. Musicians played a funeral dirge. No fewer than four ministers gave speeches. And the public enjoyed shows of military pageantry and the thumping, funereal sound of the eleven pieces of artillery lining the banks of the Potomac. There was also a riderless horse—a tradition dating back to the age of Genghis Khan. Martha, understandably, couldn't bring herself to attend such choreographed rituals. She stayed on the third floor of Mount Vernon, watching from the window.[25]

And that wasn't all. On December 23, Justice John Marshall spoke before a joint committee of both houses of the Congress. He presented a plan for the United States' first "state funeral." It was approved. The "state funeral," to be held in Philadelphia, was scheduled for December 26, 1799.

It commenced at noon. Brigadier General William Macpherson ordered his soldiers to fire minute guns and to keep firing for one hour. Church bells tolled. A military band, with fifes, wind instruments, and muffled drums, began performing George Frideric Handel's "Dead March." Meanwhile, the procession set off. It moved from the Legislative Hall and went down Walnut Street to Fourth Street, continuing along Chestnut, Market, and Arch Street to the German Lutheran Church, where Henry Lee delivered his oration, "First in war, first in peace, and first in the hearts of his countrymen." Two troops of horses flying flags of mourning followed. Brigadier General Macpherson and senior officers positioned themselves at the head of a federal battalion of cavalry, infantry, and artillery. Volunteer companies and militia followed. This was a show not only of military unity but also of hierarchy within the military.[26]

All this happened to Washington's mystical body, of course, the symbol of national unity. The terrestrial body stayed at Mount Vernon throughout. The morning of December 18, 1799, the remains lay on public display in a coffin in the portico. Not yet sealed, the coffin featured silver-plate ornaments. By the head, it bore the inscription "SURGE AD JUDICIUM" ("Rise to Judgement"). Another that read "GLORIA DEO" ("Glory to God") was placed midpoint. A procession set off at 3 p.m., and the body was deposited in the old vault, where it would remain until 1837, after which it was transferred to the new vault. On December 25, Christmas Day, since no family member had expressed a further wish to see the body, Lear called on the plumbers,

Tomb of Washington, by John Gadsby Chapman, 1834. Courtesy of Mount Vernon Ladies' Association, Mount Vernon, VA.

Washington's Tomb, by Joachim Ferdinand Richardt, 1858. Courtesy of Mount Vernon Ladies' Association, Mount Vernon, VA.

one George McMunn and his father-in-law, Isaac Sittler, from Alexandria. They came right away and sealed the inner liner of lead installed within the mahogany coffin.[27]

But this is no longer George Washington. The surveyor, the soldier, the husband, the leader, the father and grandfather, the tender man, the brutal man, the first president, the homespun and yet quite "French-like" dandy, the gifted performer, the American Moses, the slaveowner, the strong and yet weak eighteenth-century male are no more. Washington is gone forever. His entire world, too, belongs to the past.

Acknowledgments

❧

W ithout the generous support of the George Washington's Mount Vernon this book would not have been possible. I am very grateful I was selected as a fellow in 2016–17 and in 2020–21. While spending my time at the Fred W. Smith National Library trying to do my chore, I had a great time. Nadene and Doug Bradburn have been friends for many years, and their sweet company made my experience of the house on the Potomac especially enjoyable. Thanks to them, wine and conversation have flown unhampered. Curt and Cissy Viebranz have also provided friendship—and wine as well. Joe Bondi, my better alter ego, has been tremendously sympathetic. And Stephen McLeod has simply been a pleasure to team up with. At the library, I had the chance to meet and cooperate with many other wonderful persons: Mary Thompson, Samantha Snyder, Susan Schoelwer, Dawn Bonner, Adam Erby, Dana Stefanelli, Amanda Isaac, Kevin Butterfield, Jim Ambuske, Joseph Stoltz, Peter Cressy, and Julie Coleman Almancy.

Along the way, many friends, colleagues, and others who toil in the field of history have made substantial contributions to my project: Andy Burstein, Peter Onuf, Ed Larson, Ed Ryan, Matteo

Milani, John and Mary McGuigan, Charles Tharp, Bruce Rags-dale, Hubert Zapf, Enid Zafran, Arlene Shaner, Patrick Cutter, Scott D. Swank, Jennifer E. Stertzer, Sharon Kong-Perring, and Brian Muncy.

At Johns Hopkins University Press, Laura Davulis rocks. She has accompanied me, encouraged me and, often, she has led the way. Ezra Rodriguez, Juliana McCarthy, Kristina K. Lykke, Kathryn Marguy, Charles Dibble, and Hilary S. Jacqmin have similarly been effective. I'm honored that *First Among Men* ended up in such a good company.

Since I wasn't born into this wonderful, powerful, and at times a little jarring language, I had to tap the expertise of Keith Hollihan, Kenny Marotta, and M. J. Devaney. In particular, M. J. has brought my writing to another level.

My agent, Scott Mendel of the Mendel Media Group LLC, has transformed an idea into a book. I owe him. I hope this is only the first step in a much longer journey.

Serenella Iovino, my wife, is the love of my life. She has been precisely that for a long time. She will always be.

Timeline

February 22, 1732 (February 11, 1731, per the Julian calendar): Washington born in Westmoreland County, Virginia.

1738: Washington's family moves to Ferry Farm on the Rappahannock River, near Fredericksburg.

1743: Augustine Washington, Washington's father, dies. Washington becomes a slaveowner.

March 11, 1748: Washington's journey "over the mountains" begins.

1749: Washington appointed county surveyor of the frontier county of Culpeper. Suffers an episode of malaria.

September 1751–January 1752: Washington takes trip to Barbados with his half brother Lawrence. Struck with smallpox.

July 26, 1752: Lawrence dies of tuberculosis.

1753: Washington appointed adjutant of the Southern District of Virginia with the rank of major. Takes a trip to deliver a letter to the French commandant of Fort Le Boeuf.

1754: Colonel Washington sets off on the Ohio military campaign. The French and Indian War begins. Jumonville killed at the battle of May 28. Debacle at Fort Necessity.

1755: Braddock's defeat.

1756: Washington has a tooth pulled by Dr. Watson.

1757–58: Washington experiences repeated attacks of dysentery.

1758: Forbes expedition.

January 6, 1759: Washington marries Martha Dandridge Custis.

1759–75: Washington is an established "gentleman farmer" at Mount Vernon.

1761: Washington contracts malaria again.

1768: Washington suffers through repeated attacks of dysentery.

1769: Washington contracts malaria for the third time.

June 19, 1773: Martha Parke Custis, "Patsy," dies of seizures.

June 15, 1775: Congress appoints Washington commander of the Continental army.

December 26, 1776: General Washington defeats the Hessians at the Battle of Trenton.

January 3, 1777: Washington defeats British troops at the Battle of Princeton. In March, he has an attack of quinsy.

1777–78: Washington spends the winter at Valley Forge.

September 28, 1781–Oct. 19, 1781: Siege of Yorktown. General Charles Cornwallis surrenders to Washington and Lafayette.

November 5, 1781: John Parke Custis, "Jacky," dies of camp fever at Yorktown.

December 23, 1783: Washington resigns his commission as commander in chief.

1786: Washington contracts malaria yet again and experiences rheumatic pains.

1787: Washington unanimously elected president of the Constitutional Convention. Rheumatic pains persist.

1789: Washington unanimously elected president of the United States of America. Mary Ball Washington, Washington's mother, dies. A tumor is discovered on his left thigh, and he has a bout of influenza.

1790: Washington falls ill with pneumonia.

1791: The tumor returns.

1793: Washington begins his second term as president.

1794: Neoplasia appears on Washington's right cheek.

1796: Washington has a final tooth pulled by Dr. Greenwood.

1797: Washington retires from the presidency and from public life.

July 4, 1798: As the probability of a war against France increases, President Adams appoints Washington commander in chief.

July, 9, 1799: Washington signs his last will, which provides for the emancipation of the 123 persons he held in bondage.

December 14, 1799: Washington dies in his bedroom at Mount Vernon.

December 18, 1799: Washington's remains entombed at Mount Vernon.

May 22, 1802: Martha Washington dies at Mount Vernon.

Abbreviations

GWMV George Washington's Mount Vernon, Fred W. Smith
National Library for the Study of George Washington
and Museums, Mount Vernon, VA.

PGW-CFS W. W. Abbot, ed. *The Papers of George Washington:
Confederation Series.* 6 vols. Charlottesville, VA, 1992–97.

PGW-CS W.W. Abbot et al., eds. *The Papers of George Washington:
Colonial Series.* 10 vols. Charlottesville, VA, 1987–95.

PGW-D Donald Jackson et al., eds. *The Papers of George Washington: Diaries.* 6 vols. Charlottesville, VA, 1976–79.

PGW-PS Dorothy Twohig et al., eds. *The Papers of George
Washington: Presidential Series.* 21 vols. Charlottesville,
VA, 1987–2020.

PGW-RS W. W. Abbot, ed. *The Papers of George Washington:
Retirement Series.* 4 vols. Charlottesville, VA, 1998–99.

PGW-RWS Philander D. Chase et al., eds. *The Papers of George
Washington: Revolutionary War Series.* Charlottesville,
VA, 1985–.

Notes

CHAPTER I. *The American Giant*

1. This chapter discusses several myths about Washington's physique. For a discussion of other myths, see Peter R. Henriques, *First and Always: A New Portrait of George Washington* (Charlottesville, VA, 2020), 39–62. On Washington as a symbol and the creation of Washington's myth in general, see Marcus Cunliffe, *George Washington, Man and Monument* (Boston, 1958), 129–49, Bernard Mayo, *Myths and Men: Patrick Henry, George Washington, Thomas Jefferson* (Athens, GA, 1959), Daniel J. Boorstin, *The Americans: The National Experience* (New York, 1965), 337–56, Catherine L. Albanese, *Sons of the Fathers: The Civil Religion of the American Revolution* (Philadelphia, 1976), 143–81, Howard N. Rabinowitz, "The Washington Legend 1865–1900: The Heroic Image in Flux," *American Studies* 17, no. 1 (1976): 5–24, Charles Royster, *A Revolutionary People at War: The Continental Army and American Character, 1775–1783* (Chapel Hill, NC, 1979), 178–89, 255–65, Eugene F. Miller and Barry Schwartz, "The Icon of the American Republic: A Study in Political Symbolism," *Review of Politics* 47, no. 4 (1985): 516–43, Barry Schwartz, *George Washington: The Making of an American Symbol* (New York, 1987), Paul K. Longmore, *The Invention of George Washington* (Charlottesville, VA, 1999), Ar-

chie P. McDonald, "George Washington: More than Man," in *George Washington In and As Culture*, ed. Kevin Lee Cope, William S. Pederson, and Frank Williams (New York, 2001), 3–10, Joseph J. Ellis, *His Excellency: George Washington* (New York, 2004), 180–84, Adam Greenhalgh, "'Not a Man but a God': The Apotheosis of Gilbert Stuart's Athenaeum Portrait of George Washington," *Winterthur Portfolio* 41, no. 4 (2007): 269–304, John E. Ferling, *The Ascent of George Washington: The Hidden Political Genius of an American Icon* (New York, 2009), 272–77, and Edward G. Lengel, *Inventing George Washington: America's Founder, in Myth and Memory* (New York, 2011).

2. For an introduction to American and European masculinity, see David D. Gilmore, *Manhood in the Making: Cultural Concepts of Masculinity* (New Haven, CT, 1990), E. Anthony Rotundo, *American Manhood: Transformations in Masculinity from the Revolution to the Modern Era* (New York, 1993), Michael S. Kimmel, *Manhood in America: A Cultural History* (New York, 1996), Mark E. Kann, *Republic of Men: The American Founders, Gendered Language, and Patriarchal Politics* (New York, 1998), Craig Thompson Friend and Lorri Glover, *Southern Manhood: Perspectives on Masculinity in the Old South* (Athens, GA, 2004), John Gilbert McCurdy, *Citizens Bachelors: Manhood and the Creation of the United States* (Ithaca, NY, 2009), Lorri Glover, *Southern Sons: Becoming Men in the New Nation* (Baltimore, MD, 2010), Thomas A. Foster, ed., *New Men: Manliness in Early America* (New York, 2011), Lorri Glover, *Founders as Fathers: The Private Lives and Politics of the American Revolutionaries* (New Haven, CT, 2016), and Sarah Goldsmith, *Masculinity and Danger on the Eighteenth-Century Grand Tour* (London, 2020). For discussions of American masculinity as a proactive opposition to womanhood, see Joan Hoff, *Law, Gender, and Injustice: Legal History of U.S. Women* (New York, 1994), Linda K. Kerber, *No Constitutional Right to Be Ladies: Women and the Obligations of Citizenship* (New York, 1998), and Rosemarie Zagarri, *Revolutionary Backlash: Women and Politics in the Early American Republic* (Philadelphia, 2007). On homosocial culture in America, see Dana D. Nelson, *National Manhood: Capitalist Citizenship and the Imagined Fraternity of White Men* (Durham, NC, 1998). For one theory of masculinity and the idea of a "hegemonic masculinity," see Raewyn Connell, *Gender and Power: Society,*

the Person, and Sexual Politics (Stanford, CA, 1987). See also Raewyn Connell and James W. Messerschmidt, "Hegemonic Masculinity: Rethinking the Concept," *Gender & Society* 19, no. 6 (2005): 829–59.

3. On the emergence of a "masculine national character," see Michèle Cohen "'Manners' Make the Man: Politeness, Chivalry, and the Construction of Masculinity, 1750–1830," *Journal of British Studies* 44, no. 2 (2005): 312–29.

4. Willard S. Randall, *George Washington: A Life* (New York, 1997), 3. Two thorough lists of sketches and descriptions of George Washington have been compiled by historians. See Richard L. Flaig, ed., *Sketches of George Washington by Those Who Were in His Presence*, typescript, 2014, GWMV, and Mary V. Thompson, ed., "Personal Characteristics of George Washington," typescript, 2016, GWMV.

5. Paul Johnson, *George Washington: The Founding Father* (New York, 2005), 6; Ferling, *Ascent of George Washington*, 14; Richard Brookhiser, *Founding Father: Rediscovering George Washington* (New York, 1996), 111; Ellis, *His Excellency*, 68, 274. On biographers' fascination with Washington's physique and especially his thighs, see Alexis Coe, *You Never Forget Your First: A Biography of George Washington* (New York, 2020). For analyses of Washington's conspicuous masculinity, see also Jill Lepore, "His Highness: George Washington Scales New Heights," *New Yorker*, September 27, 2010, and Michiko Kakutani, "Washington's Standing in Locker Room Line-Up," *New York Times*, February 6, 1996. For an interdisciplinary study of images of bodies and bodily practices in early America, see Janet Moore Lindman and Michele Lise Tarter, eds., *A Centre of Wonder: The Body in Early America* (Ithaca, NY, 2001).

6. Ron Chernow, *Washington: A Life* (New York, 2010), 29–30, 121–22, 468.

7. On the nineteenth-century emergence of the muscular male body as normative, see Judith Butler, *Bodies That Matter: On the Discursive Limits of Sex* (New York, 1993), and John F. Kasson, *Houdini, Tarzan, and the Perfect Man: The White Male Body and the Challenge of Modernity in America* (New York, 2001). See also Thomas A. Foster, *Sex and the Founding Fathers: the American Quest for a Relatable Past* (Philadelphia, 2014), esp. 34.

8. On Washington's peers being quite "comfortable in expressing 'feminine' characteristics," see William Stafford, "Gentlemanly Mascu-

linities as Represented by the Late Georgian *Gentleman's Magazine*," *History* 93, no. 309 (2008): 47–68, 52.

9. Thad[d]eus Fiske, *A Sermon, Delivered December 29, 1799* (Boston, 1800), 10; Peter Folsom IV, *An Eulogy on Geo. Washington, Late Commander in Chief of the Armies of the United States of America* (Gilmanton, NH, 1800), 6. On Washington occupying a "transcendent status," see Ellis, *His Excellency*, 147. On the number of eulogies, see Margaret B. Stillwell, "Checklist of Eulogies and Funeral Orations on the Death of George Washington, December, 1799–February, 1800," *Bulletin of the New York Public Library* 20, no. 5 (1916): 403–41. On Washington's reputation after his death, see Matthew R. Costello, *The Property of the Nation: George Washington's Tomb* (Lawrence, KS, 2019).

10. Israel Trask, in *The Revolution Remembered: Eyewitness Accounts of the War for Independence*, ed. John C. Dann (Chicago, 1999), 408–10.

11. George Washington Parke Custis, *Recollections and Private Memoirs of Washington* (1859; rpt., New York, 1860), 519. For an account of the same episode using slightly different words see chapter 25, page 483, of *Recollections and Private Memoirs of Washington*. David Humphreys, the general's aide and early biographer, also conveyed the impression of a boorish man: "I have several times heard him say, he never met any man who could throw a stone to so great a distance as himself" (*"Life of General Washington" with George Washington's "Remarks,"* ed. Rosemarie Zagarri [Athens, GA, 1991], 7).

12. John Gadsby Chapman, "Wash[ingto]n Sketches, Forwarded to Mr. Paulding under Date 14 Nov. 1833," John Gadsby Chapman Papers, McGuigan Collection, Harpswell, Maine.

13. Custis, *Recollections and Private Memoirs of Washington*, 483–84.

14. Mason Locke Weems, *The Life of Washington*, ed. Marcus Cunliffe (1800; rpt., Cambridge, MA, 1962), 21.

15. Custis, *Recollections and Private Memoirs of Washington*, 482. For the Natural Bridge, see Humphreys, *"Life of General Washington,"* 7. For the measurements of the Rappahannock and the Natural Bridge, plus other details of the story of Washington tossing stones, see Philip Levy, *Where the Cherry Tree Grew: The Story of Ferry Farm, George Washington's Boyhood Home* (New York, 2013), 221–28.

16. See Barry Schwartz, "Social Change and Collective Memory: The Democratization of George Washington," *American Sociological Review* 56, no. 2 (1991): 221–36.

17. Schwartz himself tells the story of his daunting task in "Putting a Face on the First President," *Scientific American*, February 2006, 84–91. See also Carla Killough McClafferty, *The Many Faces of George Washington: Remaking a Presidential Icon* (Minneapolis, 2011), and Michael J. Lombardi, "Taking the Measure of Washington . . . Once More," *Colonial Williamsburg Journal* 27, no. 3 (2005): 72–78.

18. Baumgarten, "Project Report 10/19/2004," typescript, GWMV. She analyzed and measured the following objects: W-574A, W-1063, W-1514, W-754C, W-575, W-1186, W-2149, W-2673, W-574B, W-1515, W-574D-E.

19. Baumgarten, "Project Report 10/19/2004," and Baumgarten, in Lombardi, "Taking the Measure of Washington."

20. "He would have been wearing stays as a child" (Baumgarten, in Lombardi, "Taking the Measure of Washington"). See also Chernow, *George Washington*, 121.

21. George Mercer, 1760, PGW-CS 6:192n; Isaac Weld Jr., *Travels Through the States of North America, and the Provinces of Upper and Lower Canada, During the Years 1795, 1796, and 1797*, 2 vols. (1799; rpt., London, 1807), 1:105n; David Ackerson to his son, 1811, in Henry Cabot Lodge, *George Washington*, 2 vols. (Boston, 1889), 2:381; Washington, invoice to Robert Cary & Company, July 15, 1772, PGW-CS 9:66. On a hat "for a pretty large head," see also Washington, invoice to Robert Cary & Company, July 10, 1773, PGW-CS 9:274.

22. Edward Thornton to ——, April 2, 1792, in Stephen Decatur Jr., *Private Affairs of George Washington* (Boston, 1933), 268. See also S. W. Jackman, "A Young Englishman Reports on the New Nation: Edward Thornton to James Bland Burges, 1791–1793," *William and Mary Quarterly* 18, no. 1 (1961): 85–121, 104, and Weld, *Travels Through the States of North America*, 1:105n.

23. David Ackerson to his son, 1811, in Cabot Lodge, *George Washington*, 2:381; Custis, *Recollections and Private Memoirs of Washington*, 527. See also George Mercer, 1760, PGW-CS 6:192n.

24. Custis, *Recollections and Private Memoirs of Washington*, 528.

25. George Mercer, 1760, PGW-CS 6:192n; François Marbois, September 12, 1779, in *George Washington as the French Knew Him: A Collection of Texts*, ed. Gilbert Chinard (1940; rpt., New York, 1969), 75; George Washington to William Fitzhugh, August 5, 1798, PGW-RS 2:490. On the average weight in the United States today for white non-Hispanic males aged twenty and over, see https://www.cdc.gov/nchs/data/series/sr_03/sr03_039.pdf.

26. Lafayette, PGW-RWS 10:602.

27. Andreas Wiederhold, diary entry, December 28, 1776, in *The Trenton Commanders*, ed. Bruce Burgoyne (Bowie, MD, 1997), 4. On the median height of mature Virginia soldiers, see John Ferling, "Soldiers for Virginia: Who Served in the French and Indian War?" *Virginia Magazine of History and Biography* 94, no. 3 (1986): 307–28, 312.

28. George Mercer, 1760, PGW-CS 6:192n; Custis, *Recollections and Private Memoirs of Washington*, 527, italics added. For the measurements of the corpse, see Tobias Lear, *Letters and Recollections of George Washington* (New York, 1906), 136–37. This printed edition has a typo (the corpse is described as "5 feet 3 ½ inchs. exact."); the manuscript of the diary, in the Historical Society of Pennsylvania, has the correct figure. On Washington's height as six-foot-two, see also David Ackerson to his son, 1811, in Cabot Lodge, *George Washington*, 2:380.

29. Humphreys, *"Life of General Washington,"* 7; Custis, *Recollections and Private Memoirs of Washington*, 527; Weld, *Travels Through the States of North America*, 1:105n; Claude Blanchard, in William Spohn Baker, *Itinerary of General Washington from June 15, 1775, to December 23, 1783* (Philadelphia, 1892), 209.

30. Washington to Richard Washington, October 20, 1761, PGW-CS 7:81. On "Six feet high & proportionably made," see also George Washington to Charles Lawrence, April 26, 1763, PGW-CS 7:201.

31. Washington to Charles Lawrence, June 20, 1768, PGW-CS 8:98.

32. On scientific evidence linking height to life-threatening disorders, see Brian Palmer, "I Wish I Was a Little Bit Shorter," *Slate*, July 30, 2013, https://slate.com/technology/2013/07/height-and-longevity-the-research-is-clear-being-tall-is-hazardous-to-your-health.html. On the social advantages of stature, see Timothy A. Judge and Daniel M. Cable, "The

Effect of Physical Height on Workplace Success and Income: Preliminary Test of a Theoretical Model," *Journal of Applied Psychology* 89, no. 3 (2004): 428–41, and Stephen S. Hall, *Size Matters: How Height Affects the Health, Happiness, and Success of Boys—and the Men They Become* (Boston, 2006).

33. *Frederick Douglass: Selected Speeches and Writings*, ed. Philip S. Foner and Yuval Taylor (Chicago, 1999), 222, italics added.

34. See Kasia Boddy, *Boxing: A Cultural History* (London, 2008), and Elliott J. Gorn, *The Manly Art: Bare-Knuckle Prize Fighting in America* (Ithaca, NY, 1986).

35. On the importance of the leg over the arm, see Karen Harvey, "Men of Parts: Masculine Embodiment and the Male Leg in Eighteenth-Century England," *Journal of British Studies* 54, no. 4 (2015): 797–821. On the importance of the horse, see T. H. Breen, "Horses and Gentlemen: The Cultural Significance of Gambling among the Gentry of Virginia," *William and Mary Quarterly* 34, no. 2 (1977): 239–57.

36. On the myth of the calf, see https://www.atlasobscura.com/articles/colonial-calves-men-fashion-myth.

37. Custis, *Recollections and Private Memoirs of Washington*, 527; George Mercer, 1760, PGW-CS 6:193n. On Washington's legs being "rather slender" and yet "well shaped, and muscular," see Weld, *Travels Through the States of North America*, 1:105n.

38. William Hogarth, *The Analysis of Beauty* (1753; rpt., Chicago, 1908), 118.

39. On the link between dance, harmony, and military training, see Matthew McCormack, "Dance and Drill: Polite Accomplishments and Military Masculinities in Georgian Britain," *Cultural and Social History* 8, no. 3 (2011): 315–30, esp. 321.

CHAPTER 2. *Testing Himself*

1. On Washington's education being conducted by a domestic tutor, see David Humphreys, *"Life of General Washington" with George Washington's "Remarks,"* ed. Rosemarie Zagarri (Athens, GA, 1991), 6. In 1756, George Mason wrote Washington a letter in which he made a reference to one Sergeant Piper, "my neighbor and your old schoolfellow." See Willard S. Randall, *George Washington: A Life* (New York, 1997), 33.

2. On Augustine's books, see "Inventory of Colonel Augustine Washington Dec'd," *Tyler's Quarterly Historical and Genealogical Magazine* 8, no. 2 (1926): 90–92.

3. Thomas Jefferson to Walter Jones, January 2, 1814, *Founders Online*, National Archives, https://founders.archives.gov/documents/Jefferson/03 -07-02-0052; John Adams to Benjamin Rush, April 22, 1812, *Founders Online*, National Archives, https://founders.archives.gov/documents/Adams /99-02-02-5777.

4. On this first book that Washington bought, see Kevin J. Hayes, *George Washington: A Life in Books* (New York, 2017), 1–5.

5. On the libraries of Washington's mother and father, see Hayes, *George Washington*, 5–15. On Washington, his library, and his love of books, see also Paul K. Longmore, *The Invention of George Washington* (Charlottesville, VA, 1999), and Adrienne M. Harrison, *A Powerful Mind: The Self-Education of George Washington* (Lincoln, NE, 2015). See also Robin Pokorski, "George Washington's Library," http://www.mountvernon.org /digital-encyclopedia/article/george-washingtons-library/.

6. A. L. Bassett, "Reminiscences of Washington," *Scribner's Monthly*, May 1877, 78, in Hayes, *George Washington*, 9. On Mary Ball reading from Matthew Hale, see Hayes, *George Washington*, 12.

7. See Hayes, *George Washington*, 52, 118. See also Appleton P. C. Griffin, ed., *A Catalogue of the Washington Collection in the Boston Athenaeum* (Boston, 1897), 53, 67, 170, 179, 189, 192, 484, 509.

8. On Mary Ball Washington, see Philip Levy, *Where the Cherry Tree Grew: The Story of Ferry Farm, George Washington's Boyhood Home* (New York, 2013), esp. 37, 40, 54, 60. On widows' power and relative independence, see Vivian Bruce Conger, *The Widows' Might: Widowhood and Gender in Early British America* (New York, 2009), Rosemarie Zagarri, *Revolutionary Backlash: Women and Politics in the Early American Republic* (Philadelphia, 2007), and Cynthia A. Kierner, *Beyond the Household: Women's Place in the Early South, 1700–1835* (Ithaca, NY, 1998).

9. See Heidi Krofft, "Growing up a Washington: 18th-Century Childhood at Ferry Farm and Mount Vernon," paper presented at the University of Massachusetts, Boston Society for Historical Archaeology Conference, January 2012.

10. On education as ornamental, see Lorri Glover, *Southern Sons: Becoming Men in the New Nation* (Baltimore, MD, 2007), 41, 57, 84. The young George Washington has just started to elicit historians' curiosity. See Peter Stark, *Young Washington: How Wilderness and War Forged America's Founding Father* (New York, 2018), Colin G. Calloway, *The Indian World of George Washington: The First President, the First Americans, and the Birth of the Nation* (New York, 2019), and Levy, *Where the Cherry Tree Grew.*

11. For an introduction to the theory of embodied cognition, see Francisco J. Varela, Eleanor Rosch, and Evan Thompson, *The Embodied Mind: Cognitive Science and Human Experience* (1991; rpt., Cambridge, MA, 2017). See also Richard Menary, ed., *The Extended Mind* (Cambridge, MA, 2010), Margaret Wilson, "Six Views of Embodied Cognition," *Psychonomic Bulletin and Review* 9, no. 4 (2002): 625–36, Lawrence W. Barsalou, "Grounded Cognition," *Annual Review of Psychology* 59 (2008): 617–45, Edwin Hutchins, *Cognition in the Wild* (Cambridge, MA, 1995), and Michelle Z. Rosaldo, "Toward an Anthropology of Self and Feeling," in *Culture Theory: Essays on Mind, Self, and Emotion*, ed. Richard A. Shweder and Robert A. LeVine (Cambridge, UK, 1984), 137–57.

12. Thomas Fairfax, in S. Weir Mitchell, *The Youth of Washington, Told in the Form of an Autobiography* (New York, 1904), 76.

13. Levy, *Where the Cherry Tree Grew*, 42.

14. On Lawrence's aristocratic face, see James Thomas Flexner, *George Washington: The Forge of Experience, 1732–1775* (Boston, 1965), 13, and John E. Ferling, *The First of Men: A Life of George Washington* (1988; rpt., New York, 2010), 6–10.

15. Joseph Ball to Mary Ball Washington, May 19, 1747, in Philander Chase, "A Stake in the West: George Washington As Backcountry Surveyor and Landholder," in *George Washington and the Virginia Backcountry*, ed. Warren Hofstra (Madison, WI, 1998), 162. See also Levy, *Where the Cherry Tree Grew*, 64–65.

16. See Marcus Rediker, *Between the Devil and the Deep Blue Sea: Merchant Seamen, Pirates and the Anglo-American Maritime World, 1700–1750* (Cambridge, UK, 1987), and Alicia K. Anderson and Lynn A. Price, eds., *George Washington's Barbados Diary, 1751–1752* (Charlottesville, VA, 2018), 6.

17. Levy, *Where the Cherry Tree Grew*, 81.

18. On young Washington studying Leybourn, see Hayes, *George Washington*, 29.

19. See Mark E. Kahn, *A Republic of Men: The American Founders, Gendered Language, and Patriarchal Politics* (New York, 1998), 36, and Jared Orsi, "Zebulon Pike and His 'Frozen Lads': Bodies, Nationalism, and the West in the Early Republic," *Western Historical Quarterly* 42, no. 1 (2011): 55–75.

20. Washington, March 11, 13, and 16, 1748, PGW-D 1:6, 7, 11.

21. Washington, March 15 and 21, April 3 and 4, 1748, PGW-D 1:9–10, 11, 12, 18.

22. Hector St. John Crèvecoeur, *Letters from an American Farmer* (1782; rpt., New York, 1904), 69, 68. On "wilderness-temptations," see Roderick Nash, *Wilderness and the American Mind* (1967; rpt., New Haven, CT, 2014), 20, 29.

23. On maize not being a human food, see Trudy Eden, "Food, Assimilation, and the Malleability of the Human Body in Early Virginia," in *A Centre of Wonder: The Body in Early America*, ed. Janet Moore Lindman and Michele Lise Tarter (Ithaca, NY, 2001), 29–42, 37.

24. Washington, March 26, 1748, PGW-D 1:15.

25. Washington to Richard, 1749–50, PGW-CS 1:43–44.

26. See Anderson and Price, *George Washington's Barbados Diary*, 51.

27. Anderson and Price, *George Washington's Barbados Diary*, 19, 31, 33, 38, 46.

28. Anderson and Price, *George Washington's Barbados Diary*, 65. On the 1748 census, see Patricia A. Molen, "Population and Social Patterns in Barbados in the Early Eighteenth Century," *William and Mary Quarterly* 28, no. 2 (1971): 287–300.

29. Anderson and Price, *George Washington's Barbados Diary*, 62, 67, 77.

30. Lawrence Washington to William (or Thomas) Fairfax, November–December 1751, the Washingtons in Barbados, PGW-D 1:33. And see Karen Ordahl Kupperman, "Fear of Hot Climates in the Anglo-American Colonial Experience," *William and Mary Quarterly* 41, no. 2 (1984): 213–40.

31. On the Irish goose and the drink to absent friends, see Anderson and Price, *George Washington's Barbados Diary*, 85.

32. See Anderson and Price, *George Washington's Barbados Diary*, 6.

33. Washington's commission is dated December 13, 1752. See editorial note, PGW-D 1:118.

34. Robert Dinwiddie to the French commandant, October 30, 1753, editorial note, PGW-D 1:127.

35. Washington, "Journey to the French Commandant: Narrative," PGW-D, 1:152.

36. Washington, "Journey to the French Commandant: Narrative," PGW-D, 1:155. On the matchcoat, see Stark, *Young Washington*, 69.

37. Washington, "Journey to the French Commandant: Narrative," PGW-D 1:154–55.

38. Washington, "Journey to the French Commandant: Narrative," PGW-D 1:155–56.

39. Washington, "Journey to the French Commandant: Narrative," PGW-D 1:158. Upon Washington's return to Williamsburg, Dinwiddie had his journal published. It appeared as *The Journal of Major George Washington, etc.* (Williamsburg, 1754). The journal was reprinted in various colonial newspapers, giving Washington some notoriety.

CHAPTER 3. *A Taste for Cruelty and War*

1. Washington, "Journey to the French Commandant: Narrative," PGW-D 1:151.

2. Washington to Robert Dinwiddie, May 27, 1754, PGW-CS 1:105.

3. Washington, "Expedition to the Ohio, 1754: Narrative," PGW-D 1:195.

4. See David L. Preston, *Braddock's Defeat: The Battle of the Monongahela and the Road to Revolution* (New York, 2015), 351–52.

5. Washington, "Expedition to the Ohio, 1754: Narrative," PGW-D 1:195–96. See also Thomas S. Abler, "Scalping, Torture, Cannibalism and Rape: An Ethnohistorical Analysis of Conflicting Cultural Values in War," *Anthropologica* 34, no. 1 (1992): 3–20. I take my account of the Tanaghrisson killing Jumonville from John Shaw, a soldier in the ranks of the Virginia Regiment. See Hayes Baker-Crothers and Ruth Allison Hudnut, "A Private Soldier's Account of Washington's First Battles in the

West: A Study in Historical Criticism," *Journal of Southern History* 8, no. 1 (1942): 23–62. See also David Dixon, "A High Wind Rising: George Washington, Fort Necessity, and the Ohio Country Indians," *Pennsylvania History: A Journal of Mid-Atlantic Studies* 74, no. 3 (2007): 333–53. For a discussion of precise responsibilities, see "Expedition to the Ohio, 1754: Narrative," PGW-D 1:195n59.

6. Washington to John Augustine Washington, May 31, 1754, PGW-CS 1:118.

7. Horace Walpole, *Memoirs of the Reign of King George the Second* (London, 1847), 3 vols., 1:400. Washington's letter to his brother John Augustine was published in the *London Magazine* on August 23, 1754. Walpole alleges that after reading the article, King George II concluded regarding Washington's remark about bullets sounding charming that "he would not say so, if he had been used to hear many."

8. William James, "What Is an Emotion?" *Mind* 9, no. 34 (1884): 188–205, 190.

9. On Fort Necessity, see J. C. Harrington, *New Light on Washington's Fort Necessity: A Report on the Archeological Explorations at Fort Necessity National Battlefield Site* (1957; rpt., Richmond, VA, 1977), and Peter Stark, *Young Washington: How Wilderness and War Forged America's Founding Father* (New York, 2018), esp. 133.

10. Washington and James Mackay, account of the capitulation of Fort Necessity, July 19, 1754, PGW-CS 1:160–61. Washington probably inflated the estimate of the French casualties. See 164n8.

11. Benjamin Franklin, *The Autobiography of Benjamin Franklin* (1793; rpt., New York, 1932), 266.

12. See Matthew C. Ward, "Fighting the 'Old Women': Indian Strategy on the Virginia and Pennsylvania Frontier, 1754–1758," *Virginia Magazine of History and Biography* 103, no. 3 (1995): 297–320, esp. 310.

13. Washington to John Augustine Washington, July 18, 1755, PGW-CS 1:343.

14. Washington to Robert Dinwiddie, April 24, 1756, PGW-CS 3:45; *Pennsylvania Gazette* (Philadelphia), May 13, 1756. Darby McKeever's family was likely another target struck by Indians. See Washington to Henry Harrison, April 26, 1756, PGW-CS 3:53–54. Whites kept at-

tacking Indian villages well into the 1780s, and Indians, for their part, were not shy about scalping and torturing mercilessly. In 1782, for example, William Crawford, Washington's agent, attacked an Indian village northwest of the Ohio. He was scalped alive and roasted to death. See Washington to William Irvine, August 6, 1782, *Founders Online*, National Archives, https://founders.archives.gov/documents/Washington/99-01-02 -09045.

15. "Journal of Captain Thomas Morris, of His Majesty's XVII Regiment of Infantry; Detroit, September 25, 1764," in *Early Western Journals, 1748–1765: By Conrad Weiser, 1748; George Croghan, 1750–1765; Frederick Post, 1758; and Thomas Morris, 1764*, ed. Reuben Gold Thwaites (1904; rpt., Lewisburg, PA, 1998), 293–328, 315. I am indebted to Mary Thompson for pointing me to this journal entry. On the ritual torture with fire, see James Smith, *An Account of the Remarkable Occurrences in the Life and Travels of Col. James Smith* (Lexington, KY, 1799), 9.

16. Washington, remarks, 1787–88, PGW-CFS 5:522. See also David Humphreys, *"Life of General Washington" with George Washington's "Remarks,"* ed. Rosemarie Zagarri (Athens, GA, 1991), 18.

17. Washington, address to the Delaware Nation, May 12, 1779, PGW-RWS 20:447. See also Holger Hoock, *Scars of Independence: America's Violent Birth* (New York, 2017).

18. See Kevin J. Hayes, *George Washington: A Life in Books* (New York, 2017), 176.

19. Adam Stephen to Thomas Jefferson, ca. December 20, 1776, *Founders Online*, National Archives, https://founders.archives.gov/documents /Jefferson/01-01-02-0248; Washington, general orders, January 1, 1777, PGW-RWS 7:499.

20. Washington to William Livingston, March 3, 1777, PGW-RWS 8:501. On American soldiers guilty of raping American women, see Hoock, *Scars of Independence*, 173–74. For numerous examples of atrocities committed on both sides, see Samuel Kercheval, *A History of the Valley of Virginia* (1833; rpt., Woodstock, VA, 1902), 69–108. The Philadelphia *Pennsylvania Packet* and the Philadelphia *Pennsylvania Evening Post*, on December 27 and 28, 1776, respectively, published the story to which Washington referred.

21. Martin's story was made public by the Philadelphia *Pennsylvania Evening Post* on June 12, 1777, 315. On Martin, see also Washington to Charles Cornwallis, June 2, 1777, PGW-RWS 9:591.

22. *Pennsylvania Evening Post* (Philadelphia), February 27, 1777, 110. On Lieutenant Bartholomew Yates, see, for example, Washington to William Howe, January 13, 1777, PGW-RWS 8:59–61. On Mercer, see David Hackett Fischer, *Washington's Crossing* (New York, 2004), 332–33. The stories of Paoli Massacre of September 20, 1777 and the Baylor Massacre of September 27, 1778 have been recounted many times.

23. George Washington, orders, July 6–8, 1756, PGW-CS 3:239. For an interesting discussion concerning the precise number of lashes Washington may have given and a comparison between American and British standards, see Fred W. Anderson, "The Hinge of the Revolution: George Washington Confronts a People's Army, July 3, 1775," *Massachusetts Historical Review* 1 (1999): 20–48. For Washington's commitment to the practice of flogging, see Harry M. Ward, *George Washington's Enforcers: Policing the Continental Army* (Carbondale, IL, 2006). See also Stuart L. Bernath, "George Washington and the Genesis of American Military Discipline," *Mid-America* 49, no. 2 (1967): 83–100.

24. Washington, orders, July 6–8, 1756, PGW-CS 3:239; Washington, general orders, May 3, 1776, PGW-RWS 4:189; Washington, general orders, May 27, 1776, PGW-RWS 4:392–93; Washington, general orders, July 7, 1776, PGW-RWS 5:231. See also Washington, general orders, September 11, 1776, PGW-RWS 6:277–78, and Washington, general orders, August 9, 1775, PGW-RWS 1:277–78.

25. Washington, general orders, June 11, 1778, PGW-RWS 15:378.

26. Washington, orderly book, November 24, 1758, PGW-CS 6:156; Washington to Anthony Whitting, December 16, 1792, PGW-PS 11:521.

27. Washington, November 2, 1770, PGW-D 2:307–308. On Washington drowning the pup, see Washington, March 26, 1769, PGW-D 2:139. On Washington giving dogs names, see Washington, May 29, 1768, PGW-D 2:67.

28. Washington to Robert Dinwiddie, May 23, 1756, PGW-CS 3:171–72.

29. Immanuel Kant, *Grounding for the Metaphysics of Morals*, orig. pub. 1785, trans. James W. Ellington (Indianapolis, IN, 1993), 36; Wash-

ington to Robert Dinwiddie, August 3, 1757, PGW-CS 4:360. See also general court-martial, July 25–26, 1757, PGW-CS 4:329–34.

30. Washington to John Stanwix, July 15, 1757, PGW-CS 4:306; Washington to Robert Dinwiddie, September 17, 1757, PGW-CS 4:406.

31. Washington to Robert Dinwiddie, August 27, 1757, PGW-CS 4:385–86.

32. Washington to a Continental Congress Camp Committee, January 29, 1778, PGW-RWS 13:403.

33. Washington to Anthony Wayne, November 27, 1779, PGW-RWS 23:468. See also Washington, general orders, September 12, 1780, in *Writings of George Washington from the Original Manuscript Sources, 1745–1799*, 39 vols., ed. John C. Fitzpatrick (Washington, DC, 1931–44), 20:33.

34. Washington, general orders, October 1, 1780, in *Writings of George Washington*, 20:110, 111; Washington to Henry Lee, October 20, 1780, in *Writings of George Washington*, 20:223.

35. Washington, March 23, 1748, PGW-D 1:13. For similar dismissive judgments, see, for example, Washington, April 4, 1748, PGW-D 1:18, and Washington to William Cocks and John Ashby, October 10, 1755, PGW-CS 2:90–91. The best analysis so far of Washington and Native Americans is Colin G. Calloway, *The Indian World of George Washington: The First President, the First Americans, and the Birth of the Nation* (New York, 2019). See also Richard G. Harless, *George Washington and Native Americans: "Learn Our Arts and Ways of Life"* (Fairfax, VA, 2018). On Native Americans and their active role in the colonization of North America, see Daniel K. Richter, *Before the Revolution: America's Ancient Pasts* (Cambridge, MA, 2011), and Alan Taylor, *American Colonies: The Settling of North America* (New York, 2001).

36. Washington to Edmund Pendleton, January 22, 1795, PGW-PS 17:426.

37. See Washington to George William Fairfax, June 10–15, 1774, PGW-CS 10:96. See also Washington to Robert Howe, January 13, 1778, PGW-RWS 13:221–22.

38. Washington, "Expedition to the Ohio, 1754: Narrative," PGW-D 1:183, 183n37. On John Washington and Native Americans in Maryland and Virginia, see Charles Arthur Hoppin, *The Washington Ancestry and*

Records of the McClain, Johnson, and Forty Other Colonial American Families, 3 vols. (Greenfield, OH, 1932), 1:188–97.

39. Washington to John Sullivan, May 31, 1779, PGW-RWS 20:716–18.

40. Washington to Robert Dinwiddie, April 7, 1756, PGW-CS 2:333; Henry Bouquet to Washington, July 14, 1758, George Washington Papers, series 4, General Correspondence, Library of Congress, Washington, DC. See also Washington to John Robinson, April 7, 1756, PGW-CS 2:338.

41. John Benson, in Alicia K. Anderson and Lynn A. Price, eds., *George Washington's Barbados Diary, 1751–1752* (Charlottesville, VA, 2018), xl. On heads posted on chimneys, see Ron Chernow, *Washington: A Life* (New York, 2010), 111.

42. Lorri Glover, *Founders as Fathers: The Private Lives and Politics of the American Revolutionaries* (New Haven, CT, 2016), 28, italics added. The best account of Washington, slavery, and the persons he enslaved is Mary V. Thompson, *"The Only Unavoidable Subject of Regret": George Washington, Slavery, and the Enslaved Community at Mount Vernon* (Charlottesville, VA, 2019). See also Kenneth Morgan, "George Washington and the Problem of Slavery," *Journal of American Studies* 34, no. 2 (2000): 279–301, Henry Wiencek, *An Imperfect God: George Washington, His Slaves, and the Creation of America* (New York, 2003), Philip D. Morgan, "'To Get Quit of Negroes': George Washington and Slavery," *Journal of American Studies* 39, no. 3 (2005): 403–29, and François Furstenberg, "Atlantic Slavery, Atlantic Freedom: George Washington, Slavery, and Transatlantic Abolitionist Networks," *William and Mary Quarterly* 68, no. 2 (2011): 247–86. On Washington not hearing criticism of slavery until he was in his thirties, see Thompson, *"The Only Unavoidable Subject of Regret,"* 63.

43. On this figure, see Philip D. Morgan and Michael L. Nicholls, "Slave Flight: Mount Vernon, Virginia, and the Wider Atlantic World," in *George Washington's South*, ed. Tamara Harvey and Greg O'Brien (Gainesville, FL, 2004), 197.

44. On Washington, a "generous & noble master," see Eleanor Parke Custis Lewis to Elizabeth Bordley Gibson, April 29, 1823, in *George Washington's Beautiful Nelly: The Letters of Eleanor Parke Custis Lewis to Elizabeth Bordley Gibson, 1794–1851*, ed. Patricia Brady (Columbia, SC, 1991),

134. On Washington performing small acts of kindness toward "his people," see Stephen Decatur Jr., *Private Affairs of George Washington* (Boston, 1933), 50.

45. Washington to John Francis Mercer, November 24, 1786, PGW-CFS 4:394; Washington to Joseph Thompson, July 2, 1766, PGW-CS 7:453–54. On Bernard Moore, see Washington, December 8, 1769, PGW-D 2:200. On Washington selling slaves as a punishment, see Thompson, *"The Only Unavoidable Subject of Regret,"* 258–59.

46. Richard Parkinson, *A Tour in America, in 1798, 1799, and 1800* (London, 1805), 2 vols., 2:420, 419.

47. Washington to William Pearce, January 4, 1795, PGW-PS 17:365; Washington to James Anderson, June 18, 1797, PGW-RS 1:194–95. On enslaved people idling and pretending, see also Washington to James Anderson, June 11, 1798, PGW-RS 2:322–23.

48. See Thompson, *"The Only Unavoidable Subject of Regret,"* 31, for Beglair's account.

49. Washington to John Fairfax, January 1, 1789, in *Writings of George Washington*, 30:175n; John Gadsby Chapman, "Wash[ingto]n Sketches, Forwarded to Mr. Paulding under Date 14 Nov. 1833," John Gadsby Chapman Papers, McGuigan Collection, Harpswell, Maine. On Ona Judge, see Erica Armstrong Dunbar, *Never Caught: The Washingtons' Relentless Pursuit of Their Runaway Slave, Ona Judge* (New York, 2017). On Washington as a "'hands-on' manager," see Thompson, *"The Only Unavoidable Subject of Regret,"* 30. For more details about Hercules's escape, see Chelsea Lenhart, "Hercules," https://www.mountvernon.org/library/digitalhistory/digital-encyclopedia/article/hercules/#note8.

50. Washington to Anthony Whitting, December 23, 1792, PGW-PS 11:545; Washington to Anthony Whitting, May 19, 1793, PGW-PS 12:611.

51. Anthony Whitting to Washington, January 16, 1793, PGW-PS 12:12; Washington to Anthony Whitting, January 20, 1793, PGW-PS 12:34. On whipping having been a practice since at least 1758, see Humphrey Knight to Washington, September 2, 1758, PGW-CS 5:447. Anthony Whitting also whipped "Ben" for assaulting Sambo Anderson and, a few weeks later, for stealing. See Washington to Anthony Whitting, February 24 and March 3, 1793, PGW-PS 12:213 and 12:259. On Ben, see Thompson,

"The Only Unavoidable Subject of Regret," 249. Hiland Crow, another estate manager, was known for flogging slaves brutally.

52. Ann Chinn, in Thompson, *"The Only Unavoidable Subject of Regret,"* 255, 433n29. Thompson does not rule out the possibility of the story being true. See *"The Only Unavoidable Subject of Regret,"* 258. For more details and more examples of corrections by way of example, see *"The Only Unavoidable Subject of Regret,"* 432n9.

53. John Gadsby Chapman, "Wash[ingto]n Sketches, Forwarded to Mr. Paulding under Date 14 Nov. 1833," John Gadsby Chapman Papers, McGuigan Collection, Harpswell, Maine.

CHAPTER 4. *A Body in Pain*

1. Lord Chesterfield to Philip Stanhope, February 15, 1754, *The Letters of Philip Dormer Stanhope, Earl of Chesterfield, with the Characters*, 3 vols. (1774; rpt., London, 1893), 2:605.

2. For a handy account of Washington and teeth, see https://www .mountvernon.org/george-washington/the-man-the-myth/the-trouble -with-teeth/. For the persistent myth that Washington's teeth were made of wood, see William M. Etter, "Wooden Teeth Myth," www.mountver non.org/research-collections/digital-encyclopedia/article/wooden -teeth-myth. See also John M. Hyson, "George Washington's Dental History and Relics" (MA thesis, University of Delaware, 1999), 3–5. On Washington and dentures, see Jennifer Van Horn, "George Washington's Dentures: Disability, Deception, and the Republican Body," *Early American Studies* 14, no. 1 (2016): 2–47. I am deeply indebted to this study.

3. On Dr. Watson, see the entry for April 27, 1756, George Washington Papers, series 5, Financial Papers: General Ledger A, 1750–1772, Library of Congress, Washington, DC. On Greenwood, see Ann Pasquale Haddad, "Washington's Last Tooth Rests in New York," *New York Times*, March 30, 1991, www.nytimes.com/1991/03/30/opinion/l-washington-s-last -tooth-rests-in-new-york-339991.html.

4. Washington to William Stephens Smith, May 15, 1783, in *Writings of George Washington from the Original Manuscript Sources, 1745–1799*, 39 vols., ed. John C. Fitzpatrick (Washington, DC, 1931–44), 26:434; Wash-

ington to John Greenwood, December 7, 1798, PGW-RS 3:245; Washington to John Baker, May 29, 1781, in *Writings of George Washington*, 22:129.

5. Olney Winsor to Mrs. Olney (Hope) Winsor, March 31, 1788, in *The Documentary History of the Ratification of the Constitution*, digital edition, 18 vols., ed. John P. Kaminski, Gaspare J. Saladino, Richard Leffler, Charles H. Schoenleber, and Margaret A. Hogan (Charlottesville, VA, 2009), 8:523; William Maclay, *Journal of William Maclay, United States Senator from Pennsylvania, 1789–1791*, ed. Edgar S. Maclay (New York, 1890), 375. On the history of dentistry, see Christine Hillam, ed., *Dental Practice in Europe at the End of the Eighteenth Century* (Amsterdam, 2003), Bernhard W. Weinberger, *An Introduction to the History of Dentistry in America*, 2 vols. (St. Louis, MO, 1948), and John M. Hyson, Joseph W. A. Whitehorne, and John T. Greenwood, eds., *A History of Dentistry in the US Army to World War II* (Washington, DC, 2008).

6. A former enslaved person quoted in Ebenezer Porter, *The Rhetorical Reader* (1832; rpt., New York, 1852), 162. On the face and the mouth with teeth as the most important factor of human identity, see Carlos Flores-Mir, Eduardo Silva, Maria I. Barriga, Manuel O. Lagravère, and Paul W. Major, "Lay Person's Perception of Smile Aesthetics in Dental and Facial Views," *Journal of Orthodontics* 31, no. 3 (2004): 204–9. On smiles and missing teeth, see Walter Rathjen, "Dental Technology, Oral Health and Aesthetic Appearance: A Historical View," *Icon* 13 (2007): 105–24, 105.

7. Auguste Caron, *Lady's Toilette; Containing a Critical Examination of the Nature of Beauty* (London, 1808), 234.

8. On Washington buying toothbrushes, see the entry for May 23, 1755, George Washington Papers, series 5, Financial Papers: General Ledger A, 1750–72, Library of Congress, Washington, DC. On Washington buying toothbrushes and dentifrices, see cash accounts, November 26, 1773, PGW-CS 9:355.

9. John Adams, *Diary and Autobiography of John Adams*, 4 vols., ed. L. H. Butterfield, Leonard C. Faber, and Wendell D. Garrett (Cambridge, MA, 1961), 3:280.

10. Washington, invoice to Robert Cary & Company, May 1, 1759, PGW-CS 6:318; *Chronicle* (London), March 23–25, 1773, 283. On Wash-

ington buying laudanum, see Stephen Decatur Jr., *Private Affairs of George Washington* (Boston, 1933), 175.

11. *Gazette* (Boston), April 28, 1783.

12. See George Washington Papers, series 5, Financial Papers: General Ledger A, 1750–72, and General Ledger B, 1772–1793, Library of Congress, Washington, DC.

13. John Greenwood to Washington, December 28, 1798, PGW-RS 3:289. On dentures being a "luxury good," see Van Horn, "George Washington's Dentures," 12–14.

14. *Daily Advertiser* (New York), November 15, 1787; John Greenwood to Washington, September 10, 1791, PGW-PS 8:515. On Greenwood, see Malvin E. Ring, "John Greenwood, Dentist to President Washington," *California Dental Association Journal* 38, no. 12 (2010): 846–51.

15. On the London relic, see Hyson, "George Washington's Dental History and Relics," 69–73. Van Horn ("George Washington's Dentures," 6n9) attributes the Mount Vernon dentures to Greenwood.

16. Washington to John Greenwood, January 20, 1797, PGW-PS 21:540; George Washington Parke Custis, *Recollections and Private Memoirs of Washington* (1859; rpt., New York, 1860), 520.

17. Washington to John Greenwood, December 12, 1798, PGW-RS 3:245n1.

18. Washington to William Stephens Smith, May 15, 1783, in *Writings of George Washington*, 26:434.

19. On eighteenth-century transplants, see Mark Blackwell, "'Extraneous Bodies': The Contagion of Live-Tooth Transplantation in Late-Eighteenth-Century England," *Eighteenth-Century Life* 28, no. 1 (2004): 21–68.

20. *Virginia Journal and Alexandria Advertiser*, April 22, 1784; Washington to William Stephens Smith, May 15, 1783, in *Writings of George Washington*, 26:434.

21. Jean Le Mayeur to Washington, January 20, 1784, PGW-CFS 1:63–64.

22. Washington to Richard Varick, February 22, 1784, PGW-CFS 1:148–49.

23. Washington to Lund Washington, December 25, 1782, in *Writings of George Washington*, 25:472.

24. Lund Washington account book, 1774–86, May 1784, 134, typescript, GWMV.

25. See George Washington Papers, series 5, Financial Papers: General Ledger B, 1772–93, Library of Congress, Washington, DC. See also https://www.mountvernon.org/george-washington/health/washingtons -teeth/george-washington-and-slave-teeth/.

26. *Independent Journal* (New York), July 9, 1785; *Royal Gazette* (New York), July 3, 1782; *Daily Advertiser* (New York), November 16, 1787; *Columbian Herald* (Charleston, SC), October 25, 1787.

27. Washington, February 6, 1785, PGW-D 4:85. For more information on Frank Lee, see Jessie MacLeod, "Frank Lee," https://www.mount vernon.org/library/digitalhistory/digital-encyclopedia/article/frank-lee.

28. Notice placed by a patient of Philip Clumberg, *Freeman's Journal* (Philadelphia), 1784, in James Wynbrandt, *The Excruciating History of Dentistry: Toothsome Tales and Oral Oddities from Babylon to Braces* (New York, 1998), 91–92.

29. John Jones, *Plain Concise Practical Remarks on the Treatment of Wounds and Fractures* (New York, 1775), 39, italics added; Washington to John Augustine Washington, June 1, 1777, PGW-RWS 9:587.

30. On Washington's health, see Frederick A. Willius and Thomas E. Keys, "The Medical History of George Washington (1732–1799)," *Proceedings of the Staff Meetings of the Mayo Clinic* 17 (1942): 92–96, 107–12, 116–21, Jeanne E. Abrams, *Revolutionary Medicine: The Founding Fathers and Mothers in Sickness and in Health* (New York, 2013), esp. 33–78, J. Worth Estes, "George Washington and the Doctors," *Medical Heritage* 1, no. 1 (1985): 44–57, and Oscar Reiss, *Medicine and the American Revolution: How Diseases and their Treatments Affected the Colonial Army* (Jefferson, NC, 1998), esp. 219–48. See also "George Washington and Health," compiled by Mary V. Thompson, typescript, 1997, revised 2015, GWMV.

31. On Washington's malady, see Martha Washington to Mercy Otis Warren, December 26, 1789, in *"Worthy Partner": The Papers of Martha Washington*, ed. Joseph E. Fields (Westport, CT, 1994), 223–24 and 224n1. On Dr. Bard and his father, see Decatur, *Private Affairs of George Washington*, 27–28. On the tumor not being a form of anthrax, see Abrams, *Revolutionary Medicine*, 63.

32. Washington to Richard Henry Lee, August 2, 1789, PGW-PS 3:371; Washington to James Craik, September 8, 1789, PGW-PS 4:1. On Washington describing how he felt right after this operation, see his letter to David Stuart, July 26, 1789, PGW-PS 3:321. On Washington stating that he felt better, see his letter to Betty Washington Lewis, October 12, 1789, PGW-PS 4:162. On Washington trusting Dr. James Craik over the other followers of Aesculapius, see his letter to James McHenry, July 3, 1789, PGW-PS 3:112, and his letter to James McHenry, July 5, 1798, PGW-RS 2:384.

33. Washington to William Moultrie, August 9, 1791, PGW-PS 8:415; Thomas Jefferson to James Madison, July 27, 1791, *Founders Online*, National Archives, https://founders.archives.gov/documents/Jefferson/01 -20-02-0332.

34. Martha Washington to Frances Bassett Washington, August 3, 1794, in *Worthy Partner*, 272; Washington to Thomas Pinckney, February 25, 1795, PGW-PS 17:580–81; Martha Washington to Frances Bassett Washington, November 11, 1794, in *Worthy Partner*, 279. On the November payment to Dr. Tate, see Washington, cash memoranda, September 29, 1794–August 31, 1797, manuscript, John Carter Brown Library, Providence, RI.

CHAPTER 5. *Checking the Body*

1. George Washington Parke Custis, *Recollections and Private Memoirs of Washington* (1859; rpt., New York, 1860), 132–34.

2. Custis, *Recollections and Private Memoirs of Washington*, 131. For a negative assessment of Mary Ball, see Ron Chernow, *Washington: A Life* (New York, 2010), 11. For a more nuanced assessment of Washington's mother in her complex relationship to her son, see Peter R. Henriques, *First and Always: A New Portrait of George Washington* (Charlottesville, VA, 2020), 19–38. See also Martha Saxton, *The Widow Washington: The Life of Mary Washington* (New York, 2019), and Craig Shirley, *Mary Ball Washington: The Untold Story of George Washington's Mother* (New York, 2019).

3. On Washington's religious beliefs, see Mary V. Thompson, *"In the Hands of a Good Providence": Religion in the Life of George Washington* (Charlottesville, VA, 2008), and Peter A. Lillback and Jerry Newcombe, *George Washington's Sacred Fire* (King of Prussia, PA, 2006).

4. Lord Fairfax, in S. Weir Mitchell, *The Youth of Washington, Told in the Form of an Autobiography* (New York, 1904), 76–77.

5. John Locke, *Some Thoughts Concerning Education*, ed. Robert Hebert Quick (Cambridge, UK, 1880), 177.

6. On the Virginia gentleman's ideal of a mastery of self, see David Hackett Fischer, *Albion's Seed: Four British Folkways in America* (New York, 1989), 316–18.

7. Washington, general orders, July 2, 1776, PGW-RWS 5:180; Washington to Fisher Gay, September 4, 1776, PGW-RWS 6:215. On proper "manly" behavior during the war, see also Washington to John Hancock, September 2, 1776, PGW-RWS 6:199.

8. Washington, general orders, June 22, 1779, PGW-RWS 21:314. See also Washington to William Howe, April 9, 1777, PGW-RWS 9:105, Washington to John Jay, April 14, 1779, PGW-RWS 20:60, and Washington, general orders, July 1, 1779, PGW-RWS 21:314. See also C. J. Rawson, "Some Remarks on Eighteenth-Century 'Delicacy,' with a Note on Hugh Kelly's 'False Delicacy' (1768)," *Journal of English and Germanic Philology* 61, no. 1 (1962): 1–13.

9. Washington, orders and instructions for Major General Artemas Ward, April 4, 1776, PGW-RWS 4:38. Many letters of this period underscore the need for discipline and order. For Washington's ideal of bodily control, see Joseph J. Ellis, *His Excellency: George Washington* (New York, 2004), 272–75.

10. Washington, general orders, February 26, 1776, PGW-RWS 3:362. See also general orders, October 3, 1775. On habitus and embodiment, see Pierre Bourdieu, *Outline of a Theory of Practice* (1972; rpt., Cambridge, UK, 1979). See also Thomas J. Csordas, "Embodiment as a Paradigm for Anthropology," *Ethos* 18, no. 1 (1990): 5–47.

11. Washington, general orders, August 3, 1776, PGW-RWS 5:551. On overcompensation, see, for example, Jennifer K. Bosson, Joseph A. Vandello, Rochelle M. Burnaford, Jonathan R. Weaver, and S. Arzu Wasti, "Precarious Manhood and Displays of Physical Aggression," *Personality and Social Psychology Bulletin* 35, no. 5 (2009): 623–34, and Robb Willer, Christabel L. Rogalin, Bridget Conlon, and Michael T. Wojnowicz,

"Overdoing Gender: A Test of the Masculine Overcompensation Thesis," *American Journal of Sociology* 118, no. 4 (2013): 980–1022.

12. Washington, general orders, August 22, 1775, PGW-RWS 1:346.

13. Washington to James Germain, June 1, 1794, PGW-PS 16:169.

14. Washington to Patrick Henry, November 3, 1778, PGW-RWS 18:31.

15. Benjamin Franklin, "A Narrative of the Late Massacres, 1764," *Founders Online*, National Archives, https://founders.archives.gov/docu ments/Franklin/01–11–02–0012.

16. Nicole Eustace, *Passion Is the Gale: Emotion, Power, and the Coming of the American Revolution* (Chapel Hill, NC, 2008), 382. See also 154–56. On resentment as an appropriate gentlemanly feeling, see 161.

17. See Stephen Brumwell, *George Washington: Gentleman Warrior* (New York, 2012).

18. Mary V. Thompson, *"The Only Unavoidable Subject of Regret": George Washington, Slavery, and the Enslaved Community at Mount Vernon* (Charlottesville, VA, 2019), 43.

19. On the notion that the ideal woman was expected to work toward the total elimination of inner energy rather than toward its regulation, see Eustace, *Passion Is the Gale*, 191.

20. See David McCullough, *1776* (New York, 2005), 47. See also Washington to Benedict Arnold, December 5, 1775, PGW-RWS 2:493. On Addison's *Cato* in America, see Fredric M. Litto, "Addison's *Cato* in the Colonies," *William and Mary Quarterly* 23, no. 3 (1966): 431–49.

21. Washington to Sarah Cary Fairfax, September 25, 1758, PGW-CS 6:42. On Addison's *Cato* as Washington's favorite play, see also Kevin J. Hayes, *George Washington: A Life in Books* (New York, 2017), 114–15. Washington made references to Cato or quoted from Addison in many letters.

22. J. M. Plane, *Physiologie, ou l'art de connaitre les hommes, sur leur physionomie*, 1797, in *George Washington as the French Knew Him: A Collection of Texts*, ed. Gilbert Chinard (1940; rpt. New York, 1969), 114; Isaac Weld Jr., *Travels through the States of North America, and the Provinces of Upper and Lower Canada, during the Years 1795, 1796, and 1797*, 2 vols. (1799; rpt., London, 1807), 1:105n.

23. Henry Lee, *Memoirs of the War in the Southern Department of the United States*, 2 vols. (Philadelphia, 1812), 1:26; Richard Peters, "Fac-Simile

of General Washington's Hand Writing; and Sketches of His Private Character," *Memoirs of the Philadelphia Society for Promoting Agriculture*, 6 vols. (Philadelphia, 1808–39), 2:vii.

24. Thomas Jefferson to Walter Jones, January 2, 1814, *Founders Online*, National Archives, https://founders.archives.gov/documents/Jefferson/03-07-02-0052; James C. Nicholls, ed., "Lady Henrietta Liston's Journal of Washington's 'Resignation,' Retirement, and Death," *Pennsylvania Magazine of History and Biography* 95, no. 4 (1971): 511–20, 514.

25. Stephen Decatur Jr., *Private Affairs of George Washington* (Boston, 1933), 58.

26. Washington to George Muse, January 29, 1774, PGW-CS 9:460–61. On the context for this claim about land, see Washington's letter to Lord Dunmore and council, November 3, 1773, PGW-CS 9:358–66. For other examples of Washington's furious letters to overseers who disobeyed his orders, see Chernow, *George Washington*, 707–8.

27. John Adams to Benjamin Rush, November 11, 1807, *Founders Online*, National Archives, https://founders.archives.gov/documents/Adams/99-02-02-5216; Nicholas Cresswell, July 13, 1777, in *The Journal of Nicholas Cresswell, 1774–1777* (New York, 1924), 254; Lord Fairfax, in Mitchell, *The Youth of Washington*, 76; Washington to Sarah Cary Fairfax, September 12, 1758, PGW-CS 6:10; James Thacher, *A Military Journal during the American Revolutionary War, from 1775 to 1783* (Boston, 1823), 191. Although Washington was orally taciturn, he was a great and dedicated letter writer.

28. On the link between Washington's silence and violence, see Susan Burgess, "YouTube on Masculinity and the Founding Fathers: Constitutionalism 2.0," *Political Research Quarterly* 64, no. 1 (2011): 120–31, 128. See also René Girard, *Violence and the Sacred*, trans. Patrick Gregory (1972; rpt., Baltimore, MD, 1977).

CHAPTER 6. *The Love Letters*

1. Wilson Miles Cary, *Sally Cary: A Long Hidden Romance of Washington's Life* (New York, 1916), 28; Mostafa Rejai and Kay Phillips, "The Young Washington: An Interpretive Essay," in *George Washington: Foundation of Presidential Leadership and Character*, ed. Ethan M. Fishman,

William D. Pederson, and Mark J. Rozell (Westport, CT, 2001), 165–82, 166. On Washington's "unrequited love" for another young lady, Mary Philipse Morris, see Mary Calvi, *Dear George, Dear Mary: A Novel of George Washington's First Love* (New York, 2019). Part 2 of this book has benefited from a thriving discipline, the history of emotions. For an introduction, see John Mullan, *Sentiment and Sociability: The Language of Feeling in the Eighteenth Century* (Oxford, UK, 1990), Peter N. Stearns and Jan Lewis, eds., *An Emotional History of the United States* (New York, 1998), Julie Ellison, *Cato's Tears and the Making of Anglo-American Emotion* (Chicago, 1999), Barbara H. Rosenwein, "Worrying about Emotions in History," *American Historical Review* 107, no. 3 (2002): 821–45, Daniel Wickberg, "What Is the History of Sensibilities? On Cultural Histories, Old and New," *American Historical Review* 112, no. 3 (2007): 661–84, Nicole Eustace, *Passion Is the Gale: Emotion, Power, and the Coming of the American Revolution* (Chapel Hill, NC, 2008), Sarah Knott, *Sensibility and the American Revolution* (Chapel Hill, NC, 2009), William M. Reddy, *The Navigation of Feeling: A Framework for the History of Emotions* (Cambridge, UK, 2010), Jan Plamper, *The History of Emotions: An Introduction*, trans. Keith Tribe (Oxford, UK, 2015), Jonas Liliequist, ed., *A History of Emotions, 1200–1800* (London, 2016), and Katie Barclay, Sharon Crozier-De Rosa, and Peter N. Stearns, eds., *Sources for the History of Emotions: A Guide* (London, 2020).

2. Ron Chernow, *Washington: A Life* (New York, 2010), 536; James Thomas Flexner, *George Washington: The Forge of Experience, 1732–1775* (Boston, 1965), 40. On Sarah Cary Fairfax as the power beyond Washington's sense of reality and the person who taught him how to curb his emotions, see George W. Nordham, *George Washington's Women: Mary, Martha, Sally, and 146 Others* (Philadelphia, 1977), 16. On Washington's guilt over his love for Sarah, see Nordham, *George Washington's Women*, 17.

3. Washington to Sarah Cary Fairfax, September 12, 1758, PGW-CS 6:10–12 passim. See also Cassandra A. Good, *Founding Friendships: Friendships between Men and Women in the Early American Republic* (New York, 2015).

4. Cary, *Sally Cary*, 28–29.

5. On arranged marriages, see Nancy F. Cott, *Public Vows: A History of*

Marriage and the Nation (Cambridge, MA, 2000), Hendrik Hartog, *Man and Wife in America: A History* (Cambridge, MA, 2000), and Timothy Kenslea, *The Sedgwicks in Love: Courtship, Engagement, and Marriage in the Early Republic* (Boston, 2006). On love as a system of decisions, see Douglas Kenrick, "Evolution, Cognitive Science, and Dynamical Systems: An Emerging Integrative Paradigm," *Current Directions in Psychological Science* 10, no. 1 (2001): 13–17. On the volitional nature of love, see Niko Kolodny, "Love as Valuing a Relationship," *Philosophical Review* 112, no. 2 (2003): 135–89. For a survey on recent theories of love, see Robert J. Sternberg and Karin Weis, eds., *The New Psychology of Love* (New Haven, CT, 2006).

6. On the 1767 trip, see Patricia Brady, *Martha Washington: An American Life* (New York, 2005), 76.

7. The editors of the George Washington papers provide the following interpretation of the letter: "If, as is possible, GW was in September still in pursuit of the prize [Martha], this letter to Mrs. Fairfax may be read as little more than an ineptly facetious piece of banter. If, on the other hand, there was an engagement that remained something of a shared secret between him and the Fairfaxes, one is left to wonder whether Washington intended in fact to direct some of his awkward gallantries to Mrs. Custis or, as is generally assumed, only to give the impression to prying eyes that his words were all meant for his betrothed though in truth intended for Mrs. Fairfax alone" (PGW-CS 6:13n3).

8. Washington to Sarah Cary Fairfax, April 30, 1755, PGW-CS 1:261.

9. On the lost letter Washington sent George William Fairfax on September 12, 1758, see George William Fairfax to Washington, September 15, 1758, PGW-CS 6:19 and 20n1.

10. See George William Fairfax to Washington, September 1, 1758, PGW-CS 5:436–37.

11. Washington to Sarah Cary Fairfax, September 25, 1758, PGW-CS 6:41. See also Washington to Sarah Cary Fairfax, June 7, 1755, PGW-CS 1:308–9.

12. On reading aloud in public as a popular diversion, see Kevin J. Hayes, *George Washington: A Life in Books* (New York, 2017), 22, and Good, *Founding Friendships*, 108. On "public love letter," see Eustace, *Passion Is*

the Gale, 107–11. For context, see Robert Adams Day, *Told in Letters: Epistolary Fiction before Richardson* (Ann Arbor, MI, 1966), Howard Anderson, Philip B. Daghlian, and Irvin Ehrenpreis, eds., *The Familiar Letter in the Eighteenth Century* (Lawrence, KS, 1966), and Konstantin Dierks, *In My Power: Letter Writing and Communications in Early America* (Philadelphia, 2009).

13. Jonathan Swift to Mrs. Howard, August 14, 1727, in *The Correspondence of Jonathan Swift*, 6 vols., ed. F. Elrington Ball (London, 1910–14), 3:411; Mrs. Howard to Jonathan Swift, August 16, 1727, in *The Correspondence of Jonathan Swift*, 3:412.

14. See Edith B. Gelles, *Portia: The World of Abigail Adams* (Bloomington, IN, 1992), 57–58. On bantering as a method men used to assert power, see Eustace, *Passion Is the Gale*, 131. See also Good, *Founding Friendships*, 65–66.

15. James Lovell to Abigail Adams, August 29, 1777, in Gelles, *Portia*, 61.

16. See Dierks, *In My Power*, 148–52, 155.

17. See Dierks, *In My Power*, 142, 163–65. See also Anya Jabour, "Male Friendship and Masculinity in the Early National South: William Wirt and His Friends," *Journal of the Early Republic* 20, no. 1 (2000): 83–111, and Brady, *Martha Washington*, 25. For the broader context, see Andrew Burstein, *Sentimental Democracy: The Evolution of America's Romantic Self-Image* (New York, 2000).

18. Washington to Robin, 1749–50, PGW-CS 1:40–41.

19. See Richard L. Bushman, *The Refinement of America: Persons, Houses, Cities* (New York, 1993), 90–96. See also Lorri Glover, "An Education in Southern Masculinity: The Ball Family of South Carolina in the New Republic," *Journal of Southern History* 69, no. 1 (2003): 39–70, esp. 52. On the range of expression in male friendship, see E. Anthony Rotundo, "Romantic Friendship: Male Intimacy and Middle-Class Youth in the Northern United States, 1800–1900," *Journal of Social History* 23, no. 1 (1989): 1–25, esp. 2–8. On letters as "at once a part of formal schooling and a part of intimate life," see Steven M. Stowe, *Intimacy and Power in the Old South: Ritual in the Lives of the Planters* (Baltimore, MD, 1987), 142–43.

20. Washington to John, 1749–50, PGW-CS 1:42.

21. See Howard Anderson, "Sterne's Letters: Consciousness and Sympathy," in *The Familiar Letter in the Eighteenth Century*, 134.

22. See Herbert Davis, "The Correspondence of the Augustans," in *The Familiar Letter in the Eighteenth Century*, 13. The phrase "epistolary self" comes from Dierks, *In My Power*, 163–65.

23. John Arbuthnot to Jonathan Swift, August 12, 1714, in *The Correspondence of Jonathan Swift*, 2:233.

24. Washington to Joseph Reed, January 23, 1776, PGW-RWS 3:173. On the estimate, see Arthur S. Lefkowitz, *George Washington's Indispensable Men* (Guilford, CT, 2003), 4.

25. Hayes, *George Washington*, xii.

26. On Washington polishing his grammar and straightening out his convoluted syntax, see Paul K. Longmore, *The Invention of George Washington* (Charlottesville, VA, 1999), 8.

27. For more "letters of friendship," see Thomas J. Fleming, *Affectionately Yours, George Washington* (New York, 1967).

28. Washington to Lafayette, September 30, 1779, PGW-RWS 22:558–59.

29. Washington to Lafayette, March 18, 1780, PGW-RWS 25:82–83; Washington to Lafayette, July 4, 1779, PGW-RWS 21:350; Washington to Lafayette, September 12, 1779, PGW-RWS 22:405.

30. Washington to Lafayette, September 30, 1779, PGW-RWS 22:562.

31. Lafayette to Washington, April 27, 1780, PGW-RWS 25:501; Washington to Lafayette, May 8, 1780, PGW-RWS 25:571–72.

32. Washington to Lafayette, December 8, 1784, PGW-CFS 2:175.

33. Thomas Paine to Washington, July 30, 1796, in *Life and Writings of Thomas Paine*, 10 vols., ed. Daniel Edwin Wheeler (New York, 1908), 9:188–89.

CHAPTER 7. *The Meaning of Love (and Marriage)*

1. John E. Ferling, *The First of Men: A Life of George Washington* (1988; rpt., New York, 2010), 52.

2. Historian and biographer Peter Henriques argues that Mary Ball Washington underwent the same evolution, from exaggerated saintliness

to unalloyed shrewishness (*First and Always: A New Portrait of George Washington* [Charlottesville, VA, 2020], 19).

3. Patricia Brady, *Martha Washington: An American Life* (New York, 2005), 27. On Martha's sexually attractiveness, see Brady, *Martha Washington*, 233. On Martha as a sweet young woman, see also Mary V. Thompson, "'The Lowest Ebb of Misery': Death and Mourning in the Family of George Washington," typescript, 1999, GWMV, esp. 6–7. On Martha as a prized target for many suitors, see Mary V. Thompson, "'An Agreeable Consort for Life': The Wedding of George and Martha Washington," *Historic Alexandria Quarterly* 6, no. 3 (2001), 1–9.

4. On Martha's education, see Ellen McCallister Clark, "The Life of Martha Washington," in *"Worthy Partner": The Papers of Martha Washington*, ed. Joseph E. Fields (Westport, CT, 1994), xix–xx. On Martha playing the spinet and more on her education, see Polly Longworth, "Portrait of Martha, Belle of New Kent," *Colonial Williamsburg Journal* 10, no. 4 (1988): 4–11, 6. On Martha being a good conversationalist, see Olney Winsor to Mrs. Olney (Hope) Winsor, March 31, 1788, in *The Documentary History of the Ratification of the Constitution, Digital Edition*, 18 vols., ed. John P. Kaminski, Gaspare J. Saladino, Richard Leffler, Charles H. Schoenleber, and Margaret A. Hogan (Charlottesville, VA, 2009), 8:523. On Martha inspiring love from others, see Abigail Adams to Mary Smith Cranch, July 12, 1789, *Founders Online*, National Archives, https://founders.archives.gov/documents/Adams/04-08-02-0210. On Martha at Chestnut Grove, see Brady, *Martha Washington*, 22.

5. Allan Kulikoff suggests that the age of first marriage was inversely proportional to the availability of land (*From British Peasants to Colonial American Farmers* [Chapel Hill, NC, 2000]). See also Flora Fraser, *The Washingtons: George and Martha* (New York, 2015).

6. Martha Washington to Frances Bassett Washington, May 24, 1795, in *Worthy Partner*, 287. For the promulgation of the idea that Martha was much harsher than George, see, for example, Henry Wiencek, *An Imperfect God: George Washington, His Slaves, and the Creation of America* (New York, 2003), 86, 354–55. For a corrective to this myth, see Mary V. Thompson, *"The Only Unavoidable Subject of Regret": George Washington, Slavery, and the Enslaved Community at Mount Vernon* (Charlottesville, VA, 2019),

38. On Martha treating her slaves "well," whatever that means, see Brady, *Martha Washington*, 39.

7. George Washington Parke Custis, *Recollections and Private Memoirs of Washington* (1859; rpt., New York, 1860), 499–501.

8. For this trove of information, see Thompson, "An Agreeable Consort for Life." In another paper, Thompson hints at the possibility that Martha might have been the "Low Land Beauty" whom Washington mentions in a juvenile letter to his friend Robin. See Mary V. Thompson, "'Your Happiness when together will be much greater than when you are apart': The Marriage of George and Martha Washington," typescript, 2015, GWMV, 2–3. See also Washington to Robin, 1749–50, PGW-CS 1:41.

9. Robert Stewart to Washington, January 16, 1759, PGW-CS 6:187.

10. On the possibility that Martha and George were already acquainted, see Dorothy Schneider and Carl J. Schneider, "Martha Dandridge Custis Washington," *First Ladies: A Biographical Dictionary* (2001; rpt., New York, 2010), 3.

11. On Washington's visits, see PGW-CS 5:102–103n6 and 5:221n1.

12. Custis, *Recollections and Private Memoirs of Washington*, 502. On Washington's outfit at his wedding, see also James Morgan, "Along Washington's Path," *Evening Star* (Washington, DC), April 29, 1932, C-4. On the bride's outfit, see "Yr Entire Go Washington," Mount Vernon Ladies' Association of the Union, Annual Report 1976, GWMV, 22–24, 23.

13. See Washington to Martha Washington, October 1, 1782, Rhode Island Historical Society, Providence, RI. On the hundreds of letters between Martha and George, see Wendy Kail, "The Correspondence of George and Martha Washington," https://washingtonpapers.org/resources /articles/the-correspondence-of-george-and-martha-washington.

14. Martha Washington to Washington, March 30, 1767, PGW-CS 7:495; John Parke Custis to Washington, September 11, 1777, PGW-RWS 11:203.

15. Washington to Martha Washington, June 18, 1775, PGW-RWS 1:3–5; Washington to Martha Washington, June 23, 1775, PGW-RWS 1:27.

16. Elizabeth Willing Powel to Washington, March 11, 1797, PGW-RS 1:29. For Washington thanking Powel for her "delicacy" and claiming that those letters were "more fraught with expressions of friendship, than of

enamoured love," see his letter dated March 26, 1797, to her, PGW-RS 1:51–53. For more details on the transaction between Washington and Powel, see Tobias Lear to Elizabeth Willing Powel, March 9, 1797, Historical Society of Pennsylvania, Philadelphia.

17. On "old man," see Martha Daingerfield Bland to Frances Bland Randolph, May 12, 1777, PGW-RWS 9:322. On "pappa" and "general," see Stephen Decatur Jr., *Private Affairs of George Washington* (Boston, 1933), 66. On Martha unapologetic, see Anne Hollingsworth Wharton, *Martha Washington* (New York, 1897), 165–66. For "your entire George Washington," see Washington to Martha Washington, June 23, 1775, PGW-RWS 1:27.

18. On the complexities of eighteenth-century happiness, see Carli N. Conklin, *Pursuit of Happiness in the Founding Era: An Intellectual History* (Columbia, MO, 2019).

19. Washington to Richard Washington, September 20, 1759, PGW-CS 6:359. For an example of Washington describing his daily routine, see his letter to James McHenry, May 29, 1797, PGW-RS 1:159–60. See also Brady, *Martha Washington*, 71–73.

20. Washington to Burwell Bassett, May 23, 1785, PGW-CFS 3:10.

21. Washington to Elizabeth Parke Custis, September 14, 1794, PGW-PS 16:682–83.

22. On the eighteenth-century communitarian vision, see my *Nature's Man: Thomas Jefferson's Philosophical Anthropology* (Charlottesville, VA, 2013). See also Ari Helo and Peter S. Onuf, "Jefferson, Morality, and the Problem of Slavery," *William and Mary Quarterly* 60, no. 3 (2003): 583–614, esp. 611–12.

23. On the legend of Washington as a "stallion," see James Thomas Flexner, *George Washington: The Indispensable Man* (Boston, 1974), 367. On the myth of Washington ranking enslaved women, see Henriques, *First and Always*, 50.

24. See Karen Harvey, "The Century of Sex? Gender, Bodies, and Sexuality in the Long Eighteenth Century," *Historical Journal* 45 (2002): 899–916. And see Thomas A. Foster, *Sex and the Founding Fathers: The American Quest for a Relatable Past* (Philadelphia, 2014).

25. For slaveowners sexually abusing enslaved women, see Lorri Glover, "An Education in Southern Masculinity: The Ball Family of South Carolina in the New Republic," *Journal of Southern History* 69, no. 1 (2003):

39–70, esp. 56. For enslaved men becoming "prey," see Thomas A. Foster, *Rethinking Rufus: Sexual Violations of Enslaved Men* (Athens, GA, 2019).

26. See Tim Hitchcock, *English Sexualities, 1700–1800* (New York, 1997), 31, 36.

27. Michel Foucault (*The History of Sexuality*) has argued that the kind of preoccupation nineteenth-century Victorianism had with sex was entirely new. Censoring sexual acts both enhanced and universalized their importance. Jean-Paul Sartre (*Being and Nothingness*) criticizes psychoanalysis for assuming that one form of experience (determined by the sexual drive) defines the condition of all human lives. Anthropologist Bronislaw Malinowski (*Sex and Repression in Savage Society*) contends that societies handle sexuality differently. See also the *William and Mary Quarterly*'s special issue on sexuality in early America (60, no. 1 [2003]).

28. On women swooning at Washington's appearance, see Joseph J. Ellis, *His Excellency: George Washington* (New York, 2004), 11.

29. See Hitchcock, *English Sexualities*, 4.

30. See Michèle Cohen "'Manners' Make the Man: Politeness, Chivalry, and the Construction of Masculinity, 1750–1830," *Journal of British Studies* 44, no. 2 (2005): 312–29, 313. On slaveowners trying to keep the sexual exploitation of enslaved persons secret, see Joshua D. Rothman, *Notorious in the Neighborhood: Sex and Families Across the Color Line in Virginia, 1787–1861* (Chapel Hill, NC, 2003).

31. Washington to Robin, 1749–50, PGW-CS 1:41; William La Péronie to Washington, September 5, 1754, PGW-CS 1:203, 205n1. On Washington's virginity, see also Thompson, *"The Only Unavoidable Subject of Regret,"* 148, and Mark E. Kahn, "The Bachelor and Other Disorderly Men during the American Founding," *Journal of Men's Studies* 6, no. 1 (1997): 1–27. Kahn makes the convincing argument that "sexual self-restraint was a key test of manhood" (6).

32. Washington to George Steptoe Washington, March 23, 1789, PGW-PS 1:440.

33. See Anthony Fletcher, "Manhood, the Male Body, Courtship and the Household in Early Modern England," *History* 84, no. 275 (1999): 419–36, 431–32. On courtship, see also Ruth H. Bloch, *Gender and Morality in Anglo-American Culture, 1650–1800* (Berkeley, CA, 2003), esp. 78–

101, and Ellen K. Rothman, *Hands and Hearts: A History of Courtship in America* (New York, 1984).

34. Washington to John, 1749–50, PGW-CS 1:42; Frank Brady, "*Tristram Shandy*: Sexuality, Morality, and Sensibility," *Eighteenth-Century Studies* 4, no. 1 (1970): 41–56, 41. On Martha's library, see PGW-CS 6:283–97. For other books owned by Martha's first husband that reached Mount Vernon, see Kevin J. Hayes, *George Washington: A Life in Books* (New York, 2017), 96–97.

35. See Washington, invoice to Robert Cary & Company, September 20, 1759, PGW-CS 6:354.

36. Andrew Burstein, *Jefferson's Secrets: Death and Desire at Monticello* (New York, 2005), 157. Burstein insists that the eighteenth-century sexual world cannot be understand solely in psychological or psychoanalytic terms. I'm deeply indebted to this interpretation.

37. On sex "conceptualized as a problem of fluid dynamics," see Hitchcock, *English Sexualities*, 43. See also the range of discussion in Greta LaFleur, *The Natural History of Sexuality in Early America* (Baltimore, MD, 2018), 111 and 235n34. On Tissot, see LaFleur, *The Natural History of Sexuality in Early America*, 235–36n40.

38. Washington to Eleanor Parke Custis, March 21, 1796, PGW-PS 19:575.

39. On the structure of male and female genitalia, see Thomas Laqueur, *Making Sex: Body and Gender from the Greeks to Freud* (Cambridge, MA, 1990), 4–5, 23–35, and Hitchcock, *English Sexualities*, 43–44.

40. On the emergence of "separate spheres," see R. W. Connell, *Masculinities* (1995; rpt., Berkeley, CA, 2005), 68. See also Amanda Vickery, "Golden Age to Separate Spheres? A Review of the Categories and Chronology of English Women's History," *Historical Journal* 36, no. 2 (1993): 383–414, and Robert B. Shoemaker, *Gender in English Society, 1650–1850: The Emergence of Separate Spheres?* (1998; rpt., New York, 2013).

41. Benjamin Rush, in *Benjamin Rush's Lectures on the Mind*, ed. Eric T. Carlson, Jeffrey L. Wollock, and Patricia S. Noel (Philadelphia, 1981), 686, 687; Washington to Annis Boudinot Stockton, August 31, 1788, PGW-CFS 6:496.

42. See Laqueur, *Making Sex*, 46. See also Anthony Preus, "Galen's

Criticism of Aristotle's Conception Theory," *Journal of the History of Biology* 10, no. 1 (1977): 65–85.

43. On the social need to redefine women as fundamentally different from men, see Hitchcock, *English Sexualities*, 47. On the discovery of anatomical differences that certified an essential difference between women and men, see John S. Haller and Robin M. Haller, *The Physician and Sexuality in Victorian America* (New York, 1974), 24–43.

44. See Shoemaker, *Gender in English Society*, 85.

45. On the idea that women were to be loving but not have sexual needs, see Ruth Perry, "Colonizing the Breast: Sexuality and Maternity in Eighteenth-Century England," in *Forbidden History: The State, Society, and the Regulation of Sexuality in Modern Europe*, ed. John C. Fout (Chicago, 1992), 115–16. On the new hegemonic phallocentric culture and a restrictive form of masculinity, see Hitchcock, *English Sexualities*, 111–12.

46. On Martha seizing George by the button, Custis, *Recollections and Private Memoirs of Washington*, 41.

47. Brady, *Martha Washington*, 22. On Martha retaining traces of considerable beauty, see Benjamin Henry Latrobe, *The Journal of Latrobe* (New York, 1905), 57.

CHAPTER 8. *A Sentimental Male*

1. Washington eloquently defined the "Spirit of Chivalry," or simply honor, as a "virtue of such ancient date" that everyone should simply turn it "into ridicule" (Washington to Lafayette, October 4, 1778, PGW-RWS 17:249). For a criticism of "real" men and the "deep masculine," see R. W. Connell, *Masculinities* (1995; rpt., Berkeley, CA, 2005), 45. On Virginia, see Bertram Wyatt-Brown, *Southern Honor: Ethics and Behavior in the Old South* (1982; rpt., New York, 2007). On dueling in America, see Joanne B. Freeman, *Affairs of Honor: National Politics in the New Republic* (New Haven, CT, 2001).

2. William Thornton to Joseph Gales, August 13, 1823, manuscript, private collection, https://historical.ha.com/itm/miscellaneous/thornton -william-autograph-letter-signed-4-pages-9-3-4-x-7-in-248-x-200-mm -city-of-washington-13-august-1823-to-j/a/997004-1081.s. On Washing-

ton transcending stereotypes of southern honor, see William Guthrie Sayen, "George Washington's 'Unmannerly' Behavior: The Clash between Civility and Honor," *Virginia Magazine of History and Biography* 107, no. 1 (1999): 2–36. See also Mary Chapman and Glenn Hendler, eds., *Sentimental Men: Masculinity and the Politics of Affect in American Culture* (Berkeley, CA, 1999), and Robert B. Shoemaker, "Taming of the Duel: Masculinity, Honour, and Ritual Violence in London, 1660–1800," *Historical Journal* 45, no. 3 (2002): 525–45. On Washington becoming "quite merry" over a few glasses of champagne and laughing and talking a good deal, see Robert Hunter Jr., travel diary, November 16, 1785, in *The Founders on the Founders: Word Portraits from the American Revolutionary Era*, ed. John P. Kaminski (Charlottesville, VA, 2008), 495.

3. Washington to George Washington Parke Custis, January 7, 1798, PGW-RS 2:5.

4. "Mount Vernon Reminiscences," *Alexandria (VA) Gazette*, January 18, 1876. See also Benjamin Henry Latrobe, *The Journal of Latrobe* (New York, 1905), 61–62.

5. On the lack of extensive cross-situational consistency in personality, see Walter Mischel, "Convergences and Challenges in the Search for Consistency," *American Psychologist* 39, no. 4 (1984): 351–64, esp. 357.

6. On multiple masculinities within the same individual, see Sarah Goldsmith, *Masculinity and Danger on the Eighteenth-Century Grand Tour* (London, 2020), 17–18, 213.

7. James Thacher, *A Military Journal during the American Revolutionary War, from 1775 to 1783* (Boston, 1823), 191.

8. François Marbois, September 12, 1779, in *George Washington as the French Knew Him: A Collection of Texts*, ed. Gilbert Chinard (1940; rpt., New York, 1969), 75.

9. John Bell, 1779, in *Character Portraits of Washington as Delineated by Historians, Orators and Divines*, ed. W. S. Baker (Philadelphia, 1887), 12.

10. Count Segur, *Memoirs and Recollections of Count Segur* (London, 1825), 348.

11. Washington to Alexander Hamilton, October 3, 1788, PGW-PS 1:32.

12. See Richard L. Bushman, *The Refinement of America: Persons, Houses, Cities* (New York, 1993).

13. Nicole Eustace, *Passion Is the Gale: Emotion, Power, and the Coming of the American Revolution* (Chapel Hill, NC, 2008), 261. On the Quakers, see Eustace, *Passion Is the Gale*, 211.

14. See Nancy Isenberg and Andrew Burstein, eds., *Mortal Remains: Death in Early America* (Philadelphia, 2003), and Jan Lewis, *The Pursuit of Happiness: Family and Values in Jefferson's Virginia* (Cambridge, UK, 1983), esp. 69–105.

15. Washington to Burgess Ball, September 22, 1799, PGW-RS 4:318; Washington to Betty Washington Lewis, September 13, 1789, PGW-PS 4:32; Washington to George Lewis, April 9, 1797, PGW-RS 1:90; John Parke Custis to Washington, July 5, 1773, PGW-CS 9:265; Washington, June 19, 1773, PGW-D 3:188; Washington to Burwell Bassett, June 20, 1773, PGW-CS 9:243–44. On Washington crying at Patsy's bedside, see William D. Hoyt, "Self-Portrait: Eliza Parke Custis, 1808," *Virginia Magazine of History and Biography* 53, no. 2 (1945): 89–100, 92. See also Eleanor Parke Custis to Jared Sparks, February 26, 1833, in Jared Sparks, *The Life of George Washington* (Boston, 1839), 522, and Peter R. Henriques, "The Final Struggle between George Washington and the Grim King: Washington's Attitude toward Death and an Afterlife," *Virginia Magazine of History and Biography* 107, no. 1 (1999): 73–97, 89–90.

16. "Death of General Washington," December 23, 1799, in *American State Papers: Documents, Legislative and Executive, of the Congress of the United States*, class 10: Miscellaneous, 2 vols. (Washington, DC, 1834), 1:190; Benjamin Tallmadge, *Memoir of Col. Benjamin Tallmadge* (New York, 1858), 64. See also C. B. Taylor, *A Universal History of the United States of America* (New York, 1836), 233.

17. James McHenry to Margaret Caldwell, December 23, 1783, in Bernard C. Steiner, *The Life and Correspondence of James McHenry* (Cleveland, OH, 1907), 69. On weeping being manly, see also Eustace, *Passion Is the Gale*, 246.

18. See Eustace, *Passion Is the Gale*, 14, 64, 244–45.

19. William Thornton to Joseph Gales, August 13, 1823, manuscript, private collection, https://historical.ha.com/itm/miscellaneous/thornton-william-autograph-letter-signed-4-pages-9-3-4-x-7-in-248-x-200-mm-city-of-washington-13-august-1823-to-j/a/997004-1081.s.

20. See Jeremy Gregory, "*Homo Religiosus*: Masculinity and Religion in the Long Eighteenth Century," in *English Masculinities, 1660–1800*, ed. Tim Hitchcock and Michèle Cohen (1999; rpt. Milton Park, UK, and New York, 2014), 85–110.

21. On the success of "Christian masculinity," see William Van Reyk, "Christian Ideals of Manliness in the Eighteenth and Early Nineteenth Centuries," *Historical Journal* 52, no. 4 (2009): 1053–73, esp. 1056. On Christian ideals emerging in Virginia at a time when masculinity, even among the better sort, was none too secure, see Janet Moore Lindman, "Acting the Manly Christian: White Evangelical Masculinity in Revolutionary Virginia," *William and Mary Quarterly* 57, no. 2 (2000): 393–416. See also Kenneth Lockridge, "Colonial Self-Fashioning: Paradoxes and Pathologies in the Construction of Genteel Identity in Eighteenth-Century America," in *Through a Glass Darkly: Reflections on Personal Identity in Early America*, ed. Ronald Hoffman, Mechal Sobel, and Fredrika J. Teute (Chapel Hill, NC, 1997), 274–339.

22. Elkanah Watson, from *Men and Times of the Revolution; or the Memoirs Elkanah Watson*, January 23–25, 1785, in *The Founders on the Founders*, 492–93.

23. Feminist thinker Carol J. Adams asserts that "men who choose not to eat meat repudiate one of their masculine privileges" (*Sexual Politics of Meat: A Feminist-Vegetarian Critical Theory* (1990; rpt., New York, 2015), 17. See also Bruce Feirstein, *Real Men Don't Eat Quiche: A Guidebook to All That Is Truly Masculine* (New York, 1982). For the claim that foods of a light substance produced refined bodies, see Trudy Eden, "Food, Assimilation, and the Malleability of the Human Body in Early Virginia," in *A Centre of Wonders: The Body in Early America*, ed. Janet Moore Lindman and Michele Lise Tarter (Ithaca, NY, 2001), 33. On the multiple social consequences of the act of eating, including the establishment of differences and similarities, see Deborah Lupton, *Food, the Body, and the Self* (London, 1996), 15–19.

24. Washington to Anthony Whitting, June 9, 1793, PGW-PS 13:49.

25. For more details, see Eleanor Parke Custis Lewis to Elizabeth Bordley Gibson, February 23, 1823, typescript, GWMV.

26. See Stephen Decatur Jr., *Private Affairs of George Washington* (Boston, 1933), 222.

27. Marquis de Chastellux, *Travels in North-America, in the Years 1780, 1781 and 1782*, 2 vols. (London, 1787), 1:124.

28. Washington to Alexander McDougall, May 23, 1777, PGW-RWS 9:506; Washington, general orders, June 2, 1777, PGW-RWS 9:589.

29. David Humphreys, *"Life of General Washington" with George Washington's "Remarks,"* ed. Rosemarie Zagarri (Athens, GA, 1991), 36.

30. Thomas Jefferson to Abigail Adams, September 25, 1785, *Founders Online*, National Archives, https://founders.archives.gov/documents /Adams/04-06-02-0120.

31. David Ackerson to his son, 1811, in Henry Cabot Lodge, *George Washington*, 2 vols. (Boston, 1889), 2:382; Humphreys, *"Life of General Washington,"* 36. On Washington and the silver pint cup of beer, see Decatur, *Private Affairs of George Washington*, 51. On beer, porter, and cider being used extensively, see Decatur, *Private Affairs of George Washington*, 115. On Washington making a distinction between alcoholic beverages consumed during and after dinner, see his letter to Gouverneur Morris, October 13, 1789, PGW-PS 4:178.

32. *Connecticut Gazette*, February 2, 1780; Washington to Moustier, December 15, 1788, PGW-PS 1:181. See also Decatur, *Private Affairs of George Washington*, 122.

33. William Maclay, *Journal of William Maclay, United States Senator from Pennsylvania, 1789–1791*, ed. Edgar S. Maclay (New York, 1890), 177; Jonathan Bouchier, ed., *Reminiscences of an American Loyalist, 1738–1789: Being the Autobiography of the Revd. Jonathan Boucher, Rector of Annapolis in Maryland and afterwards Vicar of Epsom, Surrey, England* (Port Washington, NY, 1967), 50.

34. James Parton, *Life of Thomas Jefferson* (Boston, 1874), 369. As Peter R. Henriques remarks, "This tale is one more myth about Washington that should be discarded" (*First and Always: A New Portrait of George Washington* [Charlottesville, VA, 2020], 47). See also Mary-Jo Kline, "Gouverneur Morris and George Washington: Prodigal Son and Patient Father," in *Sons of the Fathers: George Washington and His Protégés*, ed. Robert M. S. McDonald (Charlottesville, VA, 2013), 169–88.

35. Ebenezer Denny, in Richard M. Ketchum, *Victory at Yorktown: The Campaign that Won the Revolution* (New York, 2004), 186.

36. St. George Tucker, in Ketchum, *Victory at Yorktown*, 186.

37. See A. H. Maslow, "The Dynamics of Psychological Security-Insecurity," *Journal of Personality* 10, no. 4 (1942): 331–44. On Washington embracing and kissing General Henry Knox, see Taylor, *A Universal History of the United States*, 233.

38. Benjamin Rush to Granville Sharp, April 27, 1784, in *Letters of Benjamin Rush*, 2 vols., ed. Lyman H. Butterfield (Princeton, NJ, 1951), 1:330.

39. John Adams, diary entry, September 9, 1776, *Founders Online*, National Archives, https://founders.archives.gov/documents/Adams/01-03-02-0016-0187.

40. See Michael Olmert, *Kitchens, Smokehouses, and Privies: Outbuildings and the Architecture of Daily Life in the Eighteenth-Century Mid-Atlantic* (Ithaca, NY, 2009). See also https://www.ploddingthroughthe presidents.com/2019/10/did-george-washington-poop-with-friends.html ?fbclid=IwAR2HZZHKDzTRCpvYvTm46M5_TDdolu96yeYgy8n _j3ZWqa2Xc4kbU800DEg.

41. Washington to George Gilpin and John Fitzgerald, September 1, 1786, PGW-CFS 4:234. See also Washington to John Fitzgerald, September 9, 1786, PGW-CFS 4:242.

42. See Alun Withey, *Technology, Self-Fashioning and Politeness in Eighteenth-Century Britain: Refined Bodies* (London, 2016).

43. On this last point, see Withey, *Technology, Self-Fashioning and Politeness*, 46. See also Alun Withey, *Concerning Beards: Facial Hair, Health and Practice in England, 1650–1900* (London, 2021).

44. Washington, general orders, November 9, 1777, PGW-RWS 12:177; Washington, general orders, April 8, 1778, PGW-RWS 14:422.

45. See Edward Said, *Orientalism* (1978; rpt., London, 2019).

CHAPTER 9. *A Maternal Father*

1. Henry Knox to Washington, March 19, 1787, PGW-CFS 5:96. For "the people of America look up to you as their Father," see Henry Knox to Washington, November 26, 1777, PGW-RWS 12:415.

2. Gouverneur Morris to Washington, December 6, 1788, PGW-PS 1:166. On Washington a eunuch and a woman in disguise, see James Thomas Flexner, *George Washington: The Indispensable Man* (Boston, 1974), 367. On West Ford, see Mary V. Thompson, *"The Only Unavoidable Subject of Regret": George Washington, Slavery, and the Enslaved Community at Mount Vernon* (Charlottesville, VA, 2019), 148–51, and Peter R. Henriques, *First and Always: A New Portrait of George Washington* (Charlottesville, VA, 2020), 52.

3. Washington to George Augustine Washington, October 25, 1786, PGW-CFS 4:308.

4. See Mary V. Thompson, "First Father: George Washington as a Parent," typescript, 2000, rev. 2016, GWMV, 7. For more on the suggestion that Martha Washington possibly suffered an injury in childbirth, see James Thomas Flexner, *George Washington: The Forge of Experience, 1732–1775* (Boston, 1965), 270n.

5. See Thompson, "First Father," 6–7. On the widespread use of abortifacients in the eighteenth century, see Angus McLaren, *Reproductive Rituals: The Perception of Fertility in England from the Sixteenth to the Nineteenth Century* (London, 1984), esp. 89–112.

6. See John K. Amory, "George Washington's Infertility: Why Was the Father of Our Country Never a Father?" *Fertility and Sterility* 81, no. 3 (2004): 495–99 passim.

7. On Washington suffering from Klinefelter syndrome, see M. J. V. Smith, "The Father Who Was Not a Father," *Virginia Medical Monthly* 103, no. 1 (1976): 14–22. On XYY syndrome, see Robert Marion, *Was George Washington Really the Father of Our Country? A Clinical Geneticist Looks at World History* (Reading, MA, 1994), 41–72.

8. See James Dennison, "The Experiences and Contributions of Women Following the British Army During the Seven Years' War," 2018, University of Windsor Major Papers, https://scholar.uwindsor.ca/major -papers/9. See also William La Péronie to Washington, September 5, 1754, PGW-CS 1:203, 205n1.

9. Washington to William Fauntleroy Sr., May 20, 1752, PGW-CS 1:49. On the smallpox in Barbados, see Washington, November 4, 1751, PGW-D 1:73.

10. See Amory, "George Washington's Infertility," 497.

11. "The Making of the Bronze Statues of the Washington Family," https://www.mountvernon.org/the-estate-gardens/ford-orientation-center/washington-family-statues.

12. John Parke Custis to Washington, June 10, 1776, PGW-RWS 4:485.

13. Washington's last will and testament, July 9, 1799, PGW-RS 4:489.

14. John Parke Custis to Martha Washington, July 5, 1773, in *"Worthy Partner": The Papers of Martha Washington*, ed. Joseph E. Fields (Westport, CT, 1994), 152. See also Lorri Glover, *Founders as Fathers: The Private Lives and Politics of the American Revolutionaries* (New Haven, CT, 2016), 41.

15. Lawrence Augustine Washington to Washington, July 7, 1794, PGW-PS 16:314; Harriot Washington to Washington, July 10, 1794, PGW-PS 16:328–29; Harriot Washington to Washington, February 8, 1796, PGW-PS 19:444. See also Harriot Washington to Washington, September 10, 1793, PGW-PS 14:62–63, Harriot Washington to Washington, February 9, 1794, PGW-PS 15:206, Harriot Washington to Washington, March 5, 1794, PGW-PS 15:333, and Harriot Washington to Washington, March 24, 1794, PGW-PS 15:448.

16. Washington to Harriot Washington, October 30, 1791, PGW-PS 9:130; Washington to Myles Cooper, December 15, 1773, PGW-CS 9:406.

17. See Marilyn Dell Brady, "The New Model Middle-Class Family, 1815–1930," in *American Families: A Research Guide and Historical Handbook*, ed. Joseph M. Hawes and Elizabeth I. Nybakken (New York, 1991), 98–103.

18. On the complexities of eighteenth-century American and Virginian families, see T. H. Breen, *Tobacco Culture: The Mentality of the Great Tidewater Planters on the Eve of Revolution* (1985; rpt., Princeton, NJ, 2001), Rhys Isaac, *The Transformation of Virginia, 1740–1790* (1982; rpt., Chapel Hill, NC, 1999), Daniel Blake Smith, *Inside the Great House: Planter Family Life in Eighteenth-Century Chesapeake Society* (Ithaca, NY, 1980), Jan Lewis, *The Pursuit of Happiness: Family and Values in Jefferson's Virginia* (Cambridge, UK, 1983), and Kathleen M. Brown, *Good Wives, Nasty Wenches, and Anxious Patriarchs: Gender, Race, and Power in Colonial Virginia* (Chapel Hill, NC, 1996).

19. On such "sentimentalization of home," see Konstantin Dierks,

In My Power: Letter Writing and Communications in Early America (Philadelphia, 2009), 169.

20. On eighteenth-century Virginia fathers as moved by babies, see James Marten, "Fatherhood in the Confederacy: Southern Soldiers and Their Children," *Journal of Southern History* 63, no. 2 (1997): 269–92, 270–71. On involved fathers, see Joanne Bailey, "'A Very Sensible Man': Imagining Fatherhood in England c. 1750–1830," *History* 95, no. 3 (2010): 267–92, esp. 276, 287. See also Lewis, *Pursuit of Happiness*, esp. 179–86, Jane Turner Censer, *North Carolina Planters and Their Children, 1800–1860* (Baton Rouge, LA, 1984), and Stephen M. Frank, *Life with Father: Parenthood and Masculinity in the Nineteenth-Century American North* (Baltimore, MD, 1998). For more on fatherhood, see Glover, *Founders as Fathers*, Robert L. Griswold, *Fatherhood in America: A History* (New York, 1993), and the *Journal of Family History*'s special issue on fatherhood (24 [1999]).

21. On Washington being happy at home, see Patricia Brady, "George Washington and His Family," in *A Companion to George Washington*, ed. Edward G. Lengel (Oxford, UK, 2012), 86–103, 86.

22. Eleanor Calvert Custis Stuart to Tobias Lear, July 8, 1789, and April 18, 1790, manuscript, GWMV.

23. Clayton Torrence, ed., "Arlington and Mount Vernon, 1856: As Described in a Letter of Augusta Blanche Berard," *Virginia Magazine of History and Biography* 57, no. 2 (1949): 140–175, 162.

24. George Washington Parke Custis, *Recollections and Private Memoirs of Washington* (1859; rpt., New York, 1860), 408n. On Martha Washington's "admirable management," see Torrence, "Arlington and Mount Vernon, 1856," 162.

25. Eleanor Parke Custis Lewis to Elizabeth Bordley Gibson, February 23, 1823, typescript, GWMV. See also Eleanor Parke Custis Lewis to Jared Sparks, February 26, 1833, in Jared Sparks, *The Life of George Washington* (Boston, 1839), 522: "I have sometimes made him laugh most heartily from sympathy with my joyous and extravagant spirits." On Nelly's merry pranks, see Custis, *Recollections and Private Memoirs of Washington*, 41.

26. Eleanor Parke Custis Lewis to Elizabeth Bordley Gibson, October 19, 1795, in *George Washington's Beautiful Nelly: The Letters of Eleanor*

Parke Custis Lewis to Elizabeth Bordley Gibson, 1794–1851, ed. Patricia Brady (Columbia, SC, 1991), 21.

27. Julian Ursyn Niemcewicz, *Under Their Vine and Fig Tree: Travels through America in 1797–1799, 1805*, trans. Metchie J. E. Budka (Elizabeth, NJ, 1965), 85.

28. Washington to Elizabeth Parke Custis, February 10, 1796, PGW-PS 19:445.

29. Benjamin Henry Latrobe, *The Journal of Latrobe* (New York, 1905), 58; Ron Chernow, *Washington: A Life* (New York, 2010), 739. For "father—friend—protector—and supporter," see Washington to George Cabot, September 7, 1795, PGW-PS 18:642–43. For "visible distress," see Washington to Thomas Pinckney, May 22, 1796, PGW-PS 20:184. For "modest, Sensible, & deserving," see Washington to Ségur, June 24, 1797, PGW-RS 1:209. For Washington telling the imperial ambassador in London, via Thomas Pinckney, that Lafayette's release was "*an ardent wish of the people of the United States* in wch I sincerely add mine," see his letter to Thomas Pinckney, February 20, 1796, PGW-PS 19:479.

30. Washington to Charles Carter, May 19, 1792, PGW-PS 10:398; Howell Lewis, in James Kirke Paulding, *A Life of Washington*, 2 vols. (New York, 1835), 2:196.

CHAPTER 10. *A Person of Fine Manners*

1. Benson J. Lossing, *Washington and the American Republic*, 3 vols. (New York, 1869), 3:591. See also Philip Carter, *Men and the Emergence of Polite Society, Britain, 1660–1800* (2001; rpt., London and New York, 2016). Politeness, of course, coexisted with other, impolite models of masculinity. See Paul Langford, "The Uses of Eighteenth-Century Politeness," *Transactions of the Royal Historical Society* 12 (2002): 311–31, Stephen Banks, *A Polite Exchange of Bullets: the Duel and the English Gentleman, 1750–1850* (Woodbridge, UK, 2010), Simon Dickie, *Cruelty and Laughter: Forgotten Comic Literature and the Unsentimental Eighteenth Century* (Chicago, 2011), and Karen Harvey, "Ritual Encounters: Punch Parties and Masculinity in the Eighteenth Century," *Past and Present* 214, no. 1 (2012): 165–203. As Mercy Otis Warren noted in a letter to John Adams (October 1775, *Found-*

ers Online, National Archives, https://founders.archives.gov/documents /Adams/06-03-02-0142), Washington was "one of the most amiable and accomplished gentlemen, both in person, mind, and manners."

2. See Lawrence E. Klein, *Shaftesbury and the Culture of Politeness: Moral Discourse and Cultural Politics in Early Eighteenth-Century England* (Cambridge, UK, 1994). See also Arthur M. Schlesinger, *Learning How to Behave: A Historical Study of American Etiquette Books* (1946; rpt., New York, 1968), Sarah E. Newton, *Learning to Behave: A Guide to American Conduct Books before 1900* (Westport, CT, 1994), and C. Dallett Hemphill, *Bowing to Necessities: A History of Manners in America, 1620–1860* (New York, 2002). On Washington, *The Spectator*, and other English classics, see Kevin J. Hayes, *George Washington: A Life in Books* (New York, 2017), 6–7, 41.

3. On the polite body as a contained body, see Kathleen M. Brown, *Foul Bodies: Cleanliness in Early America* (New Haven, CT, 2009).

4. See Hemphill, *Bowing to Necessities,* 71. On sensibility as a more authentic alternative to politeness, see Philip Carter, "Polite 'Persons': Character, Biography and the Gentleman," *Transactions of the Royal Historical Society* 192 (2002): 333–54, 336.

5. Kevin Hayes argues that Washington's "Rules" stem not from Hawkins directly but from William Winstanley's *New Help to Discourse,* first published in 1669 (*George Washington,* 21). For more information about the "Rules of Civility," see Charles Moore, introduction to *George Washington's Rules of Civility and Decent Behaviour in Company and Conversation,* ed. Charles Moore (Boston, 1926). See also the editorial note to Washington's school exercises, 1744–48, PGW-CS 1:1–4.

6. Austin Washington, a distant relative of Washington, has claimed that the "Rules" are of "zero value, or worse," because George was shaped by another book, Hippolyte du Chastelet de Luzancy's *A Panegyrick to the Memory of His Grace Frederick, Late Duke of Schonberg* (1713). George bought *A Panegyrick* in 1747, from his cousin Bailey Washington, together with other books. The influence of *A Panegyrick* is a "genuine secret, hidden in plain sight for two centuries," he concludes (*The Education of George Washington: How a Forgotten Book Shaped the Character of a Hero* [Washington, DC, 2014], 9). That *A Panegyrick* deeply affected Washington is certainly possible. It tells the story of the skills and accomplishment

of Friedrich Hermann von Schönberg, the first Duke of Schomberg. The duke had a brilliant military career that included a position as second in command under William, Prince of Orange, during the celebrated Glorious Revolution of 1688. The duke had integrity, a dose of Christian humility, and good manners. A fifteen-year-old kid in the eighteenth century could no doubt have found a source of personal inspiration in it.

7. John Bell, 1779, in *Character Portraits of Washington as Delineated by Historians, Orators and Divines*, ed. W. S. Baker (Philadelphia, 1887), 13; Robert-Guillaume Dillon, journal entry, January 21, 1781, "Journal of Robert-Guillaume Dillon, 1780–1781," manuscript, American Revolution Institute of the Society of the Cincinnati; François Marbois, September 12, 1779, in *George Washington as the French Knew Him: A Collection of Texts*, ed. Gilbert Chinard (1940; rpt., New York, 1969), 75. For another comment on Washington's "natural" simplicity of manner, see Moustier, April 30, 1789, in Stephen Decatur Jr., *Private Affairs of George Washington* (Boston, 1933), 7.

8. Benjamin Henry Latrobe, *The Journal of Latrobe* (New York, 1905), 54.

9. Lord Chesterfield to Philip Stanhope, January 10, 1749, *The Letters of Philip Dormer Stanhope, Earl of Chesterfield, with the Characters*, 3 vols. (1774; rpt. London, 1893), 1:190; Castiglione, in Hemphill, *Bowing to Necessity*, 25. On Washington walking the polite line between showiness and austerity, see Ron Chernow, *Washington: A Life* (New York, 2010), 76.

10. Latrobe, *The Journal of Latrobe*, 54. On Washington's hair, see George Washington Parke Custis, *Recollections and Private Memoirs of Washington* (1859; rpt., New York, 1860), 163.

11. Washington to the states, June 8, 1783, *Founders Online*, National Archives, https://founders.archives.gov/documents/Washington/99-01-02 -11404; Washington to Lafayette, August 15, 1786, PGW-CFS 4:215–16.

12. On European "promptitude to luxury," see Washington to James Duane, April 10, 1785, PGW-CFS 2:486.

13. On the persistence of Anglophilia and Europhilia, see Catherine E. Kelly, *Republic of Taste: Art, Politics, and Everyday Life in Early America* (Philadelphia, 2016), esp. 119–58, and Michal J. Rozbicki, "A Barrier or a Bridge to American Identity? The Uses of European Taste among Eighteenth-Century Plantation Gentry in British America," *Amerikastudien/American Studies* 42, no. 3 (1997): 433–49. See also Jack P. Greene,

"Search for Identity: An Interpretation of the Meaning of Selected Patterns of Social Response in Eighteenth-Century America," *Journal of Social History* 3, no. 3 (1970): 189–220. On Americans becoming French, see Michèle Cohen "'Manners' Make the Man: Politeness, Chivalry, and the Construction of Masculinity, 1750–1830," *Journal of British Studies* 44, no. 2 (2005): 312–329, 322.

14. Lord Chesterfield to Philip Stanhope, February 11, 1751, *The Letters of Philip Dormer Stanhope*, 1:405; Washington to Moustier, August 17, 1788, PGW-CFS 6:456–58. For "the quality & price of the French goods," see Washington to Lafayette, August 15, 1786, PGW-CFS 4:215.

15. Washington to Gouverneur Morris, January 28, 1792, PGW-PS 9:516; Washington to Jonathan Boucher, January 2, 1771, PGW-CS 8:426; Washington to Jonathan Boucher, May 13, 1770, PGW-CS 8:334–35.

16. Washington to Jonathan Boucher, July 9, 1771, PGW-CS 8:495; Washington to Jonathan Boucher, December 16, 1770, PGW-CS 8:411; Jonathan Boucher to Washington, December 18, 1770, PGW-CS 8:414.

17. See Amelia Rauser, "Hair, Authenticity, and the Self-Made Macaroni," *Eighteenth-Century Studies* 38, no. 1 (2004): 101–17, and Peter McNeil, *Pretty Gentlemen: Macaroni Men and the Eighteenth-Century Fashion World* (New Haven, CT, 2018).

18. For this view of polite manners, see Lorri Glover, *Founders as Fathers: The Private Lives and Politics of the American Revolutionaries* (New Haven, CT, 2016), 23. On the link between politeness and power, see Steven C. Bullock, *Tea Sets and Tyranny: The Politics of Politeness in Early America* (Philadelphia, 2017).

19. Claude-Victor, Prince de Broglie, 1782, in *Character Portraits of Washington*, 21; Richard Peters, "Fac-Simile of General Washington's Hand Writing; and Sketches of His Private Character," *Memoirs of the Philadelphia Society for Promoting Agriculture*, 6 vols. (Philadelphia, 1808–1939), 2:vii–viii.

20. Washington to William Pearce, December 18, 1793, PGW-PS 14:560. For "Be easy and condescending . . . but not too familiar," see also Washington to William Woodford, November 10, 1775, PGW-RWS 2:346–47. Kelly (*Republic of Taste*, 6) underscores the extent to which Washington's society was Janus-faced.

21. Clifford Dowdey, *The Virginia Dynasties: The Emergence of "King" Carter and the Golden Age* (New York, 1969), 343; Washington to John Augustine Washington, May 28, 1755, PGW-CS 1:290. On Washington's "Herculean efforts" to free himself from "his inferiority of station compared to most elite planters," see also John E. Ferling, *The First of Men: A Life of George Washington* (1988; rpt., New York, 2010), 97.

22. Washington to Chastellux, April 25–May 1, 1788, PGW-CFS 6:228–29.

23. Washington to Archibald Johnston, October 30, 1787, in *Writings of George Washington from the Original Manuscript Sources, 1745–1799*, 39 vols., ed. John C. Fitzpatrick (Washington, DC, 1931–44), 29:295–96. On land as "a field for manhood," see Mark E. Kahn, *A Republic of Men: The American Founders, Gendered Language, and Patriarchal Politics* (New York, 1998), 36.

24. Washington to Robert Cary & Company, September 28, 1760, PGW-CS 6:459–60.

25. See Washington to Robert Cary & Company, enclosure, May 1, 1759, PGW-CS 6:317, 318.

26. Washington to Robert Cary & Company, June 6, 1768, PGW-CS 8:92–93. For a description of the chariot made for Washington by Christopher Reeves, see the invoice from Robert Cary & Company, September 28, 1768, PGW-CS 8:135.

27. Washington to Robert Cary & Company, August 20, 1770, PGW-CS 8:370.

28. On camp furniture and rank distinctions, see Nicholas A. Brawer, *British Campaign Furniture: Elegance under Canvas, 1740–1914* (New York, 2001). On the sword, see Washington to Caleb Gibbs, August 4, 1778, PGW-RWS 16:243, and Washington to John Cox Jr. or John Mitchell, October 4, 1778, PGW-RWS 17:245. On the gold watch, see Washington to Gouverneur Morris, November 28, 1788, PGW-PS 1:135. On Washington and shoes, see Mary V. Thompson, "'By the First Ship Bound to Any Part of Virginia': Shoes for the Washington Family," typescript, 2001, GWMV.

29. Washington to John Cochran, August 16, 1779, PGW-RWS 22:141–42.

30. Washington, March 26, 1748, PGW-D 1:15; Washington, April 8,

1748, PGW-D 1:19. For "like a Negro," see Washington to Richard, 1749–50, PGW-CS 1:44.

31. William E. Woodward, *George Washington: The Image and the Man* (1926; rpt., New York, 1972), 25.

32. See Alun Withey, *Technology, Self-Fashioning and Politeness in Eighteenth-Century Britain: Refined Bodies* (London, 2016), 7. See also Richard L. Bushman, *The Refinement of America: Persons, Houses, Cities* (New York, 1993), T. H. Breen, *Marketplace of Revolution: How Consumer Politics Shaped American Independence* (New York, 2004), and Ann Smart Martin, *Buying into the World of Goods: Early Consumers in Backcountry Virginia* (Baltimore, MD, 2008).

CHAPTER 11. *The Message of His Clothing*

1. Nathaniel Hawthorne, *Passages from the French and Italian Note-Books*, in *The Complete Works of Nathaniel Hawthorne*, 12 vols. (Cambridge, MA, 1883), 10:274.

2. Kate Haulman, *The Politics of Fashion in Eighteenth-Century America* (Chapel Hill, NC, 2011), 228n8. See also Elizabeth McClellan, *Historic Dress in America, 1607–1800* (Philadelphia, 1904), Cecil Willett Cunnington and Phillis Cunnington, *Handbook of English Costume in the Eighteenth Century* (London, 1964), Merideth Wright, *Everyday Dress of Rural America, 1783–1800* (New York, 1992), Patricia A. Cunningham and Susan Voso Lab, *Dress in American Culture* (Bowling Green, OH, 1993), and Linda Baumgarten, *What Clothes Reveal: The Language of Clothing in Colonial and Federal America* (2002; rpt., New Haven, CT, 2011).

3. See "Memorandum of what clothes I Carry into Fairfax," 1748, PGW-CS 1:39n6.

4. Washington, Memorandum, 1749–50, PGW-CS 1:45–46.

5. Thomas Jefferson to David Humphreys, August 14, 1787, *Founders Online*, National Archives, https://founders.archives.gov/documents/Jefferson/01–12–02–0037. On the international success of the frock, see Cunnington and Cunnington, *Handbook of English Costume*, 16–18.

6. Washington to George Steptoe Washington, December 5, 1790, PGW-PS 7:32–33.

7. Washington to George Steptoe Washington, March 23, 1789, PGW-PS 1:439.

8. Washington to Thomas Knox, January 1758, PGW-CS 5:87–88.

9. Washington to Charles Lawrence, April 26, 1763, PGW-CS 7:201; Washington, invoice to Robert Cary & Company, enclosure, September 28, 1760, PGW-CS 6:461–62.

10. See Washington, invoice to Robert Cary & Company, enclosure, July 25, 1769, PGW-CS 8:231–32. On Washington retaining the ability later in life to name wildbores, russells, durants, moreens, tammies, thicksetts, hair plushes, shags, sattinetts, lastings, or sarsenets, and many others, see Stephen Decatur Jr., *Private Affairs of George Washington* (Boston, 1933), 63.

11. Washington to Charles Lawrence, September 28, 1760, PGW-CS 6:458; Washington to Richard Washington, October 20, 1761, PGW-CS 7:81. On Washington's complaints about Lawrence, see his letters to Charles Lawrence, August 10, 1764, PGW-CS 7:321–22, and June 20, 1768, PGW-CS 8:98.

12. Undated letter attributed to Washington to an unidentified tailor, typescript, GWMV. This letter is similar to another letter Washington sent to John Mitchell on November 5, 1782, concerning "the neatest & best Leather Breeches." See *Founders Online*, National Archives, https://founders.archives.gov/documents/Washington/99–01–02–09880. I'm indebted to Samantha Snyder for alerting me to the existence of this last letter.

13. Washington, February 4, 1770, PGW-D 2:213.

14. Washington to Thomas Gibson, July 18, 1771, PGW-CS 8:501; Washington to Thomas Gibson, July 15, 1772, PGW-CS 9:62; Washington to Thomas Gibson, July 10, 1773, PGW-CS 9:270.

15. Washington, list of suits, May 6, 1797, manuscript, GWMV. See also Washington to James McAlpin, May 7, 1797, PGW-RS 1:134–35.

16. Washington to Richard Washington, October 20, 1761, PGW-CS 7:81; Washington to Thomas Gibson, July 10, 1773, PGW-CS 9:270; Washington to Robert Cary & Company, July 26, 1773, PGW-CS 9:289n1. On the common etiquette for mourning dresses, see Anne Buck, *Dress in Eighteenth-Century England* (New York, 1979), 23, 60–63.

17. Washington to Captain Caleb Gibbs, April 22, 1777, PGW-RWS

9:236; Washington to James McAlpin, January 27, 1799, PGW-RS 3:341. See also Daniel Purdy, "The Veil of Masculinity: Clothing and Identity via Goethe's *Die Leiden des jungen Werthers*," *Lessing Yearbook* 27 (1996): 103–30.

18. William Sullivan, *The Public Men of the Revolution* (Philadelphia, 1847), 120. On the cape, see Decatur, *Private Affairs of George Washington*, 280.

19. Washington, general orders, July 24, 1776, PGW-RWS 5:439.

20. Washington to Henry Bouquet, July 3, 1758, PGW-CS 5:257–58; Washington, orders to Colonel Daniel Morgan, June 13, 1777, PGW-RWS 10:31. General Forbes likewise believed his soldiers' dressing in this garb had strategic, theatrical value. Having some of the best soldiers in every corps "go out a Scouting in that stile," Forbes wrote, would add to the final effect: "The Shadow may be often taken for the reality." Wars are always a deliberate show, at least in part: "In this country," Forbes continued, "wee must comply and learn the Art of Warr, from Ennemy Indians" (John Forbes to Henry Bouquet, June 27, 1758, in *Writings of General John Forbes Relating to His Service in North America*, ed. Alfred Procter James [Menasha, WI, 1938], 125).

21. *The Statutes at Large of South Carolina*, vol. 7, ed. David J. McCord (Columbia, SC, 1840), 412.

22. Washington to Robert Cary & Company, July 20, 1771, PGW-CS 8:506–07. For Washington's views on nonimportation, see his letter to George Mason, April 5, 1769, PGW-CS 8:177–81. For more on the age of homespun, see Laurel Thatcher Ulrich, *Age of Homespun: Objects and Stories in the Creation of an American Myth* (New York, 2001).

23. On the project of the French national uniform, see Michael Zakim, "Sartorial Ideologies: From Homespun to Ready-Made," *American Historical Review* 106, no. 5 (2001): 1553–86, 1567.

24. Washington to Lafayette, January 29, 1789, PGW-PS 1:264; Washington to Henry Knox, January 29, 1789, PGW-PS 1:260. See also the *Daily Advertiser* (New York), January 15, 1789.

25. "To the Editor of the Federal Gazette," *Federal Gazette* (Philadelphia), January 7, 1789. Washington bought the Hartford cloth. See his letter to Daniel Hinsdale, April 8, 1789, PGW-PS 2:41–42.

26. Henry Knox to Washington, February 12, 1789, PGW-PS 1:291.

27. Henry Knox to Washington, February 19, 1789, PGW-PS 1:323; Washington to Henry Knox, March 2, 1789, PGW-PS 1:353–54.

28. Jeremiah Wadsworth to Tobias Lear, February 15, 1789, in Decatur, *Private Affairs of George Washington*, 10. The two samples are attached to this letter and are well preserved.

29. Henry Knox to Washington, March 5, 1789, PGW-PS 1:365. See also Henry Knox to Washington, March 27, 1789, PGW-PS 1:451, and Daniel Hinsdale to Washington, March 23, 1789, PGW-PS 1:433.

30. Washington to Daniel Hinsdale, April 8, 1789, PGW-PS 2:41.

31. Washington to Henry Knox, April 10, 1789, PGW-PS 2:45. See also Henry Knox to Washington, March 27, 1789, PGW 1:451. On the buttons, see Decatur, *Private Affairs of George Washington*, 11.

32. "American Manufacture," *Gazette of the United States*, May 2, 1789, 27. On Washington recommending that his soldiers, the dragoons, be dressed in "Brown and White and Brown and Buff which are handsome, and good standing Colours," see his letter to James Mease, April 17, 1777, PGW-RWS 9:194. See also Washington to James Mease, May 12, 1777, PGW-RWS 9:399. The American dragoons would also be visually different from the red and blue of the British dragoons.

33. Elizabeth Parke Custis Law, transcription of a note accompanying object W-1514, GWMV.

34. Washington, January 8, 1790, PGW-D 6:4; *Pennsylvania Packet* (Philadelphia), January 14, 1790.

35. Washington, October 20, 1789, PGW-D 5:468.

36. Henry Wansey, in *Henry Wansey and His American Journal*, ed. David John Jeremy (Philadelphia, 1970), 149.

CHAPTER 12. *Astride the Great Stage*

1. Washington to officers of the army, March 15, 1783, *Founders Online*, National Archives, https://founders.archives.gov/documents/Washington /99-01-02-10840. On the Newburgh Conspiracy, see Richard H. Kohn, "The Inside History of the Newburgh Conspiracy: America and the Coup d'Etat," *William and Mary Quarterly* 27, no. 2 (1970): 187–220, and

David Head, *A Crisis of Peace: George Washington, the Newburgh Conspiracy, and the Fate of the American Revolution* (New York, 2019).

2. On Washington's spectacles, see David Cobb, November 9, 1825, in *The Life of Timothy Pickering*, 4 vols., ed. Octavius Pickering (Boston, 1867–73), 1:431. See also Samuel Shaw to John Elliot, April 1783, in *The Founders on the Founders: Word Portraits from the American Revolutionary Era*, ed. John P. Kaminski (Charlottesville, VA, 2008), 484–85.

3. Washington to David Rittenhouse, February 16, 1783, in *Writings of George Washington from the Original Manuscript Sources, 1745–1799*, 39 vols., ed. John C. Fitzpatrick (Washington, DC, 1931–44), 26:137. On Washington's difficulties with reading glasses, see also Stephen Decatur Jr., *Private Affairs of George Washington* (Boston, 1933), 48–49.

4. On this cultural transformation of spectacles, see Alun Withey, *Technology, Self-Fashioning and Politeness in Eighteenth-Century Britain: Refined Bodies* (London, 2016), 92–93.

5. Samuel Shaw to John Elliot, April 1783, in *The Founders on the Founders*, 484.

6. On Washington experiencing "the world as a stage and life as a drama," see Peter R. Henriques, *First and Always: A New Portrait of George Washington* (Charlottesville, VA, 2020), 160–61. See also Paul K. Longmore, *The Invention of George Washington* (Charlottesville, VA, 1999), 52, 182–83, 202–11. On authenticity, see Lionel Trilling, *Sincerity and Authenticity* (Cambridge, MA, 1972). On the eighteenth-century private realm as oriented to an audience, see Jürgen Habermas, *The Structural Transformation of the Public Sphere: An Inquiry into a Category of Bourgeois Society*, trans. Thomas Burger (Cambridge, MA, 1991), 49.

7. Washington to John Augustine Washington, June 1, 1777, PGW-RWS 9:586.

8. See Mary V. Thompson, "George Washington and the Theater: Plays Owned and Attended by George Washington & Other Members of His Household, 1751–1797," typescript, 2010, revised 2016, GWMV. On Washington and theaters and for a detailed analysis of the plays he saw, see Paul Leicester Ford, *Washington and the Theatre* (1899; New York, 1967). See also Odai Johnson, "Thomas Jefferson and the Colonial American Stage," *Virginia Magazine of History and Biography* 108, no. 2 (2000): 139–54.

9. "Proclamation for the Cessation of Hostilities," April 18, 1783, *Founders Online*, National Archives, https://founders.archives.gov/docu ments/Washington/99-01-02-11104. For a full list of theatrical metaphors, see Thompson, "George Washington and the Theater."

10. Washington to Martha Washington, June 18, 1775, PGW-RWS 1:3. For an account of Washington wearing this blue-and-buff uniform, see William S. Rasmussen and Robert S. Tilton, *George Washington: The Man behind the Myth* (Charlottesville, VA, 1999), 294n21.

11. On instructors advising pupils to speak aloud before a mirror, see Henry DeSaussure to John E. Colhoun, January 20, 1808, in Lorri Glover, "An Education in Southern Masculinity: The Ball Family of South Carolina in the New Republic," *Journal of Southern History* 69, no. 1 (2003): 39–70, 55. On Cicero as "the ultimate male fantasy figure," see Konstantin Dierks, *In My Power: Letter Writing and Communications in Early America* (Philadelphia, 2009), 21.

12. Longmore, *The Invention of George Washington*, 11.

13. Washington to Bushrod Washington, July 27, 1789, PGW-PS 3:334.

14. Washington to Catharine Sawbridge Macaulay Graham, January 9, 1790, PGW-PS 4:552.

15. Tobias Lear to George Augustine Washington, May 3, 1789, PGW-PS 2:248.

16. On the enslaved persons that stayed with Washington during his presidency, see Erica Armstrong Dunbar, *Never Caught: The Washingtons' Relentless Pursuit of Their Runaway Slave, Ona Judge* (New York, 2017).

17. Tobias Lear to George Augustine Washington, May 3, 1789, PGW-PS 2:248; Washington to James Madison, March 30, 1789, PGW-PS 1:464. On the dinners on Thursdays, see Decatur, *Private Affairs of George Washington*, 39.

18. See Decatur, *Private Affairs of George Washington*, 126.

19. Washington to Tobias Lear, September 5, 1790, PGW-PS 6:397.

20. Washington to James Germain, June 1, 1794, PGW-PS 16:171, 173.

21. William Maclay, *Journal of William Maclay, United States Senator from Pennsylvania, 1789–1791*, ed. Edgar S. Maclay (New York, 1890), 24–25. See also Kathleen Bartoloni-Tuazon, *For Fear of an Elective King: George Washington and the Presidential Title Controversy of 1789* (Ithaca, NY, 2014).

22. Linda Grant De Pauw, ed., *Documentary History of the First Federal Congress of the United States of America, March 4, 1789–March 3, 1791*, vol. 1: *Senate Legislative Journal* (Baltimore, MD, 1972), 45.

23. Washington to John Adams, May 10, 1789, PGW-PS 2:247.

24. Baron de Montesquieu, *The Spirit of Laws*, trans. Thomas Nugent (London, 1793), 9, 7.

25. Tobias Lear to George Augustine Washington, May 3, 1789, PGW-PS 2:248; Washington to David Stuart, June 15, 1790, PGW-PS 5:527.

26. Washington, March 19, 1790, PGW-D 6:49.

27. Washington to David Stuart, June 15, 1790, PGW-PS 5:526.

28. See Decatur, *Private Affairs of George Washington*, 73–74.

29. See Decatur, *Private Affairs of George Washington*, 73–74, 327.

30. Maclay, *Journal of William Maclay*, 351; Speculation, *Independent Chronicle* (Boston), June 3, 1790; *National Gazette* (Philadelphia), February 2, 1793, 109.

31. See Decatur, *Private Affairs of George Washington*, 172.

32. Abigail Adams to Mary Smith Cranch, January 5, 1790, *Founders Online*, National Archives, https://founders.archives.gov/documents/Adams /04-09-02-0001. See also Decatur, *Private Affairs of George Washington*, 43–44, and Rufus Wilmot Griswold, *The Republican Court: Or, American Society in the Days of Washington* (New York, 1867), 164–65. "Birth Night at St James" refers to a ball held in honor of Queen Charlotte on her birthday. On Washington's attending his wife's gatherings, which he described as being "a more familiar and sociable kind" than his own receptions, see his letter to David Stuart, June 15, 1790, PGW-PS 5:527.

33. On Washington's journey from Mount Vernon to the site of his inauguration in New York City as well as on the festivities, speeches, parades, dances, music, and food, see Stephen Howard Browne, *The First Inauguration: George Washington and the Invention of the Republic* (University Park, PA, 2020). On these trips as "political theater," see T. H. Breen, *George Washington's Journey: The President Forges a New Nation* (New York, 2015). On how Washington traveled, see Ron Chernow, *Washington: A Life* (New York, 2010), 609.

34. George Washington Parke Custis, *Recollections and Private Mem-*

oirs of Washington (1859; rpt., New York, 1860), 386. On Washington on horseback, see also Decatur, *Private Affairs of George Washington*, 92.

35. On Washington paying for dancing school, see Washington, April 18, 1770, PGW-D 2:229, Washington to Jonathan Boucher, August 15, 1770, PGW-CS 8:365, Washington, guardian accounts, May 1, 1771, PGW-CS 8:455–63, and Washington to Stephen Bloomer Balch, June 26, 1785, PGW-CFS 3:84.

36. Philip Vickers Fithian, *Journal and Letters of Philip Vickers Fithian, 1773–1774*, ed. Hunter Dickinson Farish (Williamsburg, VA, 1943), 44.

37. James Tilton to Gunning Bedford Jr., Bedford, Jr., December 25, 1783, in *The Founders on the Founders*, 488.

38. Eliza Bowen Ward, in Kate Van Winkle Keller, *Dance and Its Music in America, 1528–1789* (Hillsdale, NY, 2007), 103. On the dancing gentry, see Washington to Jonathan Boucher, April 24, 1769, PGW-CS 8:184.

39. James Tilton to Gunning Bedford Jr., December 25, 1783, in *The Founders on the Founders*, 489; Francis T. Brooke, "From 'A Narrative of My Life for My Family,'" *William and Mary College Quarterly Historical Magazine* 17, no. 1 (1908): 1–4, 2.

40. *Pennsylvania Packet* (Philadelphia), March 6, 1779; Custis, *Recollections and Private Memoirs of Washington*, 143–44.

41. See Kate Van Winkle Keller and Charles Cyril Hendrickson, *George Washington: A Biography in Social Dance* (Sandy Hook, CT, 1998), esp. 123–24.

42. Custis, *Recollections and Private Memoirs of Washington*, 144.

43. See Elizabeth Aldrich, *From the Ballroom to Hell: Grace and Folly in Nineteenth-Century Dance* (Evanston, IL, 1991), 15–16.

44. Washington to Alexandria General Assemblies Managers, November 12, 1799, PGW-RS 4:402.

CHAPTER 13. *Consummation*

1. For a good account of Washington's final years, see Jonathan Horn, *Washington's End: The Final Years and Forgotten Struggle* (New York, 2020).

2. Washington to Mary Ball Washington, February 15, 1787, PGW-CFS 5:35; Washington to George William Fairfax, June 26, 1786, in *Writ-*

ings of George Washington from the Original Manuscript Sources, 1745–1799, 39 vols., ed. John C. Fitzpatrick (Washington, DC, 1931–44), 28:470; Washington to William Pearce, November 23, 1794, PGW-PS 17:203. See also Robert F. Dalzell Jr. and Lee Baldwin Dalzell, *George Washington's Mount Vernon: At Home in Revolutionary America* (New York, 1998), 192.

3. Winthrop Sargent, diary, October 1, 1793–December 31, 1795, PGW-PS 14:208–9n3.

4. Washington to Sarah Cary Fairfax, May 16, 1798, PGW-RS 2: 272–73.

5. Washington to Sarah Cary Fairfax, May 16, 1798, PGW-RS 2:272.

6. Washington to Lafayette, February 1, 1784, PGW-CFS 1:87–88.

7. See Daniel L. Dreisbach, "The 'Vine and Fig Tree' in George Washington's Letters: Reflections on a Biblical Motif in the Literature of the American Founding Era," *Anglican and Episcopal History* 76, no. 3 (2007): 299–326.

8. Washington to Chastellux, ca. April 25–May 1, 1788, PGW-CFS 6:229. On swords turned into plowshares, see also Micah 4:3 and Joel 3:10 as well as Washington to John Hancock, December 20, 1776, PGW-RWS 7:381–86, Washington to Lafayette, September 30, 1779, PGW-RWS 22:557–62, and Washington to James Anderson, December 24, 1795, PGW-PS 19:290–93.

9. Washington to Lafayette, February 1, 1784, PGW-CFS 1:87–88.

10. See Robert P. Hay, "George Washington: American Moses," *American Quarterly* 21, no. 4 (1969): 780–91.

11. For fresh portraits of John Adams, see R. B. Bernstein, *The Education of John Adams* (New York, 2020), and Nancy Isenberg and Andrew Burstein, *The Problem of Democracy: The Presidents Adams Confront the Cult of Personality* (New York, 2019).

12. Washington to John Adams, July 13, 1798, PGW-RS 2:402–3.

13. Washington to Alexander Hamilton and Charles Cotesworth Pinckney, November 10, 1798, PGW-RS 3:192.

14. Washington to James McHenry, January 27, 1799, PGW-RS 3:342–43.

15. Washington to James McAlpin, January 27, 1799, PGW-RS 3:341.

16. Washington to James McHenry, February 10, 1799, PGW-RS 3:364; Washington to James McAlpin, May 12, 1799, PGW-RS 4:67; Washington to James McHenry, June 7, 1799, PGW-RS 4:110–11.

17. Adam Smith, *The Theory of Moral Sentiments*, in *The Essential Adam Smith*, ed. Robert L. Heilbroner and Laurence J. Malone (New York, 1986), 101. On the founders' attempt to establish a character, see Andrew Trees, *The Founding Fathers and the Politics of Character* (Princeton, NJ, 2004), and Douglass Adair, *Fame and the Founding Fathers* (New York, 1974).

18. Washington, address to the Continental Congress, June 16, 1775, PGW-RWS 1:1. For Washington telling Patrick Henry that he was about to lose his reputation, see Benjamin Rush, *The Autobiography of Benjamin Rush*, ed. George W. Corner (Westport, CT, 1970), 113.

19. Washington to James McHenry, April 3, 1797, PGW-RS 1:71; Tobias Lear, journal account of Washington's death, PGW-RS 4:545. See also Wendy Kail, "The Correspondence of George and Martha Washington," https://washingtonpapers.org/resources/articles/the-correspondence -of-george-and-martha-washington.

20. Washington to Bryan Fairfax, August 24, 1774, PGW-CS 10:155. On Washington's character being indelibly tainted by his slave owning, see Henry Wiencek, *An Imperfect God: George Washington, His Slaves, and the Creation of America* (New York, 2003). On books and pamphlets on slavery in Washington's library, see Kevin J. Hayes, *George Washington: A Life in Books* (New York, 2017), 228–41. On Washington changing his view on slavery as he matured, see Mary V. Thompson, *"The Only Unavoidable Subject of Regret": George Washington, Slavery, and the Enslaved Community at Mount Vernon* (Charlottesville, VA, 2019), 61–77. See also https:// www.mountvernon.org/george-washington/slavery/washingtons-chang ing-views-on-slavery.

21. Washington to Robert Lewis, August 18, 1799, PGW-RS 4:256– 57; William Gordon to Washington, August 30, 1784, PGW-CFS 2:64.

22. Washington to Robert Morris, April 12, 1786, PGW-CFS 4:16. Washington restates this idea that slavery can only be abolished via state intervention in his letter to Lawrence Lewis, August 4, 1797, PGW-RS 1:288–89.

23. David Humphreys, *"Life of General Washington" with George Washington's "Remarks,"* ed. Rosemarie Zagarri (Athens, GA, 1991), 78. We can't be certain that these were the precise words uttered by Washington.

24. For more on the disposition of Mount Vernon's 317 slaves at the time of Washington's death, see https://www.mountvernon.org/george -washington/slavery/washingtons-1799-will.

25. Washington to John Francis Mercer, November 24, 1786, PGW-CFS 4:394.

26. Patrick Henry to Robert Pleasants, January 18, 1773, in *The Abolitionist: or Record of the New England Anti-Slavery Society* 1, no. 10 (1833), 155.

27. Washington to George William Fairfax, February 27, 1785, PGW-CFS 2:387–88. For Washington praising Belvoir as the site where he spent "happy moments—the happiest of my life," see his letter to Sarah Cary Fairfax, May 16, 1798, PGW-RS 2:272–74.

28. Washington to Edmund Randolph, March 28, 1787, PGW-CFS 5:113; William Fogg, April 1787, PGW-CFS 5:158–59n1. On the case of malaria, see Washington to George Gilpin and John Fitzgerald, September 1, 1786, PGW-CFS 4:234–35. On aches and pains seizing Washington's body, see his letter to James Madison, November 18, 1786, PGW-CFS 4:382–83. As J. H. Mason Knox Jr. notes, "All went well until 1786" ("The Medical History of George Washington, His Physicians, Friends and Advisers," *Bulletin of the Institute of the History of Medicine* 1, no. 5 [1933]: 174–91, 176).

29. Washington, January 10, 1787, PGW-D 5:93; Washington to Lafayette, December 8, 1784, PGW-CFS 2:175. See also Jeanne E. Abrams, *Revolutionary Medicine: The Founding Fathers and Mothers in Sickness and in Health* (New York, 2013), 35. On Washington being "acutely aware" of death and for his ideas about the afterlife, see Peter R. Henriques, "The Final Struggle between George Washington and the Grim King: Washington's Attitude toward Death and an Afterlife," *Virginia Magazine of History and Biography* 107, no. 1 (1999): 73–97.

30. Washington, undelivered first inaugural address, April 30 1789, PGW-PS 2:161; Fisher Ames to George Richards Minot, May 3, 1789, in *The Founders on the Founders: Word Portraits from the American Revolutionary Era*, ed. John P. Kaminski (Charlottesville, VA, 2008), 500.

31. William Maclay, *Journal of William Maclay, United States Senator from Pennsylvania, 1789–1791*, ed. Edgar S. Maclay (New York, 1890), 257; Washington to Clement Biddle, July 20, 1790, PGW-PS 6:105–6.

Friends as well hoped that the "unfortunate change which your constitution seems to have undergone" was only temporary. See Henry Lee to Washington, June 12, 1790, PGW-PS 5:515.

32. Washington to David Stuart, June 15, 1790, PGW-PS 5:527; Frances Bassett Washington to Burwell Bassett, September 21, 1790, manuscript, GWMV. The date on the letter appears to be 1791, but it's a slipup.

33. Maclay, *Journal of William Maclay*, 375.

34. James Madison, conversations with Washington, May 5–25, 1792, PGW-PS 10:351.

35. Isaac Weld Jr., *Travels Through the States of North America, and the Provinces of Upper and Lower Canada, During the Years 1795, 1796, and 1797*, 2 vols. (1799; rpt., London, 1807), 1:104n.

36. Martha Washington to Elizabeth Willing Powel, December 18, 1797, manuscript, GWMV.

37. Washington to William Augustine Washington, February 27, 1798, PGW-RS 2:109.

38. Washington to Landon Carter, October 5, 1798, PGW-RS 3:79.

CHAPTER 14. *Giants Die as Well*

1. See Tobias Lear's accounts of the death of George Washington, PGW-RS 4:542–46 and 547–52. See also Tobias Lear's December 16 letter to Mary Lear, which was published in the 1911 annual report of the Mount Vernon Ladies' Association of the Union, 52–54, GWMV. Lear penned two versions, the journal account and the diary account. The journal account is the original version, written on December 15, now at the William L. Clements Library in Ann Arbor, MI. The diary account, entered in Lear's diary under the date December 14, which is now in the Historical Society of Pennsylvania in Philadelphia, is largely a copy of the first account with timings and events occasionally arranged in a slightly different order, with a few omissions and new information, and with altered or new quotations. In sum, it is an embellished version of the original one, clearly meant to be shared with others. James Craik, Washington's trusted doctor, endorsed the diary account as essentially correct, "so far as I can recollect." See PGW-RS 4:552.

2. Lear, diary account, PGW-RS 4:548.

3. Lear, diary account, PGW-RS 4:548.

4. See Lear, diary account, PGW-RS 4:549. See also David G. Schmitz, "Overview of Cantharidin Poisoning (Blister Beetle Poisoning)," in *The Merck Veterinary Manual*, ed. Susan E. Aiello and Michael A. Moses (Kenilworth, NJ, 2013), and David J. Karras, Susan E. Farrell, Richard A. Harrigan, Fred M. Henretig, and Laura Gealt, "Poisoning From 'Spanish Fly' (Cantharidin)," *American Journal of Emergency Medicine* 14, no. 5 (1996): 478–83.

5. See Lear, diary account, PGW-RS 4:549.

6. See Lear, diary account, PGW-RS 4:549.

7. See Lear, diary account, PGW-RS 4:550–51.

8. On the traditional body as porous and permeable, see Rudolph E. Siegel, *Galen's System of Physiology and Medicine* (Basel, Switzerland, 1968), 360–82. On the transformation of the body from porous to self-contained, see Albrecht Koschorke, "Physiological Self-Regulation: The Eighteenth-Century Modernization of the Human Body," *MLN* 123, no. 3 (2008): 469–84. Koschorke argues that even after the body was redefined as an organism, bloodletting remained a common treatment. Its meaning changed, though. No longer understood as restoring a balance of fluids, it was rather seen as encouraging the organism's self-healing process through eased circulation (476–77).

9. See J. Worth Estes, "George Washington and the Doctors: Treating America's First Superhero," *Medical Heritage* 1, no. 1 (1985): 44–57. Estes computes the amount to have been ninety-six ounces (54). In an article written six weeks after Washington's death (but published only in 1903), Dr. James Brickell estimated the quantity of blood removed to have been eighty-two ounces, which is more likely. He also expressed strong disagreement with the therapies ("Observations on the Medical Treatment of General Washington in His Illness," *Transactions of the College of Physicians of Philadelphia*, vol. 25 [Philadelphia, 1903], 90–94). On bloodletting in general, see Leon S. Bryan Jr., "Blood-Letting in American Medicine, 1830–1892," *Bulletin of the History of Medicine* 38, no. 6 (1964): 516–29. On bloodletting in Washington's case, see Michael L. Cheatham, "The Death of George Washington: An End to the Controversy?" *Amer-*

ican Surgeon 74, no. 8 (2008): 770–74, Paul J. Schmidt, "Transfuse George Washington!," *Transfusion* 42, no. 2 (2002): 275–77, P. Stavrakis, "Heroic Medicine, Bloodletting, and the Sad Fate of George Washington," *Maryland Medical Journal* 46, no. 10 (1997): 539–40, and David M. Morens, "Death of a President," *New England Journal of Medicine* 341, no. 24 (1999): 1845–49.

10. See Sissi Monteiro, Terence Pires de Farias, Marcelo de Camargo Millen, and Rafael Vinna Locio, "The History of Tracheostomy," in *Tracheostomy: A Surgical Guide*, ed. Terence Pires de Farias (Cham, Switzerland, 2018), 1–9. On Dr. Dick insisting on a tracheostomy, see Elisha C. Dick, "Facts and Observations Relative to the Disease of Cynanche Trachealis, or Croup," *Philadelphia Medical Physical Journal*, supp. 3 (May 1809): 242–55, 252–53.

11. William Thornton, in *Papers of William Thornton*, vol. 1: *1781–1802*, ed. Charles M. Harris (Charlottesville, VA, 1995), 528. See also George Paulson, "Dr. William Thornton's Views on Sleep, Dreams, and Resuscitation," *Journal of the History of the Neurosciences* 18 (2009): 25–46.

12. *Times; and District of Columbia Daily Advertiser* (Alexandria), December 21, 1799.

13. See Ben Cohen, "The Death of George Washington (1732–99) and the History of Cynanche," *Journal of Medical Biography* 13, no. 4 (2005): 225–31.

14. See Heinz H. E. Scheidemandel, "Did George Washington Die of Quinsy?" *Archives of Otolaryngology* 102, no. 9 (1976): 519–21.

15. On the laryngeal edema and streptococcus, see Walter A. Wells, "Last Illness and Death of Washington," *Virginia Medical Monthly* 53, no. 10 (1927): 629–42, and Fielding O. Lewis, "Washington's Last Illness," *Annals of Medical History* 4, no. 3 (1932): 245–48. For the argument that Washington had a streptococcal infection of the pharynx rather than of the larynx, see Creighton A. Barker "A Case Report," *Yale Journal of Biology and Medicine* 9, no. 2 (1936): 185–87.

16. The diagnosis of acute epiglottitis was first proposed in 1838. See H. Marsh, "Cases of Acute Inflammation Confined to the Epiglottis," *Dublin Journal of Medical Science* 13, no. 3 (1838): 1–23. On acute epiglottitis and haemophilus influenzae, see White McKenzie Wallenborn, "George

Washington's Terminal Illness: A Modern Medical Analysis of the Last Illness and Death of George Washington," 1999, https://washington papers.org/resources/articles/illness, and Cheatham, "The Death of George Washington." On epiglottitis, see also S. L. Shapiro, "Clinic-of-the-Month: General Washington's Last Illness," *Eye, Ear, Nose & Throat Monthly* 54, no. 4 (1975): 164–66, Morens, "Death of a President," and Scheidemandel, "Did George Washington Die of Quinsy?"

17. On the possibility that Washington experienced septic shock, see Cheatham, "The Death of George Washington," Lewis, "Washington's Last Illness," and Frederick A. Willius and Thomas E. Keys, "The Medical History of George Washington (1732–1799)," *Proceedings of the Staff Meetings of the Mayo Clinic* 17 (1942): 92–96, 107–12, 116–21. James Nydegger claimed that Washington died of diphtheria, but this is very unlikely ("The Last Illness of George Washington," *Medical Record*, December 29, 1917, 1128).

18. For comparable measurements of American beds, see Charles F. Montgomery, *American Furniture: The Federal Period* (New York, 1966), 55–68. See also Bradford L. Rauschenberg and John Bivins Jr., *Furniture of Charleston, 1680–1820* (Winston-Salem, NC, 2003).

19. See Peter R. Henriques, "The Final Struggle between George Washington and the Grim King: Washington's Attitude toward Death and an Afterlife," *Virginia Magazine of History and Biography* 107, no. 1 (1999): 73–97, 76–78. On the "grim King," see Washington to Richard Washington, October 20, 1761, PGW-CS 7:80.

20. See Stephen Decatur Jr., *Private Affairs of George Washington* (Boston, 1933), 104–5. The letter in question is Martha Washington to Mary Lear, November 11, 1800, typescript, GWMV. See also Keith Beutler, *George Washington's Hair: How Early Americans Remembered the Founders* (Charlottesville, VA, 2021).

21. Diane L. Dunkley to James C. Rees, June 3, 1994, archives (black binders), GWMV. This letter accompanied the FBI report on the hair tests dated May 31, 1994.

22. Lear, diary account, PGW-RS 4:551. In the journal account, Lear gives "two days." He also gives "two" in the letter he sent to his mother, on December 16. See also Marc Alexander, "'The Rigid Embrace of the

Narrow House': Premature Burial and the Signs of Death," *Hastings Center Report* 10, no. 3 (1980): 25–31, and Jan Bondeson, *Buried Alive: The Terrifying History of Our Most Primal Fear* (New York, 2001).

23. See Julian Litten, *The English Way of Death: The Common Funeral Since 1450* (London, 1991), 76–77, 79–81.

24. See bill from Margaret Gretter to the estate of George Washington, February 10, 1800, manuscript, GWMV. See also Mary V. Thompson, "'The Lowest Ebb of Misery': Death and Mourning in the Family of George Washington," typescript, 1999, GWMV, and Mary V. Thompson, "'In a Private Manner, Without Parade or Funeral Oration': The Funeral George Washington Wanted, but Didn't Get," typescript, 2018, GWMV.

25. Washington, last will and testament, July 9, 1799, PGW-RS 4:491. On the dirge and other details of the funeral at Mount Vernon, see Jedidiah Morse and Josiah Bartlett, *A Prayer and Sermon, Delivered at Charlestown, December 31, 1799; on the Death of George Washington* (Charlestown, MA, 1800), 34–35. See also Sterling E. Murray, "A Checklist of Funeral Dirges in Honor of General Washington," *Notes* 36, no. 2 (1979): 326–44.

26. For a detailed analysis of the many rituals and ceremonies of national mourning that followed Washington's death, see Gerald E. Kahler, *The Long Farewell: Americans Mourn the Death of George Washington* (Charlottesville, VA, 2008). See also Gerald E. Kahler, "Washington in Glory, America in Tears: The Nation Mourns the Death of George Washington, 1799–1800" (PhD diss., the College of William and Mary, 2003), and Meredith Eliassen, "Mourning George Washington," https://www.mountvernon.org/library/digitalhistory/digital-encyclopedia/article/mourning-george-washington.

27. See Tobias Lear, *Letters and Recollections of George Washington* (London, 1906), 141. On the dead Washington and his tomb as symbols, see Matthew R. Costello, *The Property of the Nation: George Washington's Tomb* (Lawrence, KS, 2019). On the coffin and the burial procedure, see Richard H. Klingenmaier, "The Burial of General George Washington: The Lesser Known Participants," *Alexandria Chronicle* (Spring 2012), 1–16. In 1830, a gardener working on the estate tried to steal Washington's skull. Instead, the thief mistakenly removed the skull from the remains of

one of Judge Bushrod Washington's in-laws. On this macabre episode see, Brady Carlson, *Dead Presidents: An American Adventure into the Strange Deaths and Surprising Afterlives of Our Nation's Leaders* (New York, 2016), 14–19. See also Thomas J. Craughwell, *Stealing Lincoln's Body* (Cambridge, MA, 2009), 77–78.

Index

civility: vs. barbarism in colonial America, 42–44, 68, 328n23; Frenchness and, 214–15; GW's conduct and, 117, 167, 210–16, 219–20; of letter writing, 136, 139, 142; macaronis as opposite of, 215–16, 230; Mount Vernon's accommodation of guests and, 277; sexual behavior and, 158. *See also* gracefulness and gentility; politeness

classism: conflicting message of hierarchy and equality, 217; emotions attributed to lower classes, 113–14; GW and, 218; land ownership and, 219; polite society and, 158, 217

Clinton, Henry, 83–84

clothing, 226–50; advice to nephews on proper dress, 229; banyan (dressing gown), 295–96, *296*; black velvet suit, 235, 238, 256; blue and buff colored uniforms, 236–37, *239*; broad cloth manufactured in Hartford, 242–43, 248–49, 369n25; brown as color of American soldiers' uniforms, 370n32; brown as color of GW's inaugural suit, 243–44, *245*; brown coat possibly worn by GW at inauguration, 247, *247*; caps worn for sleeping and during the day, 228; ceremonial costumes worn by GW, 236–38; commander in chief uniform of GW upon return to service (1798), 282–83; early interest of GW in, 227; elegance of GW for public occasions, 248–50; enslaved people's apparel, 240; federal buttons for inaugural suit, 244–45; frocks worn by gentlemen, 229, 234; grave garments, 307; homespun chosen as American fabric of citizenry, 241;

hunting or Indian shirt worn during French and Indian War, 238–40, 369n20; Lawrence as model for, 227; mourning suit, 234, 248; neck cloths worn by upper class, 228; particularity of GW in ordering from tailors, 230–31, 282, 368n12; political reasons to pick domestic fabrics, 242–43, 248–49; styles chosen by GW, 227, 230, 248; tailors as disappointment to GW, 231–35; waistcoats, 235–36, *236–37*

Clumberg, Philip, 99

Cochran, Gertrude, 223

Cochran, John, 223

Colonel Stephen Moore's House ("Red House"), 223

Colt, Peter, 242

Columbian Herald (Charleston), 98

Combs, Robert, 64

Conolly, Edward, 67

Constitutional Convention (1787), 177, 186

contemporary views vs. eighteenth century culture, 6, 131, 142, 155, 157, 166, 180

Continental Army: Congress's failure to pay, 251; Iroquois Confederacy's attacks on, 72–73; Lafayette joining, 138; Newburgh Conspiracy (1783), 251–54. *See also* Revolutionary War

Continental Congress, 67, 70, 256

Cooke, Henry, 10

Cornwallis, Charles, 64–65, 251

correspondence of GW, 125, 127–30, 137–42, 343n27; destruction of personal letters, 149–51, 284; with friends, 138, 346n19; MW-GW correspondence, 149–51, 349n16; stylistic improvements,

138, 347n26. *See also* love letters; *specific names of recipients of GW's letters*
costumes, eighteenth-century enthusiasm for, 235–38, 254, 256. *See also* clothing *for uniforms and other types of formal costumes*
Court of Assistants of the Barber-Surgeons' Company (England), 100
courtship of GW and MW. *See* marriage and courtship of GW and MW
Craik, James, 103, 138, 298–99, 301–3, 340n32
Crèvecoeur, Hector St. John de: *Letters from an American Farmer*, 42–43
Crofton, Richard, 45
cryptorchidism, 189
Cullen, William, 303
Curtius, Quintus: *History of the War of Alexander the Great*, 63
Custis, Daniel (MW's son), 146
Custis, Daniel Parke (MW's first husband), 146–48, 221
Custis, Eleanor Parke "Nelly" (step-granddaughter), 161–62, 192, 195, 199–201, 361n25
Custis, Elizabeth Parke "Eliza"/"Betsey" (step-granddaughter), 153, 195, 199, 201–2, 248
Custis, Frances (MW's daughter), 146
Custis, George Washington Parke "Washy" (step-grandson): on first meeting of MW and GW, 147; GW and MW raising, 195; on GW as authoritative figure to, 199–200; on GW breaking wild horse, 105–6; on GW's appearance on horseback, 268; on GW's body size and height, 16, 22; on GW's dancing skills, 271–73;

on GW's dentures, 93; on GW's masculinity, 7, 9; on Mary Ball Washington, 107; in sculpture at Ford Orientation Center, 192; on wedding day of GW and MW, 149
Custis, John, IV, 148
Custis, John Parke "Jacky" (stepson), 146, 149, 152, 170–71, 194–96, 201, 215, 232
Custis, Martha Dandridge. *See* Washington, Martha Dandridge Custis
Custis, Martha Parke "Patsy" (step-daughter), 146, 150, 152, 170–71, 194, 201, 232, 234
Custis, Martha Parke "Patty" (step-granddaughter), 149, 195, 199, 202
Custis Stuart, Eleanor Calvert, 195, 199, 201

Daily Advertiser (New York), 88, 98, 242
dancing, 269–74; classes to master dances, 269–70; as competitive activity, 270–71; country dances, 270, 272–73; minuets, 270–72
Dancing Assembly (Alexandria, Virginia), 273–74
David, Jacques-Louis, 241
Davis, William, 66
Declaration of Independence, 152, 217, 241
Defoe, Daniel: *Complete English Tradesman, in Familiar Letters*, 133; *Conjugal Lewdness or, Matrimonial Whoredom*, 160
de Grasse, Comte, 138, 178
Della Casa, Giovanni: *Galateo*, 207, 209
de Luzancy, Hippolyte du Chastelet, 363–64n6

Denny, Ebenezer, 178

dental problems of GW, 81–98, 336n2; appearance effects of, 84–85; barbers as dental surgeons, 82, 98–104; brutality of treatment, 81–82, 90, 102; cracking nuts as cause of, 86–87; dentures, sets and maintenance, 88–98, *89–91*, 338n13; dentures made of ivory, not wood, 82, 88, 336n2; eighteenth-century personal dental care, 81, 85, *85*, 337n8; embarrassment of GW over tooth loss, 83–84; first to final dental extractions, 82, 87–88; GW performing his own operations, 85; inability to speak clearly due to, 84, 119; last tooth extracted kept by Greenwood, 82, *83*, 86; live tooth transplants and, 95–96, 338n19; newspaper ads to find individuals willing to sell teeth, 97–98; pharmaceutical effects on teeth and, 86–87; purchase of teeth from enslaved persons, 96–97; tinctures, use of, 85, 87

dentures. *See* dental problems of GW

De Pauw, Cornelius, 42

Dick, Elisha, 18, 98–99, 299–303

Dillon, Robert-Guillaume, 210–11

Dinwiddie, Robert, 48–49, 55, 57, 61, 68–70

Dionis, Pierre, 99

Donald W. Reynolds Museum and Education Center (Mount Vernon), 12

Douglass, Frederick: *The Heroic Slave*, 20

Dowdey, Clifford, 217–18

Dunbar, Erica Armstrong, 78

Dunkley, Diane, 306

Du Quesne, Marquis, 60

Edwards, Ignatius, 69

eighteenth-century culture: Anglo-American men's appearance different from other cultures, 185; character as public performance for, 284, 376n17; clothing of, 13–14; communitarian period and, 154, 350n22; consumption and material desires of, 225; contemporary views vs., 6, 131, 142, 155, 157, 166, 180; cruelty toward sentient beings, 68; desirable body type, 17, 20; emotional sensitivity of, 170–72; fatherhood in America of, 197–99; gender differences and, 162–63; grave garments, 307; hair as mementos of the deceased, 306; happiness more important than romantic love, 151–54, 350n18; height and weight of men, 16–17, 20; letter writing and love letters, 130–34, 137, 142; novels, use of epistolary style, 132; posture of, 12–14; privacy and, 180–81; self-improvement and refinement, 169–70, 213, 217, 219, 222; sexual mores, 159–65, 352n36; simplicity and, 208, 210–13, 235

Ellis, Joseph, 5

emotions and sentimentality, 166–85; Christianity and, 172–79; clean shaven face indicating refined emotions, 183–85; contradictions within eighteenth-century men, 167–68, 172; in eighteenth-century culture, 170–72; emotional security of GW and, 179; GW as "man of great sensibility," 166–67; GW's display within his family, 198–204, 208–9; GW's favorable and approachable impression upon others, 168–69; GW's way of eating

flirting, 127, 129–31, 134, 136
Forbes, John, 128, 369n20
Forbes Expedition (1758), 127–28, 238–40
Ford, West (enslaved person), 186
Ford Orientation Center (Mount Vernon), Washington family sculpture in, 192–93, *193*
Fort Duquesne (Pennsylvania), 60, 62, 128
Fort Le Boeuf (Pennsylvania), 49–51
Fort Necessity, Battle of (1754), 59–60, 118, 330nn9–10
Foucault, Michel, 351n27
founders: body types of, 20; close-knit bond of, 178; conflicting message of hierarchy and equality, 217; slavery and, 75, 154; society at large superior to individual rights for, 154. *See also specific names*
France-U.S. relations: Adams administration and, 280, 282–83; Treaty of Mortefontaine (1800), 283. *See also* French and Indian War *for colonial period*
Franklin, Benjamin, 60, 113, 180–81
Fraunces, Samuel, 171, 259, 261
Freeman's Journal (Philadelphia), 99
French and Indian War (1754–63), 6, 56–63, 118; crossing Allegheny River, 51–52; describing sound of bullets' whistling, 57–58, 330n7; exemplary and capital punishments meted out to soldiers, 68–71; facial hair considered "unsoldierlike" by GW, 184–85; first killing by GW of a French soldier, 57; food for troops, 175–76; Forbes Expedition (1758), 127–28,

238–40; Fort Le Boeuf trip, 49–51; Fort Necessity, Battle of (1754), 59–60, 118, 330nn9–10; GW as adjutant of Southern District of Virginia, 48; GW emerging as well-known military hero, 147, 269; hardships forging GW's male identity, 52–54; health problems during, 191–92; humiliation of loss at Fort Necessity, 59–60; hunting or Indian shirt worn during, 238–39, 369n20; Jumonville's Rocks battle, 55–56; as lieutenant colonel of Virginia Regiment, 54–55; maturity and military professionalism of GW, 57, 68–70; at Monongahela River Battle (Braddock's defeat), 60–61; psychological warfare tactics, 73; upper-class masculinity and self-control in, 58, 114–18
French culture: costumes worn by Marie Antoinette, 254; country dances, 273; Frenchness as refined sensibility, 214–15, 218, 250, 307; frocks worn by gentlemen, 229; mustaches required for soldiers, 184; national uniform worn in new French republic, 241, 369n23
Fugitive Slave Act (1793), 285–86

Gaines, Gay Hart, 192
Galenic theories, 161–65
Gardette, Dr., 88
Gates, Horatio, 251–52
Gay, John, 254
Gazette (Boston), 87
Gazette of the United States, 245
gender. *See* femininity; masculinity and manliness; women

masculinity and manliness (*cont.*)
  breaking wild horse, story of, 105–7;
  brutality of GW as slaveholder, 74–80,
  117, 118; brutality of GW's military
  career, 54–74; Cato as model of, 115–18;
  Christianity and, 172–84, 356n21; dancing skills and, 269; dental and medical
  treatments as tests of, 104; diet of GW
  and, 173–76, 356n23; of eighteenth
  century, 2, 6, 108–9, 158; emotional display of affection with family and, 198–
  204, 361n20; emotional security of
  GW and, 179; emotional sensitivity
  and, 170–72; GW as model of, 2, 4–6,
  20–23, 169, 220; GW in retirement
  and old age and, 277–78, 288; hardships GW endured as forging male
  identity, 52–53; in love letters, 131;
  Middle East and Muslim male cultures, 185; military career of GW and,
  114–18; moralism and, 110–14; multiple
  forms of, 6, 168, 354n6; nineteenth-
  century stories of GW's amazing
  strength, 6–9, 13, 79; oratorical skills
  and, 257; placid and soft character of
  GW and, 169, 175; politeness and, 220,
  362n1; punishment for unmanly behaviors, 110; rage and anger as opposite of, 113–14; refashioning of GW to
  fit nineteenth-century ideal, 23; resentment and, 114, 342n16; self-control
  and, 38–40, 65, 104, 106–19, 138, 288,
  341nn6–7, 341n9; sexual aggression
  and, 164; sexualization of GW, 5, 155,
  157, 186, 350n23, 351n28, 359n2; sexual
  self-restraint and, 159, 351n31; shaven
  face and, 183–85; silence and, 119; simplicity and, 208, 220; sports and, 21

Maslow, Abraham, 179
Mason, George, 325n1
Maxfield, John, 66
McAlpin, James, 233, 282–83
McCullough, David, 115
McHenry, James, 171, 282–83
McMunn, George, 310
Meadows, Christine, 188
melioration, 169–70, 213, 217, 219, 222
Mercer, George, 14–16, 17–18
Mercer, Hugh, 65, 332n22
Mercer, John, 287
Middle East and Muslim male cul-
  tures, 185
military career of GW, 5, 48–74. *See also*
  French and Indian War; Revolution-
  ary War
military uniforms. *See* clothing
misogyny, 108, 124–25, 144
Moll (enslaved person), 259
Monongahela River, Battle of (Brad-
  dock's defeat, 1755), 60–63
Montesquieu, Baron de, 42, 263
Moore, Bernard, 75–76
Morris, Gouverneur, 178–79, 181, 187
Morris, Robert, 286, 292
Morris, Thomas, 62
Morris House (Philadelphia), 260–61
Moses, GW described as, 6, 275, 279–
  80, 288
Moultrie, William, 103
Mount Vernon: children living with
  GW and MW at, 192–99; daily rou-
  tine of GW at, 174–75; GW creating
  repository of papers at, 284–85; GW
  returning to during Congress's recess
  (1790), 290; GW's bedstead, 305–6,
  305; GW's management of, 275–76;

GW's mansion bespeaking his social dominance, 220; Lewis as manager (1797–1802), 79; New Room (drawing room) at, 301, *301*, 306; privy, 181, *182*; public nature of, in GW's day, 275–76; stagecraft of, 276. *See also* final illness, death, and funeral of GW

mourning periods, 234, 248

Muclus, Billy (enslaved person), 78

Muse, George, 117–18, 343n26

mythology of GW, 2, 80, 319n1; bedstead size needed for GW, 305; cherry tree legend, 8, 27; children treated more leniently by MW, 199–200; cold, distant personality of GW, 142; Morris-GW exchange showing GW's dislike of being touched, 178–79, 357n34; national hero and icon, 6, 9, 147, 186–87, 226, 264–67, 269, 309; nineteenth-century stories of GW's amazing strength, 6–9, 13, 79

National Gazette, 266–67

National Health and Nutrition Examination Survey, 17

National Museum of American History, 236

National Portrait Gallery, 10

Native Americans: as British allies, 56–57; as French allies, 60; GW's first encounter with, 71; GW's nickname of "conotocarious" (devourer of villages) and, 71; GW's relations with, 72, 333n35; GW's wish to live in harmony with, 72; no match for British and American troops, 74; Paxton Boys' massacre of, 113; scalping and barbarity of, 57, 60–63, 330–31nn14–15;

sense of self and manly attitude of warriors, 73–74

nature, GW's encounters with, 33, 37–38, 41–46, 106, 245. *See also* French and Indian War; surveyor, GW as

Newburgh Conspiracy (1783), 251–54

Nicholas, Robert Carter, 147–48

nineteenth-century mores: family life and fatherhood in America, 196–98; gender differences and, 162, 164; privacy and avoidance of unwanted touching, 179–80; refashioning of GW's appearance to fit, 23; sex and reproductive biology, 164; stories of GW's amazing strength and, 6–9, 13, 79

Ohio Valley, French presence in, 49–50

Onania, or the Heinous Sin of Self-Pollution, 161

opium, 87, 100

oratorical skills of GW, 257

Osborn, William, 181

Paine, Thomas, 142

Paoli Massacre (1777), 332n22

Paris (enslaved person), 259, 268

Parkinson, Richard, 76

Partnership for Research in Spatial Modeling (Arizona State University), 10

Parton, James, 177–78

Paxton Boys, 113

Peale, Charles Willson, 7–8, 88; *George Washington*, 10–12, 14, *15*

Peale, Rembrandt, 10–12

Pearce, William, 217

Pennsylvania Evening Post, 65